AS RESIDENT ALIENS

As Resident Aliens

Christian Peacemaker Teams in the West Bank, 1995–2005

Kathleen Kern

CASCADE *Books* • Eugene, Oregon

AS RESIDENT ALIENS
Christian Peacemaker Teams in the West Bank, 1995–2005

Copyright © 2010 Kathleen Kern. All rights reserved. Except for brief quotations in critical publications or reviews, no part of this book may be reproduced in any manner without prior written permission from the publisher. Write: Permissions, Wipf and Stock Publishers, 199 W. 8th Ave., Suite 3, Eugene, OR 97401.

Cascade Books
An Imprint of Wipf and Stock Publishers
199 W. 8th Ave., Suite 3
Eugene, OR 97401

www.wipfandstock.com

ISBN 13: 978-1-55635-233-1

Cataloguing-in-Publication data:

Kern, Kathleen, 1962–

    As resident aliens : Christian Peacemaker Teams in the West Bank, 1995–2005 / Kathleen Kern.

    xiv + 358 p. ; 23 cm. Includes bibliographical references and index.

    ISBN 13: 978-1-55635-233-1

    1. Christian Peacemaker Teams. 2. Peace—Religious aspects—Mennonites. 3. War—Religious aspects—Mennonites. 4. Military occupation—Social aspects—West Bank. 5. Nonviolence—Religious aspects—Christianity. I. Title.

BX8128 .P4 K48 2010

Manufactured in the U.S.A.

For Hisham Sharabati, who got us started in Hebron and helped keep us going, and for all the Palestinians and Israelis who told us when we were doing things right, helped us when we were doing things wrong, and who keep struggling for peace and justice as the principalities and powers scoff at their efforts.

Contents

Foreword / ix

Acknowledgments / xiii

Introduction / 1

PART ONE Finding Footholds 1995–1996
   ONE Hitting the Streets of Hebron 1995 / 13
   TWO New Directions 1996 / 44

PART TWO Campaign for Secure Dwellings 1997–2000
   THREE Demolitions and Death Threats 1997–1998 / 63
   FOUR Continuing the Struggle for Secure Dwellings 1999–2000 / 83

PART THREE "Things Fall Apart"—The Al-Aqsa Intifada 2000–2002
   FIVE The Al-Aqsa Intifada: September–December 2000 / 103
   SIX The Intifada Continues 2001 / 128
   SEVEN The Blood-Dimmed Tide 2002 / 160

PART FOUR Too Long a Sacrifice—The Intifada 2003–2005
   EIGHT Resistance, Repression, and Restrictions 2003 / 203
   NINE New Project in At-Tuwani 2004–2005 / 238
   TEN On the Education of Aliens: Issues Arising from CPT's Work in the West Bank / 277

Bibliography / 323

Index / 343

Foreword

IN OCTOBER 2002, THE government of Israel denied me entry into the country as I traveled to my thirteenth Christian Peacemaker Teams field assignment in Palestine. The next month, I visited the Israeli embassy in Washington, D.C., with an Israeli-American friend who eventually became my husband. Although he had called in his Israeli Identity Number and Israeli Military Serial Number to the embassy security office before we made the trip, embassy staff would not permit him to come to the meeting I had set up with Israel's Deputy Chief of Mission, Rafael Barak, and locked him in a room for the length of the meeting.

Barak and another young man, whom I assumed was a member of some Israeli intelligence branch, were hospitable and friendly. They noted they had received a great many faxes written on my behalf and the behalf of other CPTers who had recently been denied entry. I told them that the airport security people had stamped my passport and were going to allow me to enter, after I had a conversation with the Ministry of Interior people, whose English was not nearly as good as that of the security personnel. I do not think they really understood the explanation of CPT's work. (I said I was going to be joining the Rapid Response team in Jerusalem—see chapter 7—and that the purpose of the team was to try to get to the sites of bombings in Jerusalem as quickly as possible, to provide what help we could and then document the suffering of Israeli civilians as we had documented the suffering of Palestinian civilians in Hebron. For the rest of the interview, the Ministry of Interior people kept reiterating, "Bombings? I don't understand. Why do you want to go to bombings?") Both men rolled their eyes when they heard my account, suggesting that they were embarrassed by the caliber of the people who had conducted that interview.

Barak asked me to give him the contact information of four to six Israelis who could vouch for my honorable intentions. Once he had heard from the Ministry of the Interior, he said, regarding the precise reason it had denied me entry into Israel, then he would be able to proceed on my behalf. The Interior Ministry never got back to him.

For years, people within CPT and the CPT constituency had said that someone needed to write a history of Christian Peacemaker Teams. Since I had already done significant writing for the organization and had gone through the first CPT training in 1993, I was a logical candidate to undertake the task. My exile from the Hebron team suggested that the time had come to do it. I assumed the writing would take a year. Instead, it took four. Although this time included trips to Colombia and the Democratic Republic of Congo and four months of the CPT hostage crisis (see chapter 9), during which I was able to work on the history very little, for most of those four years, the primary focus of my CPT work was the history.

Given that Hebron was CPT's longest-running project, and the project on which I had served the longest, I had more Hebron-related material than I had for any other project. For the better part of 2004, I worked on the Hebron chapter, which grew to four Hebron chapters. I ended up having to cut about 200 pages on CPT's work among Palestinians from my general account of this history, *In Harm's Way*. Since 200 pages seemed a logical size for a book, I sent a dual query to Wipf and Stock Publishers, offering both the general history and a more detailed history of our work in the West Bank (by that time CPT had two Palestine projects, in Hebron and At-Tuwani.)

However, this book is not merely a receptacle for details I cut out of *In Harm's Way*. Its angle is also somewhat different. That book took an overview approach, noting how each of CPT's projects in Haiti, the West Bank, Colombia, and so on influenced the growth and direction of the organization as a whole. In this book, I take a linear approach, detailing how the Palestine projects developed, faltered, grew some more, faltered some more, and expanded. I thought this perspective might be useful to other peace teams seeking to set up projects and chart the development of their projects, as well as reassuring to members of existing peace teams who wonder whether their experiences are abnormal. Given that the last century was the most violent in human history, I hope that many such teams will develop in the next decades and demonstrate that nonviolent action is ultimately more effective than weapons.

Note to readers regarding some style and spelling issues: When I describe incidents in which I played a part, I refer to myself as "Kathleen

Kern." When I am describing the process of writing or researching this book, I refer to myself as "the author." When no footnote appears for an incident in which I took part, the reader may assume I am writing from my memory of the event.

Most CPTers are not professional writers, and spelling and grammar errors have cropped up in CPTnet releases over the years. I have chosen to correct these errors without using *sic*, unless I think preserving the original is important. This face-saving measure benefits me as well as my colleagues, since I have edited most of the releases coming out over CPTnet since 1998.

Related to these inconsistencies in CPTnet releases is the transliteration of Arabic and Hebrew words. Arabic and Hebrew both contain phonemes not present in English, and in their written forms do not generally contain vowels. Additionally, people speaking different dialects of Arabic may pronounce certain vowels and consonants differently (something that applies to most languages, including English.) Thus, transliterations of Hebrew and Arabic words can be spelled in a variety of different ways. For example, consider the different spellings of Islam's most revered prophet (Peace Be Upon Him): Mohammed, Mahomet, Muhammad, and Mohamed. Additionally, the Hebron dialect often drops the "qoph" sound, usually transliterated as "q." Thus, Medina Qadima, "Old City," becomes "Medina 'Adima," and the area of Qilqis, where the Al Atrash family had their home (see chapter 3) becomes 'Il'is, although the glottal (back of the throat) effect of the "qoph" is preserved in pronouncing the vowels. The team over the years consulted many friends about the correct way to transliterate words, but often Palestinians and Israelis fluent in conversational English were not the best sources for accurate transliterations. The reader may thus notice that certain words, especially names for people and places, are spelled differently in various Palestine releases covering the 1995–2005 period.

Acknowledgments

I AM INDEBTED TO the current and former members of CPT's Palestine teams who read chapter drafts, answered questions I had about incidents that did not appear on CPTnet or in other CPT reports, and sent me files and other useful written resources. They greatly contributed to the accuracy of this text. Particular thanks goes to Rich Meyer, the Palestine Project Support person from 2002–2007, and my former Hebron teammate, Dr. Jane Adas, who volunteered to format the chapters according to Wipf and Stock guidelines, a task that, because of an eye condition, would have been painful for me to do.

My deepest gratitude goes to my husband Michael, whose last name on my passport ushered me back into Palestine and Israel after five years of exile, and who, more importantly, ushered me into a new life of daily love, laughter, and friendship when we married in 2006.

Introduction

> Christians can hope that prophets will rise in Israel to [address Israel's denial of Palestinian rights] to their people in power. But they cannot well imagine that they themselves are the prophets. As the crucifixes drenched with Jewish blood drop from our hands, we stand impotent and wordless before this tragedy of Israel and Palestine . . . In the name of the crucified Messiah, we must struggle against the conditions which make history a trail of crucifixions. Only then, in solidarity with Jews and Palestinians, can we dream of Messianic times, of a shalom without victims.[1]

THESE WORDS BY THEOLOGIAN Rosemary Radford Ruether capture the fear and trembling with which Western Christians must enter the realm of the Palestinian-Israeli conflict. If not for the centuries of vicious Christian anti-Semitism in European countries, culminating in the Holocaust, the European Jews would probably have not felt a need for a state of their own. The Jews living in Palestine and other Middle-Eastern and North African countries would have remained members of those societies, speaking Arabic as their first language, dressing like the their Christian and Muslim fellow citizens. Religious Jews would still have flocked to the many holy sites in the region of Palestine, as Muslims and Christians would have done, and some may have chosen to settle near them, but the rancor between Palestinians and Jews would have been less by many degrees.

The legacy of Christian anti-Semitism handed a club to partisans of Israel, which they have wielded to good effect when Christians have spoken out about Israeli abuses of human rights. CPTers working in Hebron

---

1. Ruether, "Faith and Fratricide Discussion," 255–56. Note that both *shalom* (Hebrew) and *salaam* (Arabic) connote more than the English word "peace." At their root, they convey the concepts of "wholeness," "security," and "well-being."

have been on the receiving end of some of those blows, both physical and verbal. At times, they have been called Nazis on a daily basis by the Israeli settlers in Hebron, and when they have spoken in their own home communities they have had to face similar, although more sophisticated, assaults on their integrity.

Muslims in Hebron, too, have an instinctive distrust of Christians coming from Western nations, whose governments have essentially acquiesced to the Israeli occupation of the West Bank and Gaza and whose weapons bring death and conquest to Arabs and Muslims throughout the Middle East and Central Asia. They, too, remember the Crusades, when Muslim and Christian Arabs alike were slaughtered along with the Jews as European Christians pillaged and raped their way in the name of Jesus throughout the Holy Land.

Given these realities, why did a small cohort of pacifist Christians, fluent in neither Arabic nor Hebrew, decide to paddle against the currents of history and set up a project in Hebron twenty-eight years after the Israeli Occupation of the West Bank and Gaza?

A BRIEF HISTORY OF CHRISTIAN PEACEMAKER TEAMS

In 1984, Ron Sider challenged the Mennonite World Conference in Strasbourg, France, with these words:

> Over the past 450 years of martyrdom, immigration and missionary proclamation, the God of shalom has been preparing us Anabaptists for a late twentieth-century rendezvous with history. The next twenty years will be the most dangerous—and perhaps the most vicious and violent—in human history. If we are ready to embrace the cross, God's reconciling people will profoundly impact the course of world history. . . .
>
> This could be our finest hour. Never has the world needed our message more. Never has it been more open. Now is the time to risk everything for our belief that Jesus is the way to peace. If we still believe it, now is the time to live what we have spoken . . . .
>
> Even small groups of people practicing what they preach, laying down their lives for what they believe, influence society all out of proportion to their numbers. I believe the Lord of history wants to use the small family of Anabaptists scattered across the globe to help shape history in the next two decades.
>
> But to do that, we must not only abandon mistaken ideas and embrace the full biblical conception of shalom. One more thing is needed. We must take up our cross and follow Jesus to Golgotha.

We must be prepared to die by the thousands. Those who believed in peace through the sword have not hesitated to die. Proudly, courageously, they gave their lives. Again and again, they sacrificed bright futures to the tragic illusion that one more righteous crusade would bring peace in their time, and they laid down their lives by the millions.

Unless comfortable North American and European Mennonites and Brethren in Christ are prepared to risk injury and death in nonviolent opposition to the injustice our societies foster and assist in Central America, the Philippines, and South Africa, we dare never whisper another word about pacifism to our sisters and brothers in those desperate lands. Unless we are ready to die developing new nonviolent attempts to reduce international conflict, we should confess that we never really meant the cross was an alternative to the sword. . . . Making peace is as costly as waging war. Unless we are prepared to pay the cost of peacemaking, we have no right to claim the label or preach the message.

Unless we . . . are ready to start to die by the thousands in dramatic vigorous new exploits for peace and justice, we should sadly confess that we never really meant what we said, and we dare never whisper another word about pacifism to our sisters and brothers in those desperate lands filled with injustice. Unless we are ready to die developing new nonviolent attempts to reduce conflict, we should confess that we never really meant that the cross was an alternative to the sword.[2]

Sider's call sparked discussion in the historic peace churches across North America. The Council of Moderators and Secretaries (CMS) of the Mennonite, General Conference Mennonite, Mennonite Brethren and Brethren in Christ churches discussed Sider's proposal in late 1984 and asked MCC [Mennonite Central Committee] Peace Section to study the issue and bring back a proposal to the council. After the proposal had gone through many drafts, the CMS, in an October 1985 meeting, approved the concept of Christian Peacemaker Teams in principle. The council then appointed a committee[3] to oversee a yearlong process of "prayerful discussion and dialogue" in the churches.

The language in a flier put out to advertise the study guide reflected the theological emphases in Sider's presentation. The Council of Moderators

---

2. "Sider, "God's People Reconciling." Sider adapted this address into an essay for his book, *Nonviolence*.

3. Don Shafer, Lois Kenagy, Helmut Harder, Harold Jantz, Kathy Royer, and Ron Sider.

and Secretaries said that the "starting point for CPT is biblical obedience to Jesus Christ our Savior and Lord. . . . Christians give themselves for others in obedience to their Redeemer who gave himself for the sins of the world."[4]

Such language carried over to the study guide. Under the "Proposal and Goal" section the authors wrote, "The goal of CPT would be to witness to Jesus Christ as we seek to identify with the suffering, promote peace, reduce violence, identify with those caught in violence and oppression and foster justice by using the techniques of non-violent direct action."[5] Of the nine Guiding Principles of CPT, the one listed first reads, "The Central purpose of CPT is to glorify the Prince of Peace."[6]

More than 400 congregations and 700 individuals submitted responses to the study guide before the December 1986 meeting of the CMS at a retreat center in Techny, Illinois, a suburb of Chicago. The people attending (approximately one hundred) included representatives of the General Conference Mennonite Church, Mennonite Church, Brethren in Christ Church, and Mennonite Brethren Church. Church of the Brethren staff members participated as observers.

The conference issued a "Techny call" to congregations, church agencies, and conferences:

1. We believe the mandate to proclaim the Gospel of repentance, salvation and reconciliation includes a strengthened biblical peace witness.
2. We believe that faithfulness to what Jesus taught and modeled calls us to more active peacemaking.
3. We believe a renewed commitment to the gospel of peace calls us to new forms of public witness which may include nonviolent direct action
4. We believe the establishment of Christian Peacemaker Teams is an important new dimension for our ongoing peace and justice ministries

    We ask our conferences and congregations to envision Christian Peacemaker Teams as a witness to Jesus Christ by identifying with suffering people, reducing violence, mediating conflicts and fostering justice through peaceful, caring direct challenge of evil. This may include biblical study and reflection, documenting and reporting on

---

4. "Christian Peacemaker Teams: A Study Document," sent from MCC headquarters in Akron, PA and Winnipeg, MB on January 30, 1986.

5. *Christian Peacemaker Teams*, 2.

6. Ibid., 7.

injustice and violation of human rights, Nonviolent Direct Action, education, mediation and advocacy. To be authentic, such peacemaking should be rooted in and supported by congregations and church-wide agencies. We will begin in North America, but will be open to invitations to support initiatives in other places.

It is understood that in a growing emphasis on peacemaking, the Christian Peacemaker Teams vision is only one means of providing an opportunity for God's people to express a faithful witness to Jesus Christ, the Prince of Peace.

We want to acknowledge our complicity in violence and oppression. Peacemaking is most of all the work of God. The Spirit of God will nurture this work within us.[7]

Several of CPT's early founders such as Harry Huebner and Hedy Sawadsky had experience working in the Middle East and had hopes of CPT bringing a fresh approach to the Israeli Palestinian conflict. Gene Stoltzfus, who had directed the Urban Life Center in Chicago from 1980 to 1986,[8] had significant contacts with Palestinians there, including one student who was later killed in Lebanon.[9] This interest led CPT to organize two delegations to Israel/Palestine prior to the training of fulltime CPT volunteers in 1993. In June 1991, a delegation led by Gene Stoltzfus and Hedy Sawadsky visited the West Bank, Israel, and Jordan and participated in a peace walk. The next year, a second delegation participated in another peace walk with about 113 participants that crossed the border from Israel into the West Bank. Six members of the CPT delegation, including Duane Ediger, crossed the line and were among about half of the participants arrested and jailed for forty-eight hours. Among the other arrestees were Anne Montgomery and Dianne Roe who later went through training and became two of the longest-serving CPTers on the Hebron team.[10]

During the second delegation, CPTers had discussions with Zoughbi Zoughbi—who would later be instrumental in helping CPT set up the Hebron project—Naim Ateek, and other Palestinian Christian leaders about the possibility of placing a team in one of Gaza's refugee camps.

---

7. "Techny Call," 2. The Mennonite Brethren came to Techny with this call already written, and the participants largely adopted it as it was, with minor modifications.

8. See "Chicago Center for Urban Life and Culture." See also an article about CPT trainer Kryss Chupp, who met Stoltzfus at the Urban Life Center when she was a student at Bethel College, in North Newton Kansas: Melanie Zuercher, "Forum: Anabaptist at heart."

9. Stoltzfus, e-mail to author, December 1, 2007.

10. Stoltzfus, e-mail to author, August 27, 2007. E-mails from Anne Montgomery and Dianne Roe to author, August 23, 2007.

6 *Introduction*

Stoltzfus noted in his proposal for the Gaza project that CPT received "significant encouragement" to set up in a camp that continued after the delegation returned to North America.

Stoltzfus wrote:

> In brief, our basic vision would be an initial project of two months with one month additional for a one or two person advance party. One person would be designated the group leader and the other four would rotate in and out of the camps, where they would stay with the families. The group leader would be designated the specific responsibility of explaining these peacemaking efforts to local or regional leadership as appropriate, Palestinian groups, Muslim groups, Christian groups, Israel Defense Force. If and when it is desirable, the group would report on events to the press or make their observations available through Gaza and Jerusalem-based human rights offices with which we are already in touch. The team will also report to the communications offices of our various sponsoring denominations in the hope that the effort might catch the imagination of the wider church community in North America, so that the project becomes a source of inspiration for the peacemaking there.
>
> Peacemakers living in the camps would be primarily charged with a ministry of presence and observation. When violence threatens, they would be encouraged and trained to be present, and, if possible, to intervene. We are not assuming that the presences of this outside group would be respected by the authorities. The possibility exists that CPT people could be expelled at any time[;] however we believe that this would in itself be a witness in the long term [as] its own teaching appeal for those whose ears can hear.[11]

On July 2, 1993, Duane Ediger and David Weaver flew into Tel Aviv to begin doing the necessary advance work for the Gaza team. Upon Ediger's arrival, however, his arrest for crossing the Green Line during the 1992 CPT delegation came up on the immigration computer, and the Israeli authorities denied him entry. Weaver thus had to make the connections and set up housing by himself, while Ediger undertook project support from the Chicago office.[12]

The three remaining team members, Phyllis Butt, Cliff Kindy, and Elayne King arrived on July 18, 1993, and moved the next day into refugee camps. For the next two months, the team members stayed with more than

---

11. Stoltzfus, "PROPOSAL TO PLACE A FIVE PERSON TEAM," April 30, 1993.

12. Christian Peacemaker Teams, "REPORT OF FORCED RETURN OF CPT PERSON FROM ISRAEL," July 6, 1993. David Weaver, faxes dated July 6 and July 11, 1993.

twenty families in five of the eight refugee camps in the Gaza Strip. Four times, they were present in homes when Israeli soldiers raided them.[13]

While the Gaza Project was ending,[14] the news of the Oslo negotiations burst onto the world scene. On September 13, 1993, the PLO and the Israeli government signed the Oslo Declaration of Principles. CPT's Hebron team would learn in 1995 that these Accords ultimately did little to improve the lives of average Palestinians and Israelis, but in September 1993, many Israelis, Palestinians, and the internationals who cared about them held out a skeptical hope that the situation might improve.

However, to Gazans these "peace" negotiations in September 1993 did not signal a lessening of Israeli military brutality. "Israeli snipers shooting every day from rooftops in Khan Younis Refugee camp create a terrifying atmosphere," wrote David Weaver. "We are pleased that some common ground has been found in the talks, but peace is not right around the corner." Although the establishment of the Palestinian Authority to rule Gaza (and Jericho) would mean the withdrawal of Israeli troops, the people in the camps feared the desperate economic conditions brought on by border closures might lead to even greater conflict within Gaza.[15]

Three of the four people who had stayed in the camps wrote evaluations of the project. All agreed that the level of physical danger needing intervention was less than they had imagined, and expressed reservations about placing a longer-term team in the camps as a violence-deterring presence or symbolic expression of solidarity.

David Weaver wrote:

> At times in the past five weeks, I have had to ask myself what we are doing here.... Repeatedly, we have heard from Palestinians, both those living in the camps and those with well-established professional positions, that groups like ours enthusiastically come and go, and nothing changes. In fact, life has gotten worse. Will our group do this as well? What makes our work any different than the others?... I have felt at times like we are working for the headlines,

---

13. Cliff Kindy, "Indiana Peacemaker Softens Israeli Raid," August 2, 1993. Kindy, e-mail to author, August 23, 2007.

14. CPT generally refers to Haiti as the location of its "first" long-term project, even though Gaza preceded the setup in Haiti by five months. Haiti was, however, the first project staffed by CPT-trained fulltime volunteers. The interpersonal friction between the Gaza project volunteers confirmed the belief of people involved in the early years of CPT that CPTers going into the field should go through a training period first.

15. Weaver, "Gaza Team Applauds Peace Efforts," September 1, 1993.

> a confrontation or drama which will gain us some bold print. Then we can return home feeling like we were truly brave in the face of trial, like our presence somehow staved off the evil of violence one more time. However, this type of "flash in the pan" action does not provide the type of light which Palestinians need to keep hope alive. It may help us feel good, but what does it really do for them? Will we discover a way to integrate our symbolic nonviolent actions into a larger strategy which may bring real change, or will our symbolic nonviolent action become an end in itself?[16]

Weaver had no way of knowing at the time that two years later CPT's longest running project would begin among Palestinians and become a dynamic influence on the work of many different actors in the Palestine/Israel conflict.

The author has referred to CPTers who have worked in the West Bank as *ger*, translated from the Hebrew variously as "resident alien," "resident foreigner" or "sojourner." The Hebrew Bible designates *gerim* (plural) as people living among the Israelites who were not Israelites, but observed their laws. Most of the scriptures referring to these resident aliens adjured the Israelites to give them the special care that widows and orphans required and not to discriminate against them.[17]

---

16. Weaver, "CPT/CPC: What is our purpose in Gaza?" August 14, 1993.

17. See, for example, Exod 20:10; Deut 1:16, 16:14, 24:17–22, 26:12, 27:19; Num 9:14, 15:15–30; 1 Chron 29:14–15, Jer 22:3, Mal 3:5. Marilyn Rayle Kern, who has done significant research into the biblical word clusters with which *ger* is associated, wrote in a February 7, 2008 e-mail to the author,

> In the Hebrew Bible *ger* is used in proximity to the words for "widow," "orphan," "poor." These clusters are centered in the consciousness of people in a covenant relationship with their maker. They are code words that evoke sweeping theological concepts of justice and righteousness:
>
> "[God] executes justice for the orphan and the widow, and who loves the strangers *ger*, providing them with food and clothing. You shall also love the strangers *ha(the)ger*, for you were strangers *gerim* in the land of Egypt." Deuteronomy 10:18–19 NRSV (Note also, "You shall not oppress a resident alien *ger*, for you know the heart *nephesh* (soul), of an alien *ger*, for you were aliens *gerim* in the land of Egypt." Exodus 23:9 NRSV).
>
> "Render true judgments, show kindness and mercy to one another; do not oppress the widow, the orphan, the alien *ger*, or the poor; and do not devise evil in your hearts against one another . . ." Zechariah 7:10 NRSV.
>
> . . . Torah and prophets proclaim that we show whose people we are when we show Godly compassion for those who do not have land and family to support and

As such, the casual observer might think the title of this book is not especially apt.[18] CPTers have, in most cases, enjoyed special treatment by the Israeli Occupation authorities because they have foreign passports.[19] Because they are not allied with the Israeli soldiers, settlers, or their partisans, and because of traditional Middle Eastern hospitality, CPTers have also received privileged treatment from Palestinians.

But in a deeper sense of the term, CPTers are aliens in a land where the vicious attempts to obliterate "the other" have been going on for more than a century. Many Israelis and their supporters have made superhuman efforts to "prove" that Palestinians (most of whose ancestors probably were Jewish, Christian, and Muslim, at one time or another, depending who was controlling the area) were relatively recent immigrants, that they did not "love" their homeland the way that Jews did—if they had, they would not have fled in 1948. Many Palestinians and their supporters have discounted the history of Jewish suffering, primarily at the hands of Europeans, viewing the Jews who flooded into Israel because of atrocities committed against them in Eastern Europe and Germany during the first half of the twentieth century as yet one more head on the hydra of European colonialism.[20]

In this climate of delegitimization and competing claims, CPTers tell the inhabitants of Palestine/Israel that CPT has no claim on or desire for the Holy Land, that they regard every person as holy, equally loved by God, entitled to the same, exactly the same, human rights. They are taking a temporary sojourn in the land to support Palestinians and Israelis who reject violence as a means of solving the conflict, and who believe one

---

defend them. The Law specifically mentions providing a tithe of one's harvest every three years for the "The Levites, because they have no allotment [share of land] or inheritance with you, as well as the resident aliens (*ha ger*) and the orphans and the widows in your towns, may come and eat their fill so that the LORD your God may bless you in all the work that you undertake." Deuteronomy 14:29 NRSV.

I'm struck again by the emphasis in these ancient texts upon compassion, knowing it's the right thing to do, and faith that people can put themselves in the place of others to understand and feel the requirements of justice and mercy.

18. Rabbi Jeremy Milgrom, in his comments on a draft of this manuscript, wrote that the title of this book should include the rest of the phrase in Leviticus 25:23, "with me you are but aliens and tenants," referring to the Israelites themselves. "The verse," Milgrom writes, "resonates with an ironic intimacy with God—strangers, but no more or no less than everyone." Milgrom, e-mail to author, October 21, 2009.

19. Tarek Abuata, who took the position of Palestine Support coordinator in 2007, is an exception. Abuata was born in the Bethlehem area.

20. Most Palestinians, however, do not feel the same way about Palestinian Jews living in the Holy Land prior to the Zionist movement.

nation does not have the right to subjugate and exploit the other. As much as possible, in the future of the CPT's Palestine projects, they will try to follow advice CPT received from Lenore Keeshig-Tobias, a member of the Chippewas of the Nawash Unceded First Nation, who helped with the first CPT Ontario regional training in 1998. When asked what guidelines she could offer CPTers for their work in Indigenous communities, she said CPTers needed to do the work well so it didn't need to be repeated; they should prepare to step back when local people were ready to take leadership, then leave and be immediately forgotten.[21]

As resident aliens and followers of Jesus—a native of the region—CPTers who have worked in the West Bank know that not only is Palestine/Israel not their home, no nation or principality of this world is their true home. However, the world is the place where God expects them to work toward a Salaam/Shalom without victims.

---

21. Christian Peacemaker Teams, Steering Committee Minutes, April 6–8, 2000.

PART ONE

Finding Footholds
1995–1996

ONE

Hitting the Streets of Hebron
1995

"HEBRON IS THE FUSE and Jerusalem is the bomb," Zoughbi Zoughbi told Kathleen Kern and Wendy Lehman when they discussed with him in the spring of 1995 the possibility of setting up a Christian Peacemaker Team (CPT) project in Hebron. Although the two women did not fully understand that cryptic remark at the time, over the next ten years the explosive potential in both cities became evident to CPTers working in Hebron. Both had contested holy sites to which both Palestinians and Israelis felt a strong emotional connection. Both cities had small groups of Israeli settlers living in areas where Palestinians had lived for centuries. And in both cities, the full power of the Israeli military protected these settlers, creating a situation in which Palestinians had to face ongoing violent harassment from soldiers and settlers, restrictions on their movement, and other clear human rights abuses.

Zoughbi and other Christians who had met with CPT delegations to the Holy Land in 1992 and 1994 had urged CPT to send trained volunteers to document a burst of settlement expansion around Jerusalem after the signing of the Oslo Accords in 1993.[1] The Accords had had the effect

---

1. Some of these contacts included Don Wagner of Mercy Corps (later director of Middle Eastern Studies at North Park College in Chicago) and Naim Ateek of the Sabeel Liberation Theology Center. In a February 13, 2004, phone interview with the author, Gene Stoltzfus told her that since the 1990s he and others on the Steering Committee had been putting out feelers as to whether there was a place for CPT in Israel and Palestine to various organizations working on peace and justice issues in the region. Stoltzfus supplied additional information about the early explorations into Israel/Palestine work in a December 1, 2007, e-mail, writing,

of neutralizing the mainstream Israeli left and international opinion, which allowed the Israeli government to grab as much land as it could around key settlements close to the border between Israel and the West Bank (the Green Line) before final status talks. When Palestinians protested, Israel and the U.S. told them that they would need to make some sacrifices if they wanted a state. Israel had also invested itself with the sole authority to decide who was and was not violating the Oslo Accords.[2]

Kern had spent the previous year with CPT working in Haiti and Washington DC, and Lehman had just finished training when the CPT Chicago office sent them to Palestine and Israel to explore the possibility of setting up a project in the region. Basing themselves in the Bethlehem home of Zoughbi and Elaine Zoughbi, the two women traveled throughout Israel, the West Bank, and Gaza talking to Israeli, Palestinian, and international peace and human rights organizations. A number of factors kept pulling the women back to Hebron:

1. The January/February 1995 delegation of which they had been a part had visited Hebron and seen the hysterical outrage of Hebron settlers when the delegation's Palestinian driver had attempted to enter the Ibrahimi Mosque/Cave of Machpelah.[3]

2. Zoughbi Zoughbi had a friend in Hebron, Hisham Sharabati, who was active in organizing grassroots efforts against the Occupation. Sharabati

---

My only caution was that wading into a liberation situation was always difficult. Where is the credibility coming from? Could we stick with our basic grass roots goals and not be caught up in the fanfare of endorsements? Would anything resembling public displays of concern work at all? Did we have people who would engage at the grass roots? My confidence in this had grown over the time in Haiti. And that confidence was augmented by my own trips to the region with delegations which I thought went real well.

The initial CPT delegation in which Kern and Lehman participated was in the region from January 29–February 12, 1995, after which they began their exploratory project.

2. For more background on the Oslo process, see Ashrawi, *This Side of Peace*; Chomsky, *World Orders Old and New*; Said, *Politics of Dispossession*; Savir, *Process*. Those with access to back issues of *PS: The Intelligent Guide to Jewish Affairs* may wish to check out the May 13, 1998, article, "Who's violating Oslo," by Gush Shalom. *PS* ceased publication in 1998. See also an updated research paper from the Gush Shalom website, "Who is violating the Agreements?"

3. A May 1994 CPT Middle East delegation also visited Hebron and reported on the reign of terror that settlers there imposed on their Palestinian neighbors. Kern had seen CPT Steering Committee member Dale Aukerman's slides from that delegation's visit to Hebron, and his report on the thuggish behavior of settlers in Hebron made an impression.

maintained broad connections with both Israeli and international peace activists. When Kern and Lehman spent an evening in his home, he understood precisely how a small group of internationals could work in Hebron to deter and document violence. Sharabati would become CPT Hebron's earliest friend and most trusted advisor.[4]

3. On February 25, 1995, an organization called the Hebron Solidarity Committee (HSC), comprising Israeli and international Jewish activists, held a vigil in Hebron to commemorate the slaughter in the mosque a year earlier. Kern and Lehman came down to Hebron for the demonstration and had a chance to talk to the HSCers. The fact that they were publicizing the systemic brutality imposed on the Palestinians in Hebron and trying to organize solidarity visits seemed in line with much of CPT's mandate.[5]

When CPTers Wendy Lehman and Kathleen Kern wrote the proposal for the Hebron project in spring 1995, they suggested that CPT have a team there for five months only, to provide a violence-deterring presence until the Israeli military re-deployed from Hebron as part of the Oslo Peace process. Ten years later, CPT was not only still in Hebron but had a second project in Palestine based in the village of At-Tuwani, neither of which showed any sign of ending, as of this writing in late 2007. Indeed, these teams had become a fixture in the human rights landscape of Palestine and Israel, an information source for Israelis, Palestinians, and international NGOs who were looking for nonviolent ways to challenge and expose the Israeli military occupation of Palestine, and a link to other groups who were doing the same.

   4. At the time Lehman and Kern met Sharabati, he was on crutches. A journalist, he had been videotaping a demonstration protesting the 1994 Baruch Goldstein massacre (see below), when an Israeli soldier shot him, shattering his leg.
   5. In a meeting with some of the HSC members in March, Kern and Lehman said that CPT would be receiving invitations from Palestinian groups to set up a project in Hebron and that it would be helpful for the HSC to issue an invitation for CPT as well. Lehman and Kern could thus write in their proposal that CPT would be working with both Israelis and Palestinians as they set up a violence-deterring project in Hebron. The HSC members said they would be happy to work with CPT, but they believed they had no right to invite internationals to come stay in the Palestinian territories. Only Palestinians had the right to issue such an invitation, they maintained. HSC members also had strong negative reactions to Kern and Lehman referring to them as an "Israeli" group, since several of their members had made decisions not to become citizens for reasons of conscience. They further stipulated that they would not work with CPT if CPT endorsed the Oslo Process. See *Apartheid in Hebron: The True Face of Oslo.*

BRIEF HISTORY OF HEBRON[6]

About 120,000 Palestinians and 450 Israeli settlers lived in Hebron when CPT set up its project in 1995.[7] The city is also home to the il-Ibrahimi Mosque/Cave of Machpelah, where legend has it that the patriarchs and matriarchs Abraham, Sarah, Rebecca, Isaac, Jacob, and Leah are buried (see Gen 23; 25:7–10; 49:29—50:12). In the summer of 1929, a dispute in Jerusalem between Muslims and Jews over access to the Western Wall escalated and riots broke out, which left more than two hundred Jews and Arabs dead and wounded.

Inflamed by rumors that Jews had killed thousands of Arabs and tried to take over Al-Aqsa mosque, an Arab mob, many of whom did not live in Hebron, attacked Hebron's Jewish Quarter, established in the sixteenth century by Jews fleeing the Inquisition in Spain.[8] At least sixty-seven

---

6. The following are good sources for an overview of the Israeli-Palestinian conflict: Abu-Sharif and Mahnaimi, *Best of Enemies*; Avnery, *My Friend, the Enemy*; Benvenisti, *Conflicts and Contradictions*; Benvenisti, *Intimate Enemies; Sacred Landscape*; Chacour, *Blood Brothers*; Chomsky, *Fateful Triangle*; Cohen, *Israel and the Arab World*; Elon, *Blood-Dimmed Tide*; Finkelstein, *Image and Reality*; Flapan, *Birth of Israel*; Khalidi, *Palestinian Identity*; Benny Morris, *1948 and After; Birth of the Palestinian Refugee Problem*; Ruether and Ruether, *Wrath of Jonah*; Rokach, *Israel's Sacred Terrorism*; Said and Hitchens, *Blaming the Victims*; Said, *Politics of Dispossession; Question of Palestine*; Segev, *1949; Seventh Million*; Shlaim, *Iron Wall*; Turki, *Disinherited*.

7. Exact numbers are difficult to obtain, since interested parties tend to maximize their own numbers and minimize the numbers of their opponents—unless they are describing people attacking them, in which case the numbers of opponents are maximized.

8. Muslims fleeing the Inquisition also settled in Hebron during the same period. Their influence can be seen in the name of Qurtuba (Cordoba) girl's school and the Andalus mall.

A small Jewish community probably inhabited Hebron centuries earlier. The twelfth-century Christian document *Canonicus Hebronensis* records

> When they [the Muslims] came to Hebron, they were amazed to see the strong and handsome structures of the walls and they could not find any opening through which to enter; then Jews happened to come, who lived in the area under the former rule of the Greeks [that is, the Byzantines], and they said to the Muslims: "give us [a letter of security] that we may continue to live [in our places] under your rule [literally-amongst you] and permit us to build a synagogue in front of the entrance [to the city]. If you will do this, we shall show you where you can break in, and so they did.

Quoted in Gil, *History of Palestine*, 58.

The Geniza documents refer to an organized Jewish community that assisted pilgrims coming to visit "the graves of the patriarchs," prior to the time of the Crusades, as do letters from Jewish merchants and synagogue leaders of that period. Ibid., 205–7.

Jewish men, women, and children were hacked to death and many more wounded. The Arab neighbors of those living in the Jewish Quarter saved some 400 Jewish residents. But it is the slaughtered, rather than the rescued, Jews that loom large in Israeli history and the memories of the Jews in Hebron. (Muslims descended from families who rescued Jews are still proud of their families' efforts, however. "We considered them Arabs, like us," one descendant of these families told Kern and Lehman. The massacre still affects current interactions between the two groups.)[9]

Because the patriarchs and matriarchs are purportedly buried in Hebron and because of the once thriving Jewish Quarter there, when Israel's settlement policy began to take root after the 1967 war, the Hebron area became a special target for the rightwing religious adherents of Gush Emunim (Bloc of the Faithful).[10]

Rabbi Moshe Levinger and a band of armed supporters took over the only hotel in Hebron in 1968 and refused to leave. To appease them, the army gave them a Jordanian army camp on the outskirts of Hebron that later became the settlement of Kiryat Arba. In 1979, Levinger's wife, Miriam, and a group of women and children moved into Hebron's Old City under the protection of the Israeli military and over the protests of the local Palestinian inhabitants. In 1980 a militant wing of the Palestinian Liberation Organization killed six yeshiva students in Hebron.[11] Israeli

---

9. Segev, *One Palestine, Complete: Jews and Arabs Under the British Mandate*, 314–27. "Jewish History records very few cases of a mass rescue of this dimension," notes Segev on 326.

Oded Avissar wrote a history of the Hebron Jewish Community, *Sefer Hevron*, which included the names of both those slaughtered and those rescued, as well as the names of the rescuers. Yona Rochlin, a descendant of the pre-1929 Jewish community who opposes the presence of the settlers in Hebron, told the team that the settlers had bought all available copies of *Sefer Hevron*, now out of print, and burned them. (Other descendants of the pre-1929 community do support the Hebron settlers.)

The grandfather of Hisham Sharabati (see below) had worked as a "shabbos goy" for the Jewish community (i.e., he turned out their lights for them on the Sabbath.) He told Lehman and Kern that on the day of the massacre he witnessed the British officers opening the gate leading into the Jewish for the Arab mob. The author has found no written source that verifies this claim, but many other Palestinians in Hebron also blame the British.

10. Founded in 1974, Gush Emunim was an organization for people who believed that settling the West Bank and Gaza would help hasten the coming of the Messiah. Not all who belonged to the organization were violent. Some thought that the coming of the Messiah would benefit the Palestinians living in the Occupied Territories as well.

11. The attack was launched from Dubboya Street (see below), which may have factored into settlers targeting the people living there at the time that CPTers began their presence on the street in the summer of 1995.

military response was swift: Miriam Levinger's "unauthorized" settlement of Beit Hadassah, next to the pre-1929 Jewish synagogue, became authorized, and two more settlements appeared in the center city.

Relations between the settlers and Palestinians continued to deteriorate throughout the period of the first Intifada[12] and culminated in the February 1994 massacre in the il-Ibrahimi mosque/Cave of Machpelah.[13]

According to reports of the massacre, settler Baruch Goldstein, a medical doctor born in Brooklyn, NY, began spraying Muslim men and boys with bullets at 5:30 in the morning as they prayed. Twenty-nine worshippers died in the mosque before two Palestinians (subsequently shot by Israeli soldiers), subdued him with a fire extinguisher and others beat him to death.[14] The Israeli Defense Force (IDF) killed another twenty-nine

---

12. "Intifada" means "shaking off" in Arabic and refers to Palestinian attempts to "shake off" the Israeli military occupation of the West Bank and Gaza. Most of the resistance in the first Intifada (1987–1993) was nonviolent and included refusing to pay taxes, boycotting Israeli goods, and conducting mass demonstrations. The Intifada that began at the end of September 2000 is called "the Al-Aqsa Intifada" because it began after Ariel Sharon, surrounded by hundreds of riot police, visited the Haram al-Sharif compound, which includes the Al-Aqsa mosque, the third holiest site of Islam.

13. In March 1994, Christian Peacemaker Teams put out a paper entitled, "Discussion Points for Middle East Peacemaking Hebron Ibrahimi Mosque Massacre" developed in consultation with Mercy Corps International. The points included:
  1. The tragedy in Hebron suggested that the Occupation must end in "specific phased withdrawal strategies" based upon U.N. resolutions.
  2. U.S. aid to Israel needed to be reviewed.
  3. The Palestinian population must be protected and settlers disarmed.
  4. An independent international inquiry should investigate the Hebron massacre.
  5. Financial support for anti-Palestinian hate groups, such as Kach and the Jewish Defense League needed to be investigated.
  6. Israel and the PLO should reiterate their commitment to the Fourth Geneva Conventions and
  7. "The goal of these processes should lead to an internationally sanctioned State of Palestine based upon international law."

14. Goldstein's tomb became a shrine in Kiryat Arba, complete with shelves of prayer books and votive candles. The inscription on his stone reads, "Here lies the saint, Dr. Baruch Kappel Goldstein, blessed be the memory of the righteous and holy man, may the Lord avenge his blood, who devoted his soul to the Jews, Jewish religion and Jewish land. His hands are innocent and his heart is pure. He was killed as a martyr of God on the 14th of Adar, Purim, in the year 5754." Team members visited the tomb frequently with delegations and other guests in the first year of the Hebron project, before Kiryat Arba security began keeping them out. Translation of the Hebrew is from Winslow, *Victory for Us*, 184.

Accounts of the massacre differ wildly due to partisanship and to the panic and mayhem that occurred at the time. The author's description of the massacre is based on conversations with dozens of Palestinians and Israelis, as well as on her reading different accounts of what happened.

Palestinians in the demonstrations that followed—including one notorious incident when soldiers shot Palestinians standing in line to donate blood to the injured victims. The army put all Palestinians in Hebron under curfew for approximately six weeks,[15] while allowing the settlers to roam the streets freely. By the time Wendy Lehman and Kathleen Kern arrived there a year later, people expressed as much bitterness about the collective punishment imposed upon them as they did about the massacre.

The official invitation for CPT to set up a project in Hebron came after Kern and Lehman had met with the Public Relations director of the Hebron municipality, Ahlam Muhtasib. She asked about CPT's work on other projects. When Kern explained what she had done with CPT in Haiti, Muhtasib exclaimed, "That is just what we need here, people who will live in the Old City and report what the settlers and soldiers are doing there." She gleefully described what it would look like if Americans dressed as Palestinians documented the behavior of soldiers and settlers.

Accordingly, on April 3, 1995, the Mayor of Hebron, Mustafa Al-Natshe, faxed the following invitation to CPT's Chicago Office:

> April 3, 1995
>
> Dear Sir,
>
> As mayor of Hebron city, I'd like to express the wish of our citizens to receive a team of your [illegible] to accompany the people here as they struggle with the daily violence caused by the Israeli occupation. We hope that the team will report the truth of what it sees to the people in Canada and the United States. Thank you for your cooperation and understanding.
>
> Yours Sincerely,
> Mayor of Hebron
> Mustafa Natshe[16]

---

15. "Curfew" to those unaware of the realities of military occupation, summons up images of teenagers having to be home at a certain time. In Hebron, "curfew" means that soldiers will not let Palestinians leave their homes, even to buy food or for medical emergencies. American missionaries in Hebron, Ervin and Susan Voth, told team members that when Israel imposed curfew on Palestinians during the first Gulf War in 1990, they had known that it would be imposed and were able to stock up on food supplies. Since no Palestinians anticipated the Goldstein massacre, two months of curfew meant that many families went hungry.

Some sources report that the Israeli military imposed curfew on Hebron for fifty days and others for two months. Forty days is a common mourning period for Muslims.

16. Mustafa, Natshe, Fax to Chicago Office, April 3, 1995. Given Natshe's role as a member of the political establishment in Hebron, this invitation came from the least

In their proposal drawn up at the Zoughbi home in Bethlehem, Lehman and Kern suggested that CPT send a team of four people to Hebron from June 1995 until October 1995. Since Israeli Prime Minister Yitzhak Rabin had scheduled a pullout of Israeli troops from Hebron in late summer or early fall, and since it was unclear whether the Israeli government would remove the Hebron settlers, Kern and Lehman suggested that CPT stay for a period of five months. They reasoned that having international observers for a month or two after the army redeployed might make the transition smoother.

In late May and early June 1995, Cliff Kindy, Kathleen Kern, Wendy Lehman, and Jeff Heie set up the project in Hebron. Later in the summer, Kathy Kamphoefner, a Communications professor at Manchester College and Carmen Pauls, who had worked with Mennonite Board of Missions in Galilee, joined the team.[17]

The team spent most of the summer building relationships with Palestinians whose proximity to settlements in Hebron and on the outskirts of Hebron left them vulnerable to attack. They also developed significant relationships with Palestinian journalists and Hebron University students and professors.

Initially, the team hoped the journalists would lead them to direct interventions in violent situations. During one such incident on June 2, 1995, the Israeli military destroyed a home because a Palestinian militant

---

"grassroots" source of any CPT project. However, Lehman and Kern viewed Muhtasib as the real source of the invitation. She put them in touch with many families in Hebron who were losing their lands to settlement expansion and who were facing soldier and settler violence on a daily level. Although the team in Hebron as of 2008 still makes regular visits to the Hebron municipality to report on events happening in their neighborhood, the municipality could not be called precisely a "partner" in the same way that the Hebron Rehabilitation Committee, Sabeel, Holy Land Trust, the Hebron Land Defence Committee or the Israeli groups Ta'ayush, Israeli Coalition Against House Demolitions, and Bnei Avraham/Breaking the Silence are partners.

17. Kindy had not yet gone through training in 1995, but served on the CPT steering committee and had been part of a two-month CPT presence in Gaza in 1993. See chapter 13 of *In Harm's Way*. Kamphoefner had lived and studied for some years in Egypt and could speak conversational Arabic. She went through CPT training in 1997. Pauls would later work for Mennonite Central Committee in Jerusalem and Iraq and also spoke some Arabic. Given that the team expected the project would last for only five months, the others did not put serious effort into learning the language other than as a method of socializing. (Asking for help with a language is a good way of building relationships in almost any culture. Given that Arabic is considered a difficult language even by Arabs, Palestinians are especially pleased when internationals make an effort to learn it.)

had taken refuge there. Helping to rebuild the home was one of the team's first acts in Hebron. On June 29, 1995, soldiers destroyed two Palestinian homes at the entrance to Hebron, when they discovered Palestinian militants in a vineyard near the houses. After the Israeli army assassinated one militant, they demolished the houses with bulldozers and hand-held missile launchers. Soldiers also bulldozed twenty hectares of the family's vineyard and farmland and destroyed their tractor with a pile driver.[18]

The first team soon learned, however, that in order to really address the violence in Hebron, they would have to build relationships with ordinary Hebronites. Drinking tea and listening to the stories of people suffering the effects of the Israeli occupation was more important work, long-term, than following journalists.

HEBRON UNIVERSITY

The relationship with Hebron University students and professors led to the first official arrests of team members in July 1995.[19] During the first Intifada (1987–1993), the Israeli military sealed the front gates of Hebron University with concrete and metal. Even after Arafat, Rabin, and Peres signed the Oslo Accords in 1993, the Israeli authorities refused to allow the university to open the gates, claiming that opening the gate would allow students to throw stones or Molotov cocktails at passing Israeli jeeps. However, the university was nowhere near the Israeli settlements in Hebron or official checkpoints, so patrols passed it rarely.[20] Keeping the front gate closed meant that students, staff, and teachers had to climb over the fence or walk to the back campus entrance, a considerable distance from the main road. The closure thus seemed to serve no other purpose than collective punishment.

After the team made contact with professors at the university, one of them volunteered to help team members set up their computer. Upon

---

18. See Lehman, "Christian Peacemaker Team Lays Foundation in Hebron"; Lehman, "One Man Killed. Two Houses destroyed in Hebron." The detail of the pile driver is from the author's memory, not from the release.

19. A week earlier, Israeli soldiers detained Cliff Kindy and Jeff Heie while they were accompanying a truck bringing water to Palestinian families living near the settlement of Tel Rumeida. That incident will be described in further detail below under the discussion of settler violence.

20. Lost in this concern for soldiers' safety was the fact that settlers had attacked the university in 1983, killing three students and wounding thirty-three students, teachers, and staff. Friedman, *Zealots for Zion*, 29.

hearing about CPT's work in Haiti, he spoke with students and other professors and then approached the team, asking if they would help take down the gate.

CPTers met up with the Hebron Solidarity Committee in Jerusalem to finalize plans for the July 22, 1995, action at the Hebron University gate. Hillel Barak and Maxine Kaufman from the HSC came to participate. For reasons of safety, Palestinians organizing the event planned to provide the tools and let the Israelis and CPTers do all the work, but when no Israeli patrols showed up, students joined them in chiseling through the welds on the metal gate and breaking the concrete seal with sledgehammers. When the army did arrive an hour later, students and staff fell back, and soldiers, under the command of Captain Eyal Ziv, arrested Cliff Kindy, Kathy Kamphoefner, Wendy Lehman, and Maxine Kaufman. The police took the women to Abu Kabeer prison near Jaffa, and Kindy to the Russian Compound in Jerusalem, where he spent the night in a cell next to some Hebron settler youth who had been arrested for assaulting a police officer the day before.[21]

Linda Brayer, a lawyer who had put her services at the disposal of the team after the water truck incident at Tel Rumeida (see below), once again represented the team members and got them released. Israeli Yochanan Lorwin of the Alternative Information Center, posted their bond.[22]

All four of the arrestees arrived in shackles for their hearing. A representative of the American Consulate in East Jerusalem vigorously intervened when an officer refused to uncuff Lehman long enough for her to go to the bathroom. Later, referring to the arrests at Tel Rumeida ten days previously, the chief officer at the Consulate told team members, "Try to wait at least another couple of weeks before you get arrested again, okay?"[23]

---

21. This incarceration happened after Kindy had begun receiving death threats from the Hebron settlers, because they thought he was a member of Hamas. See below.

22. Lorwin was a religious Jew who worked as an editor at the Alternative Information Center, an organization committed to publishing information about Israel and the Occupied Territories censored or overlooked in the mainstream media. He and two other AIC staff members died on January 24, 1999, when a flash flood overtook them as they were hiking. He had been a helpful source to the Hebron team on how Judaism could provide spiritual resources for human rights work.

23. The Hebron team would continue to have a cordial working relationship with representatives of the U.S. Consulate in Jerusalem during subsequent years. Since they dealt with the rights of Palestinian Americans as well as Israeli Americans, consulate members were generally sympathetic to the team's work. They especially appreciated CPT funneling information about land confiscation and settlement building to them. However, meet-

Lehman noted in her unpublished report about the action and the arrests that Captain Eyal Ziv repeatedly told them that the students at the university were angry with the CPTers and HSCers for destroying the gate. However, the students and faculty gave the team members who had not been arrested a tea and cookie reception at the university to thank them for their efforts and told them that a chant—"Jeff and Cliff did more than the TIPH"—was circulating in their honor.[24]

Lehman and Kern later went in to talk to Captain Eyal, as he said they should call him. They told him what CPT had done in Haiti and why they were in Hebron. When they asked why the army wanted the gate closed, he smiled tolerantly and said essentially that the closure was for security reasons that Lehman and Kern could not understand. He also told them that representatives of the university had been in dialogue with the Israeli Civil Administration about opening the gate and that CPT had ruined negotiations. Later, the team's contacts at the university told them that Captain Eyal was lying. Administrators had never come to the Civil Administration to plead for the doors to be opened. "It is not for them to give permission. It is our right," one of these administrators told team members.

NETWORKING WITH ISRAELI GROUPS

That first summer, the team also assisted Israeli human rights organizations seeking to document settler and soldier abuses in Hebron. In particular, the team connected Israeli groups with Palestinians in Hebron living near the Hebron settlements. Many Israelis, even those sympathetic to the plight of Palestinians in Hebron, perceived of Hebron as a dangerous place and felt safer traveling there with CPTers.

In early September 1995, Shmuel David from B'tselem, Israel's premiere human rights organization, came to Hebron along with other progressive Israelis to visit families living near the settlements of Beit Hadassah and Tel Rumeida and document their stories. CPTers asked the families living there to allow David to interview them; they grudgingly agreed.

---

ings in which controversial issues were discussed generally happened in secrecy, and team members never received permission to quote Consulate representatives.

24. TIPH is an acronym for Temporary International Presence in Hebron, a group of European observers who set up a monitoring presence in Hebron after the Goldstein massacre. The Israeli government refused to renew their mandate after three months, saying they were biased on behalf of the Palestinians. However, after the Hebron Accords were signed in 1997, TIPH returned as part of the agreement and remain in Hebron as of this writing in 2007. Unfortunately, few rhymes exist for "Kathy," "Wendy," or "Maxine."

Persecution by soldiers and settlers had made them distrustful of all Israelis, and the CPTers were aware that they were cashing in chips they had accrued from accompanying the families who lived in these neighborhoods.

Team members held their breath as David introduced himself to the families in competent Arabic and then, rather than asking about human rights violations, told them he had heard that Hebron had better kanafi—a cheese dessert—than Nablus. Palestinians immediately began a discussion of where he could find the best kanafi in Hebron and then drifted easily into a discussion of attacks settlers had made against them and their homes. Kern watched in awe as David, who introduced himself only as "Shmulik," engaged a Palestinian patriarch living near the Tel Rumeida settlers who had regularly told team members about the vast Jewish conspiracy to dominate the world. David and the old man found that they both had ancestors who had come from Greece and began speculating on how they might be related. At the end of the day, as the CPTers went to search for the Israelis to get them onto a taxi back to Jerusalem, Shmulik and his friends pulled alongside them in a car filled with new Palestinian acquaintances, informed them that they were going off in search of kanafi, and drove away. Soon afterwards, B'tselem put out a thirty-four page report about human rights abuses in Hebron entitled "Impossible Coexistence: Human rights in Hebron since the Massacre at the Cave of the Patriarchs."[25]

SETTLER AND SOLDIER VIOLENCE

The most pressing work that the team undertook in the summer and early fall of 1995 revolved around street violence committed by both Israeli settlers and soldiers.

The Murder of Ibrahim Idreis

On July 1, 1995, witnesses from the Tel Rumeida neighborhood told the team that Hebron settler Baruch Marzel and an Israeli soldier had assassinated sixteen-year-old Ibrahim Khader Idreis. The boy, who lived with his family in Jordan, was visiting relatives near Tel Rumeida. During breakfast, the extended family ran out of bread and sent him to buy more at a shop around the corner. He slipped on his aunt's shoes for the trip, which were several sizes too small. Palestinian witnesses said that the boy refused to

---

25. B'tselem, *Impossible Coexistence*.

stop when Marzel called to him and was subsequently shot once in the leg and once in the chest. A soldier then shot him again in the stomach.

The Israeli military told an uncle visiting from the U.S. that his nephew had attempted to stab a soldier, but soldiers produced no knife as evidence. When Idreis's uncle picked him up to take him to the hospital, he saw that the shots to the leg had nearly amputated it below the knee. The boy died in the car on the way to the hospital. The IDF refused to allow family members to enter the hospital to see the body.

Lehman, who went to investigate after hearing of the incident, saw soldiers and settlers laughing together as one settler, Noam Federman, pushed a baby stroller through a large smear of the young man's blood. The team watched that evening as settlers gathered outside an apartment building in the Old City[26] and toasted the soldier who had shot Ibrahim Idreis (according to Palestinian residents of the building who were providing translation).

Two days later, Lehman interviewed the uncle, Yunis Idreis, who had held Ibrahim in his arms as he died. He said the family had not responded as quickly to the gunshots as they might have otherwise, because they never dreamed Ibrahim would be a target. If he were going to attack someone, the uncle asked, why would he do it in broad daylight in front of a soldier camp and in shoes four sizes too small? He told the CPTers that he did not think people would believe his story when he returned to his home in Seattle, Washington.[27]

Water Delivery to Abu Haikel Family

One of the team's most significant relationships with Palestinians living near settlements in the summer of 1995 was with the Abu Haikel family, who for years had resisted harassment from settlers and soldiers surrounding their property on Tel Rumeida.[28] Fluent in Hebrew, Hani Abu Haikel

---

26. The Hebron team eventually moved into this building in October 1995. Their first apartment, found for them by Palestinian journalist friends, was a 10–15 minute walk away from where most violence in Hebron happened.

27. See two reports written by Wendy Lehman, "Israeli settler and soldiers assault Palestinians, one killed," and "Uncle of slain Palestinian teenager talks about attack." July 3, 1995. The comment regarding how people would respond in Seattle is from the author's memory.

28. One could write a full-length book describing the assaults and the indignities this family has faced since the settlement of Tel Rumeida moved in next door in the mid-1980s. The family resisted these pressures with a certain *joi de vivre*. Once, after settlers hit

had also established meaningful relationships with the Hebron Solidarity Committee. Soldiers forbade the team to stay in the home of the Abu Haikels their first week in Hebron, which of course meant that the team sought out as much contact as possible with the family in ensuing weeks.

The delivery of water in the summertime is a pressing issue for all families in Hebron who live on hills. The Israeli government diverts most of the water from the West Bank aquifers to Israel and Israeli settlements in the West Bank.[29] Consequently, for five months out of the year people living on hills (which includes most Palestinians in Hebron) do not have enough pressure in their pipes for water to flow from their taps. Those who can afford to do so buy water from the municipality or private sources. The Abu Haikels paid about $28.00 for each water truck delivery to their home on the summit of Tel Rumeida.

However, after settlers had broken one too many windshields on water trucks coming up to Tel Rumeida, the municipality announced it would no longer deliver water there. The team told the Abu Haikels they would be happy to accompany the truck. On July 12, 1995, ten days before the team worked on opening the gates of Hebron University, Cliff Kindy and Jeff Heie got the call that the water truck was ready to go. They dropped what they were doing and walked with the water truck through the settlement of Tel Rumeida. Soldiers at the checkpoints detained them both, emphasizing that they meant "detention" and not "arrest."[30] As the CPTers stood in the July sun for an hour, two settlers walked past and threatened to kill Kindy.

---

his mother in the head with a rock, Hani Abu Haikel called the Israeli police, who refused to come out. He then walked over to the soldiers' camp with a metal pipe, told the soldiers there that he intended to hit a settler with it, and then walked back to his house and waited for the police to arrive. They took him and his mother to the police station where he was able to make a statement. The Shin Bet (roughly equivalent to the FBI in the U.S.) officer who took his statement appeared sympathetic to the Abu Haikels and wanted more information on the settler attacks.

29. See Center for Economic and Social Rights, "The Right to Water in Palestine: Fact Sheet #1"; "The Right to Water in Palestine: Crisis in Gaza, Fact Sheet #2." See also Tolan, "Mideast Water Series: Collision in Gaza"; "Mideast Water Series: The Politics of Mideast Water."

30. The distinction is important. Arrests generate paper work and a record that Israeli authorities can use later to deny internationals entry into the country. Detentions are more common. Before the outbreak of the Al-Aqsa Intifada in September 2000, soldiers would detain CPTers and then hand them over to the civilian police. The police, in turn would hold the CPTers for hours or even overnight and then release them. Generally, the civilian police worked hard *not* to arrest CPTers and other internationals. After the outbreak of the Al-Aqsa Intifada, the Israeli authorities began using a record of detentions as a reason to deny internationals entry into the country.

The police eventually took Kindy and Heie to the Civil Administration and questioned them further. Kindy tried to explain to the officer interrogating him that the Abu Haikels had been without water for over a week.

The officer said, "But why do you care? Why are you doing this?" Kindy told the officer that if he had been in Germany during the time of the Third Reich, he would have done the same thing on behalf of the Jews.

"Are you calling me a Nazi?" the officer asked.

Soldiers later told the two men that they were being held on charges of entering a closed military zone, assaulting an officer, and calling soldiers Nazis.

Israeli friends from the Hebron Solidarity Committee called the team to tell them that they, too, had been arrested for making statements nearly identical to the one Kindy made about the Third Reich. Kern was touched and surprised by their concern, not realizing the impact the Nazi remark would eventually have.

The official IDF report on the incident said that Kindy and Heie had called the soldiers Nazis and "cursed them in every known language." In the following weeks, if settlers saw team members having friendly conversations with soldiers, they would draw them aside and tell them something involving the word "Naziim"—presumably informing them that these were the people who called soldiers "Nazis."

However, the water truck incident also had four positive outcomes. First, Linda Brayer, a lawyer who had founded the Society of St. Yves in Jerusalem volunteered to represent CPT. She and her legal staff also eventually provided free legal help to several of the families in Hebron that team members knew.

Secondly, a *Washington Post* reporter came to spend the day with the team (Heie had worked on CPT's Washington DC project, and the reporter's editor told him to work the local angle).[31] One of the Israeli settlers living at Tel Rumeida approached the reporter and told him, when Kindy was out of earshot, that he had not wanted to talk to him in front of Kindy because Kindy was a Muslim-American activist who had come to raise money to kill Jews. "That's funny," Lancaster told him. "He told me he was an organic farmer from Northern Indiana. He's Christian."

"Church of the Brethren," Kern chimed in, handing the man a CPT business card. The settler, a British immigrant whom the Abu Haikels

---

31. Lancaster, "Hebron Daunting for Ex-DC Activist." See also Lehman, "Military Detains Two American Members of Christian Peacemaker Teams."

said was not involved in violent attacks on Palestinians in the neighborhood, looked stunned. He had obviously believed the information about Kindy, who had an Amish-style beard similar to those worn by religious Muslims.

The conversation thus dispelled rumors about Kindy being a Hamas activist, and the sporadic death threats that Kindy and the team had been receiving became less frequent.[32]

Third, the incident made the team think more seriously about the approach they should take to these threats, and they wrote the following release for CPTnet:

> STATEMENT FROM HEBRON CPT TEAM
>
> In response to death threats the Christian Peacemaker Team in Hebron, West Bank Israel has called for the rejection of the use of violence in the settlement of all disputes including punishment of anyone who would be responsible for casualties to members of the Christian Peacemaker Team itself.
>
> On July 11, two members of the team were detained by Israeli security forces while they tried to help a Palestinian move water to his home. The team has enjoyed positive relationships with most people in the tense city of Hebron including selected members of the Israeli Defense Force. Militant Israeli settlers have accused the team members of membership in Hamas, a Muslim grouping.
>
> The statement calls for the removal of all persons who have guns and encourages an end to all U.S. aid to Israel. The team urges all persons committed to nonviolence to take the same risks that soldiers are asked to take in order for peace to be established.
>
> HEBRON CHRISTIAN PEACEMAKER TEAM'S
> STATEMENT OF CONVICTION
>
> Two members of our team have recently received death threats from several of the local settlers here in Hebron. While we do not wish to blow these threats out of proportion, they have prompted us to consider the consequences of being attacked, injured, killed or kidnapped. We would like our wishes, as stated below, to be respected in the event such a crisis occurs.
>
> We utterly reject the use of force to save our lives should we be caught in the middle of a conflict situation or taken hostage. In the

---

32. Hani Abu Haikel found the idea of Kindy being a member of Hamas hysterically funny. When team members told him that the settlers had told Lancaster that Abu Haikel was also a member of Hamas, however, he became highly indignant. "I am Fatah!" he said. "I used to be part of Arafat's bodyguard."

event that we die as a result of some violent action, we reject the use of violence to punish the people who killed us.

Should our deaths come as a result of attacks by soldiers or settlers in Hebron, we ask that our deaths be regarded as no more tragic than the murders of dozens of Palestinians who have died here in the last decade. We ask that all legal nonviolent means be taken to ensure that these deaths do not continue. We ask that the government of Israel follow the principle of logical consequences. People with guns who kill other people should be removed from society for that society's protection. Whether those people are soldiers, rabbis or students should make no difference.

We ask that the United States, which has funded the militarization of this society, immediately cut all aid to Israel that is used for the manufacture and purchase of weapons and for the expansion of settlements in the West Bank and Gaza.

At present, we feel much safer walking through Palestinian neighborhoods than we do when we walk past the Israeli settlements in Hebron. However, should our lives be threatened by Palestinians, we ask that they be treated by the authorities in the same way as those authorities would treat Israelis intent on harming us. If more Palestinian blood is shed by Israelis on our account, then our deaths will indeed be in vain. We think it is possible that a collaborator or unstable individual could be encouraged by Israeli intelligence to harm us, and ask that this possibility be investigated in the event of our death. We also ask that the people who care about us look into the root causes of violence found amongst oppressed peoples struggling for liberation.

All of us who joined Christian Peacemaker Teams recognized there are certain risks inherent in this work. We believe that until people committed to nonviolence are willing to take the same risks for peace that soldiers are willing to take for violence, people will always choose violence as the most viable solution to their problems. If our deaths promote the sort of soul-searching that leads to a rejection of armed conflict characteristic of this occupation then our deaths will indeed have redemptive value. Following the central tenet of our faith, we do not hate the people who have harmed us (Matthew 5:44–45). We believe that those best able to love their enemies will ultimately emerge the victors in this bloody conflict.

Cliff Kindy, North Manchester, IN
Wendy Lehman, Kidron, OH
Kathy Kamphoefner, N. Manchester, IN[33]

Kathleen Kern, Webster, NY
Jeff Heie, Washington DC

33. CPTnet, "CPT HEBRON DEFINES NONVIOLENCE," July 20, 1995 (the release was dated July 16, 1995.)

Over the years, as new threats arose, CPTers in Hebron, Chiapas, Colombia and Iraq adapted the statement to address these dangers.[34]

Finally, the subsequent publicity drew both Israeli and international attention to the water shortage in Hebron. Many in the Israeli public expressed outrage when they saw footage of the settlements in the West Bank with swimming pools and well-watered lawns and then learned that Palestinians in Hebron did not have enough water for drinking and washing. Prime Minister Rabin sent a fact-finding mission to Hebron to determine the extent of the problem—even though the West Bank cities had complained for years of water shortages.[35]

Shakir Shukri Dana Family

The relationships the team fostered with professors and students at Hebron University led to an involvement with the Shakir Shukri Dana family. Dana, a telephone operator at the university, had been a construction worker who helped build the settlement of Kiryat Arba, the border of which was adjacent to his neighborhood. He was fluent in Hebrew and had developed relationships with some of the people there. He told the team that in the past when boys stoned his home, he was able to call out their names, and they would stop, but by the summer of 1995, he did not know any of the

---

34. The most recent use by the Hebron team, as of this writing, was in August 2001, after verbal threats and physical attacks by settlers on the team had increased and bullets fired from the settlement of Avraham Avinu had hit the women's apartment. See CPTnet, "CPT Hebron Statement of Conviction," August 29, 2001. The Colombia team adapted the statement after they learned that paramilitaries had plans to kill a member of the team. See Kern, *In Harm's Way*, and CPTnet releases, "Colombia: CPT learns of alleged paramilitary plan to kill team member," August 12, 2002; "COLOMBIA: Statement of Conviction from CPT Colombia. 'Life will claim victory over death,'" August 13, 2002; "COLOMBIA: CPT calls on all armed actors to love their enemies and leave the civilian population in peace," August 17, 2002. The Iraq team, in 2004, also adapted portions of the statement when they returned to Baghdad after having left because their Iraqi coworkers deemed the situation too dangerous there for the team to be able to work. They reissued the statement in 2005 after Iraqi militants kidnapped two CPT delegation members, Norman Kember and Harmeet Singh Sooden and CPTers Tom Fox and Jim Loney. See CPTnet releases, "IRAQ: Christian Peacemaker Teams to Return to Iraq on May 3, 2004," and "IRAQ: Christian Peacemaker Team in Iraq releases 'Statement of Conviction,'" November 29, 2005. Tom Fox signed the Iraq team's version in March 2005. One year later, he was murdered by members of a militant group that had kidnapped him, CPTer James Loney, and two CPT delegates, Norman Kember and Harmeet Singh Sooden. See CPT Iraq, "CPT in Iraq Statement of Conviction."

35. See Kern, "From Haiti to Hebron," 189–90. See also Lehman, "Military Detains Two American Members of Christian Peacemaker Teams." July 12, 1995.

teenagers who were stoning his home, and the psychological pressure and actual damage to his home were becoming intolerable. In a particularly vicious attack at 12:30 AM, approximately twenty-five to thirty settlers went through the Danas' neighborhood and stoned many homes. One Palestinian threw a stone back. An Israeli settler fired his Uzi and then called the IDF.

When the IDF arrived, they searched the entire Palestinian neighborhood, said Dana. While they were searching the house of Dana's brother, an Israeli soldier told Dana's brother, "You are responsible for this neighborhood. If any stones are thrown at Kiryat Arba, we will arrest every one of you." Shakir Dana told the team he would like to move he said, but who would buy a house that settlers stoned constantly?

"I think I may explode one day," Dana told the team. "There should be a solution to this problem. But no one can help."

The team visited the Danas on several occasions to document the stoning and the damage—and to enjoy the hospitality of the Danas; the parents and their eleven children currently living at home were an affectionate family. Team members witnessed several incidents of stoning and received threats from the settlers throwing the stones. Since Captain Eyal Ziv told the team they should call him if they had problems, they spoke to him about the Danas' situation and he told them it was not the IDF's "business" to protect Palestinians. The team also intervened with the municipality about the family's electric bills—unpaid because the family had put the money toward protective grillwork around the house—and connected him with Attorney Linda Brayer.

After apprising the Hebron Solidarity Committee about the Danas' situation, the team was set to do a public witness with the HSC that involved laying protective screens and shingles to fix the damaged, leaking roof—but Dana ended up using the materials the HSC had bought to fix the roof himself before they could do it publicly. When CPTers said they would initiate a regular presence, sleeping at his house during the night, he told them the neighbors might think ill of him if he had single women sleeping there. In the end, his desire not to incur the wrath of settlers and the Israeli authorities or the judgment of his neighbors made contacts between the family and the team less frequent.[36]

36. CPTnet, Kamphoefner, "Life in Hebron for a Family of Fourteen," August 1 1995; CPTnet, Lehman, "CPT members witness settler harassment of Palestinian family," August 12, 1995. The team later renewed their acquaintance with the extended family

Qurtuba School

September 10, 1995, was the first day of school for Palestinian students throughout the West Bank. Since the Israelis had handed over responsibilities for education to the Palestinian Authority over that summer, thousands of schools raised the Palestinian flag for the first time. But when the flag was raised over Qurtuba school, settlers from Beit Hadassah charged onto the school grounds, seized the flag, and burned it. They then attacked the school headmistress, Fariel Abu Haikel, striking her in the chest.

A half hour later, Abu Haikel, several teachers, and about a hundred and fifty students from the school marched to the Palestinian Education Department to make a complaint. As they passed Beit Hadassah, the settlers attacked again. One of the aggressors, an adult male, seized a Palestinian flag from the girls, swung it around, and then ran at them with it. A female settler threw glass liter bottles at the girls.

Ambulances took ten girls to the hospital where they were treated for minor injuries. Many others fainted. The newspaper the next day printed pictures of the girls with eyes rolled up in their heads lying limp in the arms of the men who had rushed to help them. For months, the team had seen settler boys making slashing motions across their throats when Palestinian children walked past them. The settlers had also sprayed "Death to the Arabs" graffiti in dozens of places around the area of the school, leading the team to wonder if the girls who had fainted thought that the settlers from Beit Hadassah were finally making good on their threats.

As it happened, a friend from Hebron University had insisted that the CPTers take their first day off as a team that summer and come with him to Jericho, so they were not in Hebron when the attack happened. For the first week after the attack, however, members of CPT and representatives from the Hebron Solidarity Committee met at the school in the morning. Since Dubboya Street, site of many settler attacks, was en route from the team's apartment to the school, they would wait there for a group of girls to gather and then accompany them and about a dozen fathers past the settlement of Beit Hadassah.

---

after a Palestinian gunman tried to sneak into the south entrance of Kiryat Arba from the Dana's neighborhood. The Israeli government sought to demolish homes in the neighborhood to prevent further attacks. CPTnet, Greg Rollins, "HEBRON: The scenery around an expanding settlement," April 26, 2003; CPTnet, "HEBRON URGENT ACTION: Stop demolition of homes near Kiryat Arba," April 26, 2003. See also Palestinian Human Rights Monitoring Group, "Criminal Negligence?"

On the day after the attack, the flag was raised again and the girls began their morning assembly with singing. Using a loudspeaker, settlers from Beit Hadassah began blaring music from a right-wing Israeli pop singer in an attempt to drown out the girls. Four or five jeeps appeared at the foot of the steps leading up to the school. Anat Cohen, one of the settlers most actively involved with Kach, began videotaping team members and HSC members. The police, backed up by several army officers, came up and took the flag down. One of the team's friends from Dubboya Street protested loudly when the soldiers came for the flag. They immediately arrested him. He spent a week in jail and paid a fine of 3,000 shekels (around $1,000).

The next morning, garbage was strewn all over the school grounds, with big piles in front of the door and the gate. On the door was a sign in Hebrew: "There will be no school today." The Palestinian flag went up and again the police came and took it down.

The next day the team found dirty diapers thrown in the school's foyer. Someone had tried—unsuccessfully—to seal the front door shut with bathtub caulking. The flag went up. The police took it down.

The authorities then declared the school a closed military zone and told CPTers and the Hebron Solidarity Committee to leave. Later CPTers and HSCers watched two young settler women reading aloud from prayer books. At certain intervals, they would stand and wave towards the school. An Israeli reporter told the team that they were putting curses on their enemies—the elementary school girls sitting in their classes at Qurtuba School.

Fearing that the HSC and CPT presence might provoke the settlers, Headmistress Abu Haikel asked them not to come to the school in the mornings anymore. They made a point, however, of arranging to walk by the school in the morning and around noon when school let out. The fathers of the neighborhood continued to stand guard and would wave as the CPTers walked by.[37]

Dubboya Street Saturdays

By far the team's biggest exposure to settler harassment and intimidation happened on Dubboya Street, which ran by the settlement of Beit Hadassah. Every Saturday afternoon, settler men would march up the street attacking Palestinians and breaking anything they could. By the time team

---

37. Account of Qurtuba attack adapted from Kern, "Hebron's Theater of the Absurd," 5–6.

members became aware of the problem, neighbors had stopped replacing glass in the windows.

Hisham Sharabati introduced the team to the neighbors at an evening meeting. One family brought forth a four-year-old boy who had stitches near his eye from a metal projectile that a settler had launched at him with a slingshot. Another family introduced the team to a twelve-year old son in a full-leg cast. He told the CPTers that settler boys had pulled him to the ground and jumped on his leg until it broke.

The team thus began a Saturday afternoon presence on Dubboya Street that lasted for several months, recording what they saw and heard and, when possible, standing between Palestinians and settlers in order to prevent assaults.

These Saturday afternoons took on a surreal quality; Miriam Levinger, in particular, contributed to this atmosphere. Early in the summer, she had tried to warn Lehman and Kern about plans the Arabs with whom they were fraternizing had for raping them. After a mentally disabled boy pointed to a broken weapon button Kern had pinned to her shirt, gesturing that he wanted her to give it to him, Levinger told Kern later, "I saw that Arab grabbing for your breast." In ensuing weeks, she said, "Don't say I didn't warn you," every time she passed team members. The hostility then edged up a notch, when she began asking questions like, "I hear you sleep with Arabs for money." Lehman responded by saying she did not, in fact, sleep with Arabs for money, to which Levinger rejoined, "Oh so you do it for free."

Kern wrote about these Saturday afternoons in an article for *The Link*, a magazine put out by Americans for Middle East Understanding:

ONE SATURDAY AFTERNOON ON DUBBOYA STREET[38]
by Kathleen Kern

I.
Early in the afternoon, I was sitting outside an Arab home on Dubboya Street. At any given time, there are twelve or more children in the three-story house, many of whom peer through the bars of

---

38. Ibid., 11–13. The descriptions of that September 23, 1995, afternoon appeared in a form closer to the original in Kern's 2003 novel, *Where Such Unmaking Reigns*. Scene X never appeared in print. Hisham Sharabati was the "journalist friend" referred to in the original piece, so the author has substituted his name for the "journalist friend" in this chapter.

a small bay window and drop things—sometimes by accident and sometimes to see if the people below will pick them up.

As three adult male settlers were passing by on the opposite side of the street, one of the children dropped an empty plastic soda bottle from the window. It landed directly under the window, about twenty feet from the settlers. Nevertheless, one of them hailed a passing military jeep, pointed at the bottle on the ground, and insisted the soldiers do something about it. Reinforcements arrived about four minutes later, and eight heavily armed soldiers got out of their jeeps and sent a young man who lived there inside to fetch his father. The father came to the window to speak to the soldiers, which seemed to satisfy them. They left after barking what sounded like a stern warning.

II.

Two male settlers in their late teens or early twenties walked past singing in Hebrew, with mocking expressions on their faces. One then began singing in nearly perfect English, "All we are singing is 'Give war a chance.'" When he passed by again about two hours later, he sang, "If I had an Uzi, I'd shoot 'em in the morning. I'd shoot 'em in the evening, all over my land." Then, speaking, he said, "It's MY land. It's not their land. "It's MY land." He later identified himself as Azrael Ben Israel.

III.

Between 2:00 and 2:30 pm, a confrontation occurred between Palestinian youth and Israeli soldiers near the checkpoint at one end of Dubboya St. This was one of several clashes that erupted after the settler attack on Qurtuba girls' school. As I watched, some soldiers shot in the air and threw sound bombs [percussion grenades]. One soldier smiled and waved at two settlers who approached the checkpoint. A few minutes later, Azrael Ben Israel walked past me briskly, muttering, "There should have been fifty or sixty dead Arabs by now."

IV.

Another young Israeli also became interested in events at the checkpoint and asked me about the explosions. "They were sound bombs," I said. He asked for a definition of sound bombs and then inquired whether the army or the Arabs had thrown them. I told him that only the army uses sound bombs. "It doesn't matter," he said. "Pretty soon the Mashiach [Messiah] will come and [the Arabs] will all move to Jordan. I'm not like the others," he continued. "I don't want to kill them. I only want them to leave."

Then he asked, "Are you Jewish?"

"Christian," I replied. His face stiffened. "The Messiah will come and kill all the goyim—Arabs and Christians—and drink their blood," he said as he walked away.

V.

The young messianic hopeful was joined by Ben Israel. He noticed a group of Palestinians watching him and his friend. "Why don't we invite ourselves for coffee?" Ben Israel asked. "I hear they are very hospitable people." Abruptly changing his tone, he pointed at them and said, "First, we'll deal with you, and then we'll deal with the Germans."

"They are the same people," his friend said.

"Let's go," Ben Israel said. "It's making me sick to look at them."

As he walked away, he called over his shoulder, "Go back to Greece."

VI.

Around 3:45 pm, about eight girls walked onto the street from the settlement of Beit Hadassah and began yelling insults at Palestinians watching from balconies across the street. Several began throwing stones at their homes. A soldier tried to cajole the girls into leaving. They ignored him and continued shouting and throwing stones.

They were joined by several small boys and a teenager in a prayer shawl who began reading from a prayer book. Another soldier approached the group, and the two of them ordered the children to leave. They ignored both soldiers. The girls began chanting the name of Baruch Goldstein [the man who committed the massacre in the mosque in February 1994] and saying, "Goldstein is our father" in Hebrew. Then they began throwing rocks and spitting in our direction.

A visiting Quaker professor engaged one of the settler men who was watching the children, and told us later, "I asked him how he, as a parent, felt about the children throwing rocks at Arabs and yelling, 'Goldstein, Goldstein.' He spent the next twenty minutes not answering my question."

VII.

After the girls dispersed, Carmen Pauls, Wendy Lehman, Hedy Sawadsky, and I sat near the Beit Hadassah checkpoint. Ben Israel and the young man who had talked about the Messiah again passed the group. Ben Israel proclaimed loudly, "We should gas them all. Does anyone know where we can get Zyklon B? I heard you can get it in Germany. I think we should take some Zyklon B, put all these—I don't know what you call them—they're not human. Take all of them and put them into little camps and gas them."

Joe, the visiting Quaker professor, asked, "So you think what the Germans did to the Jews justifies the Jews using the same tactics against the Arabs?"

"Absolutely. We've learned our lesson. I'm a member of the Jewish Nazi party." His friend tried to hush him. "I'm not," the friend said. "Well, I am," Ben Israel said. "I'm a Jewish Nazi."

He then told the CPTers that he had no particular desire to kill Arabs. "We'd be much happier shooting Rabin and Peres."

After a pause, Ben Israel told us that the people living on Dubboya Street had roots that went back only about 100 years. "They're not from Ishmael. They're mixed. Mostly they're from Greece. The Ottoman Turks brought them over."

"Where are you from?" Wendy asked.

"I'm from here," he said.

"I mean, where were you born?"

"I was born in Romania," said Ben Israel, "but I don't see what that has to do with anything."

Carmen and I went further up the street at this point and the two young men continued their conversation with Wendy and Hedy. "We're at war. We are at war with these people," Ben Israel told them, pointing at the Palestinians up the street.

Hedy tried to tell him that all people—Jews, Arabs, Christians—have the breath of God in them. "So does a dog or a goat," said Ben Israel's friend. "These people are immoral," added Ben Israel. "Terribly immoral. Homosexuality came from these people."

He continued, "We know what we're doing is between us and God. If I kill an Arab, I will know I am doing it for the right reasons. Not because I hate him, but because he'll kill me."

Ben Israel ended the conversation by saying he had one uplifting thing to share. "We're going to rebuild our temple. We're going to keep our land. They can't take our land. The world can't take our land. We are going to retake Jordan, retake Lebanon, retake Syria."

"Soon," his friend added.

"Yes," agreed Ben Israel. "Very soon."

VIII.

A young man dressed like the settlers had watched quietly while the girls from Beit Hadassah had shouted insults and thrown rocks. He came over to a group of Palestinians on the street and began talking to them in fluent Arabic. At first skeptical, the Palestinian young people began asking him rapid-fire questions. Hisham Sharabati, interpreting, told us that he was telling the group that his family had come from Iraq, but that he had been born in Jerusalem. A young woman brought a newspaper out of her house and asked the young man to read aloud to test his Arabic.

Sharabati shouted, "What do you think of the situation in Hebron?"

"It is very beautiful here," he said. "But Nablus is more beautiful."

Soldiers approached and tried to drag the young man away. I called out "Shabbat shalom."

"God helps you," he called back.

He resisted the soldiers' attempts to remove him. "But they're my friends!" he protested. As the two soldiers each took one of his arms and physically forced him to walk away, he called back to the assembled Palestinian young people, "Come visit me in Jerusalem."

It was the only time that long afternoon that the soldiers intervened to prevent an Israeli from making contact with Palestinians.

Sharabati, as he watched the young man being dragged away, said, "He was very crazy."

IX.

At 4:35, four male settlers walked past. One of them has become known to CPT members as the "Kill the Arabs" guy;[39] as is typical, he shouted these words as his group walked past.

---

39. The team later found out that this man was Avishai Raviv, an agent the Shin Bet sent to infiltrate the settlers. After the Rabin assassination, he was investigated for not

Another of the men called, without waiting for a response, "Why are you interviewing Arabs when you should be interviewing Jews?

"Kill the Arabs," the first man said.

"Thank you very much," Sharabati responded.

"F*** you," one of the men said. CPTers witnessed this particular settler assault a seventy-five-year-old man ten minutes later, after the man became angry at comments this settler was making about the reputations of the old man's wife and daughters.[40]

X.

As CPT members Carmen Pauls and Hedy Sawadsky returned from a "night patrol" to the mosque at 7:35 pm, one of the settlers from Beit Hadassah called out to them, "Watch out! Wearing a keffiyeh like that you will be stabbed." [A keffiyeh is a scarf that older Palestinian men typically wear on their heads. CPTers wear keffiyehs tied to their backpacks so that they will not be mistaken for settlers.]

On September 30, just hours before Kern was scheduled to leave the country, Lehman and Kern arrived early for the Saturday afternoon presence on Dubboya Street. Lehman heard shouting coming from around the corner, went to investigate, and saw some settler teenagers throwing bottles at people in the marketplace. She called for Kern to follow her. As Kern turned to walk in her direction, she heard people further up the street calling, "Kathy. Don't go. They are coming."

Kern turned and saw about twenty men appearing to range in age from mid-twenties to early forties walking purposefully up the street. She began walking up the street toward the people who had called her. A cry went up behind her and she heard running. Someone yanked at the red-

---

having reported the intentions of Yigal Amir to kill Rabin. The Israeli left pointed out that perhaps the Shin Bet should not use agents sympathetic to the settlers' agenda if it wanted reliable information.

40. When Kern and Lehman accompanied the old man, Mahmoud Al-Bayed, to the police station later, they were interviewed separately by the same Shin Bet agent who had assisted Hani Abu Haikel after settlers attacked his mother (see n. 28). Mr. Al Bayed had not mentioned the physical attack; he wanted the police to do something about the insult to his daughters and wife. The agent then spoke to him again, at which point the elderly man confirmed that the settlers had assaulted him. When the agent asked Kern to tell him more about CPT, she told him that the organization had received an invitation from mothers of Russian soldiers and Chechen women's groups to go to Chechnya. He told her, "Don't go to Chechnya. We need you here."

checked keffiyeh[41] Kern had tied to her backpack, pulling her over onto her back. Several men spit on her and kicked her as she lay on the ground.

The men ran past and began breaking the windows on all the cars parked on the street. When Kern began taking pictures, a very large man turned around and shouted, "No. No pictures."

Five or six men tried to grab her camera. One of the men punched her in the ear and knocked her to the ground. As the men dragged Kern around on the ground by the camera strap, she noticed that there were no soldiers at the Beit Hadassah checkpoint, and she began screaming in order to attract attention. (Kern later regretted doing so. Palestinians watching from their homes on Dubboya Street could not see her because of all the settlers clustered around her and they thought the men were torturing her. Years after the incident, neighbors on Dubboya kept expressing sorrow that they had called her to come toward them, because they assumed settlers would not attack her.)

Lehman returned from around the corner, saw the men who were attacking Kern, snapped a picture of Kern's chief assailant, and joined her in trying to retain the camera. They both were pushed to the ground again. Lehman was kicked in the back and head and the man who had socked Kern stomped hard on Lehman's hand, which made her release the straps. He ran toward the settlement of Beit Hadassah, holding the camera high above his head. His co-assailants ran with him, laughing and cheering.[42]

---

41. Many of the settlers had strong reactions to them. One woman said wearing keffiyehs was the equivalent of wearing gang colors. Even one of the team's Israeli peace activist friends told them he felt uncomfortable with them when team members displayed them. He said it showed CPT had "sided" with the Palestinians. CPTers eventually decided to stop wearing them, because they felt they had built enough trust with Palestinians and they were unnecessarily alienating to soldiers and settlers.

42. See Reuters news brief, "Hundreds of settlers rampage in Hebron." In May 1996, Kern and Lehman gave early testimony in court against the man who had assaulted them, Natan Levy (of whom Lehman had taken a photo). The police wanted him for violent assaults in other locations as well. After seeing how the lawyers, judge, and translator treated him, the team realized Levy was mentally slow and had probably been manipulated by more intelligent people, such as Baruch Marzel, who was standing with Levy when Lehman and Kern walked into the court that day. Both women felt almost sorry for him. Later, after the Rabin assassination, Lehman read in the *Jerusalem Post* that Levy was Avishai Raviv's roommate (see n. 39). He told the Associated Press that he would turn himself in only if he could see a lawyer immediately, "not after 48 hours," and would be questioned without physical violence. Wendy Lehman, e-mail to author, November 12, 1995. See also the United Nations, "Report of the Special Committee to Investigate Israeli Practices Affecting the Human Rights of the Palestinian People and Other Arabs of the Occupied Territories," which refers to both Levy and Raviv as Kach activists.

A little over a month later, on November 4, 1995—the same day Yigal Amir assassinated Yitzhak Rabin—CPTer Dianne Roe was also assaulted by settlers on Dubboya Street. Roe, who would go through training in January 1996, had befriended a Palestinian teenager, R., and agreed to meet the girl's sister, W., in front of Qurtuba school, so she could see W.'s scrapbook on Bosnia.[43] Settlers were threatening the children in Qurtuba—preventing them from leaving school—as often happened on Saturday afternoons. Wendy Lehman was videotaping them when a settler kicked W. As Roe attempted to intervene, settlers knocked her down. When R. came to Roe's aid, settlers knocked her down as well. Then they began dragging R. along the ground by her hair braid, kicking her as she screamed until an Israel soldier rescued her. After the situation had calmed down, an adult settler who had earlier threatened Lehman told her, "You will pay a very high price if you help these Nazis," and gestured toward the Palestinians. When Roe asked him where he was from, he said. "It's not your business. This is my country and any foreigner who comes to be with these Nazis will pay with their life."[44]

The New York Times later conflated the two attacks in an article about Yigal Amir, the young man who assassinated Prime Minister Rabin on November 4, 1995:

> Such trips to Hebron were one of the [Amir] brothers' frequent activities. Several weeks ago, witnesses say, the two swaggered in the lead of such a group, some of whom broke ranks and attacked a line of Christian women peace activists who regularly placed themselves between the Jews and Palestinians, knocking two of them down and dragging them by their hair.[45]

Several hours after the assault on Roe and the two girls, more than 100,000 people gathered at Kings of Israel Square in Tel Aviv in support

---

43. Since the girls' family was sensitive about their coming to public notice, the author has used initials instead of names. They later forbade the girls from associating with CPT, because CPT had introduced them to some young Israelis.

44. Dianne Roe, e-mail to author, November 22, 2003. See also Lehman and Roe, "Israeli Settlers attack Palestinian Girls and Christian Peacemaker Team Member," November 5, 1995. Lehman captured most of what happened on videotape, although a settler threatened her for doing so. Reuters cameraman Mazen Dana begged to use the footage and then claimed to have lost it. Dana was later killed by U.S. forces in 2003 while working for Reuters in Iraq.

45. John Kifner, "The Zeal of Rabin's Assassin springs from Rabbis of Religious Right." Since the article notes this attack as happening some weeks before Rabin's assassination, it probably refers to the assault on Lehman and Kern.

of the Rabin government's policies. The organizers felt they needed to respond to the numerous settler rallies and demonstrations against the Oslo Accords that had taken place that summer. The turnout was beyond what any of the organizers had imagined, and affirmed that the majority of Israelis supported Rabin's policies to dismantle at least some of the settlements. Jeremy Milgrom, a Rabbis for Human Rights activist and friend of the team, told Kathleen Kern later that the gathering was an emotional high for him—which made what followed all the more traumatic. (He and Amos Gvirtz, another early Israeli friend of the Hebron team, were selling t-shirts at the gathering with the Hebrew slogan, "Human Rights: From Way Back and Forever," using the font and colors the Hebron settlers used for their logo, "Hebron: From Way Back and Forever.") As Rabin left the rally, Yigal Amir shot and killed him.[46]

The assassination had immediate consequences for the work of the Hebron Team. Since Amir had strong ties to the Hebron settlers, public outrage was directed toward them and other right-wingers who had called for the death of Rabin and Shimon Peres.[47] The Israeli police and prosecutors, who had watched the complaints filed against the Hebron settlers go down a big black hole for decades, because of influential friends the settlers had in the Knesset, suddenly had the green light to follow through on charges pressed. Several of the Hebron settlers, as well as other settlers who

---

46. Jeremy Milgrom, e-mail to author, November 8, 2007.

47. The Jewish Community of Hebron immediately went into spin control mode and issued the following statement:

> The Jewish Community of Hebron renounces all acts of violence by Jews and Arabs alike, against all people of all races and religions. The murder of Prime Minister Rabin is a continuation of the violence commencing with the outbreak of the Intifada, that has peaked over the last year and a half, since the signing of the first Oslo Accords.
>
> The Jewish Community of Hebron joins all Am Yisrael in calling for national unity. The sad and tragic events that have culminated with the killing of a nationally elected leader by one of his countrymen demands a public accounting by the national leadership, whose decisions and declarations have led to overwhelming despair among large segments of the Israeli population. This has resulted, unfortunately, in an unwarranted and unjustified act of aggression and desperation by a lone gunman.
>
> The Jewish Community of Hebron sends condolences to Mrs. Lea [sic] Rabin and the entire Rabin family. We hope and pray for an end to all killing and violence.

From the Hebron settlers e-mail newslist, *Hebron Today*, November 5, 1995.

had conspired against the government and carried out violent attacks on Palestinians, were put under administrative detention.[48]

With Amir in jail and the political climate having become hostile toward them, the Hebron settlers and their supporters no longer conducted the Saturday afternoon rampages. This lack of activity led the team eventually to modify the Saturday afternoon presences. Instead of remaining in one place on Dubboya Street, they made a point of patrolling the area on Saturday and visiting the people who lived on the stretch of road between the settlements of Beit Hadassah and Tel Rumeida. The team also sought to build on Israeli and international outrage at the Rabin assassination by calling attention to settler violence against Qurtuba Girl's school, the Abu Haikel family, and the Shakir Shukri Dana family.[49]

The team would not see the summer 1995 level of settler street violence again until the summer of 2000, just before the Al-Aqsa Intifada broke out.

---

48. Right-wing U.S. Senator Jesse Helms, in an interview with a journalist from the settler news venue Arutz-7, spoke out against these detentions as a violation of democratic rights. Kern sent him a letter saying she was glad to hear that he felt so strongly about such detentions and hoped that he would also speak out against the administrative detentions of the 3,000 or more Palestinians currently in Israeli jails. She later received a letter from Helms's office telling her he was glad to know they were "on the same team."

49. See, for example, CPTnet, "HEBRON ACTION ALERT," November 13, 1995.

TWO

New Directions
1996

Although the team no longer had to deal with frequent, egregious street violence after the Rabin assassination, the winter and spring of 1996 was a busy time. During CPT director Gene Stoltzfus's first visit to the Hebron team, he and the team, in consultation with Hisham Sharabati and Fahmi Shahin (a journalist active in the Palestinian People's Party) decided formally to extend the project until, as Sharabati and Shahin suggested, the Israeli government definitely decided to remove the Hebron settlers or leave them in place.[1] The decision meant that CPT-Hebron was to keep running, as of this writing, for another twelve years, with no end in sight. Even though the settlers remained entrenched, new opportunities for violence prevention kept cropping up. Team members monitored the first Palestinian election, pulled off a successful public witness, and were arrested or detained by the military and police in three separate incidents.

The first of these arrests happened on January 8, 1996, the day after Palestinians in Hebron's Old Market, where the team apartment was located, spontaneously pulled down the turnstile gate at one of the access points into the market that the Israeli military had installed for crowd control. These gates impeded both Palestinians living in the Old City and those coming from surrounding villages, transporting vegetables and other goods in donkey carts.

---

1. At the time, Haiti and the D.C. project were still going. Cole Hull, as the team discussed what to do with Hebron, said, "We've got to start learning how to close down projects." Instead, CPT began extending projected times or leaving project proposals more open-ended.

The team asked Hisham Sharabati and Fahmi Shahin on the evening of January 7, 1996, whether they ought to help in the gate removal. The two advisors told them that they should only give support to locals initiating the action and take care not to initiate actions themselves.

Accordingly, the team split up the next day to stand by the gates and see if people made further efforts to take them down. After Kindy and Kern had waited by one gate for a half hour, Kindy began shaking it and examining it for weak points. A few minutes later, Palestinians arrived with power tools and began to cut it up. The action at this gate appeared to ignite a spark that resulted in crews of Palestinians taking apart all the gates in the Old City. Soldiers at the checkpoint opposite the entrance of the alley in which the CPT apartment was located saw the crowd gathering, but could not see the actual work on the gate closest to the CPT apartment.

Eventually the soldiers approached the crowd, saw the gate come down, and detained Kindy, Art Gish, and two Palestinian boys watching the work, whom they grabbed at random.[2] They also grabbed Cole Hull, who had been videotaping the event.

The Israeli police released Kindy and Hull after viewing a tape. (Hull had managed to switch the tape recording the incriminating actions with a tape containing innocuous Hebron street scenes and a puppet show put on by Carmen Pauls when the team was learning how to use the camera.) Gish remained in prison for three days, during which time he refused to eat or drink. After he finished interrogating Gish on the first night, an Israeli officer told him that he would be deported the next day. Instead, the authorities released him without further charges.[3]

Captain Eyal Ziv told the team that although the Oslo II accords signed by Israel and the PLO in Washington on September 28, 1995, had stipulated that the gates in the market should be removed, the gates would now be reinstalled. Like his assertion that the Hebron University students and faculty were angry with CPT for breaking the seal of the main entrance to their campus, this information was not true. The passageways into the Old City would remain open until another commander ordered new gates installed in 2003, during the Al-Aqsa Intifada.

2. Kern had been standing near them, stroking the rabbits at the shop of a vender who sold primarily poultry and eggs, and saw that they had nothing to do with actually removing the gate. When the soldiers saw Kindy and Gish removing the gate with Palestinians, they turned to Kern and said, "What are you doing!?" She said, "I'm petting the bunnies."

3. Gish, "Hebron: Opening Gates to Freedom," 1–2. A more detailed account of the incident may be found in Gish's *Hebron Journal*.

On January 20, CPTers helped monitor the first Palestinian elections, which would ultimately have little effect on the lives of Palestinians. As Cole Hull noted in an article about the event:

> As redeployment approaches, the Hebron settlers' belligerent rhetoric is increasing. Permanent military checkpoint buildings are replacing temporary tents. Bypass roads are being constructed right through some of the most productive grape vineyards in the West Bank . . . Confiscation of Palestinian homes and land continues. Intimidation and harassment persist. The construction crane for [Beit Romano, a yeshiva academy] is still in place, despite the Oslo Accords, which call for the school's closure.[4]

To mark yet another stipulation of the Oslo Accords left unfulfilled, the team sold tomatoes on February 9, 1996, in the vegetable market near the team apartment and the settlement of Avraham Avinu. The team sent out a press release prior to their action:

> Oslo II Market Grand Opening Sale
>
> "Measures and procedures for normalizing life in Hebron's Old City and on the roads of Hebron will be taken immediately after the signing of this Agreement, as follows:
>
> a. opening of the wholesale market—Hasbahe as a retail market"
>
> These are the words of the Oslo II accords, ratified by then Prime Minister Y. Rabin and Y. Arafat on Sept. 28, 1995.
>
> In the interest of helping the peace process move ahead smoothly, and in recognition of the tremendous overwork and backlog of duties that the local authorities must attend to; and realizing too that the Accords, at over 400 pages of small type, and summaries and maps is a difficult document to wade through, the local members of the Christian Peacemaker Team will seek to assist in the transition to compliance with the Oslo Accords.
>
> As such, the Oslo II market stand will begin operation this morning at 11 am, accepting all customers without regard to ethnicity, religion, or historical origin . . .
>
> The market will be located as specified on p. 53 para. 1 of the Accords (English copy: Article VII: Guidelines for Hebron) in the old city area of Hebron adjacent to the current vegetable market, the IDF checkpoint, and the Avraham Avinu settlement.
>
> We invite your patronage.[5]

---

4. Hull, "Signs of the Times in Hebron," 3.
5. CPTnet, "Oslo II Market Grand Opening sale," February 9, 1996.

People from the Hebron Solidarity Committee and various press agencies came down and surrounded the CPTers as they plied their wares in the "Oslo II Market." Pressure from the Hebron settlers on the Israeli military had kept the vendors from selling vegetables there since the Goldstein massacre. The team ran out of tomatoes just as the army moved in to stop the action, which received good coverage in the Israeli and Palestinian media.

Immediately following the action, settler news releases condemned the "Arab demonstration" instigated by several Americans from a Christian group sympathetic with Hamas tactics. The issue of the Oslo Accords was never mentioned, and the demonstration described as more of an effort to block access to the Avraham Avinu settlement (which had not occurred). The settler releases also condemned the complicity of "hundreds of Arabs."[6]

Several weeks later, on February 25, 1996, the Palestinian militant group Hamas blew up the #18 bus in Jerusalem as well as a bus in the Israeli city of Ashkelon. The bombings marked the one-year anniversary of Baruch Goldstein's slaughter in the Ibrahimi mosque and the fiftieth day since the assassination of Yahye Ayyash, "the Engineer," who had masterminded several other bombings.[7]

Kathleen Kern wrote about the event,

> I first heard about the bombings during the morning service at the Lutheran Church when the pastor asked the congregation to pray for the families of the victims. Several people told me afterwards that they had heard the explosion but assumed it was a sonic boom.
>
> I needed to run an errand to Jerusalem's International Convention Center after church,[8] three blocks away from the site of

---

6. CPTnet, "Update from Hebron," February 17, 1996. Bearing Hull's explanatory note, "an occasional piece reading the signs of change, both good and ill, and revisiting stories we have previously reported on," this release was the first CPTnet update. Originally intended to serve the function of recording events and conversations that did not merit a full release, Updates have been adopted by all Christian Peacemaker Teams in the field and adapted to fit nature of each project. See also CPTnet, "Hebron: News of the Week of Feb. 1–7," February 9, 1996.

7. Shimon Peres obliquely admitted to ordering the assassination. A Palestinian collaborator handed Ayyash a cell phone, saying he had a call, which then exploded. The Palestinian Authority, Hamas, and Israel had been observing a ceasefire since December 1995, when the Palestinian Authority and Hamas conducted negotiations in Cairo. Hamas used the assassination as proof Israel could not be trusted and began attacking civilians inside Israel once again.

8. Kern was signing up for a Christian Zionist tour of Kiryat Arba. See her articles, "Ambassadors for the End Times," and "Under-cover with Christian Zionists at Kiryat Arba."

the bombing. Listening to the Hebrew commentary playing on the radio of the Egged bus, I heard the words "Machpelah" and "Ayyash." . . .

As the people on the bus listened to the radio, the lines on their faces seemed to deepen. A man sitting across from me said, "Zeh Shalom?" to his friend in exactly the same tone of voice that I have heard Palestinian men in Hebron say "Hada salaam?" ("This is peace?") after witnessing acts of violence committed by the Israeli military and Israeli settlers living in Hebron.

On the way back from my errand, I stopped at the site of the bombing. There was no indication that a bus had ever been there. Dozens of Orthodox Jewish men wearing rubber gloves were picking up fragments of charred flesh still lying in the road or stuck to cars. Across the street, one young man was up in a tree carefully trying to reach ashy tatters draped over twigs and branches. A boy in a black velvet yarmulke said to his friend, "They found a really big piece of skin hanging up there." Over on the next street I saw more men carefully scanning the street, walls, bushes and trees for human remains—so that they could have a decent human burial.

In the evening, the rest of the team went to visit a friend whose house frequently gets stoned by settlers in Kiryat Arba [Shakir Shukri Dana.] I stayed home to write this story. At 7:30, I received a call from the team asking me to call the police because our friend's house was being stoned again. The policeman at the civil administration told me I had to go to the station near the mosque. As I stepped outside, a soldier from the checkpoint near where we live approached me.

"Why are you living with terrorists?" he asked. "Did you hear what they did?"

I told him about what I had seen in Jerusalem.

"They are animals. They are shit," he said. "They want to kill you and you just don't know it."

He kept yelling as I walked away—long after I had stopped understanding what he said.[9]

The Hebron team put out a release denouncing the terror attacks, noting team members were "sick at heart" over the bombings and rejected "violent sacrifice of human life to achieve political aims or to express rage over previous injustices." They noted that devout Muslims they knew in Hebron condemned the bombing and asked their constituency not to "condemn an entire nation for the actions of a few."

---

9. Kern, *Where Such Unmaking Reigns*, 276–77.

"Pray that God, who loves each human being more than any political cause, will work through this tragedy and inspire both Israelis and Palestinians to seek justice, practice kindness and resolve to treat no one with contempt, hatred or violence," the release concluded.[10]

On February 28, the Wednesday after the bus bombings, Yiphat Susskind of the Hebron Solidarity Committee called the team and said she had heard that the Israeli military was demolishing homes between the Israeli settlements of Kiryat Arba and Givat Ha Harsina on the outskirts of Hebron.

After wandering around the area for an hour and a half, the team came to a house that had furniture, appliances, and sleeping mats strewn around the yard. Two brothers and their families—twenty-two people in all—lived in the five-room house. Because of impossible overcrowding in their parents' home, the Zalloum brothers had built the house in 1991. Soldiers had given them one hour to remove their possessions before they returned with a bulldozer to destroy their home.

One of the brothers gave team members Anne Montgomery, Dianne Roe, Bob Naiman and Kathleen Kern permission to climb up on the roof of the house along with a couple of BBC and AP journalists. A Palestinian journalist, Kawther Salam, told one of the sons to hide the ladder in the vineyard.

Soon, people from the Hebron municipality, including the mayor, showed up soon along with the neighbors. By the time the soldiers arrived with their jeeps and bulldozer, dozens of people surrounded the house. An Israeli friend gave Cole Hull, who was videotaping from the roof of another house, the number of an official from Meretz, one of Israel's most progressive political parties, who said he would pressure Shimon Peres to call a halt to the demolition. Eventually, the military said that anyone who did not come down from the roof immediately would be arrested. The journalists left. A dozen or more soldiers climbed on to the roof.

"Why are you doing this?" Kern asked them.

"Because of what they did to us in Jerusalem and Ashkelon," one said, referring to the bus bombings.

"Because it's our land and we can do whatever we want," another said.

"Because they built without a permit,"[11] a third one responded.

10. CPTnet, "CPT Condemns Jerusalem Bus Bombing," February 25, 1996.

11. Since 1967, the Israeli authorities have not issued building permits for Palestinians who have had the bad luck to have Israeli settlements built near their land. Jeff

One by one, the four CPTers, Bob Naiman, Dianne Roe, Anne Montgomery, and Kern were carried off the roof. The soldiers pushed Bob Naiman's head into the ground and told him to eat dirt. The soldier that approached Kern, the last CPTer left on the roof, had tears in his eyes. "Please come," he said.

"It's not their fault that the bus was bombed," she told him.

"I know," he said. "Please come."

Once the roof was clear, the team watched as the bulldozer plowed into a corner of the house. As the roof slowly wilted to the ground, the women of the household likewise crumpled to the ground sobbing, and the soldiers standing around the CPTers broke into cheers, ululations, and laughter.

The police arrested Roe and Naiman when they followed a young Palestinian man whom police were taking away. They charged the CPTers with incitement. According to Roe, to bolster the latter charge the police kept asking her if she had made eye contact with any Arabs in the course of the three hours team members were up on the roof. The police told Roe that normally Arabs did not get so upset when their houses were demolished, so the team must have caused the resistance. The police charged Naiman with being a member of Hamas when he attended Bir Zeit University in the 1980s. This accusation was ridiculous for a number of different reasons, not the least of which was that Hamas had not existed when Naiman had attended Bir Zeit.

Roe and Naiman were held at the Russian Compound in Jerusalem (former property of the Russian Orthodox church that Israel converted into courtrooms and prison). Israeli lawyer and Hebron Solidarity Committee member Allegra Pacheco released their statements as they waited arraignment.

Halper, head of the Israeli Committee Against House Demolitions, wrote about houses demolished for lack of a permit,

> Normally they are carried out at dawn, after the men have left for work and only the women and children remain at home. And they are randomized so as to diffuse the fear and uncertainty, to deter people from building at all. Once a demolition order is confirmed by the court, the bulldozers could arrive the next morning, or next week, or next year—or never. It is like a reverse lottery you do not want to "win." In the end the policy of house demolitions makes life so unbearable that those who have the means (especially the educated middle classes so critical for Palestinian society) are driven from the country altogether.

Halper, "A Most UnGenerous Offer."

Diane Roe's statement reads as follows:

> I wish to challenge military laws when they are breaking laws of human conscience and violating Palestinian human rights. Actions like house demolitions escalate the violence, and it does nothing to contain the violence. These actions by the military make people angrier and strengthen terrorist organizations, as the people involved find that they have no hope for the future. I want the violence on all sides to end.
>
> The Israeli police have informed me that I am being held for 48 hours and then will be deported. Apparently, my crime is attempting to stop the illegal demolition of a Palestinian home. Whatever happens I hope that this will not discourage others from nonviolently opposing the illegal policies of the Israeli occupation, which continue to this day despite the signing of the Oslo peace agreements.[12]

Connecting the home demolition to the bombing, the team also put out the following "Prayer to Beget Peace":

> The CPT Team in Hebron requests prayers especially in these days following the tragic bombings in Israel. From soldiers, settlers, and Palestinians we hear the sorrow, but also the message that those on the other side do not want "real" peace and that two peoples cannot live together on the same land. On February 28, five Palestinian homes near Kiryat Arba were demolished. This is not land for peace but a reinforcement of a policy, which refuses building permits to Palestinians while it expands settlements like Kiryat Arba.
>
> Even a minor event—recently the discovery of a dropped knife—can cause a humiliating roundup of innocent people, a reminder of all the injustices that give birth to more resentment and desperate acts on the part of a few. We cannot undo acts, but we can counter the spirit of fear and revenge. We can meet low-intensity warfare with the high-intensity prayer required to cast out self-destructive spirits (Mk. 9:29). We can call upon the one Spirit who can touch the deep places of the heart, "who intercedes for us with groans that words cannot express" (Rom. 8:27).
>
> CPT Hebron asks that prayers for the victims and perpetrators of the violence we see here every day. We ask for prayers for those imprisoned unjustly, for those [made] homeless without recourse, for the innocents killed by political expediency and moral torpor. We ask for prayers especially at this tense time when so

---

12. CPTnet, "Update on CPT Members now Held at Russian Compound," February 29, 1996.

> many people seem ready to see danger and respond to violence or the perception of violence in kind, when soldiers step up their patrols, and people polish their weapons. Pray for true peace, peace of heart, mind, and soul. Peace between families, between faiths, between neighbour[s].[13]

On the day of Naiman and Roe's hearing, the police never showed up—possibly because of a torrent of e-mails and faxes from the CPT constituency—so the judge dropped all charges.[14]

The team found out later from friends at the Hebron municipality that the Meretz pressure on Israeli Prime Minister Peres had been successful. He had called to issue a desist order on the demolition of the Zalloum family home. But Captain Eyal Ziv refused to take the cell phone until his soldiers completed the demolition. However, the rooftop witness tied up the Israeli military for long enough that the soldiers were not able to destroy six more houses in the area also scheduled for demolition. The action also alerted a number of Israelis—who had no idea these demolitions were happening—to the problem. Their pressure on the government caused Prime Minister Shimon Peres to call an end to all home demolitions in April 1996.[15]

The Sunday after the Zalloums' house went down, Hamas bombed the #18 bus in Jerusalem again, at approximately the same time in the morning as the previous Sunday. The team decided to undertake a witness against this violence by riding the #18 bus during the hours that the other #18 buses had been bombed the following Sunday and posted the following on CPTnet:

> CPT has been in Hebron since June 1995. The team has worked to deter violence in Hebron by intervening between soldiers, settlers and Palestinians, accompanying Palestinian children who have been the target of settler attacks, demonstrating a non-violent response to the Israeli occupation, and reporting their experiences in Hebron to people in North America, Israel and around the world.
>
> "Unlike many of the somewhat predictable acts of violence to which we have responded in Hebron, such as house demolitions by the Israeli army and harassment of Palestinians by Israeli settlers, acts of violence by the Islamic Resistance Movement have generally

---

13. CPTnet, "Prayers for Peacemakers," February 29, 1996.

14. See CPTnet, "HEBRON URGENT ACTION: CPT THREATENED WITH DEPORTATION," March 1, 1996.

15. See "Collective Punishment," 1–2. See also "Confiscation Protest."

been unannounced, making it difficult for CPT Hebron to try to prevent them," wrote the CPT Team in announcing its plans to the local media. "In this instance, however, we feel that the repeated attacks on bus #18 constitute an implied threat for next Sunday morning. Therefore we feel called to respond to this threat by stating publicly that if bus #18 is attacked next Sunday, CPT Hebron will be on it."

The loss of life as a direct result of these bombings has been painful and tragic. Moreover, the cycle of retaliation following each bombing has threatened the fragile process of peace and reconciliation between Israelis and Palestinians. Nowhere is this more evident than in the city of Hebron, where the first bombing was followed by a wave of house demolitions. It was in the course of these demolitions that two members of CPT were arrested and threatened with deportation. At this writing, the whole city of Hebron is tense.

Yesterday, two yeshiva students were stabbed, Israeli settlers rampaged through the Hebron market, and the Palestinians were placed under curfew. Today part of the market remains closed. Many Palestinians are staying away from the city center for fear of further Israeli reprisals. Moreover, the Israeli government has announced that the already limited "redeployment" of the Israeli army in Hebron, scheduled for March 27, is being "reconsidered.

Copies of this announcement were shared with the Israeli police and all Palestinian political movements. The announcement concluded, "We invite Palestinians and Israelis of conscience to take a strong, public, and principled stand against all violence and to support this action by participation, statements of support, and prayer.[16]

The spring 1996 bus bombings in Jerusalem, Ashkelon, and Tel Aviv were to have fateful consequences for Israelis, Palestinians, and the work of the team. Binyamin Netanyahu of the Likud Party used footage from the bombings on TV and in movie theaters to convince Israeli voters that Shimon Peres and the Oslo process had brought these calamities to Israel. Israeli Arab voters boycotted the elections for several reasons: Shimon Peres

---

16. See CPTnet releases: "Hebron: Clarifying the Status of the CPT Team," March 6, 1996; "CPT Hebron Vows to Ride Bus #18 in Jerusalem Next Sunday," March 6, 1996; "Christian Peacemaker Team—Hebron Responds to Bombings," March 7, 1996; Diane Roe, "PERSONAL REFLECTIONS ON RECENT EVENTS," March 8, 1996; "BUS #18 RIDE FOR PEACE CONCLUDES WITHOUT INCIDENT," March 10, 1996.

The day after the team rode bus #18, Israeli plain-clothes authorities ransacked the office of Defense for Children International in Hebron, taking the files of juvenile clients. Anne Montgomery connected the two events in CPTnet, "LESSONS FROM THE CHILDREN," March 12, 1996.

had ordered the assassination of Yahye Ayyash in Gaza at a time when Hamas was observing a ceasefire, thus causing the chain reaction that led to the bus bombings. He had authorized the April 18, 1996, bombing of the U.N. compound in Qana, Lebanon, in which hundreds of civilians had taken refuge, and, as was true for all Israeli governments, he had generally ignored the needs of the Israeli Arab sector.[17] Thus, Binyamin "Bibi" Netanyahu—who had complained at the time of the Tiananmen Square massacre in 1989 that the Israeli government had lost a chance to conduct mass expulsions of Palestinians from the Occupied Territories—won the election.[18]

Since one of the bombers who had participated in the Jerusalem bus attacks was from the Al Fawwar Refugee camp just south of Hebron, the Israeli military demolished his family's house and put the rest of the camp under total curfew, allowing no food to enter even via U.N. vehicles for two weeks. On March 16, 1996, the Hebron Solidarity Committee organized a food delivery to Al-Fawwar, and CPTers sat with the food for five hours until the military finally allowed a representative from inside the camp to come and fetch it.[19]

---

17. The amount of money Israel allocates to Arab towns and neighborhoods for schools and infrastructure is far lower than amounts allocated to Jewish areas. See Nir, "Anti-Arab Policy bias worsens"; Cook, "'Democratic' racism"; Human Rights Watch, "SECOND CLASS."

In general, Palestinians have told CPTers they see no difference between Likud and Labor governments. Both have supported the expansion of settlements and the confiscation of their land. Some even say they prefer Likud governments because Likud leaders are at least open about their intentions. Although this opinion is largely valid, CPTers have found that Labor governments usually have progressive parties like Meretz in their coalition, which creates more avenues for appeal.

18. "Israel should have exploited the repression of the demonstrations in China, when world attention focused on that country, to carry out mass expulsions among the Arabs of the territories." Benjamin Netanyahu to students at Bar Ilan University (cited in Drake, "A Netanyahu Primer.") It is unlikely that Palestinians would have cooperated with the transfer, as they have learned from history that leaving one's land means losing it. Additionally, Jordan or other Arab countries would probably not have allowed the Palestinians to be forced into their territories.

19. As they waited, other Palestinians outside of the camp spontaneously began donating food. Other Palestinians began aggressively begging for the food as well, but the team told them it had to go to an authorized representative inside the camp. Some CPTers found turning the young men down distressing, but Hull and Kern thought that the pressure paled beside what they had experienced in Haiti. See CPTnet, Hull, "AL-FAWWAR REFUGEE FOOD DELIVERY PLANNED," March 14, 1996; CPTnet, "Food Delivered to Al-Fawar Refugee Camp Under Curfew," March 17, 1996.

The bombings also led to a closure of Palestinian universities throughout the West Bank. Despite the fact that no faculty, staff, or students from Hebron University were ever implicated in the bombings, the Israeli government sealed the university on March 5, 1996, forcing students to meet in schools and other buildings scattered throughout the city of Hebron. CPT began meeting regularly with students and faculty in spring 1996 to discuss strategies for re-opening the university. Team members provided accompaniment for several student marches protesting the closure and for "teach-ins" in front of the sealed campus.

On April 8, CPT taught a "Nonviolent Strategies for Social Change" class on the sidewalk outside the university campus. The next day, students held a sit-in on the campus without notifying the CPTers. Israeli soldiers attacked them, pounded the heads of some into the ground, and chased others, raiding a restaurant in which some had sought refuge. The seven students arrested were beaten in jail.

The students regrouped and backed off from their protests, partly because they did not want anyone else to get hurt and partly because the Israeli military had threatened to close their alternative classrooms. In the months that followed, at the request of students and faculty, the Hebron team sent out urgent action alerts asking its constituents to call for the reopening of the school.[20] The next phase to re-open the university would occur nine months later in December 1996.

While the University resistance movement was on hiatus, the team participated in another action on behalf of a Hebron University professor that was to have a negative impact on the work of the team. On May 28, 1996, CPTers Randy Bond, Wendy Lehman, Tom Malthaner, and Bob Naiman accompanied an eccentric American woman who called herself Sister Ellen[21] to the land of Musallem Shreateh, south of Hebron, to re-

---

20. See Kern and Lehman, "Teaching Nonviolence in Hebron." See also "Collective Punishment" and six releases related to the university witnesses in the March 1996 CPTnet archives.

21. Her real name was Ellen Rosser and she called her one-person operation in Hebron, "The Hebron Center for Friendship, Peace and Human Rights." Sister Ellen was not a nun, but claimed that she was Jewish, Christian, and Muslim. She sought to promote dialogue between settlers and Palestinians and succeeded only in making herself an object of contempt. At the time of the settler attack on Qurtuba school in September 1995, she blithely suggested that the school fly both the Israeli and Palestinian flags, which enraged the parents and teachers still distraught by the attack on the girls. Nevertheless, she intervened vigorously for the human rights of Palestinians when she saw soldiers mistreating them. She also once protected Israelis—wearing clothing distinguishing them as settlers—

move olive trees that settlers from Susia had planted in his wheat field. Shreateh taught Arabic at Hebron University and Sister Ellen had come to know him when she taught English for one semester there.

Shreateh's land had been in his family for many generations at the time that the settlement of Susia moved next door. Settlers had repeatedly destroyed his crops and harassed his family as they tried to work their land. Members of the team had already helped Sister Ellen, at Shreateh's request, take down a fence that settlers had erected around the wheat field during Passover a few weeks earlier.[22]

Sister Ellen did not like the idea of killing the seedlings, so she proposed that they replant the trees across the road near the settlement. Unfortunately, the ground was hard and the team had not brought the appropriate tools. Worse, they had accidentally left their cell phone at Sister Ellen's office.

Eventually, soldiers arrived and detained Rosser and the CPTers after they had planted only one or two trees. While the group was under detention, armed settlers approached, threw stones at them, and tried to spit on them, while the soldiers stood between them and the settlers. The police arrived four hours later, around midnight, and brought Bond, Naiman, Malthaner, Lehman, and Sister Ellen to the Hebron police station, locking them in a staircase and interrogating them for the next fifteen hours.

Team members were able to borrow a cell phone from a Palestinian prisoner and call lawyer and HSC member Allegra Pacheco. However, she was dealing with the eviction of the Jahalin Bedouin from their encampment near Maale Adumim,[23] and was not able to inform the Chicago Office about the arrests until three days later.

Police took the men to a prison near Dura, west of Hebron. Lehman and Sister Ellen were taken to a prison in Ashkelon. When their cellmates began smoking a white powder they put on tinfoil and heated with a flame, Sister Ellen openly reported them to the guards, which resulted in one of the Israeli women pulling a knife on her.

The police said the CPTers could leave if they signed a statement saying they would not return to Hebron. Sister Ellen signed it immediately.

---

who made a wrong turn and ended up among hostile Palestinians in downtown Hebron. Rosser put her body between the settlers' car and the stones being thrown at it.

22. The team left a note for the settlers and the military on a fence post explaining why they had done so. They decided not to write a release about it, because Sister Ellen and Shreateh wished to maintain a low profile.

23. See Applied Research Institute-Jerusalem, "The Jahalin vs. Ma'ale Adumim."

Lehman—left alone with the Israeli prisoners who had not forgiven her for the drug episode and questioned why she would not sign the paper—began to fear for her physical safety. She was also worried about how the news of her imprisonment would affect her father, who had recently suffered a heart attack. When she was finally able to talk to Pacheco, whom police had been misdirecting for several days, she advised Lehman to sign the statement, saying that Lehman could appeal the ruling later. The police told Naiman, Malthaner, and Bond that Lehman had signed and that they should sign, too. Palestinian prisoners in the cell with them also encouraged them to sign, although Naiman, Malthaner, and Bond suspected that the Israeli guards were pressuring the Palestinians to do so. Malthaner chose to remain in prison, but acquiesced when Pacheco encouraged him to sign a few days later.

After consulting with Palestinian Christian supporters, Hebron co-workers, members of the CPT constituency, and Israeli activists, Naiman and Bond returned to Hebron openly on June 12, 1996, joining new team member Bruce Yoder, who had arrived while the rest of the team was in prison. They sent a letter to the police explaining why they were returning, along with a renewed invitation from the Hebron municipality, Lehman returned after a few days of further discernment,[24] and Malthaner flew home on the date he had originally planned to leave the country.

CPT staff and most of Hebron CPTers agreed that the team had made some mistakes when they chose to accompany Sister Ellen. This attitude was reflected in the summer 1996 issue of *Signs of the Times,* which ran a sidebar with the title, "It could have been worse." The sidebar listed all the terrible things that had *not* happened as a result of the abortive olive tree replanting, e.g., serious injuries to CPTers, parents demanding immediate evacuation, etc. The most serious consequence of this action came later—in December 1996 and April 1997 when the Israeli government denied entry to Bob Naiman and Wendy Lehman respectively into Israel.[25]

---

24. At the time, Lehman was still shaken by her experience with her cellmates. She also told the author later that she regretted that her decision to sign the paper had resulted in the men signing as well. However, after reading an excerpt from Daniel Berrigan's *No Bars to Manhood* in Wink's *Engaging the Powers,* she felt empowered to return. See "CPTers Imprisoned, released and resuming work in Hebron."

In a September 7, 2004 e-mail to the author, Lehman corrected some factual errors in the newsletter and other team releases that the author used to write about the incident. They have been incorporated into the manuscript.

25. Lehman's denial of entry was particularly difficult for the team at that time. Mark Frey and Sara Reschly were still worn out from the Fast for Rebuilding (see chapter 3). The

For much of December 1996, Netanyahu and Arafat were negotiating what would become the "Protocol Concerning the Redeployment in Hebron." The Protocol divided the city into H-1, which the Palestinian authority would govern, and H-2—the area around the Old City where the CPT apartment was located—which the Israeli military would control. Although the parties called the removal of an Israeli military presence in H-1 "redeployment," the number of Israeli soldiers in Hebron remained about the same; they were just more concentrated in the Old City.

On December 9, 1996, the Israeli military extended the closure of Hebron University without giving reason for doing so. The students began a concerted campaign to end the closure. After an initial occupation of the campus on December 9, 1996, they began meeting every day outside the gates from about 8:00 AM to 11:00 AM. Some of the slogans on their signs included, "We only want to study," and "We did not kill Yitzhak Rabin," referring to the fact that Bar Ilan University, Yigal Amir's school, remained open after he assassinated Rabin.

Student organizers maintained careful control of participants in their witness, limiting the numbers present and restraining those who responded to soldier provocations. When the soldiers were behaving in a particularly insulting manner, the students would sit down to defuse the tension. Some days, professors came and taught courses such as Applied Statistics in the middle of the street that ran past the front entrance of the university.

CPTers showed up to accompany the students every day, but did not participate much in the planning—with an important exception. One of the organizers, as the soldiers became more aggressive each day of demonstration, asked if the team had thoughts on how to respond to the soldiers' behavior. The team suggested that the organizers include more women students and put them in front of the men. The male students were shocked at the idea of putting women in danger and said they thought the women would refuse. With excitement and bemusement, they reported to the team later that the women students were eager to stand in front.

The move proved to be a good strategy—soldiers were indeed much more reluctant to push the women around. In one instance, soldiers told a professor who spoke Hebrew to tell the women students to move back about a meter; they were too close to the soldiers and the soldiers did not

---

fast also had prevented them from meeting many of the CPT contacts with whom Lehman was familiar. Thus, when Lehman was not able to join them, Frey, Reschly, and Jeremy Bergen (who had joined the team at the recommendation of his aunt, former MCCer Kathy Bergen) were left somewhat adrift.

want to touch them. The professor talked to the women and then came back to the soldiers and said, "The women say you are standing much too close to them. You need to move back to here," the professor gestured to a spot about a couple meters away from the students. The soldiers moved.

On December 28, 1996, Hebron University re-opened. Whether the students' public witnesses were a reason for the re-opening is unclear. Netanyahu was facing international pressure to finalize redeployment in Hebron and criticism of his hard-line policies in the Occupied Territories. A Palestinian journalist told the CPTers that the negotiations for redeployment—to be finalized on January 17, 1997—had caused the Israeli authorities to "permit" the university to open, since the university was in H-1. On the other hand, at the time the demonstrations began, the students, faculty, and staff did not know when or if redeployment would occur. They decided to resist whatever the consequences, and the administration followed the students' lead by terminating the leases on rented classrooms.

On the day that the Hebron University campus finally opened, a student told the team, "This is the result of our peace." Another added, "And our determination."[26]

---

26. For a more thorough discussion of the Hebron students' resistance, see Kathleen Kern and Wendy Lehman, "Teaching Nonviolence in Hebron: Christian Peacemaker Team's Experiences with Palestinian High School and University Students." This article also describes the team's experience teaching about nonviolence to Palestinian boys in a putative English class the summer of 1995. One of these boys, Osaid Rashid, eventually became a regular translator for the team.

PART TWO

Campaign for Secure Dwellings
1997–2000

THREE

Demolitions and Death Threats
1997–1998

On January 1, 1997, Noam Friedman, an Israeli soldier, opened fire with an M-16 in the market near the Hebron team's apartment in hopes of preventing the redeployment of the Israeli military from Hebron. Another soldier subdued him before he killed anyone, although he shot and injured at least five people. Wendy Lehman, Anne Montgomery, Pete Byers, and Lehman's mother Ella Mae Lehman then witnessed soldiers pushing the crowd back and beating some of the Palestinian onlookers a number of whom required hospitalization.[1]

Despite the shooting, the redeployment of Hebron followed through as planned on January 17, 1997—ten months after the date stipulated by the Hebron Accords. In the part of Hebron handed over to the Palestinian Authority, H-1, Palestinians filled the streets waving Palestinian flags—forbidden by the Israeli occupation authorities in the past—and welcomed the newly arrived Palestinian police force. In H-2, which remained under Israeli control, boys began throwing stones at soldiers stationed in front of Avraham Avinu settlement, and the military immediately closed the produce market (where CPT conducted the tomato action a year earlier) and placed all Palestinians under curfew.[2]

---

1. Lehman, "Israeli Soldier opens fire on Palestinian marketplace," 3. See also Contreras, "Radicals in the ranks," 40–42. After the press referred to Friedman as mentally ill, Palestinians in Hebron commented to team members that when Israelis like Baruch Goldstein and Friedman attacked large numbers of Palestinian civilians they were judged mentally unbalanced. When Palestinians did so, they were called terrorists.

2. Rempel, "Redeployment and division of Hebron," 1–2. Rempel would go on to be a founding member of Badil, an organization that deals with Palestinian refugee issues.

CAMPAIGN FOR SECURE DWELLINGS

In spring 1997, the team began an initiative that was to become the primary focus of the Hebron team until the Al-Aqsa Intifada broke out in September 2000. The Netanyahu government had instituted a new campaign of home demolitions. Houses that were "saved" because of Meretz pressure on Shimon Peres in the spring of 1996 were now under threat of demolition again. Hundreds of other families received additional demolition orders. For nearly all the homes, the legal reason for their demolition was that they had been built without a permit.[3] The actual reason was that they belonged to Palestinian families who had had the bad luck to have an Israeli settlement move in nearby. The settlements typically expanded onto Palestinian farmland, and confiscating this land was easier when houses were not on it.

Terry Rempel, Art Gish, Dianne Roe, Mark Frey, and Cliff Kindy initiated the Fast for Rebuilding to impress upon the North American churches the urgency of the issue. Originally, the team decided to fast for 700 hours—one for each house threatened with demolition in the West Bank[4]—and end it on Easter Sunday. "We have stood with Palestinian families as the bulldozers reduced their homes to rubble," wrote the team

---

3. Before Israeli groups had done their work educating the Israeli public, a large portion of the Israelis believed that all home demolitions occurred because the people who lived in them had been involved in some sort of Palestinian military operation. The team witnessed one such demolition on June 29, 1995, when Israeli soldiers destroyed two Palestinian homes at the entrance to Hebron, after they discovered Palestinian militants in a vineyard near the houses. The Israeli army assassinated one militant, then demolished the houses with bulldozers and hand-held missile launchers. Soldiers also bulldozed twenty hectares of the family's vineyard and farmland and destroyed their tractor with a pile driver. (See chapter 1.)

4. Someone told them halfway through the fast that the number was closer to 1,500. According to the Israeli Committee against House Demolitions, during the Oslo negotiations (1993–2000), some 740 homes were demolished. Another 5,000 homes were demolished from the start of the second Intifada (October 2000) through 2004. See Israeli Committee Against House Demolitions, "Frequently Asked Questions." Amnesty International, in its 1999 report about home demolitions in the West Bank noted,

> The number of demolition orders in force in March 1997 was 850. Despite many requests Amnesty International has been unable to obtain more recent figures from the authorities. Since that date, many more orders have been issued than houses demolished, and about 1,300 houses may be under threat of demolition at the present time. These might have a population of perhaps 9,000, or almost a quarter of the entire Palestinian population of Area C.

Separating the West Bank from East Jerusalem, Amnesty International said that 12,000 homes in East Jerusalem were under order of demolition. See its December 8, 1999 report, "Israel and the Occupied Territories."

members. "We know what demolitions will mean for these 700 families [with demolition orders] and feel keenly their despair and hopelessness." Fasting, they said was a way to "move to deeper levels of spiritual nonviolence, to embody solidarity with the Palestinian people, and to allow an inflowing of God's spirit to provide clarity of vision and direction."[5] Sara Reschly and Anne Montgomery also participated in the fast when they joined the team shortly after it began.

Friends of the team set up a fasting tent in H-1, the Palestinian-controlled area of Hebron. In addition to providing a shelter for the public witness, the tent symbolized the Red Cross/Red Crescent tents that Palestinian families received after the Israeli authorities demolished their homes. Palestinian, Israeli, and International groups began making solidarity visits to the tent. Scores of villagers came to share their own stories of house demolitions, land confiscations, arrests, and raids on their homes by the Israeli military. After an Israeli friend, Harriet Lewis, witnessed a home demolition while she spent a week fasting with the team, she went on to mobilize Israeli groups around this issue and planted the seeds for what became the Israeli Coalition Against House Demolitions. Thousands of people from at least eight different countries fasted in solidarity with the team in Hebron.[6]

The fasting tent also resulted in the team developing valuable new contacts in Hebron. A group of young men put themselves at the service of the team, providing help with the logistics of life in Hebron and Arabic-English translation.[7] Through the fasting tent, the team also came

---

5. "Peacemakers Fast for 700 hours," *Signs of the Times*, 1.

6. Ibid., 1–2. Rich Meyer, who would later direct the Campaign for Secure Dwellings and become the Palestine teams' Project Support Coordinator, did a parallel fast in Lafayette Park outside of the White House. He became part of a community of "chronic" protesters in the park, who helped watch each other's exhibits to prevent the National Park police from confiscating them. Homeless people in the park would also help by staying with the exhibits while the protestors went to the bathroom.
On March 20, Art Gish, Wendy Lehman, Bob Naiman, and Jeff Heie accompanied Meyer to the U.S. State Department, bringing rubble and photos from demolished homes. They asked an official there why the U.S. had vetoed the U.N. Security Council resolution calling on Israel to halt settlement expansion. "They essentially said that for policy to change we should be directing our appeal to Congress," said Rich Meyer in a January 18, 2005, phone interview with the author. "The guy we were talking to spent forty-five minutes agreeing with us about what we were saying and then sighed and said, 'It's sometimes hard to defend U.S. policy in this area of the world.'"

7. They were also very helpful in dealing with a young man who sexually harassed Reschly continually and egregiously.

to know members of the Atta Jaber family, who would become some of the team's closest friends.[8] Zleekha Muhtasib, a teacher who spoke nearly fluent English and Abdel Hadi Hantash, the cartographer of the Hebron district, changed from casual acquaintances of the team into friends and co-workers.

The tent also exposed the team to local Palestinian politics. The fasting effort had originally received support from members of The Prisoners Club, a group of men who had served time in Israeli prisons. Because Palestinian political parties were outlawed under the Israeli Occupation, those in the Prisoner's Club had not been able to identify themselves as members of Fatah, Yasser Arafat's political party within the PLO. However, after redeployment, they were free to identify themselves as such. They made most of the logistical arrangements for the team's fast, providing the tent and a doctor to check on the team's health daily.

Arafat's Fatah people, who were trying to solidify their hold on H-1, tried to claim credit for the tent, which upset the members of the Prisoner's Club. They took down the tent on the last day of the Fast in order to spoil the press conference that Abbas Zaki, Arafat's man in Hebron, had arranged at the site.[9]

Near the end of the Fast on March 29, 1997 (Good Friday), the team and about forty Palestinians, Israelis, and other internationals cleared rubble in preparation for rebuilding the Zalloum family home that the team had unsuccessfully tried to save a year earlier. Israeli police arrested Cliff Kindy, Rabbi Arik Ascherman, co-director of Rabbis for Human Rights, and two nineteen-year-old Palestinian youth, Imad Mohammed Shawer and Mamdoh Abd Al Asem Zaatari. The young men were held for

---

8. During the fast, the team heard that his home was about to be demolished in the Beqa'a Valley, east of Hebron and headed out to the location. Frey, Anne Montgomery, and Kindy stayed with the Jabers while the rest of the team followed the bulldozer to the house of the unfortunate family that the Israeli military demolished instead.

9. Intra-Fatah politics had also victimized Zoughbi Zoughbi (see chapter 1) in 1996. The local Fatah people in Bethlehem had nominated him as their candidate for the Palestinian parliament—something of a groundbreaking achievement, given that Fatah members were overwhelmingly Muslim and Zoughbi was Christian. Near the time of the elections, Arafat's people replaced him with their own candidate—much to the anger of the party members.

One could argue that the tensions occurring between the Prisoner's Club, the Bethlehem Fatah people, and Arafat's people symbolized what had happened during the first Intifada, which began as a broad grassroots movement. When Arafat's people took control of it, they quashed many of the democratic reforms for which the Intifada's organizers had called.

a week and tortured. Ascherman's wife bailed him out so he could perform Shabbat services that evening, and Kindy remained in jail for four days until his departure date. Israeli police drove him out onto the tarmac of Ben Gurion airport, dumped the contents of his backpack on the ground, and gave him barely enough time to scoop them back inside the pack before they escorted him onto the plane. The rest of the team broke their fast on Easter Sunday with members of Sabeel, a Palestinian Christian organization, in Jerusalem.[10]

As houses continued to go down, CPT started sending Rebuilders Against Bulldozers (or RAB) delegations to the West Bank, the first ones occurring in June and October 1997. Participants in these delegations spent the first week touring Israel and Palestine and the second week in Hebron, meeting people facing demolition or whose homes were already demolished. When possible, these delegations assisted families in rebuilding the homes or agricultural terraces destroyed by the Israeli military.

In the fall of 1997, CPT launched the Campaign for Secure Dwellings (CSD) to address the growing number of demolitions under the Netanyahu government. The Campaign took its name from Isaiah 32:16–18:

> Then justice will dwell in the wilderness, and righteousness abide in the fruitful field.
> The effect of righteousness will be peace, and the result of righteousness, quietness and trust forever.
> My people will abide in a peaceful habitation, in secure dwellings, and in quiet resting places. (NRSV)

CSD was one of three organizations focusing on the home demolition issue. Its two partners, founded at roughly the same time, were the Israeli Committee Against House Demolitions (ICAHD) and the Palestine Land Defense Committee. Congregations participating in CSD were matched with Palestinian families in the Hebron area facing home demolition. The congregations and families exchanged profiles, letters, and photographs. The North American families wrote letters to their representatives, the Israeli government, and the U.S. State Department describing the threat that their partner family faced. Canadian and U.S. churches and organiza-

---

10. Anglican priest Naim Ateek had founded Sabeel in order to put Liberation Theology—developed in Africa, Asia, and Latin America—into a Palestinian context. The team regularly participated in discussion groups organized by Sabeel after worship at St. George's Cathedral on Sundays, until church politics forced Ateek to leave his position at St. George's.

tions also held vigils and witnesses outside Israeli Consulate offices and the local offices of their senators.[11]

As thousands of Israelis became more aware of this issue, the pressure on the Israeli government likewise grew. ICAHD made a provisional commitment to Palestinian families facing these demolitions that it would rebuild the homes of any family whose home was demolished, at their request. The provisos were that the Palestinian Land Defense Committee had to authorize the rebuilding, the rebuilt homes would be simple cinderblock structures, and the rebuilding had to be a public act of resistance. Most families did not make the request because they feared reprisals from the military.

Home demolitions proved to be an effective entry issue into the Israeli-Palestinian conflict for both internationals and Israelis. Although some people might have believed the Israeli government's propaganda about Arafat and demanded "balance" when referring to the culpability of both Israelis and Palestinians for perpetuating the conflict, almost no one thought demolishing Palestinian homes so that Israeli settlements could expand was a good idea. The movement thus quietly began gathering steam.

1998

On Sunday, January 18, 1998, CPTnet editor Kathleen Kern came home from church and found that the following message from someone with the E-mail ID "AL SHEKHTMAN" had bounced to her address:[12]

> Subject: From KACH International
> Date: Sat, 17 Jan 1998 10:01:25–0600
>
> 3 of your members: Cliff Kindy, Pierre Shantz and Sara Reschly are aiding and abaiting violent moslem terrorists against heroic Jewish Community of Hebron, Israel. Information has been forwarded to

---

11. In a November 15, 2007, e-mail to the author, Doug Pritchard wrote, "For the public action at the 1998 CPT training in Canada we tried to get a real bulldozer but couldn't because all the contractors we contacted were afraid that Jewish builders would cause problems for them in the future. So we used a toy bulldozer at the Israeli consulate action. The media were quite annoyed. Then at the MC Canada annual assembly in Stratford ON in July 1998 we did get a real bulldozer and parked it in front of the conference entrance with the banner ['Stop the demolitions'] and a prayer tent using the . . . theme 'Roses not Rubble.'"

12. When people hit "reply" to CPTnet postings during this period, the messages bounced to one of four addresses authorized to post releases on CPTnet during this period. (Note: all misspellings in these e-mails are *sic*.)

the appropriate offices of Jewish self-defense organizations. It is advised that these 3 persons leave Land of Israel in the next 96 hours.

She forwarded the message to CPT Director Gene Stoltzfus and called him. He told her to call the team in Hebron, although it was 1:00 in the morning there.

Another message soon followed, repeating much of the same information, with the more specific assertion that Reschly, Kindy, and Shantz were themselves terrorists and that they had "help[ed] and assist[ed] arab terrorists in smuggling explosives used in recent bombings of the Hebron Jewish Community in Israel."

Kern wrote the following response that evening:

> Subj: Re: SWIFT PUNISHMENT!
> Date: Sun, 18 Jan, 1998 7:23 PM EDT
>
> Dear Mr. S.,
>
> Please look up "Anabaptism," "Mennonite," "Quaker," or "Church of the Brethren" in an encyclopedia. We are the spiritual descendants of people who were burned alive, drowned, and tortured to death in other ways for refusing to participate in violence at any level—which includes participating in the military.
>
> We believe that all human beings were created in the image of G-d, and loved by G-d, and that no one has the right to harm any human being for that reason. Participating in any action that would physically harm a human being for us is trayf [the opposite of "kosher"]
>
> It would be more likely that the settlers in Hebron would start serving ham sandwiches at bar mitzvahs than it would be for anyone serving with Christian Peacemaker Teams to become involved with explosives or other objects that could bring harm to others.
>
> Thank you for bringing this to our attention.
>
> Sincerely,
> Kathleen Kern

To which Shekhtman responded,

> Date: Mon, Jan 19, 1998 12:38 AM EDT
>
> Ms. Kern,
>
> I am on a humanitarian mission to save the lives of those 3 members of your organization in Hevron.
>
> People are not stupid, nor can you fool anybody. Nobody will go figure if all of your members are stupid/naiive or 1 or 2; are all of them sympatize with Hamas or PFLP or . . . ?

Fact is: they assisted in smuggling explosives later used against Jewish Community of Hebron. People not connected with the Hebron Jewish Community nor with the Israeli Government are angry and the accusing fingers are pointed at those 3. Federal Laws specifically prohibit assisting terrorism overseas: looks like your church choose to violate those laws.

Time to get the 3 to Europe ASAP, before it is too late.

Stoltzfus found a message repeating the same information on the Chicago office answering machine, including the phrase, "This is a warning. This is the last warning." The following message then bounced to his e-mail address:

Subject: Bombing in Hevron!!!
Date: Mon, 19 Jan 1998 06:38:05 –0600

Grieving parents of Cliffy, Pierry and Sari sent their precious darling ones to a very dangerous place. Brainwashed by the church fathers, who themselves were taught that the real menno-, anabapto- and quaker- men were persecuted, burned at stake and murdered by their pseodo-christian bretherin, they must not fear death and do what Jesus tells them to do.

Guess what? Everyone in the Middle East dies w/o fear. This is the end of this argument.

3 poor naiive darlings came to a wolf's den, called "casba". Immediately, certain people became interested and made friends. Unfortunately, on the Middle East, even among "certain" people, there are some who tell other people about what is going on. And other people tell things about those people, too. That's how it happens that some people know more then others. To keep the long story short, there is a higher possibility on "casba" then anywhere else, that during certain illegal activities, carried out behind locked doors of "casba" shops by the abovementioned "interested certain" people, things go wrong and some pieces begin to travel at speeds around 20,000 feet per second with temperatures reaching 5,000 degrees C. At that time many other things around start going wrong and people get hurt.

But the most funny thing will be if in their naiivity and stupidity, the 3 darling ones unwittingly participated in hurting themselves by helping certain people to get things they were not suppost to have! Of course, the fault is not only theirs: their grieving parents are fools, along with the stupid people who sent them there along with the most stupid of all: their church doctrines.

The team began forwarding the messages to Jewish friends and acquaintances to ask their advice regarding how to respond. Mark Levine a contributing editor to *Tikkun* magazine who had visited with the Hebron team,[13] sent a long letter to Shekhtman, ending with an encouragement to read the Hebrew prophets. He closed his January 20, 1998, e-mail message with

> having spent time with cpt in hebron I will say to you that they are doing the work that jews should be, in the spirit of the prophets, preaching peace and trying to stop violence and oppression, period. (isn't that what Judaism should be about?) they would not work with anyone preaching violence, it's simply ludicrous. So I implore you and your organization to leave them alone, or better yet, to use them and their actions to see a spark of Judaism that I fear you have lost.

He received the following response:

> Subject: Re: is this judaism?
> Date: Mon, 19 Jan 1998 22:33:29 –0600[14]
>
> Wednesday is fast approaching and the 3 explosive-smuggling Hamas assistants got to be back home by that time. All shmocks with ideas better put their efforts where their big mouths are and help pay for the airfares.
> All bullshit is ignored.

At a press conference in Hebron on Tuesday, January 20, 2004, the Hebron team issued a statement:

> The only explosive force we believe in is the power of love—stronger than hatred, fear, or the enmities they create. . . [The threats have] interrupted our regular work. We're scared. But we refuse to let this fear stop our witness against injustice and dominations. We also recognize that the fear we feel is only a taste of the fear that Palestinians live with every day under Israeli occupation—fear that soldiers might beat them, fear that bulldozers might arrive at their door to knock down their family home. It also the fear that some

---

13. Levine wanted to set up a Jewish Peacemaker Team that would do work similar to what CPT was doing in Hebron. Around the same time, an American Israeli, Charles Lenchner, had a similar idea and actually fielded a group of young Israelis to come to Hebron and paint over racist settler graffiti in June 1998. Lenchner also organized "Olive Tree summer" in 2001, which brought Jews from around the world to stand in solidarity with Palestinian families facing violence and the loss of their land.

14. Although the dates of the e-mails appear to be out of order, Shekhtman's response to Levine, dated January 19, did follow Levine's message, dated January 20. Levine travels frequently and may have been in another time zone.

Israelis have when they walk through Mahanea Yehuda Market in West Jerusalem, site of the most recent suicide bombing.[15]

After a several-day hiatus, a new threat arrived on January 22, 1998:

> To: Kathleen Kern
> Date: 98–01–22 12:34:38 EST
>
> Rabbi Meir Kahane, ZT"L, taught Jews never to stand silent when other Jews are threatened. Unfinished hitlerites of the mennotite faction, of which your are one, openly engaged in a persecution of the heroic Jewish Community of Hevron will learn that thare are plenty of Jews willing to stand up for their People.
>
> Mutherfucken scum like you, threatening the expulsion of Jews from their homes, engaged in bombing of a kindergarten in Hevron will end up like your spiritual father: hitler.

Also on the 22nd, Doug Pritchard, the CPT Ontario coordinator, posted his weekly "Prayers for Peacemakers" on CPTnet:[16] "Pray for the safety and steadfastness of the Christian Peacemaker Team in Hebron, West Bank. They have received death threats from the Israeli terrorist group Kach."

To which he received the following reply two days later from Wim and Irene Kortenoevan, writing from an address in the Netherlands:

> Subj: Re: Prayers for Peacemakers, Jan. 22
> Date: Sat, 24 Jan, 1998 11:29 AM EDT
>
> We prefer to pray for the survival of the Jewish community of Hebron, which is threatened by your Christian anti-semitic terrorist group and its Arab allies. You are inciting to violence against and the murder of Jews, just like your ancestors did in Germany. You are Amalek. You are Amalek. But you will not succeed. [See Exodus 17:13–16.]

The final communications from Shekhtman were forwarded by other CPT supporters who had tried to engage him in dialogue:

15. "CPTers Defy Death Threat, Stay in Hebron," 1. "Lives in Jeopardy," 1–2. CPTnet, "Hebron/Chicago: Update from team and background on Kach," January 22, 1998. See also Finch-Durichen, "K-W man on peace team threatened with death"; "Hebron peace workers take precautions but opt to stay." Both articles in *the Kitchener-Waterloo Record* focused on CPTer Pierre Shantz.

16. Pritchard began posting weekly "Prayers for Peacemakers" in February 1996 for those people of faith who supported CPT's work and wanted to target their prayers. The prayers also proved to be popular with people who found the number of releases coming in from CPT projects overwhelming, but still wanted to support CPT's efforts.

Subject: Re: Bombing in Hevron!!!
Date: Sat, 24 Jan 1998 05:30:55 −0600

As with all people, there is a dark side to Christianity, too. We identified hypocrites of mennonite/anabaptist/quacker persuasion who talk sweet non-violence but have a leftist political agenda. They sent a Mennonite Bombmaking Team to Hevron, Israel, that smuggles explosives, acts as a lookout for bloodthirsty terrorists, helped to bomb a kindergarten, instigates mobs for attacking small Jewish community, hides criminals and provides other logistical and financial help to Hamas, Islamic Jihad and PFLP.

Already, every 4th member of Jewish Community of Hevron was attacked, stabbed, or beaten in past 2 years. 17 were brutally murdered by terrorists. G-d commanded us not to stand idly by our brothers' blood. The clock is ticking.[17]

Subject: Re: Bombing in Hevron!!!
Date: Sat, 28 Jan 1998 01:59:35–0600

Creatures like you can do anything: write to anyone, even smuggle explosives to bomb kindergartens. [The recipient of this message had told Shekhtman he would continue write his congressperson expressing his concern about U.S. military support of the Israeli military machine.] Truth is: Mennonite church is full of Nazis (nuts: crazy people). Clock is ticking: answer is on the way. Poor darlings: we tried to save them!!! May you abandon idolworship and see the light before it is too late![18]

On January 27, 1998, a car full of young settler men followed JoAnne Lingle and Dianne Roe while they were on night patrol.[19] When it pulled up beside them, a young man with an American accent called out, "Go back to America, you scumbags, before we kill you." As the car pulled away slowly, the same voice repeated more loudly, "We will kill you!"[20]

---

17. Al Shekhtman, e-mail to EJERALEIGH@(domain withheld), January 24, 1998.

18. Al Shekhtman, e-mail to gillham@(domain withheld), January 28, 1998. All other e-mails to and from Shekhtman are listed in the bibliography.

19. Team members typically circled the area between Beit Hadassah and the Il-Ibrahimi mosque/Cave of Machpelah at nights to monitor soldiers' checkpoints. Because so few Palestinians were out at that time, the team was able to have extended conversations with soldiers during these patrols.

20. E-mail from JoAnne Lingle to the author, January 31, 1998. The team in Hebron believed that the interaction confirmed a connection between the e-mails and the Hebron settlers.

The fallout from the threats was largely positive. The Jewish constituency following the work of CPT sent messages of support and progressive Israeli groups made solidarity visits to the team in Hebron.[21] Many of them had also received threats from Kach and the Jewish Defense League. The fact that rightwing settler partisans had never followed through on these threats helped alleviate the anxiety of the team and staff.[22]

After deliberation and consultation, staff at the Chicago office decided to notify the FBI about the E-mail and telephone threats to the team.[23] An agent arrived and interviewed them, but CPT reservist Pierre Gingerich was the first person to find the location of Shekhtman—Des Plaines, Illinois—after researching the computer codes Kern had sent him. CPT submitted Gingerich's research to the FBI, who, several months later told the Chicago office that the agents had found Shekhtman themselves (where Pierre Gingerich said he was located.) They asked Stoltzfus if he would consent to the tapping of the office phone in order to entrap Shekhtman. He, along with other CPT staff and advisors, decided this collaboration with the FBI went one step too far and the FBI dropped the case.

For the remainder of 1998, the team mostly focused on building the Campaign for Secure Dwellings network. Team members became especially involved with the Jaber and Al Atrash families and those living near them on the eastern and southern borders of Hebron respectively.

The Al Atrash family first had their home demolished in 1988, because it was too close to a bypass road that the Israeli authorities had not yet

---

21. After the Chicago office received the bomb threat on April 5, 1998, Jews in the Chicago area affiliated with *Tikkun* magazine also came to serve as a violence-deterring presence at the office on W. Polk Avenue.

22. The team felt sheepish about calling attention to themselves in this manner. Given the ongoing brutalization of Palestinian friends in Hebron and the number of houses the Israeli government was demolishing, the threats seemed minor by comparison. In a letter to his supporters Pierre Shantz wrote, "the violence that these threats represent is the violence that we are here to stay against . . . We now have a taste of what Palestinians feel every day, except they don't have the protection of a foreign passport." Finch-Durichen, "Hebron Peace workers take precautions but opt to stay."

A few months later, when the team received another death threat via E-mail, they called Harriet Lewis to report it and she told them she thought they were overreacting.

23. For older CPTers who remembered the FBI targeting antiwar and civil rights activists in the 1960s and 1970s as part of its COINTELPRO program, seeking help from the FBI seemed like making a deal with the devil. Additionally, as pacifists, some thought it might be hypocritical to seek help from people committed to using violence to achieve their ends, however noble. But, as Gene Stoltzfus told Kern when he consulted her about the threats, "This really is their job."

built. Yussuf al Atrash had again built on his property in 1995. Many other families living in Area C—the 70 percent or more of the West Bank that remained under Israeli control after the Oslo Accords were signed—had also chosen to build in 1995, because the Oslo process led them to believe they would soon be living in their own state. Al Atrash had expended an enormous amount of effort and money to receive a building permit for the home, hiring an architect, paying the licensing fee, presenting the plans to the Planning commission at the settlement of Beit Il. However, the Israeli Civil Administration had stymied all of his efforts to receive a permit.

Seventy soldiers under the command of Captain Tzvika, who would figure heavily in most subsequent home demolitions in the Hebron area during this period, arrived at the house on March 3, 1998. Yussuf's wife, Zuhoor, locked herself inside with the youngest two her ten children, Ra'ad and Wa'ad. The soldiers broke in, threw the children outside of the house, and attacked their mother in front of them. When Yussuf and Zuhoor's brothers arrived and tried to intervene, soldiers arrested them.

Jeff Halper, head of the Israeli Committee Against House Demolitions used the case of the Al Atrash family as a template for the issue of home demolitions in a letter to the British Ambassador to Israel at the time:

> To: His Excellency the British Ambassador, Mr. David Manning
>
> A Protest Against the Brutal Treatment of the Al-Atrash Family of Hebron by the Israeli Authorities
>
> The Israeli Committee Against House Demolitions wishes to register its protest against the brutal treatment, going back over ten years, of the Palestinian Al-Atrash family of Hebron by the Israeli authorities.
>
> . . . There cannot be a better example of arbitrary and completely superfluous cruelty as this case. Here is a family with 10 children, reduced to poverty by what is euphemistically called "the closure," the forbidding of most Palestinian workers to come into Israel during the day for purposes of employment—even though Israeli policy of the past 30 years was designed to transform them into a work-force completely dependent upon Israel by preventing the development of Palestinian industry, agriculture, business or even an adequate infrastructure in the West Bank and Gaza. Yusef Al-Atrash, an experienced construction worker, now sews boots in Hebron for a salary of $350 per month. All he wanted to do was build a house for his family ON HIS OWN PROPERTY which has been in his family since Ottoman times (and for which he has all the proper documentation). No politics involved, in a rural area

far from any Israeli settlement, army base or by-pass road, yet on a hillside from which he could point out another eight or nine houses also slated for demolition, and a school building the Israelis will not allow to be completed.

Why was he denied the permit? Well, the reason given by the Civil Administration was that only one house was permitted on "his" property according to the 1942 British planning policy—and a relative of his had already built one. But what is "his property?" The Mandate plan was intended to ensure that agricultural land was not overwhelmed with building—although the Al-Atrash property is on a steep and rocky slope that has never been cultivated. As time passed fathers passed on their holdings to their children, thus subdividing the land as happens naturally in every country. Yusef inherited his plot of six acres from his father, had it carefully surveyed and marked with border markings and officially registered with the authorities. When he traveled to the Israeli Civil Administration to obtain a building permit, however, he was told that the boundary is not recognized and that all the land going back 100 years was recognized as one undivided unit, upon which a house had already been built, thus foreclosing any other building in the future. Taking out his maps, Yusef protested that his plot was legally marked and registered, but was waved out of the office of the Israeli clerk Yossi Hasson (who has a reputation of dealing curtly with Palestinian petitioners seeking permits), who told him: "I don't care." The trek to the Civil Administration north of Jerusalem, the wait to see Hasson and the trip back took between 7–8 hours; the meeting with Hasson took less than a minute.

... The Israeli Committee Against House Demolitions protests this action on the part of the Israeli authorities and calls on people and governments of good will to raise their voices as well. Indeed, we should together raise the issue of mass house demolitions—a cruel and completely unnecessary application of a Kafkaesque policy of planning in which Palestinian homes are demolished because they are "illegal" yet making it virtually impossible for Palestinians to obtain building permits—onto the international agenda. Over 1000 Palestinian families on the West Bank and in Jerusalem face the loss of their houses in this increasing aggressive campaign to clear most of the West Bank of its Palestinian residents.

Simply on a human level it is one of the most shameful aspects of Israeli occupation, one that violates fundamental rights of people to decent shelter as guaranteed in human rights covenants signed by Israel itself. And it victimizes primarily the poor and defenseless, causing untold suffering as it destroys any possibility of reconciliation between Israelis and Palestinians. The policy of home demolitions for punitive and political reasons (Israel being the only country in the world following such practices) illustrates more than [any] other element of our tragic situation how good people with their own history of persecution and suffering can so easily become the perpetrators of persecution and suffering when they gain power over others. We seek in our efforts not only to end the gratuitous pain and misery caused by our government's actions, but to try to reclaim that basic humanity that we ourselves invoked as a justification for having a state of our own.

We call on you and your government to aid us, Palestinian and Israeli together, in combating this inhumane policy that only undermines any chance for peace. Protesting the brutal and arbitrary treatment of the Al-Atrash family is a place to start.

THE ISRAELI COMMITTEE AGAINST HOUSE DEMOLITIONS[24]

As the family tried to rebuild, the team began sending one member every night to stay with them. Rich Meyer spent several weeks camping with the family in a large tent supplied by the Red Cross.

Continuing a twenty-four-hour presence with the Al Atrashes, however, proved stressful for the team. By 1998, the team's work had expanded to include visiting dozens of other families who belonged to the CSD network. The team was also conducting regular tours for Israeli, Palestinian, and international delegations and individuals seeking to understand the situation in Hebron and the rest of Palestine. They had to visit regularly with families affected by soldier and settler violence and conduct regular patrols past military checkpoints in their neighborhood. Daily meetings and writing required a significant block of time. Team members had also begun establishing relationships with Palestinians, Israelis, and internationals in Jerusalem and Bethlehem and taking Arabic lessons from Selwa Awad in Bethlehem.

Although Meyer did not mind staying with the Al Atrashes indefinitely, he could only work in Hebron for shorter stints, given his family and farm responsibilities at home in the U.S. Other team members felt isolated when they stayed there for more than a day. Given these realities, as well as the inconvenience of having one of their cell phones dedicated to the Al Atrash site,[25] the team began gradually diminishing the twenty-four hour presence.

24. Halper, ICAHD e-mail newslist, March 23, 1998. Also reprinted in Kern, *Where Such Unmaking Reigns*, 111–15.

25. As of 2007, cell phones had become cheap enough that fulltime CPTers working

On March 22, 1998, the team went to the monthly hymn sing at the Mennonite Central Committee office in Jerusalem hosted by MCC country representative Patty Shelly. On their way to Jerusalem, Meyer and Kern received a phone call from Bassam Eid. Eid, who worked with the Israeli Human Rights organization B'tselem at the time, told them that soldiers had arrived at the Al Atrashes, attacked and then arrested the parents, Yussuf and Zuhoor Al Atrash, and their two oldest children Hussam (18) and Manal (17). They also confiscated the cement mixer the family was using to rebuild.

Meyer and Kern immediately returned to Hebron and found the younger children wandering about the site of their demolished home in a daze. The rest of the team in Jerusalem made the decision to cut short the hymn sing and returned, along with Gordon and Rhonda Brubacher and their two children.[26]

Not only had the Israeli military performed these strong-arm tactics in the presence of Eid, they did so in front of Gideon Levy, a journalist for the Israeli newspaper *Ha'aretz*. Levy posted bail for the Al Atrashes and wrote a stinging article entitled, "The cement mixer is in our hands"—meant to evoke the radioed message that Israeli forces sent when they captured the Western Wall in Jerusalem in the 1967 war.[27] Video of the Al Atrashes that showed Zuhoor and daughter Manal being dragged along the ground in a way that exposed their bare stomachs—extremely shameful in conservative Palestinian culture—appeared on Israeli television and drew offers of help from sympathetic Israelis.

The attack exacerbated existing tensions among family members. The stress caused a debilitating outbreak of shingles in Yussuf Al Atrash. Manal, who had been separated from her mother for six hours at the prison, began having seizures every time she saw the videotape or people pressed her to tell them about her experience. Her incapacity meant that fourteen-year-old Wila', the second oldest daughter, had to take on by herself the enormous housework and childcare burdens that the two sisters had previously

---

in Palestine were allocated their own phones, which they carried with them, traveling to and from their assignment.

26. The Brubachers were spending a year at the Tantur Ecumenical Institute on the border of Jerusalem and Bethlehem. They had already established a relationship with the Al Atrashes on previous visits.

27. Israeli activist Harriet Lewis told Kern what the title meant in Hebrew. In the English edition of Ha'aretz, the article appeared under the title, "All in order," 3.

shared. The Al Atrash's distress, in turn, affected the team because staying with the family struggling with these crises was difficult emotionally.

On June 11, 1998, when team members were not present, the Israeli military demolished the Al Atrashes' partially rebuilt home again. As soon as the bulldozers were out of sight, Wila' Al Atrash ran to see if her rose bush had survived. It had been uprooted but rescued during the previous demolition.

Building on the symbolism of the surviving rosebush,[28] CPT started a "Roses not Rubble" campaign as part of the other CSD efforts. The team encouraged constituents to plant a rosebush that would serve as a reminder to pray for the Al Atrash family and visit their legislators, bringing both roses and rubble symbolizing a demolished home.

In the summer, the team's focus shifted from the Al Atrash family to the extended Jaber family. The shift was partially due to the wishes of the Al Atrashes, who felt that the extra attention CPT had brought to their plight might have made the Israeli authorities target them.

In June 1998, the Israeli military built a road through the land of Abdel Jawad Jaber, Atta Jaber's father, destroying two-and-a-half acres of terraced orchards. Three months later, they uprooted one hundred more olive and fruit trees. On August 4, 1998, when the Israeli military arrived to remove irrigation hoses from the families' tomatoes, they detained CPT reservist Jim Satterwhite as he tried to collect the hoses and return them to the families. He wrote about the experience,

> It is interesting that the army officer who first detained me (technically soldiers cannot make a formal arrest—they have to hand you over to the police for that) said: "I've just been waiting for the chance to arrest one of you from CPT—you cause us so many problems!"
>
> While in the field and later by the police jeep waiting to be taken in, I had the chance to talk with some of the African workers who had been hired to tear up the pipe. At first they were defensive when we told them that they were contributing to the destruction of the family's livelihood, but while I was being detained at the jeep they brought me food and drink and told me that they felt bad about what they had been hired to do.
>
> The Israelis use a disproportionate amount of the available water, drawn from two main aquifers under the West Bank. When the

---

28. According to CPT reservist Jane Adas, who proofread the manuscript for this chapter in 2004, the rosebush ultimately died.

Palestinians try to build on land which the Israelis want to control (regardless of who holds title to it), or use more water than the Israelis want to allocate them, then their houses or irrigation pipes are destroyed. Many of the families in the Beqa'a valley whose irrigation systems have been destroyed also have home demolition orders outstanding (including the Fayez Jabber family where CPT maintained a presence against bulldozers last week).

The police station resembled police stations everywhere—a front desk, a lot of coming and going, etc. The only difference from the basic North-American pattern was that many police officers also carried submachine guns, and soldiers sometimes came in with a prisoner. This difference only served to underscore for me how both the police and the army here are instruments of control— these are truly the "occupied territories." It was thus ironic when— as I insisted on signing the personal recognizance form only in English—the interrogating officer said: "You don't have to be so nervous. We are the police, and Israel is a democracy."[29]

Two weeks later on August 19, 1998, the Israeli military destroyed the home of Atta Jaber's family, along with eight other homes at disparate locations in the Hebron District. The catastrophic effect the demolition had on the Jaber family was a huge emotional blow to the team. They had built close relationships with members of the family, partially because Atta shared with them a vision for coexistence and nonviolent change reflected in his quotation that appeared in CSD materials:

> We have everything here: land, water; it could be very beautiful. What we are missing is love between people. There is enough for everyone if everyone is willing to share. Engineers should be studying how to grow bread in the desert, not inventing new weapons. Palestine needs factories to make medicines to heal diseases, not to manufacture weapons.[30]

The charisma of the Jaber family inspired Israelis, Palestinians, and internationals to flock to the Jaber land and help them rebuild, but less than a month later, on September 16, 1998, the military demolished the Jaber home once again. When 'Atta tried to get his five-month-old son Rajah out of the house, soldiers arrested him and charged him with "assault by infant," because he thrust Rajah into the arms of an Israeli Border Police

---

29. CPTnet, "HEBRON: Reflections on Water," August 5, 1998. See also Steiner, "History Prof held, released from Hebron jail," 3.

30. Quotation from Campaign for Secure Dwelling materials. Original notes at CPT Hebron, "Atta Jaber Family."

and said, "You raise my child, I cannot." They damaged 'Atta's windpipe when they put him in a chokehold, for which he sought medical treatment in Jordan. Because of injuries sustained when soldiers beat her, Rodeina Jaber suffered blinding headaches for weeks afterwards. The couple's oldest daughter, Amooni, became withdrawn and depressed.[31]

Since the Jabers had welcomed so many people into their home and served dinner to several CPT delegations, the subsequent campaign "Reduced to rubble. Whom shall I send?" garnered numerous responses. CSD coordinator Rich Meyer sent to constituents photos of two-year-old Dalia Jaber, the couple's second child, and her three-day-old brother Rajah with the message, "Because you have not demanded an end to the Israeli policy of home demolitions, these Palestinian children were made homeless on Wednesday, August 19, 1998 and again on September 16, 1998 in the Beqa'a Valley east of Hebron." The CSD participants then sent them to congressional and U.S. State Department representatives.

The Campaign for Secure Dwellings celebrated its first anniversary in December 1998. In total, fifty-eight churches had been matched with families who had experienced or were facing home demolition. Many of the matches had their roots in the participation of church members in CPT-RAB delegations. After helping to rebuild homes or farming terraces that the Israeli military had destroyed, the delegates went home and persuaded their churches to join the Campaign for Secure Dwellings.[32] A surprising number of people whose churches were matched with CSD families sight unseen also eventually participated in delegations to visit the families with whom they and their churches were matched.

The pressure on the Israeli and American governments from letter writing and fax campaigns—undertaken by people who were part of the CSD and ICAHD networks—began to have an effect in 1998. Friends from the Israeli Committee Against House Demolitions reported that Secretary of State Madeleine Albright had begun to issue great, though unpublicized, pressure on the Israeli government to stop demolishing homes. The ICAHD representatives also told the team that a contact in the U.S. State Department told them that the Department received more letters on the issue than it did for any other issue in the entire Middle East.

---

31. CPT Hebron Chronology February 1995–September 2003.

32. As of January 2005, two rabbis (without their congregations) also participated in the Campaign for Secure Dwellings.

Atta Jaber began rebuilding his home for yet a third time in 1999, but did so quietly, asking that CPT not draw attention to him anymore. The house remains standing as of October 2009.[33]

---

[33]. Sara Reschly, who edited a draft of this chapter in 2004, wrote the following comment on the manuscript, "Apparently one of the ICAHD folks was good friends with the Heb district commander's wife. She became aware of Atta's situation, was moved, and advocated on behalf of him to her husband, who made a deal with Atta—that his home would never be destroyed. Who knows if the agreement will be honored, but it is there. I'm not sure if it was ever written down or if it was just verbal."

FOUR

Continuing the Struggle for Secure Dwellings, 1999–2000

JUST AS THE DEATH threats at the beginning of 1998 had diverted the Hebron team's attention away from home demolitions for a brief period, the team's intervention to prevent soldiers from firing on unarmed demonstrators shifted their focus at the beginning of 1999.

On January 10, 1999, a group of Palestinian men belonging to the Fatah party organized a nonviolent demonstration protesting the closure of the Ibrahimi Mosque and the curfew placed on the 30,000 Palestinians living in the part of Hebron under Israeli control. The Israeli military had imposed the curfew a week earlier after two Israeli settler women were injured, one seriously, when Palestinian militants shot at their van near the Mosque. The Christian Peacemaker Team in Hebron heard about the demonstration and went to observe.

Holding long banners reading, "No For Closure of Ibrahimi Mosque," and "No for Collective Punishment," a group of 70–100 Palestinians marched from the Hebron municipal offices to the border that separates the Palestinian and Israeli-controlled areas. As the marchers approached, the Israeli soldiers and border police—armed with rubber-coated metal bullets, tear gas, and sound grenades—took positions behind large cement barriers, ready to fire.

CPTers Pierre Shantz, Sara Reschly, and Joanne "Jake" Kaufman jumped in front of the soldiers and their guns, crying, "This is a nonviolent demonstration! They are not throwing rocks!" The soldiers, not knowing how to respond, tried to push the CPTers away. Some lowered their M-16s, but other soldiers threw sound grenades that sent the crowd scurrying.

After the demonstration's leadership calmed the Palestinians observing and participating in the demonstration, the crowd returned, standing face to face with the soldiers.

Older Palestinians leading the procession circulated among the youth, telling them not to throw rocks. After about thirty minutes of this standoff, soldiers began pushing the Palestinians. The marchers started to run away and some threatened to stone the troops. Soldiers quickly moved into firing positions. CPTers again got in the way, standing in front of the rifles and saying, "This is a nonviolent demonstration!" Only a couple of rocks were thrown before the Palestinian leaders restrained the youth. No one was injured.

One of the military officers, furious with the CPTers for interfering, began shouting at CPTers Mark Frey and Shantz, telling them to leave the area. Shantz retorted that the demonstration was nonviolent, and the officer slapped him twice. At another point, a soldier physically restrained Kaufman as she tried to stand in front of soldiers taking aim. When the Israeli civilian police arrived, the enraged officer demanded that they arrest Shantz and Reschly. The police also detained Sydney Stigge-Kaufman for a short time on location, and then released her.

The remaining CPTers circulated among the crowd or positioned themselves between soldiers and Palestinians. About an hour and a half after the demonstration began, the Palestinian leadership called for everyone to pray in the street to defuse the mounting tension. The older men knelt on the prayer rugs they had brought with them, calling for the younger ones to join them. An Israeli Druze officer circulated among soldiers, telling them to stay calm; in Arabic, he encouraged Palestinian youth to join the prayers. After praying, the leaders declared the demonstration finished and called for everyone to return to the Palestinian area. No clashes developed after the demonstration ended. A Palestinian leader formally thanked CPTers after the march, saying, "Thank you. You have done your work."

"The success of the intervention was due to three things," Shantz reported later. "The discipline of the men on their way to pray, the efforts of the Druze Border Police officer and our standing between the soldiers and the demonstrators. If any one of those three things had been missing, someone would have gotten shot. There was one officer there who obviously wanted to shoot someone."[1]

---

1. The soldier, known to the team as "Avi," was to have several negative interactions with the team in the next few years. See chapter 7.

The authorities charged Shantz with "pushing two border police and hitting one on the helmet" and "interfering with police doing their duty." They charged Reschly with "yelling 'don't shoot' at soldiers," and "assaulting a soldier" (pushing him). Reschly and Shantz told the court their commitment to nonviolence would prohibit them from pushing or hitting anyone. A third charge by a Russian-speaking soldier that Reschly called him a Nazi was dropped after the court discovered that he did not speak English. Video footage of the event later shown on Israeli TV proved that Reschly and Shantz had intervened nonviolently. The court told Shantz and Reschly to hand in their passports and 2,000 shekels bail each while the police investigated the incident for two weeks. After that time, the police returned the passports and money (which had been raised on the spot at their hearing by Israeli and international supporters) and dropped all charges.

The subsequent arrests—for "interfering with a soldier's duty"—and acquittal enhanced the team's credibility with both Palestinians in Hebron and the Israeli and international peace communities.

In many ways, the action was a defining moment for the Hebron Team—the vision of what CPT was meant to be, the essence of what CPTers are trained to do. As lawyer Jonathan Kuttab told them, "You have a lot of moral power that both sides recognize . . . Running around without guns throws [both sides] off and gives you leverage."[2]

The team's releases from January 1999 contain hints that the praise and notoriety heaped on the team because of the incident made them uncomfortable. In a piece describing the outcome of their court appearance and subsequent release, Joanne "Jake" Kaufman wrote,

> After the court hearing, team members and a Palestinian friend relaxed in a restaurant where Shantz talked about his night in an Israeli prison where he had been well-treated. CPT's Palestinian friend then shared about his 18-day administrative detentions and torture experiences in Israeli prisons, putting the events of the last two days into perspective.[3]

---

2. CPTnet, Kaufman, "HEBRON: Update on Shantz and Reschly's arrests," January 11, 1999.

3. Ibid. CPTer Jane Adas noted to the team some months after the incident that the Associated Press photo showing Reschly standing in front of the soldiers with arms outspread also showed a Palestinian municipal observer beside her, doing the same thing, but no one had bothered to take his name down. In reality, he had stood a much greater chance of getting shot than Reschly did.

In a posting meant to express their gratitude for the support received, team members wrote,

> Dearest friends and supporters,
>
> "As long as [peacemakers] look at resistance as performing individual acts of heroism, there won't be many peacemakers who will survive the enormous pressures put upon them. Without community, we will be quickly sucked back into the dark world of needs and wounds, of violence and destruction, of evil and death." Henri Nouwen
>
> CPT Hebron is grateful for the outpouring of support we received over the course of the past week in response to the arrest of two of our members for intervening when Israeli soldiers were about to fire on a nonviolent Palestinian demonstration.
>
> The solidarity of our Christian, Jewish, and Muslim communities witnessing on our behalf in the courtroom struck deep into our souls. This distinct support community, comprised of [sic] varied skin colors, varied languages, and varied prayer styles bore witness to God's inclusive love. It is in this solid community that we CPTers find witness of God's strength, love, and nearness. We thank you for your witness of love. We thank God for our community.
>
> We were very pleasantly amazed at how quickly the bail money was raised by people digging within their own pockets outside the courtroom—thank you. Additionally, thank you to all those who helped us contact Jonathan Kuttab, our lawyer . . . Once again, thank you dear friends, for your consistent support and prayers. We feel most wonderfully blessed by you, for it is with your backing that we speak and act boldly.
>
> Christian Peacemaker Teams, Hebron[4]

After the January 11, 1999, action and arrests, most of the team's energy again went into the issue of home demolitions. On February 4, the Israeli military demolished the homes of Fayez Jaber in the Beqa'a Valley and Leyla Sabarneh in Beit Ummar (a village north of Hebron). In both cases, the team arrived too late to intervene. As a response to these demolitions, the team again initiated a "Tent for Lent" campaign on March 9, 1999, to call attention to the issue of home demolitions. Using materials from the Coordinating Committee of the Campaign Against the Permanent Occupation,[5] the team noted that the Netanyahu government

---

4. CPTnet, "HEBRON: Thanks from CPT Hebron," January 19, 1999.

5. Groups belonging to this umbrella organization included The Israeli Committee Against House Demolitions, Rabbis for Human Rights, Gush Shalom, Peace Now, Bat Shalom, Yesh Gvul, Netivot Shalom, Alternative Information Center, Hebron Solidarity

had accelerated the demolitions of Palestinian homes and the confiscation of Palestinian land since the signing of the Wye River Memorandum in October 1998. They encouraged their constituents to set up tents in their homes and at church, and outside the offices of legislators whose policies supported Israel, and hence, home demolitions. The campaign also urged constituents to write elected representatives in Canada and the U.S. to apply pressure on Israel to stop home demolitions and land confiscation.

In addition to visiting families who were part of the ever-widening CSD network, the team also participated in rebuilding homes when they had a chance. In one notable effort on April 17, Sara Reschly, Michael Goode, and Jamey Bouwmeester helped Israeli activists from ICAHD rebuild the home of Hassan Daoud, demolished the previous August.

By the time workers had bolted down the last corrugated steel sheet on the roof of Daoud's house, about thirty-five Israeli military personnel had arrived. They began collecting passports and IDs, paying special attention to the two Palestinian men working on the roof. After the military ordered everyone to leave the area, Jeff Halper stalled the soldiers while family members quietly slipped away across the hills to homes of neighbors.

On their way back to Jerusalem, the Palestinians, Israelis, and internationals who had participated in the rebuilding of Daoud's home stopped in to visit the tent of Atta and Rodeina Jaber, who were celebrating their son Rajah's first birthday. Police who followed the activists told Halper in Hebrew, "We ordered you to leave one demolished house and you drive right to another!"

Halper, enraged, shouted back, "It's a BIRTHDAY PARTY! A birthday party for an infant who has had his house demolished twice. See, here's the present I'm bringing him!" When the police continued to argue, Halper turned to the rest of the group and said, "Come on. We don't need to waste time with these people."

The activists went up the hill to the tent where the family and their guests were celebrating and the police stayed at the bottom of the hill. Atta Jaber asked why they had not invited the police to the party. Bouwmeester replied, "Because they haven't learned to play nicely with others yet." The group later learned that the police fined one of their Palestinian drivers the equivalent of fifty dollars because he stepped out of his van to speak to the other driver.[6]

Committee, The Student Committee of the Hebrew University, Campus Tel Aviv and Green Action.

6. Bouwmeester, "Hebron: Building, Birthdays, and the Occupation," 2–3.

On May 19, 1999, Dianne Roe, Bourke Kennedy, and Jamey Bouwmeester arrived at the home of Ramadan Rajabi, just as the Israeli military was about to demolish a reservoir he used to irrigate his fields. Bouwmeester sat between the reservoir and the front-end loader.

After a soldier told him, "Get up. Go. Leave here," Bouwmeester told him, "I'll leave after you, okay?"

The soldier once again ordered him to leave. Bouwmeester pointed to Rajabi's elderly father, who had smiled approvingly and told Bouwmeester "Tamam, tamam" (perfect) when he first sat in front of the machinery. "Do you see that man over there?" he said. "I get my orders from him."

Four soldiers grabbed each of Bouwmeester's limbs and a fifth jerked him up by his ears. In the process of dragging him away, one of the soldiers knocked Roe over and damaged the digital camera she was holding.

After the soldiers finished demolishing Rajabi's reservoir, they moved in a convoy to the home of Kaied Jaber and began again. Jeff Halper, head of the Israeli Committee Against House demolitions arrived, spoke to the officer in charge, handed Bouwmeester his camera and said, "Jamey, I think it's time for a little civil disobedience."

Bouwmeester reported that he felt a "sense of déjà vu" as he watched Halper sit in front of the loader. After a short argument in Hebrew, soldiers handcuffed Halper, dragged him back up the hill and dropped him in the dirt. Later they stuffed him on the floor of their jeep. When Bouwmeester tried to help Halper onto the seat, a soldier elbowed him in the gut and two others pushed him back on the ground.

The loader and bagger then moved on to demolish Ismael Jaber's reservoir. As it happened, a camera crew from BBC was following Halper around on that day and documented the destruction of Kaied Jaber's cistern and the cistern of Ismael Jaber, cousin and neighbor of Atta Jaber. In a subsequent documentary, *Reservoir Raiders*, released in 2000, the documentary-makers noted that all three cisterns were built with funds donated from the European Community. They also interviewed Peter Lerner, the spokesperson for the Israeli Civil Administration, who said that the owners were "stealing water" by tapping into the nearby water main. However, when the camera people asked him to show them where pipes from the cisterns were connected to the water main, he was unable to do so.[7]

7. CPTnet, Bouwmeester, "Hebron: Time for a little civil disobedience," May 19, 1999. Given that the military had confiscated the Jabers' irrigation hoses, leaving them to rely on rainwater, the destruction of the cisterns meant to catch the rainwater seemed especially nasty.

The next day, the team issued an urgent action release calling for an end to "Lame Duck" demolitions. They asked their constituents to write Prime Minister-elect Ehud Barak and ask him to call for an end to land confiscation and home demolitions ordered by the defeated Netanyahu government.[8]

The extended Jaber family suffered further losses in spring 1999 when the military bulldozed farmland to install a gas station on bypass road 60 as well as erecting a wall almost on top of the house belonging to Abdel Jawad Jaber—Atta Jaber's father. The wall, built over bulldozed Jaber olive groves, marked the new boundary of the settlement of Givat Ha Harsina. A spring RAB delegation held a press conference on the confiscated Jaber land. On the way, they marched past Israeli soldiers and police guarding a gas station—also built on confiscated Jaber land—with a banner declaiming, "This Gas Station is Built on Confiscated Palestinian Land; it fuels Occupation and Pollutes Peace."

When the Israeli Labor Party candidate Ehud Barak became Prime minister in the summer of 1999, hopes were high that he would roll back the expansion of settlements in the West Bank. However, the building of roads and settlement housing on land already confiscated actually increased, and the military continued to hand out demolition orders.[9]

In November 1999, while a delegation led by Kathleen Kern ate a meal served by 'Atta and Rodeina Jaber among the rubble of their two demolished homes, team and delegation members observed a group of men with equipment arrive at a spot about half a kilometer up the road. When team and delegation members went to investigate, they found out that Arab laborers and their settler overseers had come to turn off the water main, because Palestinian families had tapped into it to irrigate their crops.

The Israelis explained that the farmers in the Beqa'a Valley were stealing water from Palestinians in Hebron. When pressed, they admitted that half the water went to the 120,000 people in Hebron and half went to the approximately 6,000 people in Kiryat Arba. Keri Holmes, Ben

---

8. Team members also mentioned that the team's digital camera had been irreparably damaged when Israeli soldiers pushed Dianne Roe to the ground and asked for donations to replace it. They encouraged people to send checks to the Israeli Committee Against Home Demolitions if they wanted to support rebuilding efforts. CPTnet, "HEBRON URGENT ACTION: Stop "Lame Duck" Demolitions," May 20, 2004.

9. Jamey Bouwmeester reflected on the lack of progress by the Barak government toward a peaceful resolution in "In Sharm's Way." "Sharm" referred to the Sharm al Sheikh Memorandum signed by Arafat and Barak that basically updated the Wye Memorandum, unilaterally halted by Israel. See also Meyer, "Bulldozers and Steamrollers," 2, in the same issue of *Signs of the Times*.

Kenagy, Joanne Kaufman, and Kathleen Kern took turns sitting on the pipe. Eventually the police pulled Kern out of the hole and detained her, Kaufman, and Kenagy, as well as Natasha Krahn and CPT intern Reinhold Kober, who had tried to leave the scene. Delegation member Keri Holmes wrote on a "gravestone" after the police left, "'29 November; Irrigation Pipes shredded; the Earth Wept; Occupiers Laughed. Documented [by] CPT."

During Kern's interrogation by police, they asked her, "What brought you to Kiryat Arba today?" She told them she had come in the police jeep, but then felt suddenly chilled by the realization that they meant the Jaber lands—a couple kilometers from the high-rise apartment buildings of Kiryat Arba. The whole of the Beqa'a Valley was obviously still at risk for confiscation.

The police released Kern, Kaufman, Kober, Kenagy, and Krahn without charges after Hisham Sharabati came to sign for them. They seemed especially anxious about helping Kern make her flight leaving that evening.[10]

During the rest of autumn 1999, Israeli settlers in the Hebron area—annoyed by the refusal of the Barak government to let them continue confiscating land in the Beqa'a—took matters into their own hands and began staging nightly demonstrations in the valley for two weeks, beginning on November 30, near the home of Omar and Lamia Sultan. Like the Al Atrashes and the Jabers, the Sultans had documents for their land dating back to the time of the Ottoman Empire. In their vigils, the settlers demanded that the Israeli government demolish the Sultan house, where fifteen people lived.

On December 21, 1999, the settlers began a twenty-four-hour presence near the Sultan home, after taking over a neighboring house that was unoccupied. One settler tried to enter the Sultans' home and pushed Lamia Sultan. Israeli police took Omar Sultan and his son to the police station after they tried to intervene and the settler claimed they had struck him. Two days later, the team put out an urgent action release asking that constituents write to Ehud Barak and Canadian and U.S. diplomatic officials concerning the settler harassment. Art Gish moved into the Sultan

---

10. The police had detained Kern and most of the delegation a few days earlier for trying to sell tomatoes in the vegetable market that the Oslo Accords had stipulated should be open to Palestinian vendors. (See CPTnet, "HEBRON: ISRAELI POLICE DETAIN ELEVEN CPTERS FOR SELLING TOMATOES," November 26, 1999.) A Palestinian friend had also given her a replica of the Dome of the Rock made by his brother who was in an Israeli prison for his membership in Hamas. Miraculously, none of these factors led to extra hassling by airport security that evening.

home to establish a twenty-four-hour CPT presence in the area. Kathy Kapenga, a friend who attended the Lutheran Church in Jerusalem, also spent time there.[11]

On December 25, about 100 settlers charged up the hillside to the Sultan home with flaming torches, destroying property and frightening the family. They announced they would return the following Tuesday to demolish the house, confiscate the property, and start constructing a settlement there—theoretically an extension of the Kiryat Arba/Givat Ha Harsina complex—although the Sultan home was more than two kilometers away from the inhabited area of Kiryat Arba.

On the evening of December 27—the day before settlers threatened to demolish the Sultan home themselves if the government did not do it—several Israeli peace activists joined the team and spent the night at the house. The next morning, soldiers told the Israelis and CPTers to leave. When they refused, the soldiers told the oldest son, Fahed, that if the peace activists remained in the "closed military zone" around the house, the settlers could insist on remaining too. "These are our guests." Fahed Sultan responded. "Our culture does not allow us to ask guests to leave."

Journalists arrived as well as a busload of Israelis with signs and banners to show solidarity with the Sultans. Settlers showed up later in the afternoon and exchanged words with Israelis who had remained.

Shortly after CPTers left the next day, a busload of settlers set up banners on an old Palestinian house near the Sultan home. They then rushed the Sultan house, but soldiers stopped them from reaching it.

Two weeks later, Rich Meyer posted a thank-you note to those who had responded to the urgent action release. He told them that because of the international letter writing, the Israeli government promised the Sultans that their home would not be destroyed and that it would thwart the attempt of the settlers to establish a new settlement near the Sultan home. Meyer also noted that the campaign around the Sultan home had brought Jews, Christians, and Muslims together in a show of solidarity. However, the prefatory comment attached to Meyer's posting noted that the Israeli government continued to refer to the Sultans' land and the rest of the Beqa'a Valley as part of the municipality of Kiryat Arba.[12]

11. Kapenga became a CPT reservist after going through training in 2003.
12. See CPTnet releases: "HEBRON URGENT ACTION: Family Under Siege in Beqa'a," December 23, 1999; "Prayers and Speeches, Destruction and Hope on Christmas Day," December 26, 1999; "House under siege in the Beqa'a Valley: A Question of Hospitality," January 2, 2000; "Hebron: A Big Thank-You to the Campaign for Secure

The travails of the Sultan family illustrated that families living near settlements at the end of 1999 still lacked real security. However, Rich Meyer, in the fall 1999 *Signs of the Times*, noted that under Barak's administration the Israeli authorities had demolished only four homes in the Jerusalem area and none in other regions of the West Bank.[13] Unwittingly, Interior Minister Natan Sharansky provided proof that the efforts of CPT, the Israeli Committee Against House Demolitions, and the Palestine Land Defence Committee had influenced Israeli government policy. The December 1, 1999, *Jerusalem Post* quoted Sharansky as complaining, "Every house demolition becomes an international incident."[14]

2000

By 2000, many CPTers working in Hebron felt that the Campaign for Secure Dwellings had stagnated. Families with whom the team had worked most closely—and who had suffered the greatest losses in terms of home demolitions and harassment of the Israeli military—no longer wanted their names used in releases. They felt that if they rebuilt furtively, their houses might have a greater chance of remaining standing. Communications between Palestinian families and North American churches seemed to be mostly one-way, from North America to Palestine, which made congregations less likely to participate.

Since threats to homes in the Beqa'a Valley (where the Jabers lived), Qilqis/Al Sendas (where the Al Atrashes lived), and Beit Ummar, north of Hebron, seemed less imminent under the Barak government, the team began to focus more on ongoing land confiscation. On February 11, 2000 the team, along with Israeli activists, Palestinian farmers, and a CPT-RAB delegation held an action in the Beqa'a Valley. The group carried buckets

---

Dwellings and CPT Network," January 13, 2000. Se also Gish, "Love Overcomes Fear in Hebron," *Signs of the Times*, 4–5. The College Mennonite Church of Goshen, Indiana, partnered through CSD with the Sultan family, sent about seventy-five faxes to Israeli prime minister Ehud Barak.

13. Meyer, "Bulldozers and Steamrollers," 2. The lack of demolitions probably had more to do with the pressure of progressive parties like Meretz in Barak's coalition than Barak's own convictions.

14. Cited in "Demolition Season Reopened," 14. The quotation appeared in a story about the demolition of two East Jerusalem homes at the end of October. A third was also scheduled to go down, but Israeli activists mobilized a worldwide protest against the demolitions and Meretz Party Whip Zehava Gal'on was able to persuade Barak that the protests from grassroots organizations and representatives of the European Union were a good reason to call a halt to further demolitions.

of soil brought from Palestinian lands to the gates of the settlement. As they walked they unfurled a banner that read, "Land Confiscation Is Not Peace," in English and Arabic.

Israeli police and military personnel stopped them after a few meters and informed them that they would not be allowed to proceed, because the entire area had been declared a "closed military zone"—the catch-all order the Israeli military uses when they want to remove people from an area.[15]

The demonstrators then proceeded, one at a time, to dump their buckets out onto the confiscated ground. In his release about the witness, Jamey Bouwmeester explained the biblical basis for the action:

> "If someone sues you for your coat, give up your shirt as well. If a soldier orders you to carry his pack one mile, carry it two. When someone slaps your right cheek, turn and let that person slap your left." If Jesus were alive and living in Palestine today, he might well say, "When Occupation forces take your land to expand and build new settlements, bring them a few buckets more."

When all of the buckets had been emptied, Abdel Jawad Jaber planted the remains of one of his olive trees into the pile of soil at the feet of the soldiers. Israeli peace activist Harriet Lewis then spoke of her Palestinian friends. "No matter how many times the bulldozers come," she said, "each time they wonder again how it could happen. They can't believe that something that evil could happen. They never lose hope."

The team followed up the public witness with an urgent action release, asking people to send packets of soil from their homes to Israeli consulates and communicate the following:

> Ask Israeli officials how they reconcile talking peace with Palestine while, at the same time confiscating more land. State your objection to the Israeli government's expropriation of far more land than it has turned over to the Palestinians under the Wye and Sharm al-Sheikh agreements. Demand that no more Palestinian lives, homes and lands be sacrificed to the annexation of territory, which Barak has labeled "peace."[16]

---

15. Israeli activists told the team that, technically, soldiers have to show people a map with the closed military zone clearly marked for the order to be valid, but the IDF routinely ignores this stipulation.

16. CPTnet, "HEBRON: Buckets of Soil Campaign Against Confiscation Begins," CPTnet, "HEBRON URGENT ACTION: Send packets of soil to Israeli Gov't," February 11, 2000.

The theme of the 2000 Tent for Lent campaign was "Under One Tree," derived from Omar Sultan's statement, "If they destroy my house, I will not leave. I will be under the sky. Under one tree I will live." The team observed the period by fasting and staying overnight with families who had experienced or were facing the demolition of their homes.[17]

At the end of March 2000, members of the team were present at the Israeli Supreme Court in Jerusalem when a judge handed down a decision stipulating that 700 Palestinians, whom in November 1999 the military had expelled from their homes in the southern Hebron District, could return to their lands.[18] The families had lived in caves near the town of Yatta for hundreds of years, but the caves lay in an area that the settlement of Susia wanted to confiscate.[19] Intense lobbying on behalf of the families by Israeli groups like the ICAHD and Rabbis for Human Rights finally paid off. On April 9, 2000, the families killed a sheep and invited their Israeli friends and CPT for a feast.

In an April 10, 2000, reflection on the court ruling, Dianne Roe wrote,

> "The other peace process" has not been taking place in fancy resorts in Sharm El Sheikh or Wye River. These meetings have been taking place in Red Cross tents set up after a house demolition, or in cinder block shells. Or in a cave warmed by a small wood fire. The security interests of this "other peace process" are not served

---

17. See "Under One Tree," 5; Krahn, "Now I Lay Me Down to Sleep," 8, and "Tent for Lent 2000," 8. CPT's Chiapas team also mounted a Tent for Lent campaign in 2000. See chapter 7 of Kern, *In Harm's Way*.

18. See background of the cave-dwelling families in CPTnet, "HEBRON DISTRICT URGENT ACTION: Stop the expulsion of cave dwellers from South Hebron," March 23, 2002.

19. The Hebron team had had contacts with Palestinians facing settler violence and land confiscation in the southern Hebron district since 1996. See chapter 2 for an account of the arrests of CPTers near the settlement of Susia in May 1996. For other examples of the team's involvement with the area, see CPTnet releases: "The Wheat Harvest Near Hebron," May 13, 1996. McClanen, "Plowing Musallem's land," October 27, 1996; "HEBRON DISTRICT: August 1997 Land Confiscation Report," September 8, 1997; "Hebron: Delegation Rebuilds Destroyed Fence," December 29, 1997; "Hebron: Update December 24 [1997]-January 4, 1998," January 6, 1998; Adas, "HEBRON/YATTA: BETWEEN SETTLER AND SOLDIERS," April 18, 1998; HEBRON: YATTA FARMER LOSES ENTIRE WHEAT CROP TO ARSON," June 27, 1998; "Hebron Update: October 27-31, 1999," November 9, 1999.

Transportation difficulties and the needs of families living closer to Hebron prevented the team from undertaking sustained humanitarian interventions on behalf of families living in this area of the Hebron District, prior to the team setting up the At-Tuwani project there in 2004 (See chapter 10).

by walls of separation, by checkpoints, by closures or by weapons. Instead, this security will be one of friendship and mutual trust. Amos Gvirtz, an Israeli activist who worked tirelessly on this issue, had tears in his eyes as he embraced us.

Later, as he introduced CPT to author David Grossman, Amos credited CPT with providing the inspiration that led to the formation of the Israeli Committee Against House Demolitions. Activist Beate Zilverschmidt added that CPT had provided a framework for them to meet Palestinians. "There have been dialogue groups before," she said. "But CPT found the burning issues and put them on our table.

"Thank you for having that table," we said.[20]

Reading through the newsletters and CPTnet archives for spring and summer of 2000, one notes the relative paucity of material from the team. Most CSD families in the areas around Hebron continued to eschew publicity so as not to attract attention to their rebuilding efforts. This desire for a lower profile was shared by Palestinian families living in the Qilqis area. However, the families there made an alternative request of the team. Instead of CPT drawing attention to their homes, the families asked the team to help advocate for the their unfinished elementary school—destined for demolition by the Israeli authorities. Hundreds of children from the area had to walk three miles to school each way along the dangerous settler bypass road. The team thus asked the CSD network to send letters to the Israeli authorities asking that it grant permission for the school to be finished. They posted a sample letter in a follow-up release:

> Dear Ambassador (or Minister of the Interior; or Senator, or Minister of Foreign Affairs):
>
> Why is it that the Israeli authorities are preventing the people of Qilqis from building an elementary school?
>
> Just south of Hebron there is a half-finished elementary school. Many children walk past this every school day, and then keep walking, another 5km, to the nearest school. This school was being built by the community, at their own expense, but the Israeli government has put a stop-work order on the project.

---

20. CPTnet, "Hebron: The Other Peace Process: Dispossessed Families Return to Land," April 10, 2000. Photos of these homes, including those demolished by the Israeli military, are available at Applied Research Institute-Jerusalem, "People of the caves targeted by the Israeli occupation forces." The website also includes an update of the inhabitants' legal status as of June 2004. Unfortunately, as chapter 9 demonstrates, the legal victory for these families was short-lived.

> It is usually considered one role of government to provide for education. In this case, not only is the Israeli government not providing schools, but the Israeli government is even stopping people from meeting this need themselves.
>
> Can you please find out why the Israeli authorities are blocking the construction of Qilqis elementary school? I look forward to your reply . . .

Congregations responded in greater numbers than expected. An Italian church even put the request for letters in its parish newsletter. However, as of September 2000, none of the letter writers had received a reply.[21]

The U.S. President Bill Clinton-sponsored Camp David negotiations between Barak and Arafat began on July 11 and lasted until July 27, 2000, at which point the parties broke without having come to an agreement. Arafat's refusal to sign the agreement—which would have left the largest settlements in Israeli hands and solidified Israeli control of Jerusalem—was depicted by the U.S. press and government as yet another example of Palestinian intransigence and refusal to compromise.

In an August 2, 2000, urgent action release, the team encouraged its constituents to write a variation of the following letter:

> Dear Editor,
>
> At Camp David, President Clinton and Israeli Prime Minister Ehud Barak pressed Palestinian leader Yassar Arafat to agree to a settlement reflecting Israel's superior power, not an agreement based on principles of justice. While Israel talks about making concessions for peace, they [sic] continue to flout international law, creating facts on the ground that make a just and lasting peace more and more difficult to envision.
>
> Today, Israel continues to build new settlements and expand those that already exist. Not only is Israeli settlement expansion illegal according to international law, but it results directly in land confiscation and home demolitions for Palestinians in the area. While Israel continues to build new Jewish-only settlements on occupied territory, the Israeli army bulldozes Palestinian homes, evicts entire villages from their ancestral homesteads and uproots olive trees and grapevines.
>
> In the Beqa'a valley east of Hebron, more than 50 families have been issued home demolition orders. More than a dozen homes

---

21. CPTnet, "HEBRON: Internationals advocate for Qilqis School," September 4, 2000; CPTnet, "HEBRON: Contact information for those writing on behalf of Qilqis school," September 5, 2000.

have been razed by the Israeli military. Palestinians are forbidden to cultivate and irrigate farmland that has belonged to their families for generations. At the same time, the Israeli settlement of Kiryat Arba/Harsina is in the process of building more than 200 new housing units on land confiscated from these same Palestinian farmers. In currently existing settlements, the residents lounge on green lawns and swim in private pools while some of their Palestinian neighbors are not given enough water to drink.

Israel fails to implement U. N. Resolutions, ignores world opinion and pursues unjust policies that would give a fraction of the Palestinian people a fraction of their rights on a fraction of their land. Future negotiations between Israel and the Palestinians must be based on International law and the principles of justice.[22]

In the late summer of 2000, for the first time since 1995, street violence in Hebron began to occupy most of the team's energy. Some of the street violence had to do with the Camp David negotiations. As Palestinians heard that Arafat might sign the agreement that would make aspects of the Occupation permanent, they stepped up street clashes, throwing stones at soldiers stationed on the border of H-1 and H-2. Soldiers generally responded by shooting rubber-coated bullets.[23]

The Camp David negotiations may have been responsible for an upsurge in settler violence as well. On August 10, Amos Harel wrote in *Ha'aretz*, the Israeli "newspaper of record," that, according to the Palestinian press, Barak offered to evacuate the settlements in Hebron as a concession to the Palestinian authority. (Barak denied the allegation.)

Whatever the reasons for the settlers' behavior, the team increasingly found themselves standing between settlers and Palestinians in an effort to prevent these assaults in July, August, and September 2000. Hebron updates covering the period between July 18 and August 15, 2000, record eight instances in which settlers attacked Palestinians, CPTers, or both. In one notable incident on July 21, 2000, about thirty inebriated settler men surrounded Grace Boyer and Sara Reschly when they attempted to intervene on behalf of two young Palestinian boys whom the settlers were pushing. Boyer later told Kathleen Kern that if a TIPH car had not arrived

22. CPTnet, "HEBRON URGENT ACTION: Telling the truth in letters to Editors," August 2, 2000. For a progressive Israeli perspective on the Camp David negotiations, see Gush Shalom, "Barak's 'generous' offer."

23. Clashes were a feature of life in Hebron since the beginning of the project, but were not a central focus of the team's work. See an analysis of these clashes and the team's response to them in chapter 10.

at that moment, she and Reschly probably would have been seriously hurt. When the car arrived, the settlers surrounded it instead, kicking it and beating it with their hands. Ten soldiers arrived and took the settlers back to Beit Hadassah. Reschly asked the soldiers why they had not called the police, and a soldier told her it would make the situation worse.[24]

The venue for many settler assaults was often the vegetable market around the corner from the team's apartment.[25] When the Israeli authorities allowed the market to open over the years, it became a particular target for settlers any time a settler or soldier was attacked by Palestinians. Although no vendors were ever implicated in these assaults, the common settler response was to go into the market, physically abuse the vendors, and overturn vegetable carts and stands. Usually settler women and children did most of the attacks, because male soldiers had to wait for female civilian police or female soldiers to arrive and deal with them.

Attacks in the market became more frequent as the summer passed. On August 10, Michael Goode, Nait Alleman, Jeremy Bergen, and Bob Holmes tried to stand beside the vendors and take pictures of the adolescent settler women attacking them. The teenagers surrounded Bergen, cursed him, stole his CPT hat, kicked him, and tried to grab his camera. When an IDF soldier intervened, he said he would arrest Bergen if he took any more pictures. Israeli border police and soldiers began to push the vendors away from their carts; Goode and Alleman stood between the vendors and the soldiers and tried to pick up the produce. After soldiers and settlers had driven all the vendors out, the settlers prayed and celebrated with snacks and beverages.

On August 19, settlers attacked the market again, allegedly because a taxi driver hit a settler boy. The team spent several hours maintaining a presence there. As soldiers used their rifles to push back Palestinians, Natasha Krahn and Bergen were also knocked to the ground. After a soldier had told Goode, Bergen, and Bob Holmes several times they would be

24. CPTnet, "HEBRON UPDATE: July 18–30, 2000," August 7, 2000.

25. Earlier that summer, the team had conducted yet another tomato sale as part of a delegation witness. (Each delegation was supposed to include an act of public witness, and over the years, when no obvious alternative action presented itself, the team by default set up a time to sell tomatoes. See chapter 2.) In its release regarding the action, the team noted that Israel had signed three separate agreements that included opening the wholesale vegetable market. The most recent Sharm el-Sheikh agreement stipulated in article 7, item b that "the wholesale market Hasbahe will be opened not later than November 1, 1999." But the part of the market closest to Avraham Avinu usually remained closed. CPTnet, "Hebron: CPT sells 'Tomatoes for an Open Market.'"

arrested if they did not leave the area, Goode told the soldier that the team needed to be there. "I'm concerned that the IDF's response here is provoking more violence," he said. Soldiers then detained Goode for "inciting a riot," but released him five minutes later.

When a large group of settlers entered the market, the Palestinians fled while settlers fought with the soldiers. Palestinian children then began throwing fruit and stones at settlers and soldiers from the interior of the market, and Palestinian youth began throwing stones from a block near the border of the H-1 area up the street. The *Jerusalem Post* reported that three settlers and ten Palestinians were arrested.[26]

During this period, settlers also began holding regular demonstrations in the Beqa'a Valley, near the homes of the extended Jaber family, demanding that the IDF close the road to Palestinian traffic. The residents of the valley found these demonstrations frightening. (Their fears proved well-founded when the settlers conducted a pogrom there in 2001. See chapter 6.) Since the team felt at a loss when they tried to think of effective responses to this settler violence on the street and outlying regions of Hebron, they decided to initiate a period of fasting and prayer, posting the following on CPTnet:

> Therefore, CPT in Hebron has decided to fast and pray on Saturdays for the next six weeks as a response to the violence, and also as a way of being open to the Spirit's guidance in this troubled time.
>
> We will have a peace candle burning all day and continue with our patrols in Hebron, being aware of what is happening on the streets. We will be breaking our fast on Sunday morning with communion at the church where we worship . . . Let us call on the power of these two important spiritual disciplines not only to move our own hearts and minds, but also to transform the atmosphere of violence and fear pervasive in Hebron.[27]

In an accompanying release, Bob Holmes noted that incidents of settler violence on Saturdays in September had decreased in comparison to Saturdays in August. Israeli newspapers had reported the Israeli military had told settlers that it would not tolerate further attacks. However, he wrote, the newspapers also reported that the IDF was assisting the settlements in acquiring more arms to counter anticipated Palestinian violence

26. CPTnet, Goode, "HEBRON: Settler violence increases tension," August 16, 2000; CPTnet, Bergen, "HEBRON: Violence in the market," August 23, 2000.

27. CPTnet, "HEBRON: Calling on the Power of God—An Invitation to Fast and Pray," September 22, 2000.

following the completion or collapse of the peace process. "My prayer is that my next few weeks in this holy and conflicted city will not be a repeat of my first few weeks," wrote Holmes, in a CPTnet release posted on September 22, 2000.[28]

Seven days later, Ariel Sharon would visit the Temple Mount in Jerusalem, setting events in motion that would create an outcome breathtakingly different from the one for which the Hebron team was praying.

---

28. CPTnet, "HEBRON: Shabbat Shalom? Not in Hebron!"

PART THREE

"Things Fall Apart"
The Al-Aqsa Intifada
2000–2002

> . . . Things fall apart; the center cannot hold;
> Mere anarchy is loosed upon the world,
> The blood-dimmed tide is loosed, and everywhere
> The ceremony of innocence is drowned;
> The best lack all conviction, while the worst
> Are full of passionate intensity.
> Surely some revelation is at hand . . .
>
> W. B. Yeats, "The Second Coming"

FIVE

The Al-Aqsa Intifada
September–December 2000

W. B. YEATS'S POEM, "The Second Coming," evokes images of the Israeli-Palestinian conflict for many people who have lived in the region. The poem captures their feelings of powerlessness as they watched the peace and reconciliation work undertaken over the years recklessly destroyed by craven politicians.[1] The Al-Aqsa Intifada only deepened their despair, as it plowed under modest advances toward mutual understanding among Israelis and Palestinians and small legal victories some Palestinians living near settlements had won regarding their land and their homes.

On Friday, September 29, 2000, Ariel Sharon, surrounded by hundreds of riot police, visited the Haram al-Sharif compound, which includes the Al-Aqsa mosque, Islam's third holiest site after Mecca and Medina.[2] The visit characterized Sharon's historic bent for displaying flagrant domination in Palestinian areas. For example, his house in the Muslim Quarter of Jerusalem's Old City—in which he spent little time—boasted a two-story Israeli flag draped out of the window and a giant Menorah on the roof.[3]

---

1. Israeli writers make frequent reference to the poem, for example, see Elon, *Blood-Dimmed Tide*; Rubinstein, "Slouching toward Jerusalem," and "Things fall apart"; Stein, *Widening Gyre of Negotiation*.

2. Muslims believe that Muhammad made a journey from Mecca to Al-Aqsa ("The farthest") in a single night on a winged steed brought to him by the angel Gabriel. From a rock there, he ascended to heaven, accompanied by Gabriel, received the commandments—including the traditional Muslim five daily prayers—before returning to Mecca and communicating them to the faithful.

3. For more insights into Ariel Sharon's character, see Benzimann, *Sharon*.

PART THREE: "THINGS FALL APART"—THE AL-AQSA INTIFADA

To Palestinians in Jerusalem, the September 29 visit clearly signaled Israel's intent to assert sovereignty over the Haram al-Sharif/Temple Mount, and rioting erupted.[4] By the time Sharon left, hundreds of Palestinian worshipers and Israeli police officers had sustained injuries.

Although commentators pointed to Sharon's visit on the Temple Mount as "the start" of the Intifada, in reality Sharon merely threw a figurative match on a pool of gasoline. Settlement expansion and land confiscation had continued throughout the Oslo, Wye, Sharm al Sheikh, and Camp David negotiations. Checkpoints had made travel increasingly more onerous for Palestinians. Jerusalem had become closed to all but a few Palestinians who had Jerusalem identity cards. Israel continued to hold political prisoners in its jails. Furthermore, U.S. President Bill Clinton had pushed an agreement through that would have made no provision for refugees, would have allowed Israel to annex large settlement blocs, and legalized Israel's hegemony over Jerusalem. By signing the Oslo Accords, Arafat had essentially signed over 78% of historic Palestine to Israel, so Palestinians felt they had already made major compromises. Sharon's visit to the Temple Mount was one more proof to Palestinians that Israel was negotiating in bad faith.

The clashes that began in Jerusalem spread to the whole of the West Bank and Gaza by Saturday. On Sunday, clashes between Palestinian citizens of Israel and Israeli police began in Israel proper.[5]

Hebron team members and fellow Redeemer Lutheran Church congregants[6] were returning from a church retreat at the Sea of Galilee that

---

4. Jews view the area of Al-Aqsa and Haram al-Sharif as the location of Herod's temple, of which only one wall—popularly called "The Wailing Wall"—remains. When Israel captured East Jerusalem in 1967, the government left the administration of the Muslim holy site in the hands of Muslims, fearing further attacks from the entire Arab/Muslim world. Since that time, rightwing Jews and their Christian Zionist sidekicks have advocated removing the Muslim structures, which they call "the abomination on the Temple Mount," by violence, if necessary.

Interestingly, many attribute the 1929 massacre in Hebron (see chapter 1) to altercations on the Temple Mount between Jews and Muslims as well. After several days of violence in Jerusalem, on Friday, August 23, 1929, rumors spread that the Zionists were killing Arabs there. Segev, *One Palestine*, 318–24.

5. The Adalah Legal Center for Arab Minority Rights in Israel wrote in its "Summary Report to the United Nations Human Rights Commission Emergency Session on Israel/Palestine, 17–18 October 2000" that thirteen Palestinian-Israeli citizens were killed by police during the first two and a half weeks of the Intifada and about a thousand received treatment for their injuries at hospitals.

6. The team in Hebron attended several different churches in the Jerusalem and Bethlehem area over the years. Most went to St. George's Anglican cathedral until a political

Sunday. The drive to Jerusalem, which would have normally taken two hours, took nine as their driver found road after road closed. The team spent the night in Bethlehem after learning the entire West Bank was under closure.

Natasha Krahn wrote the first team release describing the change in the status quo, entitled "Fury, Fear and Faith." In it, she reported hearing gunshots and percussion grenades from a clash between soldiers and Palestinian youth in the distance, and settler youth attempting to smash the windshield of a van parked just outside the team apartment.[7] This ambience was to mark the team's life in Hebron for the next year, as they were forced to switch from the long-term strategizing they had done as part of the Campaign for Secure Dwellings to one crisis response after another.

CLASHES: OCTOBER–DECEMBER

From the beginning of the CPT Hebron project in 1995, clashes were a regular, if sporadic, feature of life. Usually occurring on the border between H-1 and H-2, they often happened after a particular incident—such as when settlers attacked the Qurtuba Girls' School in 1995 or when a young Israeli woman hung flyers depicting the Prophet Muhammad as a pig writing the Quran in 1997. They also occurred after Israeli and Palestinian negotiators set up an agreement detrimental to Palestinian residents of Hebron. The clashes would last hours, days, or weeks, depending on the degree of anger simmering within the populace.

The team had learned early on that standing between soldiers and stone-throwing shabab (young Palestinian men) did not prevent a clash. Often Palestinian women and children trying to move out of the clash zone were hit by rocks and bottles thrown by other Palestinians. The team tried to deal with the issue, by noting that the clashes—while they made good news footage—distracted from the real issues of the occupation and the reconciliation work that Israeli and Palestinian activists were doing.[8]

---

struggle between Bishop Riah and Father Naim Ateek caused a split in the church in 1997. Afterwards, most members of the team attended the English services at Redeemer Lutheran Church in Jerusalem's Old City, when they were able to travel.

7. CPTnet, "Fury, fear and faith," October 3, 2000.
8. See Kern's "Sobbing on the Stairs":

When the Al-Aqsa Intifada broke out in the fall, most representatives of the Israeli peace groups stopped coming to Hebron. But after a few weeks, Israeli women from Bat Shalom began visiting—often riding alone in Palestinian taxis to visit

All clashes contained a certain degree of predictable theater. Young men would begin taunting soldiers at a checkpoint and throwing rocks, bottles, and Molotov cocktails. Soon, younger boys would join in. Soldiers would send for reinforcements and then begin shooting percussion grenades, tear gas, or rubber-coated metal bullets (called "rubber bullets") into the crowd, not necessarily in that order. Bystanders and people happening to leave shops or their homes often got hit.

With the coming of the Intifada, the clashes happened on a daily basis for months. The rocks and glass shards on the streets near the border of H-1 and H-2 literally became ankle deep at times.

While observing these clashes in fall 2000, the team for the first time became a target of hostile behavior from Palestinian strangers because some team members were citizens of the United States. During one tense encounter, Hani Abu Haikel (see chapter 1) limped by and told hostile youth that the team was not there to spy on them.[9]

As clash after clash dragged on, certain aspects became more surreal. Team members trying to get through a clash zone experienced the shabab and soldiers pausing, gallantly waving them through, and then resuming their stone throwing and shooting. Zleekha Muhtasib, who translated for the team, told them she had tried to get to the city center from her home in the Old City and realized she would not be able to get past the clash zone. She and several other women turned to go back to their homes when one of the soldiers shouted to the young men in Arabic, "You stupid people! Can't you see there are women trying to pass?" The boys stopped, and the soldiers waved the women through.[10]

Palestinian families like the Abu Sharabatis [Kern gave Atta and Rodeina Jaber pseudonyms in the article.]

I think these visits are big news. But showing Israeli and Palestinian women sitting together drinking tea is not as "hot" as stone-throwing, so the women remain invisible.

9. CPTnet, "HEBRON UPDATE: October 13–16, 2000," October 17, 2000. Having Canadians on the team like Anita Fast, Bob Holmes, and Natasha Krahn proved helpful in these encounters, since Palestinians did not perceive the Canadian government as having a knee-jerk pro-Israel stance. Israeli soldiers had shot Abu Haikel in the foot on the previous day. See below.

10. CPTnet, "HEBRON UPDATE: November 8–11, 2000," November 17, 2000. The team also observed on October 3, 2000, soldiers telling a group of about twenty-five young Palestinian men and boys who were calmly watching the clash from the sidelines that they could join the stone throwers on the other side. Soldiers called for a brief cease-fire so that some of the boys could cross over. A Palestinian journalist told the team that soldiers had allowed the young men to cross so they could shoot at greater numbers of shabab. CPTnet,

Although some of the clashes seemed spontaneous (for example the ones that occurred just as Palestinian boys were leaving school), after awhile the team began to wonder if the Palestinian Authority (PA) was encouraging and directing them to some extent. When shop owners near the H-1/H-2 boundary told the PA that they were suffering staggering financial losses because of the clashes, and when there seemed to be some progression in negotiations between Barak and Arafat, the Palestinian policemen came in to prevent the stone-throwing. Osaid Rashid, a CSD translator and nurse at a local hospital, once watched—along with CPTer Rich Meyer—young men making Molotov cocktails. Rashid told Meyer they were receiving orders "from above" to make them. When Meyer asked Rashid—as they watched the young men—whether nonviolent direct action could be promoted among the Palestinians, Rashid told him, "That would be like trying to teach breathing exercises to a woman in labor. She can't hear you. You needed to do that two months ago."[11]

On the whole, CPTers and the observers from TIPH found the clashes dispiriting and detrimental to the Palestinian cause. However, given the ongoing soldier and settler violence and land confiscation, they understood the rage as well. Anita Fast, in a reflection written on the team's third Saturday of fasting in October (see chapter 4), spoke of neighbors in the Old City going hungry because of the curfew the Israeli military had imposed on the 35,000 residents since the beginning of the Intifada. When Hebron municipality workers tried to deliver emergency food aid to these families, soldiers denied them access. Fast, Krahn, and Holmes took the food and delivered it to some of the families.

"My own hunger vanished as I took the small offerings of food to those who really needed it," Fast wrote.

> But the joy of fulfilling the one family's need was diminished by other hungry eyes, children watching from windows of homes for which we could not supply food.
>
> Knowing first-hand the suffering of those under curfew in H2, it is easy to get angry at those Palestinians in H1 who are throwing stones at soldiers and shooting at Jewish settlements, thereby providing justification for the curfew. I mourn the choice of many Palestinians who respond to violence with violence. Yet as I laid in

---

"HEBRON UPDATE: September 30–October 6, 2000," October 9, 2000.

11. CPTnet, "HEBRON UPDATE: October 28–November 1, 2000," November 7, 2000. Meyer relayed some of this conversation to the author at the time, so the incident is partially described from the author's memory.

bed Saturday night, the words of Jesus from the Gospels echoed in my mind: which one of you, when someone asks for bread, would give them a stone? And I remember that the Palestinian people have long been asking for bread—for the ability to live lives of dignity, self-determination, safety and freedom. Yet Israel, the U.S. and to a large extent, the entire international community has given them stones instead: hardened promises; firm and inflexible ultimatums; uncompromising policies of home demolitions and land confiscation; collective punishment; severe restrictions on movement . . .

I have never, nor God willing, will ever condone the use of violence, even in revolt, but I wonder, what right has the hand that gives stones in the place of much needed bread to condemn and demonize God's children when they take the stones they have been given and begin to throw them.[12]

HOME/SCHOOL OCCUPATIONS

As a result of the clashes and nightly shooting, the Israeli military began to occupy homes, shops, and schools situated near the H-1/H-2 border or at other strategic vantage points.

Rooftop outposts caused significant disruption in the lives of the families living in the homes. Some IDF units confiscated the upper floors of a building, crowding the families into one or two rooms below. Soldiers often broke furniture in the household, cut lines connecting satellite dishes to TVs, defecated and urinated on roofs (and sometimes in families' water tanks), shouted sexually suggestive remarks at the women in the household, and made insulting comments about Islam and the prophet Mohammed.[13]

12. CPTnet, "HEBRON: Calling on the Spirit of God. Week Three—Bread not Stones," October 16, 2000. In a letter to family and friends published in *Signs of the Times*, Kathleen Kern recorded that Fast, during another worship session, had reflected on Amos 5:24, "Let justice roll down like waters and righteousness like an everflowing stream." Fast noted Amos's proclamation described a scary image:

> Justice is like a flash flood causing chaos and destruction in its path. Maybe that is the way to look at the recent violence. The false peace of the Oslo Accords that institutionalized Israeli economic, political and military hegemony of the region and facilitated the ongoing confiscation of land, had to be crushed and destroyed and swept away.

K. Kern, "Rage Rocks Hebron," 1–2.

13. See CPTnet releases: "HEBRON UPDATE: September 1–15, 2000," September 26, 2000; Anita Fast, "HEBRON: The Martyrdom of Innocence," October 4, 2000 [incorrectly dated as September 4 in the text of the release]; "HEBRON UPDATE: September 16–29, 2000," October 9, 2000; "HEBRON UPDATE: October 17–19 [2000]" October 22, 2000; "HEBRON UPDATE: January 6–11, 2001," January 23, 2001.

Having a soldier outpost on the roof also made a house the target for stones and Molotov cocktails thrown by youth during clashes. Some Palestinian families thus had rooms facing the street ruined by other Palestinians.

The Israeli military took over eight schools in Hebron to use as military outposts. One of them, Osama Bin Munqeth, had been built years earlier to accommodate the students displaced when the Hebron settlers took over the school they renamed "Beit Romano." The school takeovers resulted in the displacement of thousands of children. Other schools in Hebron began teaching in shifts to accommodate the teachers and students displaced from their former schools. In later years of the Intifada, accompanying children to schools on the outskirts of the Old City would become a central part of the team's work.

CURFEW

As noted above, the clashes and the shooting led to the imposition of curfew on Palestinian residents of H-1 that lasted for weeks. The military had little incentive to lift the curfew, because imprisoning the residents of the Old City in their homes made their jobs easier. They did not have to worry about settler/Palestinian altercations or someone attacking them from within a throng of civilians.

Sometimes, the military would lift curfew for a few hours so people could buy food (but as time passed and people were unable to get to their jobs, they had no money with which to buy food). Team members often found themselves negotiating with soldiers at checkpoints, persuading them to allow residents of the Old City to pass through who had not gotten back before the military re-imposed curfew.

The team also intervened when people told them they needed to get to the hospital. Whether soldiers let people pass for medical treatment generally depended on the unit staffing the checkpoints. In one case, soldiers told a woman whose daughter was having severe abdominal pain that they would not permit an ambulance through and that she must watch her daughter die. The mother hailed a garbage truck, which soldiers let through, because these trucks picked up the soldier as well as Palestinian trash. She and the driver laid the sick woman on top of the garbage and the man took her into the Palestinian-controlled section of Hebron, where she found a car to take her to the hospital in Jerusalem.[14]

---

14. CPTnet, HEBRON UPDATE: October 20–22, 2000," October 25, 2000. The team found out about this incident after it happened. Some soldiers, particularly the

On November 1, Israeli journalist Amira Hass wrote a story about the curfew in Hebron, beginning,

> How perfectly natural that 40,000 persons should be subject to a total curfew for more than a month in the Old City of Hebron in order to protect the lives and well-being of 500 Jews. How perfectly natural that almost no Israeli mentions this fact or, for that matter, even knows about it. How perfectly natural that 34 schools attended by thousands of Palestinian children should be closed down for more than a month and their pupils imprisoned and suffocating day and night in their crowded homes, while the children of their neighbors—their Jewish neighbors, that is—are free to frolic as usual in the street among and with the Israeli soldiers stationed there. How perfectly natural that a Palestinian mother must beg and plead so that an Israeli soldier will allow her to sneak through the alleyways of the open-stall marketplace and obtain medication for her asthmatic children, or bread for her family.[15]

Hass wrote that the curfew in Hebron was a microcosm of the occupation as a whole, showing that the Israeli public could accept with ease the intolerable suffering the occupation imposed on Palestinians. On the day her article appeared in *Ha'aretz,* Israeli military officials told her that it had lifted the forty-day curfew on Hebron. She called the team in Hebron to see if it had indeed been lifted. Had she known the article would be so effective, she told them, she would have written it much sooner. In spring 2002, as curfew was again imposed for great lengths of time, she would apologize to the team for not being able to write another piece about it, given the Israeli assassinations of Palestinian militants and the siege on Arafat's compound in Ramallah.[16]

SETTLER VIOLENCE

Curfews never applied to Hebron's Israeli settlers—not even after the Baruch Goldstein massacre in the Il Ibrahimi Mosque in 1994 (see chapter 1). The Hebron settlers took the advantage the curfew afforded in the first months of the Intifada to vandalize homes, shops, and cars belonging to Palestinian owners trapped in their houses. The violence that the team sought to ad-

---

Nahal unit, were more accommodating to sick people and often let children play outside undisturbed.

15. Hass, "The Mirror Doesn't Lie."
16. CPTnet, "HEBRON UPDATE: March 7–12, 2002," March 21, 2002.

dress pre-Intifada continued unabated. During times that the military lifted curfew, settler women and children would rush into the vegetable market, overturn stalls, and steal merchandise until the military declared curfew again. Ultimately, the settlers won what they wanted on November 27, 2000, when the military cleared away the stands from that portion of the market. Although soldiers told CPTers they did so to create a "buffer zone," settlers swiftly began to build their own structures in the market.[17]

Settler youth continued to assault team members physically and verbally. For example, youth from Beit Hadassah told Bob Holmes and Andrew Getman on October 10, "Why don't you go home? You are Nazis. We are Jews. We killed Jesus." The youth then pushed Getman and kicked Holmes before soldiers intervened.[18] Settlers also threw rocks and shot marbles with sling shots at the team's windows, occasionally cracking the glass. They punctured the PVC-plastic water pipes that ran up the sides of a building near the CPT apartment. USAID had installed water infrastructure in 1997 to fulfill a U.S. commitment stipulated in the 1996 Hebron Protocol (see chapter 2). Water poured out of the punctured pipes for days before the team thought to call the USAID representative who attended the Lutheran church in Jerusalem. As it happened, the engineer, David Muirhead, who had originally supervised the USAID renovations on Shuhada Street, happened to be in town, and he put in an irate call to the Israeli military, who immediately had someone fix the pipes.[19]

A more serious incident for the work of the team happened in early December 2000, when settlers cut more than 1100 phone lines used by residents in the Old City. E-mail became difficult. (The box where they cut the phone lines was several feet away from a checkpoint. They clearly could not have accomplished the vandalism without soldiers observing them.) Team members put releases on disks and sent them out from Internet cafes in H-2, but the address lists and other vital information for releases were

---

17. CPTnet, "IDF closes vegetable market following settler demands," November 27, 2000. Another soldier told a CPT delegation member that the military was confiscating the market "to build offices and apartments."

18. CPTnet, "HEBRON UPDATE: October 9–13, 2000," October 13, 2000.

19. CPTnet, "HEBRON UPDATE: December 11–14, 2000," December 16, 2000. For an account of how settlers and Israeli military policy sabotaged Muirhead's work in 1997, see chapter 10.

CPTnet, "CPT Hebron Update: August 29–September 2, 1997," September 8, 1997. See also CPTnet, Dianne Roe, "HEBRON: Turquoise awnings and the failure of the Hebron Protocol," July 22, 2003. For more information on USAID, see www.usaid.gov.

on the non-portable computers at the team's office, making responses to e-mail difficult.[20]

The settler violence on the outskirts of Hebron also increased as settlers sought to close Bypass Road 60 to Palestinian traffic—even to Palestinians through whose land the road passed. Beginning in November, hundreds of settlers began massing nightly on the road in front of the homes of the extended Jaber family, throwing rocks at their houses and setting fire to their vineyards.[21] Police and soldiers more or less kept these demonstrations contained until December 8, when Palestinian gunmen shot and killed settlers Rina Didovsky and Eliyahu Ben Ami on the bypass road near the village of Bani Naim, several miles away from the Jaber families. After the killings, Israeli settlers invaded Atta and Rodeina Jaber's home, burning most of their possessions, including photo albums and important documents. When team members, watching events unfold from the home of Abdel Jawad Jaber, asked why the police were not removing the settlers, an officer replied, "The army is in charge here and the army says they can stay."

The next day, more settlers streamed up the hill to the house for Saturday prayers. Then, around 10:00 AM, settler men and youth began fanning out to the other Palestinian homes and bombarding them with stones. One settler shot thirteen-year-old Mansour Jaber, a nephew of Rodeina Jaber, in

---

20. CPTnet, "Hebron Update: December 1–10, 2000," December 11, 2000. CPTnet, "HEBRON UPDATE: December 29, 2000-January 4, 2001, January 15, 2001. On January 2, the team put out the following to its direct e-mail list:

> January 2, 2001
>
> On the evening December 7, the phone line to the CPT Hebron apartment stopped working. Friends of the team called PalTel repeatedly, explaining that CPT could not get out its human rights reports if the phone line was not fixed.
>
> A few days later, the team found out that their line, along with more than 1100 others in Hebron's Old City had been cut by settlers. Because of the curfew imposed by the Israeli military on the Old City, PalTel workers were not able to work on these cut lines. Team members walking past the men working on the lines across from the settlement of Avraham Avinu observed a huge snarl of wires in the metal box, and understood the immensity of the repair job.
>
> Some of you may be getting very old mail from us. Hopefully, new releases will be coming your way soon! Thank you for your patience.
>
> CPT Hebron

21. See CPTnet releases: "Hebron Update: November 2–3, 2000," November 7, 2000; "Hebron Update: November 8–11, 2000," November 17, 2000; "HEBRON UPDATE: November 12–15, 2000," November 19, 2000; "Settler Attack in the Beqa'a valley," November 27, 2000.

the stomach. At that point, the police did move in and arranged for an ambulance to take the boy to Jerusalem. The settlers, still under the protection of the Israeli military, returned to Atta and Rodeina Jaber's house. Later that day, four members of the Israeli Committee Against House Demolitions arrived with court orders for the army to remove the settlers. After they did so, soldiers told Atta Jaber that his home was a closed military zone—meaning the family could not return to it—until March.

Later, on December 14, Atta Jaber told the team that the Israeli Druze officer who had protected his house from the settlers over the previous month had been on leave the weekend that settlers had occupied his house. When the officer returned on December 10, according to Jaber, he had wept when he saw the damage.[22]

After the team publicized what had happened to the Jaber home, they received an irate e-mail from a partisan of the Hebron settlers noting they had not reported that the pogrom in the Beqa'a Valley had occurred because two settlers had been shot. The team put out the following response:

> It has been brought to our attention that in our most recent update we neglected to mention the murders of two Israeli settlers by Palestinian gunmen on Thursday, December 7, near the village of Bani Naim, east of Hebron. It was inexcusable for us not to have included this information.
>
> The settlers occupied the house of Palestinian [CSD] partner family Atta and Rodeina Jaber and burned all their possessions, using the murders of the two settlers as justification for their actions.
>
> We regret the time it has taken to provide this correction. Our email link is no longer available to us because settlers cut the phone lines to many residents in Hebron.[23]

---

22 CPTnet, "HEBRON UPDATE: December 11–14, 2000," December 16, 2000. The military allowed Atta and Rodeina Jaber to move back into their home in January 2001. See below under "Land confiscation 2001."

23. CPTnet, " Hebron: Correction Hebron Update Dec. 1–10," December 13, 2000. The hastily and snidely written correction echoed one that Mark Frey had written in 1998, after settlers burned the harvested wheat of Palestinians living near the settlement of Susia:

> In a recent CPT release we reported that Ibrahim Abu Jendia, a farmer near Yatta in the southern West Bank, told the team that last Friday evening settlers from Ma'on settlement burned his entire wheat crop of 150 dunams. The team was careful to clarify with Jendia at that time that it happened on Friday night, and he responded affirmatively.
>
> Numbers of inquires [sic] to the team questioned whether this would actually happen since lighting a fire on Shabbat is a complete violation of Jewish Law. As

Although the Israeli police and military continued to protect Atta Jaber's house because of a lawsuit that ICAHD had helped him bring against the Israeli military and police, settlers continued to hold demonstrations, attacking Palestinian cars and homes in the Beqa'a over the next weeks and months.[24]

GUN BATTLES

Although Palestinian gunmen, Israeli soldiers, and Israeli settlers had shot at each other sporadically since the Hebron Project began in 1995,[25] during the Intifada there were nightly gun battles between gunmen and soldiers for the first time in the history of CPT's Hebron project.

The barrages usually started late afternoon/early evening and followed a predictable progression. The team would hear sporadic gunfire from the light weaponry of Palestinian militants firing at settlements and soldier encampments. Israeli soldiers responded with heavy, automatic weapons fire and then the team would hear the loud boom of tank fire. Sometimes Israeli forces shot into neighborhoods without any precipitating Palestinian fire as retaliation for violence that had occurred elsewhere. For example on November 1, 2000, Adam Keller, co-editor of *The Other Israel*, called the team at 12:30 AM, saying, "I want to make sure you know that the Israeli military has told Palestinians to evacuate the neighborhoods of Harit iSheikh and Abu Sneineh. They are threatening retaliation because three Israeli soldiers were killed today." Two of the three soldiers killed were

---

one of our Jewish readers noted, "There is nothing in Jewish Law which would allow such a thing except to a save a life."

We spoke with Jendia again today (June 29) and asked him to clarify yet again when the fire happened. He said, it happened around 1 a.m. Thursday night/Friday morning—NOT on the Sabbath, Friday evening.

We sincerely apologize for this misinformation and thank our readers for raising the question. Settlers did not burn his entire wheat crop on the Sabbath. They burned it on the night before the Sabbath.

24. See for example, CPTnet, Gish, "Hebron: Donkeys and Bulldozers," December 29, 2000. Team members were able to stay out in the valley for short periods, but found they could not keep people in the Beqa'a indefinitely and deal with disturbances in the city at the same time.

25. Team members learned at one point that the gunfire that they heard on Fridays was a traditional part of Palestinian wedding celebrations. Zleekha Muhtasib once told Kathleen Kern that she thought the shooting was a stupid and dangerous custom. Even though men shot into the air, she said, every year someone would get hurt or even killed by falling bullets at a wedding

engaged in a firefight at Al Khader, near Bethlehem and one was killed in a battle near Jericho.[26]

In the first few nights of shooting, the team huddled in the windowless kitchen of the apartment. Gradually, they realized that since they lived in a neighborhood with Palestinian families, Palestinian gunmen were unlikely to shoot at them. Since they had an Israeli soldier camp on one side of their apartment and the settlement of Avraham Avinu on the other, soldiers were unlikely to shoot at them. As the nightly shelling continued over the next months, the team and their neighbors began going up on the roof of the apartment building during the gun fights to figure out the locations from which Palestinians and Israeli soldiers were firing the shots.

These gun battles began to claim casualties connected with the team's work. On October 9, Israeli snipers shot the brother of Tarik Sharif, one of the team's translators in its Campaign for Secure Dwellings, as Shehab Sharif walked home through the neighborhood of Haret iSheikh, located in the H-1 section of Hebron. Exploding bullets hit him in the back and hand. Twenty-nine fragments embedded themselves in Sharif's flesh. Doctors were able to remove only a few of them. When Dianne Roe called Tarik Sharif on October 13, as he sat by his brother's bedside in a Jerusalem hospital, he told her, "You know me. You know I have always been for peace. You know I have always wanted to work for peace with you. Use my name and tell everyone I am not for peace anymore. Tell them that now I am for war."[27]

Also on October 13, shots fired from the settlement of Beit Haggai hit Ibrahim Abu Turki, uncle of CSD participant Nabil Abu Turki. Both men were returning from Hebron to their homes in the Qilqis/Al Sendas area. Having heard that the military had lifted the curfew in Hebron, they had taken a donkey into town and loaded the animal up with bread for their families. The uncle was put on life support systems in Jerusalem's Hadassah Hospital and later sent to Saudi Arabia for further treatment, but one arm and both legs remained paralyzed. (Nabil Abu Turki escaped injury by diving behind some rocks.)

On the same morning in downtown Hebron, team friend Hani Abu Haikel emerged after a clash from his shop in the Al Andalus mall to deliver coffee when Israeli snipers shot him in the foot. A twenty-two-year-old

---

26. CPTnet, "Hebron Update: October 28–November 1, 2000." November 7, 2000. Bethlehem, Beit Jala, Beit Sahour, and Jericho also underwent heavy bombing that night.

27. CPTnet, "Use my name, Mom," November 8, 2000.

father of three, who had also been waiting for the clashes to end, left the mall at the same time that Abu Haikel did, and an exploding bullet hit him in the abdomen. Abu Haikel told the team he heard nothing before he felt the pain in his foot and saw the young man, Mansour Saied Ahmad, fall. According to Hisham Sharabati, a neighbor of Ahmad's, the soldiers held the ambulance bringing blood for Ahmad from Ramallah for four hours, not letting it through until after Alia hospital declared the young man dead.

That evening, in the Al-Fawwar refugee camp, soldiers killed Shadi al-Wawi as he stood on the roof of his house, where cellphone reception was better, to call his uncle in Gaza.

Sharabati brought Kern to meet a Palestinian field researcher who worked for the Israeli human rights organization, B'tselem, the next day. The field researcher, who lived across the road from the Al-Fawwar refugee camp, told Kern that al-Wawi had come home for a four-day visit to Al-Fawwar. The young man was calling his uncle to tell him that he would not be able to visit before he returned to his university in Sudan. Soldiers shot flares into the sky—illuminating al-Wawi and his brother—and then shot al-Wawi in the back. Because the military refused to allow an ambulance from Yatta to take al-Wawi on the direct road to the hospital in Hebron—a ten-minute drive—the ambulance took a dirt road and broke down. By the time another ambulance came and got him an hour later, he had died from blood loss. Doctors said they could have easily saved his life had he gotten to the hospital earlier.[28]

On October 23, Andrew Getman and Dianne Roe heard shots in Bab iZawwiye twice in one morning. Following the crowd after the second shooting, they came to the place where a taxi driver had been shot in the back of the head. He had been cleaning his taxi at least eighty meters

---

28. CPTnet, Sharabati, "View from Within," October 30, 2000. In a unique departure from CPTnet posting policy, the team put out Sharabati's release at his request. See also CPTnet, "Hebron Update: October 13–16, 2000," October 17, 2000. CPTnet, Getman, "HEBRON: Calling on the Spirit of God. Week Four—A day for prayer," October 20, 2000. (Getman, the son of the World Vision director in Jerusalem, volunteered time in autumn 2000, although he never went through training.) CPTnet, Holmes, "God's Tears," October 18, 2000. Holmes's release notes that a settler youth had killed the brother of Ibrahim Abu Turki (the man bringing bread to his family) two years earlier along the same stretch of road by putting a board out the window of a car as it whizzed past him.

See also Ben Lynfield, "In Mideast, crossfire more careless." Lynfield covered the shooting of Ibrahim Abu Turki and the army's lack of interest in pursuing the matter. He noted that during the first Intifada, the Israeli military investigated every death—of Palestinians not classified as terrorists—at the hands of Israeli soldiers.

away from where a clash had been taking place and one hundred and fifty meters from the nearest Israeli soldier station. Getman and Roe saw pieces of his brain lying in the street. They later learned that Fayez Mohammed Al-Qemari—a thirty-year-old father of three—was one of the men who regularly drove team and delegation members out to the Beqa'a Valley for CSD visits.[29]

On October 25, Israeli machine gunfire raked the hillside of Abu Sneineh, across from the team's apartment. When the phone rang during the shooting, fifty-five year old Abdul Aziz Abu Sneineh reached for it, and, according to his family, his head "exploded." The houses were on the opposite side of the hill from the settlements and the team apartment and thus could not possibly have been the source of shots fired at the settlements, to which the IDF said soldiers were responding. Since Aziz and Qemari were both active members of Fatah, rumors began to circulate that the Israeli military was intentionally targeting Arafat's people in Hebron.[30]

Also on October 25, a cousin of some CSD families in the village of Beit Ummar, Ibrahim Al-Alameh, was shot in the back of the head by Israeli soldiers when he failed to stop at a newly-installed checkpoint.[31] On November 4, soldiers shot fourteen-year-old Ghazala Jaradat. She was wearing the distinctive striped tunic that all Palestinian schoolgirls wear when a bullet hit her in the eye as she walked past clashes on her way home from school. She lived near the Beit Hanoun checkpoint at the entrance to the Beqa'a Valley that the team often used as a back route when soldiers closed the bypass road.[32]

Residents of Hebron sustained fewer casualties than those living in Gaza, Nablus, Ramallah and Jenin. However, Hebronites participated in the agony of other Palestinians as they watched the deaths and the funerals replayed on Palestinian television. In particular, the videotaped shooting of eleven-year-old Mohammed al-Dura in Gaza on September 30, 2000, played dozens of times every day on Palestinian TV. A cameraman working for French television had shot footage of the boy and his father (who had gone shopping together and had gotten caught in an armed clash) crouched

29. See CPTnet, Getman and Roe, "Tonight it will be worse," October 23, 2000.

30. CPTnet, Holmes, "A Spiral of Violence," October 31, 2000. See also CPTnet, "HEBRON UPDATE: October 23–27, 2000," November 2, 2000.

31. CPTnet, "Hebron Update: October 23–27, 2000," November 2, 2000.

32. The November 8–11, 2000, update refers to the incident in a "November 4 Update" that never appeared on CPTnet or was lost in the process of archiving Hebron team releases.

against a wall in the midst of the shooting. The father periodically waved his arm over a barrel that offered poor protection, shouting "walid, walid" (boy) to alert the soldiers that they were shooting at a child. The shooting continued as the father placed his arm protectively across his son and viewers watched Mohammed slump—after being hit multiple times—in his father's lap. The father, too, teetered to the side, semiconscious from loss of blood. Soldiers also killed the ambulance driver, Bassam al-Balbisi, as he tried to get to the father and his son. The Israeli military claimed that Palestinian gunmen shot the boy. However they destroyed the wall against which the father and son had crouched, so independent investigators could not examine it for ballistic evidence.

The relentless replaying of the boy's death and other casualties began to take a psychological toll on Palestinian friends of the team. One man told CPTers Natasha Krahn and Bourke Kennedy that his nephew had told his father (the man's brother) that he preferred to stay with his mother rather than go out on an errand with his father because, "fathers cannot protect their sons."[33]

Facing the prevailing rage and despair over the killings of civilians and decimation of neighborhoods by Israeli barrages, the team struggled to respond in an appropriate way. Their work on the mornings after heavy gunfire barrages involved walking around the neighborhoods of Harit iSheik and Abu Sneineh to document the damage done there. In homes and shops, they saw burned bedding and furniture, shattered mirrors and windows, bullet holes through steel doors and concrete and marble walls. Rockets left holes a foot in diameter. Bowls that used to hold flowers, cookies or fruit on decorative tables now held a variety of bullets and other projectiles that had hit the houses. One family in the Old City made a necklace of hundreds of spent M-16 shells that fell in their courtyard after soldiers fired from their roof into Abu Sneineh.[34]

After the team made several visits to the Qawasme family in Harit iSheik, one of the men in a household particularly hard-hit by Israeli barrages suggested that team members spend the night to get an idea of what life under fire was like. (Anita Fast had already spent the night with team friend Nisreen Abu Mayaleh in Abu Sneineh. She reported hearing the "sharp crack of live fire and the deep, breathy push of air as missiles cut

---

33. CPTnet, "Hebron Update: November 2–3, 2000," November 7, 2000.

34. CPTnet, "HEBRON UPDATE: October 7–9, 2000," October 9, 2000. See also Kern, "Hebron–H2: The Necklace of Umm Yusef."

through the darkness" and then feeling a sense of guilty relief when she found out that Israeli soldiers were aiming at Harit iSheik.)[35]

Accordingly, the team delivered the following letter to the soldiers' camp next to their apartment, shortly before Dianne Roe and Kathleen Kern left to spend the night in Harit iSheik:

> November 2, 2000
>
> To Noam Tibon, Commander of Hebron District:
>
> The Christian Peacemaker Team in Hebron, which has had a continuous presence here since June 1995, is saddened by the many deaths this month; whether Palestinian or Israeli, armed or unarmed, we believe that each killing destroys part of God's good creation, each killing is a loss for the entire human family. We are appalled by the dramatic escalation of violence the Israeli military is engaged in with indiscriminate fire from heavy weaponry in Bethlehem, Beit Jala, Beit Sahour, as well as throughout the neighborhoods of Hart-iSheik and Abu Sneineh here in Hebron. Accordingly, members of our team will be staying with families in the Hart iSheik neighborhood this evening, Thursday, November 2. As pacifists, we have asked the families to assure us there are no guns in their homes and they have done so.
>
> We are aware that the authorities of the Israeli occupation may accuse us of shielding terrorists, and we know there have been shots fired from these neighborhoods over the past month. However, no one from these neighborhoods has strafed Israeli neighborhoods with missiles and automatic weapons fire, and the vast majority of people in these neighborhoods are not gunmen. We believe that collective punishment against a whole people, whether they be Israeli or Palestinian, is morally wrong. In 1996, we rode the #18 bus in Jerusalem on the third Sunday after it had been bombed the two previous Sundays to protest the collective punishment of Israeli civilians. Tonight, we are staying in the Hart iSheik neighborhood to protest the collective punishment of Palestinian civilians. By the time you receive this, members of our team will be in this neighborhood and our consular representatives will have been notified.
>
> With hopes for a just and lasting peace for both Palestinians and Israelis,
>
> Christian Peacemaker Teams[36]

---

35. CPTnet, "God protect us." Fast's release was dated October 28, 2000, although it did not appear on CPTnet until November 6, 2000.

36. CPTnet, "CPTers Stay in Neighborhoods Under Fire," November 2, 2000.

The first night Roe and Kern spent with the Qawasme family passed in a festive atmosphere of jokes and small talk after Roe had videotaped damage done to the house, including a refrigerator in an inner room punctured by bullets. Once the shooting started, Kern called the U.S. Consulate in Jerusalem and told the Marine Guard on duty that she and Roe were staying in a neighborhood under fire. He asked her if she were aware that the U.S. Embassy had ordered all U.S. citizens to leave the West Bank, Gaza and East Jerusalem. She said they were aware of this order and that they just wanted the embassy to be aware of their presence. The entire family then moved to a back part of the house, on the other side of a courtyard, which was not vulnerable to Israeli shooting. Andrew Getman and Roe spent the night of November 4 in the same household and saw more extensive damage the next morning—windows that had not been bricked up were shattered and bullet holes riddled the children's clothing in their closet. Roe noted in her report on the second night in Harit iSheik that she and Getman had heard no shots from Palestinian gunmen emanating from the part of the neighborhood in which they were staying. "This contradicts the IDF's contention that they wait to shoot until Palestinian shots are fired," wrote Roe, "and that they fire only on homes that are sheltering gunmen."

The team's overnight visits did not appear to protect the neighborhoods in which they stayed. As the nightly shellings continued, they began to experience animosity from people living in Abu Sneineh and Harit iSheik. Palestinian boys in the neighborhoods began throwing stones at them. After a relative of one woman heard the CPTers offer to spend the night with her and her two sons, he asked what the visit would accomplish. Rich Meyer and Roe told him that the team could write a report and he said,

> What good is your report? We have enough reports to fill this whole house from floor to ceiling or more! Listen, your government is supporting these criminals, giving them the very weapons they are using to shoot at us. It is only my religion, Islam, that keeps you safe here, and someone else who is too angry could try to hurt you.[37]

The nights team members spent with families under fire were not entirely useless, however. The families involved appreciated the gesture of solidarity. They understood the accompaniment had been an experiment, and did not blame CPT when their presence did not prevent their homes from attack. The experiment also helped inform those who set up the Beit Jala project in December 2000.

37. CPTnet, "Hebron Update: November 8–11, 2000," November 17, 2000.

BEIT JALA

Since the beginning of the Hebron project, the team had had a special relationship with people in the Bethlehem area. Zoughbi Zoughbi, one of the people who had invited CPT to become involved with human rights work in the West Bank, had his home there, as did many internationals working for various relief and development organizations. In 1997, the team began taking weekly Arabic lessons from Selwa Awad at Bethlehem Bible College, which further strengthened ties the team had to people there.

The magnitude of the Israeli military's shelling of Bethlehem and the adjacent villages of Beit Jala and Beit Sahour[38] in the first months of the Intifada far exceeded the shelling in Hebron. CPT received repeated requests to put an emergency team in that area. Accordingly, Hebron team support person and CSD coordinator Rich Meyer came over in November 2000 to do the scouting work necessary to set up a project in the Bethlehem area.

Beit Jala was especially hard hit by Israeli shells because it sat across a valley from the settlement of Gilo, built between 1973 and 1979 on land confiscated from Beit Jala residents.[39] Palestinian gunmen shot from the neighborhoods of Beit Jala at Gilo, and the Israeli military fired tanks in response.

Two newspaper photos perhaps encapsulated the situation best: In the first week of major shooting between Beit Jala and Gilo, the *Jerusalem Post* showed a picture of an Israeli girl holding two bullets that had come through the living room window in her Gilo home. An Arabic language paper the team saw in Hebron with the same date showed a little Palestinian girl holding two missile shells. Her torso and head were framed by the gigantic hole the shells had blasted into the wall of her home in Beit Jala. Amnesty International condemned both the gunmen and the Israeli military for shooting at civilians, but called the response of the Israeli military "excessive."[40]

---

38. Rich Meyer, the Hebron team support person at the time, described the geographical relationship between the towns in terms of Mickey Mouse's head: Bethlehem is the face, Beit Sahour the left ear and Beit Jala the right ear.

39. Part of a ring of Israeli settlements built around Jerusalem, Gilo is referred to by politicians and even by progressive Israelis as "within the consensus," meaning that they no longer view it as a settlement, but part of Israel proper. Israeli sources generally call it a "neighborhood" of Jerusalem.

40. Amnesty International, "Israel and the Occupied Territories." Team reports from this period, and the Winter 2001 *Signs of the Times* quotes Amnesty International as having said Israel's use of lethal force was "grossly excessive," but a contemporary web search

The team's goal in Beit Jala was thus more nuanced than in Hebron. Although team members condemned all the shooting, they sought to publicize that Israeli retaliation to Palestinian gunfire was grossly disproportionate. One of the most technologically savvy militaries in the world with the capacity to pinpoint gunmen at night was collectively punishing entire neighborhoods. Like the residents of Haret iSheik and Abu Sneineh in Hebron, the residents of Beit Jala sincerely wished that gunmen would not shoot from their neighborhood, but were nearly powerless to stop it.[41]

Anne Montgomery and Pierre Shantz were the first CPTers to staff the house of Umm Elias Kunkar at the corner of Intifada and Martyr Street in Beit Jala. The basement apartment had three bedrooms and north/northeastern exposures that faced the settlement of Gilo.

Montgomery and Shantz spent their days networking with residents of Bethlehem, Beit Jala and Beit Sahour. They attended one meeting on December 5, 2000, in which local residents met with the mayor of Beit Jala and demanded that the local police stop gunmen from shooting at the settlements. Shantz and Montgomery also visited homes that the Israeli military had shelled, helping residents put sandbags in their windows and sweep up glass.

The most serious attacks on their neighborhood happened on December 5 and 11, 2000. Shells gouged holes in the streets and damaged three sides of the house. Both times, the gregarious Shantz was playing cards in another house with friends, leaving Montgomery by herself.

On December 5, she called the U.S. Consulate to tell them she was in the house and she had heard no gunfire coming from that section of the neighborhood. The shelling soon stopped. On December 11, Montgomery heard a machine gun firing outside the window of the kitchen where she was reading a novel and bolted to the bathroom. She called the consulate again, informing personnel that she had heard firing from the neighborhood. The shelling continued, aiming directly at the house. The next day she found a tank bullet had hit the wall where she had been standing before she fled to the bathroom. After the second incident, Montgomery (74) and Shantz (26) moved into the same bedroom and stuck together nights.[42]

---

does not reveal Amnesty International using that description in its reports. The original report the team read possibly was different from the official report on the web.

41. Some residents did try to do street patrols at one point to shoo the gunmen away, which in the end proved ineffectual. A discussion of their attempts appears below.

42. CPTnet, "BETHLEHEM DISTRICT UPDATE: December 1–14, 2000," December 20, 2000. (The team wanted to say that the releases came from Beit Jala. CPT's

Shantz accompanied neighborhood patrols Beit Jala residents organized to get the shooters out of their neighborhoods. These met with mixed success. After a while, the gunmen started coming out at odd hours, like 4:00 AM, and once, gunmen threw rocks at the neighbors who were yelling at them to get out of the neighborhood.[43]

In the second two weeks of the Beit Jala project, Kathleen Kern and Bob Holmes took the places of Anne Montgomery and Shantz, who, having spent the previous year with the team in Chiapas, was anxious to get to Hebron and catch up on his relationships with friends there. These two weeks passed relatively quietly, although the number of interviews with press increased as Christmas approached.

On December 18, 2000, Zoughbi Zoughbi warned the team that the American and Israeli press were trying to put the shootings into the context of Christian/Muslim tensions. These tensions did enter into the situation in a small way. Many gunmen were Muslim residents of the heavily-bombed Aida refugee camp in Bethlehem. The homes in Beit Jala sustaining the worst damage belonged to affluent Palestinian Christians. Thus, a certain amount of bitterness regarding class differences did exist. However, three days later, when the *New York Times* called and asked Kern and Montgomery about the Christian/Muslim tensions, they told him what most Palestinians believed: Gunmen chose to shoot from locations where they had the best vantage point to aim at settlements and soldier outposts. The situation of people living in the all-Muslim neighborhoods in Hebron did not differ significantly from those of the people living in Beit Jala. The team's Muslim friends and acquaintances in Hebron never talked to CPTers about the Israeli military

---

Chicago Office wanted the releases to come from Bethlehem—to tie constituent churches to the project during the Christmas season— so staff and the team compromised by saying the releases were from the Bethlehem district.) Some details are from an undated note that Montgomery sent the author in 2004 after she read a draft of this chapter.

See also Christine Hauser, "U.S. Nun plays witness to Israeli-Palestinian strife." Honest-Reporting, an Israeli partisan group, referred to Hauser's article in its "Dishonest Reporter 'Award' 2001," claiming that her Reuters story totally ignored the plight of Israeli civilians in Gilo living under fire of Palestinian terrorists.

The critique article has no date, but refers to *USA Today* posting the Hauser story on December 7, 2000 and removing it from its online edition on December 8.

43. The stories of these patrols did not appear in the Beit Jala Updates. Kathleen Kern referred to them in a response to an e-mail query from Rabbi Yehudai-Rimmer (a progressive British Rabbi normally supportive of CPT's work) in the "Dialogue" section of the Winter 2001 *Signs of the Times*, 8. Her account was based on what Shantz had told her. She concluded the response with, "There are a lot of rumors about [the gunmen] being collaborators or even Israeli secret police. I think it's just too many guns in too many hands."

shelling "Christians" in Beit Jala. They viewed them as fellow Palestinians suffering the same collective punishment for the actions of gunmen who did not live in their neighborhoods.[44]

When the team returned to their Beit Jala apartment on the evening of December 22, 2000, from a dinner engagement, Palestinian policemen were present on most major intersections in Beit Jala. As team members approached each corner, policemen stopped and questioned them. Yasser Arafat had announced that the police would enforce a ceasefire order by arresting gunmen shooting from Beit Jala and other locations. While the respite from shelling was welcome, Arafat's actions demonstrated that he had had the power to stop the gunmen from shooting before and chose not to intervene.

One of the outgrowths of the Beit Jala team's work was the "No Christmas in Bethlehem" campaign that sought to involve the CPT constituency in the plight of Bethlehem-area residents. On December 3, 2000, the team put out the following release:

> NO CHRISTMAS IN BETHLEHEM: CPT CALL FOR
> SOLIDARITY WITH THE PEOPLE OF BETHLEHEM,
> BEIT JALA AND BEIT SAHOUR
>
> Since the beginning of the new Intifada, or Uprising, in early October, the town of Bethlehem and the adjoining, predominantly Christian, villages of Beit Sahour and Beit Jala have suffered from repeated bombings by the Israeli military. Many Beit Jalan families facing the Israeli settlement of Gilo and Beit Sahourian families whose houses are next to a military camp have fled their homes. Additionally, the military has sealed off even the side roads into the area, which is leading to the economic strangulation of the three towns.
>
> The annual Christmas festivities in Bethlehem's manger square have been canceled, because the organizers have deemed it inappropriate to celebrate when Palestinians all over the West Bank and Gaza are being killed. The current 60% unemployment rate in the area is making it nearly impossible for Christians and Muslims to buy what they need for Christmas and Ramadan feasts and gifts.
>
> Christian Peacemaker Teams is calling on the churches of North America to show solidarity with the Christian and Muslim residents of Bethlehem, Beit Sahour and Beit Jala by sitting in darkness and silence for five minutes during their annual Christmas services. Ask the members of your congregation to pray for the families living

---

44. William J. Orme Jr. quoted Kern about the Christian vs. Muslim issue in Orme, "Jerusalem Christians Now Back Palestinian Sovereignty."

in the war zone that encompasses Bethlehem, Beit Jala and Beit Sahour and for an end to the Israeli military occupation of the West Bank and Gaza.

Additionally, CPT is asking U.S. residents to write their legislators and President Clinton, notifying them that their congregations will be remembering the struggles of people living under the Israeli occupation in the three villages during their Christmas services. You may refer to the work of Christian Peacemaker Teams, which is in the process of setting up a new project in a neighborhood in Beit Jala, which has been repeatedly bombed. Note that CPT's presence in Hebron has helped to reduce violence there, and request that all Palestinians and Israelis receive more comprehensive international protection.

Canadian citizens should write to the Prime Minister and their members of Parliament commending the government for its recent vote in the U.N. Security council that condemns Israel's use of excessive force against Palestinians. Describe the intolerable conditions that the residents of Bethlehem, Beit Sahour and Beit Jala are living under and ask your legislators to support the sending of unarmed international observers to provide protection for the Palestinians in the West Bank and Gaza.[45]

The celebration of Christmas 2000 by the Hebron and Beit Jala teams would prove especially meaningful. The teams spent December 24 and 25 together at the Beit Jala apartment. In a reflection on the holiday, Kern wrote:

> "Christmas gloomy in Bethlehem," read the front page headline of the Israeli newspaper, Ha'aretz, on December 25. The Associated Press story beneath it began, "Soaked by cold rain and saddened by three months of wrenching violence, crowds of Palestinians and a thin trickle of foreign tourists joined in subdued Christmas Eve commemorations yesterday in Bethlehem."
>
> Those of us who have worked with CPT in Hebron and Bethlehem for the last few months have known that this Christmas would not be a festive occasion in Bethlehem. With unemployment at 60 percent because of the Israeli closure on Bethlehem, and the shelling by Israeli military of civilian homes in Bethlehem, Beit Jala and Beit Sahour, few of the area's Palestinian Christians felt they had much to celebrate.
>
> The Christmas spirit was likewise not in large supply within our two teams. Those in Beit Jala had experienced several nights of heavy Israeli shelling and watched their landlady burst into tears

---

45. CPTnet, "No Christmas in Bethlehem," December 2, 2000.

when she saw the piles of broken glass, bullet and missile holes in the house where she and her late husband brought up seven children. The Hebron team came to Bethlehem feeling helpless from watching families we love coming apart at the seams from the stresses of home demolitions, poverty, soldier and settler violence. Neighborhoods in Hebron, too, had experienced severe shelling the evenings before the team came up, and the curfew on the Old City of Hebron, imposed since October with devastating consequences for its residents, was still in place when they left.

On Christmas Eve, the Hebron and Beit Jala teams attended the five o'clock service at the Christmas Lutheran Church. We slogged through the downpour to get there, and by the time I arrived, my feet were soaked and I had to wring out my socks. I felt the discomfort was worth it, though, once we began singing, in Arabic, English and German, the opening hymn, "O Come All Ye Faithful."

I know this Christmas hymn so well that I can nail the alto part in any key. The full impact of its words, however, never hit me as they did on Christmas Eve. Tears filled my eyes as I looked around and saw that it was indeed the faithful who had come to church in Bethlehem that evening.

There are more people from the Bethlehem district now living in Santiago, Chile than there are in Bethlehem. The pressures of the Israeli Occupation have made hundreds of thousands of Palestinian Christians emigrate. Those who were worshipping in their church this Christmas Eve had stayed, in part, because they want the oldest Christian community in the world to continue, because they want there to be Living Stones in the Holy Land, not just monuments and shrines for tourists.

Among the dozens of internationals present were those who had chosen to stay in the West Bank and Gaza even though their governments had told them to leave once the new Intifada had started. Still more had come via complicated routes into the city when Israeli soldiers told them Bethlehem was closed for the holiday. Two friends from the English-speaking Lutheran congregation in Jerusalem had been turned away by soldiers, but noticing that the soldiers let a car driven by the pastors of that congregation pass, gunned their motor and ploughed through the checkpoint immediately behind them. Given that Palestinians have been killed for doing the same thing, it was not a smart thing to do, but their hunger to be in Bethlehem made them feel it was worth the risk.

Looking around at my teammates, I realized that we, too, were part of the faithful. We had come to church because we wanted to, not out of a sense of obligation, but nevertheless, we had come to Bethlehem to join that long line of faithful and fallible witnesses who had come to meet Jesus when he shared our human condition.

Later in the service, we sang "O Little Town of Bethlehem" which I have always considered too schmaltzy, but after the familiar first stanza, the second, alternative, stanza brought on fresh tears:

"O little town of Bethlehem, the organs still do play
Of Jesus in a manger and angels on the way;
Our music and our singing is louder than a gun,
And church bells in their ringing remind us we have won."

From that moment, the weight of the misery here lifted from my heart—or perhaps I should say that I found fresh confidence to face it and know that it would not have the last word.

This confidence lasted through the prayers, sermons and singing in different languages until the end of the service, when the children of the Palestinian congregation of the Lutheran church began lighting the candles of all the worshippers. As I saw their eyes shining, from both the reflected light and their own awe and wonder, I thanked God once more for the reminder that the prayers and songs of the faithful are stronger than weapons, and that where Jesus is concerned, joy can happen in the most unexpected times and places.[46]

After four weeks in which no shelling of Beit Jala occurred, Jamey Bouwmeester, Bob Holmes, and Anne Montgomery closed down the Beit Jala project on January 12, 2001. Since most of the neighbors left at night to sleep in safer locations, the project had also lost its *raison d'etre*: accompaniment of people under fire. Members of the Beit Jala team rejoined the team in Hebron, where shelling of neighborhoods had stepped up.

---

46. From the Hebron/Beit Jala Teams' direct mail list. A shorter version of the reflection appeared on CPTnet: "O Come all Ye Faithful," December 26, 2000. December 2000 CPTnet archives.

Had team members known that the Intifada would still be going on, as of this writing, for the next eight years, and that the death toll of Israelis and Palestinians would rise from hundreds to thousands, perhaps neither the rainbow that had appeared earlier in the day (See CPTnet, Beit Jala Update: December 23, 2000–January 12, 2000," January 18, 2001) nor the Christmas Eve service would have sufficed to allay their sorrow.

SIX

The Intifada Continues
2001

For much of 2001, Hebron team members dealt with the same issues as they had for the first three months of the Intifada: clashes, gun battles curfews, closures, settler violence, etc. However, with the exception of clashes, the grimness of all these aspects seemed to intensify, and the mean streets of Hebron became progressively meaner.

The team's update covering January 4, 2001, captured some of the despair and helplessness felt by Palestinian colleagues. A social worker at the Woman's Counseling Center tearfully told Anita Fast and Kathleen Kern that she was afraid of the Intifada's long-term effects on children, given the number of young people who had died. She and her husband had taught their own children about the importance of co-existence with Israelis, but influences outside the home had had their effect. Her eight-year-old son had told her he wanted to die as a martyr. Her daughter told her that she would like to throw stones at soldiers as Palestinian boys did. When the social worker told her that throwing stones would not change anything, the daughter said, "Then I want to make a bomb."[1] Dr. Tayseer Zeahda, whose home at Tel Rumeida had had soldiers stationed on the roof since the beginning of the Intifada, told the team on February 5, 2001, "The problem is not a broken door or window. This we can get fixed. The problem is that our children now think about killing. They are suffering in their minds and I do not know what they are thinking. My Palestine is my rooftop. I only want to have the soldiers leave my house."[2]

---

1. CPTnet, "HEBRON UPDATE: December 29–January 4, 2001," January 17, 2001.
2. CPTnet, "HEBRON UPDATE: January 27–February 6, 2001," February 7, 2001.

CLASHES

Clashes continued at various friction points in Hebron and its surrounding areas throughout 2001. When school was letting out in the Abu Sneineh neighborhood, for example, Palestinian boys almost routinely threw rocks at the checkpoint in the area the settlers called Gross Square, which bordered the former vegetable market. Major clashes were, however, no longer daily occurrences. When team members did record these clashes in their updates, they usually connected them to specific events. For example, when Israeli forces for the first time used American-made F-16 warplanes to bomb Palestinian population centers like Nablus, Gaza, Ramallah, and Tulkarm, clashes on the border of H-1 and H-2 lasted for a couple hours the next day, May 19, 2001.[3] The team also noted clashes that precipitated a curfew on July 29, 2001, that were sparked by the announcement that right-wing Israelis intended to lay the cornerstone of the Third Temple in Jerusalem.[4]

LAND CONFISCATION

With the diminution of clashes came an increase in the rate of land confiscation and home demolitions throughout the West Bank and Gaza. In early January, soldiers began building a road circling the hill on which the longsuffering Atta Jaber family had its home. One officer told the CPTers who came out to the site after receiving a call, "This is a compromise. We are building a road to separate the Israeli land from the Palestinian land. We are giving the Jabers their home."[5] After the military finished its work on the road, destroyed several gardens, further flattened Jaber's two demolished houses, and confiscated thirty dunams (about eight acres)[6] of land

---

3. CPTnet, "Hebron Update: May 16–29, 2001," June 5, 2001. The team mentioned only bombings of Nablus and Gaza, but the planes bombed Tulkarm and Ramallah also on May 18, 2001. On May 19, Israel bombed Tulkarm once again and Jenin. The attacks were a retaliation for the suicide bombing, that earlier that day killed five Israelis and injured ninety-six in Netanya's central shopping mall.

4. CPTnet, "Hebron Update: July 30-August 11, 2001," August 26, 2001.

5. CPTnet, Rebecca Johnson, "Hebron: A curious road to peace," January 10, 2001. Johnson, who became a CPT reservist after going through a CPT regional training in Toronto, would later become the head the World Council of Churches' Ecumenical Accompaniment Program in Palestine and Israel (EAPPI), which modeled itself on CPT's Hebron team. See below. In 2007, she became the CPT Canada Administrative Coordinator and in 2008 the CPT Canada Program Coordinator.

6. One dunam equals one fourth of an acre.

behind Fayez and Huda Jaber's house, they allowed Atta and Rodeina to move back into their house from which they had been barred in December 2000 following the settler invasion (see chapter 5).[7] Even more dramatic confiscations of land, duly reported to the team by the Hebron District's chief cartographer, Abdel Hadi Hantash, were taking place south of Hebron near the Israeli settlement of Susia and the Palestinian town of Yatta.

The team put out an urgent action release regarding this confiscation on October 8, 2001, noting that the Israeli government was taking advantage of the world's current focus on Afghanistan to plant and expand settlements. The sample letter offered in the team's urgent action release captured the team's undercurrent of anger against the U.S. government's lack of initiative in challenging Sharon:

> Dear [elected representative],
>
> We have just received word that Israeli settlers are still building new settlements in the occupied territories—four new settlements this month already. On Sunday October 1, settlers seized a plot of land in the south Hebron district, and (with Israeli military support) placed a mobile home and water tank. Three more settlements are slated to be planted this month. These new settlements are in addition to the twenty-five new settlements built in occupied territory since Sharon was elected Prime Minister in February.
>
> There is no reason for more Israeli settlement construction in occupied territory. The settlements are built on land seized without due process. They are a provocation and a security nightmare. Yet, it is clear that more settlements are part of Sharon's plan. What is our country's role in this continuing violation of human rights? Have we, have YOU, made it clear to Israel that we oppose more settlements? Have we given the Israeli government any sense that there are costs to heading farther down this dead-end street?
>
> (For US partners:) If we continue to send billions of dollars to Israel while they continue to build settlements, we are like friends of a drunk buying them drinks.[8]

HOME DEMOLITIONS

Home demolitions, which had almost ended under Barak due to sustained grassroots resistance, resumed dramatically in 2001. Most of these demoli-

---

7. CPTnet, "Hebron Update: January 6–11, 2001."

8. CPTnet, "HEBRON URGENT ACTION: NO MORE SETTLEMENTS!" October 8, 2001.

tions happened in the Jerusalem area, but people in the Hebron area soon learned that their homes also were no longer safe. On February 10, the Israeli military demolished two homes in Beit Ummar—one of which had received neither a "stop work" order nor a demolition order. On March 13, the military destroyed the Love and Peace greenhouse, a landmark on the road between Hebron and Bethlehem.

Fifteen homes in the Jerusalem and Hebron areas—including four in the Beqa'a Valley—fell on April 4. When Pierre Shantz, Rick Polhamus, and Greg Rollins arrived in the Beqa'a, Shantz climbed on the roof of a house he mistakenly thought was next in line for demolition. Avi—the Israeli border policeman whom Shantz and Sara Reschly had stood in front of in January 1999 as he prepared to fire on unarmed demonstrators (see chapter 1)—kicked Shantz, slapped him across the face, and pushed him down the stairs. Later, Polhamus, who had taken photographs of the confrontation between Avi and Shantz previously, chatted with Shantz, whom the police were detaining. When Polhamus began walking back up a hill toward Rollins, who was videotaping, Avi ran up behind Polhamus, hit him on the back with his gun butt, and kicked him in the leg hard enough to cause bleeding.[9]

In a subsequent urgent action release release, the team speculated that the Sharon government felt free to resume demolitions because Bush had vetoed a U.N. Security Council resolution calling for international observers in the Occupied Territories. The release noted

> In the words of the Israeli peace group Gush Shalom, "The houses destroyed yesterday and today belong to ordinary Palestinian citizens

---

9. CPTnet, "HEBRON/JERUSALEM: Eight homes destroyed in one morning; more demolitions to come," April 4, 2001. Avi turned Shantz over to police because he had "incited" the crowd to resist by calling Rollins to join him on the roof. The police, as was often the case in their interactions with the team, treated Shantz cordially and took his statement. They wrote down Shantz's suggestion that Avi take anger-management classes and then released him without charges. On May 9, 2002, Rick Polhamus testified in a Jerusalem court about Avi's actions. The prosecutor lost two copies of the videotape Polhamus had taken of Avi and insinuated that the defense had deliberately lost the second copy. Someone from the prosecutor's office later told Polhamus that Avi would lose rank and/or be stationed somewhere inside Israel as a result of the hearing. E-mails from Polhamus to the author, January 27, 2005, and January 25, 2008.

Also demolished, for the third time, on April 4, was the home of Salim Shawamreh, which had become the highest profile house in the movement to end home demolitions. He and Jeff Halper, director of the Israeli Committee Against Home Demolitions, had done several speaking tours of the U.S., and Shawamreh had dedicated the house as a "House of Peace" where Israelis and Palestinians could meet. The Hebron team had helped rebuild the Shawamreh home in 1998, 1999, and 2003.

whose only crime is the wish to have a roof over their heads. In this case, there isn't any pretence of 'security interests' or 'military targets.'" This is the consequence of [the] willingness of the world to tolerate (and of the U.S. Congress to support) the violence of continued Israeli military occupation.[10]

Because of the April demolitions, the Campaign for Secure Dwellings sought more North American congregations to match with families facing home demolitions. Given that the team had found family-to-family matches too difficult to keep up, the new Campaign for Secure Dwellings matched newcomers with villages and neighborhoods, specifically, those in the Beqa'a, Beit Ummar, and the Al Sendas/Qilqis area.

The team put out another urgent action release in July after the Israeli military had demolished, over a period of days, dozens of homes, cave dwellings, tents, wells, and animal shelters near the Israeli settlement of Susia.[11] The team took pictures of goats and sheep that Israeli soldiers crushed to death when they bulldozed the pens with the live animals inside. Rabbis for Human Rights estimated that the demolitions left as many as a thousand people homeless.[12] Further demolitions of cave dwellings in the area happened on September 18, 2001, Jewish New Year's Eve, leaving sixty-five people homeless.[13]

Home demolitions of another sort happened in August 2001, when the Israeli military blew up two houses after a day of heavy shooting in the Abu Sneineh neighborhood. (See below.)

CURFEWS/CLOSURES

In 2001, curfews in the Old City and road closures continued to devastate the Palestinian economy. The team's updates recorded roadblocks between

---

10. CPTnet, "HEBRON URGENT ACTION: Fifteen homes demolished in southern West Bank," April 4, 2001.

11. See chapter 4, particularly footnotes 18–20.

12. "CSD URGENT ACTION: Revenge demolitions and arrests," July 2001. The team used the term "revenge" because they speculated that the military targeted the families because Israeli groups had helped them get a court order allowing them return to their homes in March 2000. The place where the Israeli and international activists had feasted with the families in celebration was demolished. See chapter 4. When the urgent action release appeared on CPTnet, it was titled, "Devastation in Yatta Area," July 6, 2001.

13. CPTnet, Cockburn, "HEBRON DISTRICT: Happy New Year or Just Another Day?" September 22, 2001. Although "cave dwellings" sounds primitive, they were actually more comfortable than most Palestinian homes in winter and summer. Most of them had house-like facades built over the front.

Jerusalem and Hebron gradually increasing in size and new dirt mounds appearing on side roads and the trails that Palestinians used to avoid checkpoints. The team had to allow two hours to get to Bethlehem for language lessons—a trip that had taken twenty minutes before the Intifada. At times, they had to take five taxis to get there. Drivers would go to a barricade, team members and other passengers would climb over and then take a different taxi to the next barricade.

Often at these barricades, passengers and drivers would look hopefully at them when soldiers approached, or even order them to talk to the soldiers. Their interventions with these soldiers became progressively less successful. Taxi drivers and others trying to evade the checkpoints by taking trails through agricultural areas often had their tires slashed or keys confiscated by soldiers. (Once, a driver handed his keys to Kathleen Kern near the Jerusalem checkpoint and told her to hide them to prevent their confiscation.)[14]

Harriet Taylor wrote in July 2001,

> While the international community congratulates Israel on its "restraint" (i.e., no shelling of Palestinian areas) after the suicide bombing of the disco in Tel Aviv on June 1st, the Israeli government has imposed even more egregious measures of collective punishment and control on the Palestinian people in the Occupied Territories.
>
> Villages and towns are under siege, completely closed off by barricades, often made more intimidating by the presence of the Israeli military. Palestinian workers are forbidden to go to Israel to their jobs and are subject to arrest and imprisonment if they are caught trying to do so. Although settler roads remain open, there are checkpoints every few miles; and since no one except certain taxi drivers are permitted to leave their home territories, Palestinians found traveling in private cars or taxis are forced from their cars and stranded wherever they happen to be. International borders are closed, and international mail and money transfers into the West Bank and Gaza are cut off. Many Palestinians receive financial sup-

---

14. Because the Israeli government repeatedly denied that its soldiers confiscated keys, some soldiers from a Nahal unit hung a display of confiscated keys at a 2004 exhibit, "Breaking the Silence," in Tel Aviv. See CPTnet, "HEBRON/TEL AVIV: "'Breaking the silence' about Israeli soldiers' experiences in Hebron," June 25, 2004. Yehudah Shaul, a soldier who befriended the team in 2002, was the chief organizer of the exhibit, which also contained photos and video clips of soldiers and settlers abusing the human rights of Palestinians in Hebron.

port from family members abroad, without which they may literally starve. The Israeli closure is strangling the Palestinians.

Monday night CPTer Gene Stoltzfus and delegate Bill Rose watched as soldiers re-established huge barricades of dirt and concrete blocks on the secondary roads in the Baqa'a and set up checkpoints on the main settler by-pass road through the Valley. They saw private Palestinian cars at the barricade whose tires had been deflated by the military, and heard that the IDF had confiscated the air pump the Palestinians tried to use to re-inflate the tires.

While the world looks for images of bomb damage and tank fire, which have been largely absent for the last several days, the Israeli Knesset on Saturday tightened the silent, virtually invisible noose of control and deprivation that is the occupation. When will the world hear the strangled cries of the Palestinians?[15]

Israeli military curfews imposed on the Palestinian residents of the Old City were also devastating. Often the military lifted the curfews on the Old City only to reimpose them again swiftly—usually because of settlers attacking vendors in the marketplace. People who had left before the imposition of curfew would come back to their homes in the Old City and find themselves forbidden to enter. Ten minute walks to homes and jobs began to take an hour as Palestinians walked circuitous routes via back alleys. Team members often found themselves negotiating passage into and out of the Old City for women and children—many times so they could get to the hospital.[16]

The team also frequently intervened on behalf of a neighbor who sold chickens and more exotic birds in their alley. Soldiers would forbid him and his nephews to feed and water the birds; he would pugnaciously stand his ground and eventually one of the team members would come downstairs to plead on the chickens' behalf. Often the compromise reached was that he could lock his nephews inside the shop for a half hour, then come back and unlock the door so they could return home.[17]

15. CPTnet, "HEBRON: The Strangulation of the Occupied Territories," July 2, 2001. July 2001 CPTnet archives.

16. On one occasion, Pierre Shantz and Bob Holmes interceded on behalf of an elderly woman laden with groceries whom soldiers would not let pass by the Beit Hadassah settlement. Eventually, the woman was forced to climb rickety stairs that detoured around Beit Hadassah while Shantz and Holmes carried her groceries past the settlement. When soldiers threatened to call the police, Holmes retorted, "Good, maybe they will be more reasonable." "HEBRON UPDATE: January 6–11," January 17, 2001.

17. On June 28, 2001, soldiers beat, with gun butts and hands, one of the chicken shop owners and his brothers. They banged the owner's head against a wall, causing an

When the soldiers rejected any compromise, the chickens died. On July 21, 2001, Kathy Kamphoefner met with three chicken shop owners after a curfew period during which electrical transformers supplying energy to the Old City had been destroyed in a shootout. Four days without electricity meant chickens inside refrigerators spoiled and live chickens died due to lack of ventilation, food, and water. They estimated their losses from curfews since September 2000 had come to $52,400.[18]

Families and shop owners with the financial means or family outside of H-2 began to leave *en masse*. Those remaining, with a few exceptions,[19] simply stayed and went hungry. The soup kitchen near the Ibrahimi Mosque/Cave of Machpelah found the number of families depending on its food grow from fifty to one hundred by July 2001. During curfew, families had no access to food.

A journalist friend of the team, Kawther Salam, showed up one day at the team's apartment in tears. She asked Kern to write a letter in English to the military commander of Hebron. It read, in part,

> Yesterday, 27 August, I was following the army who were searching the apartment of Afifa Herbawi. She is 92 years old. I noticed this woman collecting stale bread from the garbage in the street. She soaks it in water for a couple hours to prepare it for her daily meal . . . I stopped being a journalist and broke down emotionally, crying in front of the soldiers. I demanded that the soldiers kill me, because I don't want to film or write any more stories like this in the 21st century.

Salam then asked Commander Weinberg to permit the Islamic Waqf soup kitchen to begin operating again, since it was the primary source of food, according to her, for 570 families in the Old City. On the next day, she reported to the team that Weinberg passed the letter on to the head of the Israeli Civil Administration, Dov Tzedekah. He promised to lift the curfew and said if it were reimposed, he would allow the soup kitchen to operate for two hours every day.[20]

---

injury that required four stitches. CPTnet, "HEBRON UPDATE: 1 July–8 July 2001," July 9, 2001.

18. CPTnet "HEBRON UPDATE: July 19–21, 2001," August 9, 2001.

19. The team's upstairs neighbors found ways of getting to jobs by leaving at odd hours and monitoring soldier patrols from their window. However, they too finally gave up in March 2003 and left the neighborhood.

20. CPTnet, "HEBRON UPDATE: August 29–September 3, 2004," September 14, 2004. The sheikh who gave Grace Boyer and Kathleen Kamphoefner a tour of the

Salam also organized a demonstration on August 28, 2001,[21] of children in the Old City who had been forced to remain inside their homes for approximately 183 days with brief respites. Holding signs reading, "Can we come out to play?" and "I need to go to school," about forty children assembled in the Old City in front of soldiers and journalists. The soldiers demanded that the children disperse and asked Salam, "Do you want me to shoot the children?" A British visitor of the team, Angie Zelter, told a soldier it was not right to punish the entire Old City of Hebron for the violence of a few. The soldier told her he had seen gunmen run into the Old City and that he had a right to defend his soldiers. "But we have IRA terrorists in Britain," she said, "and the British government doesn't put all of Belfast under curfew when the IRA commits acts of terrorism."

The incident culminated with Greg Rollins standing between soldiers and the children and telling them, "You don't have to shoot them, they're just kids." The soldiers then began to harass Palestinian journalists who had covered the demonstration by trying to confiscate their Israeli Press credentials. The officer told them that the military must have issued the credentials by mistake. "But you say you have to follow orders even if they are mistaken," Rick Polhamus told them. They returned the credentials. Rollins then stood between the soldiers and boys who wanted to throw stones at the soldiers, refusing to budge even after the boys motioned him to move out of the way.[22]

In their last urgent action release release for 2001, the team chose to address the issue of the curfew, noting that imposing it during the last week of the Muslim holy month of Ramadan was particularly difficult for families. They could not attend worship or prayer services, buy food to prepare the feast that concludes Ramadan, or travel to visit family celebrations—all integral parts of observing Ramadan. "The curfew is especially cruel for

---

soup kitchen on July 23, 2001, gave them the "100 families" figure. CPTnet, "HEBRON UPDATE: July 22–28, 2001," August 16, 2001. August 2001 CPTnet archives. Salam's figure is not substantiated anywhere else, but it is possible that she meant five hundred and seventy people instead of families.

21. The team's writings make determining the exact date of this demonstration confusing. Releases written by Dianne Roe and Greg Rollins about the event are dated September 10 and 14, 2001, respectively. The Hebron update covering August 28 refers to the demonstration happening on that date. Since the updates are usually based on the team's log, that date is probably more accurate. However, the "August 29–September 3 Update" refers to the demonstration happening on August 27.

22. CPTnet, "HEBRON UPDATE: August 20–28, 2001," September 4, 2001; CPTnet, Rollins, "Curfew Babies," September 14, 2001.

Palestinians when they see that Israeli settlers are allowed to move freely in the Old City for their celebrations of Hanukkah, which began Sunday evening," the team wrote.[23]

SOLDIER VIOLENCE

Although gun battles in Hebron happened with less frequency in 2001, they still racked up a major death toll. CPTers found themselves pinned down by gunfire several times, both in Hebron and as they traveled to and from the Jerusalem and Bethlehem areas.[24]

On New Year's Eve, a particularly heavy shelling attack killed an eleven-year-old boy, Moath Ahmed Abu Hadwan, and wounded several other children who were hurrying home on narrow streets leading into the Old City. They had considered the streets safe, because of tall buildings on either side, but the shrapnel from a shell hit the boys as well as a fourteen-year-old girl standing on the steps of her home.

Six days later, on January 6, sisters-in-law Ahlam and Areeg al-Jabali went to the rooftop of their building in the southern part of Hebron to bring in laundry. Machine guns from the Israeli settlement of Beit Haggai opened fire, and the two women ran into the stairwell. As they embraced each other in fright, a bullet went through Areeg's back and into Ahlam's abdomen. They ran down to the second floor and fell through the door to their second floor apartment. Areeg died from the bullet hole in her heart. Ahlam was hospitalized because of the bullet wound in her abdomen.[25]

---

23. CPTnet, "HEBRON URGENT ACTION RELEASE: Pressure Israeli authorities to lift curfew in Hebron," December 13, 2001.

24. See CPTnet, Shantz, "Wedding Bells and Bullets," February 16, 2001. CPTnet, "HEBRON UPDATE: February 14–20, 2001." "HEBRON: CPTers caught in crossfire on road from Jerusalem to Hebron," April 19, 2001. CPTnet, Mortellito, "BETHLEHEM DISTRICT: CPT Delegation under fire in Beit Jala," August 19, 2001.

25. Rebecca Johnson and Bob Holmes, "HEBRON: The Women and Children Weren't Shooting," January 14, 2001. January 2001 CPTnet archives. Holmes and Johnson incorrectly reported that Areeg had died at the house instead of at the hospital and that Ahlam had died two days later. (Kawther Salam may have given them the erroneous information.) Holmes noted in the release that Areeg's fiancé had arrived on January 6 from Haifa, bringing gold jewelry to finalize their marriage contract. He attended her funeral instead.

Human Rights Watch reported the two incidents as follows (note different dates and variants in spelling—always a challenge for the Hebron team, because Arabic uses a different alphabet and systems of transliteration vary):

> On December 31, IDF fire into the Haret al-Sheikh neighborhood of Hebron injured eighteen-year-old Arit al-Qawasma in her bedroom, injuring her in the

Of particular consequence to the residents of Hebron was the March 26, 2001, shooting of ten-month-old Shalhevet Pass, the daughter of a Hebron settler Yitzhak Pass, who was also shot as he was pushing her stroller in the Avraham Avinu settler enclave. The IDF retaliated by bombarding houses in Abu Sneineh for two hours while settlers ransacked the Palestinian market, closed because of a curfew.

The next morning, settlers invaded homes on Abu Sneineh. When the army turned them around, the settlers began shooting randomly into the neighborhood.[26]

Four months later, a seven-year-old girl in Abu Sneineh, a relative of the team's friend Nisreen Abu Mayaleh, would die when an Israeli bullet hit her in the head during a shooting exchange. The team later learned that the girl's grandmother died of heart attack one hour after she left her dead granddaughter in the hospital.[27]

---

right shoulder and face. As she was being evacuated from the house, renewed IDF fire killed eleven-year-old Muath Abu Hadwan, who had come to watch the evacuation, and wounded another boy. During the same period, IDF fire injured thirteen-year-old Abir Salameh as she went to feed her chickens on the roof of her house, injuring her in the stomach.

On January 5, IDF fire from the Beit Haggai settlement hit eighteen-year-old Ahlam al-Jabali and her eighteen-year-old sister-in-law, Arij al-Jabali, as the two were seeking shelter in the stairwell of their home. A single bullet penetrated the body of Arij al-Jabali, who was killed in the incident, and lodged in the body of Ahlam al-Jabali, who recovered. According to the family, the IDF was responding to fireworks fired at Beit Haggai from the family's neighborhood. Arij al-Jabali was expecting to get engaged on the day of her death.

Human Rights Watch, "Israel/Palestine: Armed Attacks on Civilians Condemned."

26. CPTnet, Roe, "HEBRON: Baby killed; Army and settlers retaliate," March 27, 2001. The Arab-American Institute published a report comparing media coverage of Shalhevet Pass's murder with that of a four-month-old Palestinian girl killed by Israeli troops in Gaza on May 7, 2001. It noted that *The Washington Post* and *New York Times* invariably write more sympathetically about Israeli victims of Palestinian violence than they do about Palestinian victims of Israeli violence. Morey, "A Tale of Two Killings." Shalhevet Pass's photo was prominently displayed on a banner at the Avraham Avinu settlement for many months afterward (when the author inquired of the team in August 2004 whether the banner was still up, Dianne Roe replied in an August 7, 2004 e-mail, "Kathy, I am pretty sure it is gone, but we are no longer allowed to be in that area, so there is no audience for such a banner. I have seen posters in Jerusalem, I think. dianne").

27. CPTnet, "HEBRON UPDATE: August 12–19, 2001," August 30, 2001. The fact that the team did not write a special release regarding the death of the girl—the relative of a friend—shows, to some extent, the amount of suffering that the team had been reporting. Consigning the girl's death to an update also relates to the sheer volume of releases the team had been putting out over the summer. In July 2001, they put out seventeen releases, in August, eleven.

Israeli shooting began to target systematically Bab iZawiyya, the central commercial district in Hebron in 2001, as well as other locations in Hebron not previously targeted. On May 20, soldiers shot into Alia Hospital for the second time during the Intifada, hitting a patient. Twenty-two-year-old Majdaleen Alrai, undergoing treatment for diabetes, suffered extensive damage to her liver, kidney, and intestines.[28] On June 25, when Palestinian gunmen in Abu Sneineh—after a lull lasting several weeks—shot and wounded a seven-year-old Israeli settler boy and four soldiers near Avraham Avinu, the Israeli military pounded Bab iZawiyya and Abu Sneineh with shells. Palestinian Authority officials evacuated their headquarters in Hebron, fearing a retaliatory air strike as had occurred in Nablus and Ramallah following a suicide bombing in the northern coastal town of Netanya the previous month.[29]

After months of Hebron CPTers assuring family members and supporters that their apartment was quite safe from all the shooting—given its location in a Palestinian neighborhood between a settlement and a soldier camp—bullets finally hit close to home on July 19, 2001. Several CPTers and their upstairs neighbors were on the roof, listening to the shooting as they usually did when they heard gunfire. A bullet hit the wall—against which Rick Polhamus was propping his chair—inches away from his shoulder, covering him with concrete dust. The next morning women on the team found six bullet holes in their apartment. One pierced the metal door and went through boxes and sheets stacked on a nearby shelf. When they looked through the bullet hole in the door, team members saw that it framed the roof of Avraham Avinu. A low caliber bullet shot from the roof of Avraham Avinu went through the glass in the door on August 20, 2001.[30]

28. CPTnet, Jane Adas, "Let the World Know," June 8, 2001. For the previous incident, see CPTnet, "HEBRON UPDATE: November 8–11, 2000," November 17, 2000.

29. CPTnet, Anita Fast, "Hebron: Heavy gunfire erupts," June 25, 2001. CPTnet, "Hebron Update: June 24–30, 2001, July 17, 2001.

30. CPTnet, "HEBRON: Christian Peacemaker Team Apartment in Hebron hit during firefight," July 21, 2001. The release incorrectly reports the date the team found the hole as June 20, 2001. CPTnet, "HEBRON: More settler attacks; CPT apartment hit by bullet once again," August 21, 2001.

Interestingly, Polhamus almost getting shot did not make it into the team's update or merit a special release. The writer contacted him about the date and he said he had photos dated June 19 showing him with dust on his back and holding a shell fragment. When she asked if he remembered why the team had not written about it, Polhamus (known for his twisted sense of humor) wrote,

> I seem to remember either Dianne or JoAnne or one of those ANN people suggesting that we not mention me almost getting hit for the following reasons: We

Releases and updates from the spring and summer of 2001 reflect growing anguish, anger, and a sense of powerlessness within the Hebron Team about the relentless juggernaut of violence crushing both Israelis and Palestinians. Greg Rollins, in a September 15, 2001, release, described following drops of blood leading to the house where a seventeen-year-old boy had been shot in the head. He passed crying children running away from the house. "The moment I saw the children running down the street, I knew there was nothing we were going to be able to do," he wrote. "Part of me still wishes I had followed them to wherever they were running."[31]

The team began to look for creative ways to throw a wrench into the cycle of violence or at least hold warmongers accountable. On April 11, 2001, the team hung a banner on top of Abu Sneineh mountain reading "The Veto Kills," referring to the U.S. veto of a December 2000 U.N. Resolution calling for unarmed observers in the West Bank and Gaza strip. In June, the team called for a July 27–August 8, 2001 Emergency Peacemaker Witness delegation to the West Bank to serve as a violence deterring presence in locations around the West Bank suffering most from Israeli assassinations, shellings, and full scale military invasions.[32]

---

weren't sure if that shot was Palestinian or Israeli. It was just a stray shot for sure while the ones to the women's apartment were from the settlement area and were probably deliberate. It would just disappoint many people to know the shot came close but missed me. Take care, Rick.

May 11, 2004, e-mail to author.

31. CPTnet, "HEBRON: Finding the Dead," September 15, 2000. See also Montgomery, CPTnet, "HEBRON: More than watchmen wait for morning," September 16, 2001. CPTnet, Kern, "HEBRON: 'Israelis and Palestinians must stop killing each other,'" August 10, 2001. Kern quoted Atta Jaber (anonymously) in the release as saying

I am so sad. I was just watching the television and 19 Israelis are killed [in a Jerusalem suicide bombing.] I want to call all my Israeli friends and make sure they are all right. I want to run into the streets of Jerusalem and shout that the killing must stop. Maybe people will think I am crazy, but I just want to keep shouting that Israelis and Palestinians must stop killing each other.

32. CPTnet, "HEBRON UPDATE: April 3–15, 2001," April 30, 2001. CPTnet, "CHICAGO: CPT calls for Emergency Peacemaker Witness delegation to West Bank," June 12, 2001. The fourteen-member delegation included reservists Tracy Hughes, Ron Forthofer, Elayne McClanen, CPT Steering Committee member, and Dorothy Jean Weaver. It also included Char Smith, Le Anne Clausen, Quaker peace activists Bill and Genie Durland, and Sis and Jerry Levin who would eventually go through training in 2003 (see Mortellito, "West Bank: Under Fire in Beit Jala," 12, for a complete list of delegates).

Levin had been in charge of CNN's Beirut bureau when he was kidnapped by Hezbollah in the 1980s. His wife, Sis, had managed to get him released through back channels before the Iran-Contra scandal hit, after which the other foreign hostages became a valuable

Major gun battles continued throughout the summer, although not daily. The Israeli military repeatedly destroyed electrical transformers in these shootouts, and the Hebron municipality began alternating current to different parts of the city. The public relations director for the municipality told the team, "Our hopes are getting smaller and smaller. First, we wanted to end the Occupation. Then we just wanted them to clear the rubble away. Now we just want electricity. Soon, it will be just to see our children."[33]

On August 23, 2001, after a day of heavy fighting which injured a twenty-one-year old and an eleven-year-old settler, Israeli forces entered Abu Sneineh and simultaneously detonated two houses at the top of Takrouri mountain. Because they provided good vantage points, Palestinian gunmen often used these homes for cover. Throughout the night, the team witnessed Israeli vehicles entering the neighborhood while an Israeli helicopter flew overhead dropping flares. Soldiers and gunmen then battled in the streets of Abu Sneineh for most of the night.

Soldiers again moved into Abu Sneineh on October 5, 2001, two days after Palestinian gunmen shot and wounded two Israeli women. Around 4:00 AM, helicopter gunships began circling above, without lights, and the military cut off power to the entire city. At 5:00 AM the team heard several loud explosions, one of which shook the team's apartment, presumably caused by the gunships firing rockets into homes. Bulldozers and tanks then entered the neighborhood and began demolishing homes, crushing cars, and knocking over stone walls that stood in their way. Two of the five Palestinians killed in the incursion were crushed to death when shells destroyed their houses. Soldiers forced twenty families from their homes so they could use the buildings as outposts. They remained in Abu Sneineh until October 15. Friends from the neighborhood expressed mixed reactions to the ten-day military takeover. The soldier outposts restricted their freedom of movement, but they no longer had to fear the shelling while the military commandeered the neighborhood.[34]

---

commodity. See Sis Levin's book, *Beirut Diary*. Jerry Levin was to become a CPT full-timer and Sis Levin a reservist. In a Beit Jala home under fire in the summer of 2001, Levin was telling the story of his kidnapping. He was just getting to the part about tying his blankets together to escape out a window in his stocking feet when a bullet hit a propane tank on the outside of the house. He left the story unfinished, much to the disappointment of his Palestinian and international listeners.

33. CPTnet, "HEBRON UPDATE: July 15–18, 2001," July 28, 2001.

34. CPTnet, Fast, "HEBRON: Abu Sneineh invaded by Israeli forces," October 5, 2001; CPTnet, "HEBRON UPDATE: September 26-October 5, 2001," October 19,

The assassination of right-wing Tourism minister Rehavam Zeevi by the Palestinian Front for the Liberation of Palestine on October 17 prompted fresh invasions into Palestinian cities.[35] The team's friends in the Bethlehem district reported their dire predicament as tanks fired into civilian neighborhoods, hotels, and hospitals. In response, the team put out an urgent action release, asking its constituents to demand that President George Bush, Secretary of State Colin Powell, Canadian Prime Minister Jean Chretien, and Canadian foreign minister John Manley call for Israeli troops to pull out of Palestinian cities and implement the provisions of the Mitchell report that would reduce violence (e.g., placing unarmed observers in the Territories and freezing settlements). "You may note," the team wrote, "That the U.S. war against Afghanistan is giving Prime Minister Sharon both cover and a precedent for increased attacks on Palestinians."[36]

In the midst of all the shooting, the team continued to interact with soldiers in more mundane ways every day. As mentioned earlier, much of this communication involved negotiating with them to allow people to get to their homes or to the hospital during curfew and monitoring treatment of people soldiers detained at checkpoints. Most often, the team simply documented stories of soldier abuse days or even weeks after they had happened.[37]

Some egregious abuses the team documented involved soldiers throwing stones at a widow who lived alone in the Old City (injuring her eye),

---

2001. CPTnet, "HEBRON UPDATE: October 14–20, 2001," November 10, 2001. Comment on the benefits of occupation versus shelling from author's memory.

35. As far as killings go, the Ze'evi murder was a measured response. The PFLP specifically stated that they killed the cabinet minister in retaliation for Israel assassinating the PFLP's Secretary-General, Abu Ali Mustapha, on August 27, 2001. Ze'evi was notorious for advocating that Israel expel Palestinians from the Occupied Territories and was considered an extremist even by many right-wing politicians. Yassir Arafat outlawed PFLP and arrested thirty-three PFLP militants after Ze'evi's death, but Sharon invaded because Arafat did not turn over the men wanted for Ze'evi's death to Israel.

36. CPTnet, "HEBRON/BETHLEHEM URGENT ACTION: STOP THE ISRAELI INVASIONS INTO PALESTINIAN CITIES," October 22, 2001.

37. However, in at least one instance a CPTer was in the right place at the right time to intervene. In September 2001, on her way to a meeting in Bethlehem, Le Anne Clausen tried to get in the way of soldiers who were beating a Palestinian employee of Save the Children. (The West Bank was under closure at the time, but the U.S. Embassy had received authorization for the man to travel because Save the Children facilitated projects with USAID funds.) Clausen was able to stand by the man and get the team to call the Israeli police to come to the man's rescue. CPTnet, "HEBRON: 'Save the Children' Worker Beaten at Checkpoint," September 5, 2001.

breaking into and looting shops,[38] and dragging a man they had shot in H-1 into the settlement of Beit Hadassah while soldiers and settlers spit on him and strangled him. The last incident, occurring on January 12, 2001, evidently must have been videotaped or photographed, because the team reported reading the following letter in the January 17, 2001, edition of *Ha'aretz*:

> As a Jew and ex-IDF officer, I was shocked to see IDF soldiers dragging a bleeding young Palestinian in the streets of Hebron. The shocking image showed our soldiers as sadists who rejoice over the killing of a young man, and drag his body to our settlers to rejoice, dance, exchange candy and congratulations and kick the not-yet-dead body.
>
> It reminds me of cheetahs and hyenas, which kill and drag their prey. The problem is that these animals kill to survive. Our soldiers kill to maintain the occupation, an apartheid system.
>
> It seems to me that our society has become increasingly violent and moved away from Zionist principles. When the Arab crowd lynched our soldiers in Ramallah, it was criminal, and they were savage, and when our disciplined soldiers do it, it is heroism and civilized.
>
> I strongly believe that their blood is as red as ours and equally sacred. Our army's actions in the West Bank and Gaza amount to crimes against humanity. The Israel Defence Forces should investigate in a fair way and punish these soldiers before the world wakes up and put most of us on trial for crimes against humanity.
>
> Rafi Miller, California[39]

People whose homes became soldier outposts in 2001 continued to suffer in particularly onerous ways. The presence of the outposts made their homes the target for Palestinian gunmen, and soldiers often made all but one room in the household off-limits to family members. The team recorded soldiers cutting antennas and cables, throwing their trash—including soft drink bottles filled with urine—down into the families' rooms, urinat-

---

38. Doctors Without Borders treated the woman with the injured eye and videotaped the soldiers throwing stones and large pieces of metal at people in the neighborhood. When Kawther Salam summoned other soldiers for help, they arrested a twelve-year-old boy instead of disciplining the soldiers. CPTnet, "HEBRON UPDATE: June 9–16, 2001," June 23, 2001. For an account of soldiers burglarizing shops, see CPTnet, "HEBRON UPDATE: "September 26– October 5, 2001," October 19, 2001. Incidents of soldiers vandalizing and looting shops would increase dramatically in 2002.

39. CPTnet, "HEBRON UPDATE: January 12–16, 2001," January 27, 2001.

ing on their roofs, and wrecking the family's furniture. Journalist Kawther Salam rented an apartment close to a soldier outpost and for several weeks was able to call the team when soldiers were invading homes and abusing residents in the buildings around her. She had to move out in October 2001 when soldier harassment, which included invading her home and destroying furniture, became too emotionally difficult for her.

SETTLER VIOLENCE

Settler attacks continued to increase dramatically in 2001. All but one of the team's updates for 2001 contain some incident of settler violence.[40] These incidents included attacks on Palestinian homes and cars in the Beqa'a Valley.[41] In one particularly vicious example, a settler deliberately drove his car into four-year-old Mahmoud Jaber—son of CSD partners Ismael and Fatmi Jaber—crushing both of his legs. The settler also killed three sheep that the child was shepherding across the road, and then drove into the gate of Kiryat Arba without stopping.[42] Many of the updates have accounts of settlers attacking the homes of the Sharabati family next to Avraham Avinu, and the Abu Haikel and Baatsch family homes on Tel Rumeida. Settlers threw Molotov cocktails into homes in the Old City, in one incident nearly killing a newborn and during another narrowly missing an old woman who was a neighbor of the team.[43] Repeated assaults on vendors in the marketplace near the team's apartment continued as well as assaults on pedestrians—including women and children—and shooting into Palestinian neighborhoods.

Team members found themselves the target of attacks more often than in previous years and, depressingly, found that their presence with

---

40. The lone exception, covering February 7–12, 2001, contains the following entry for February 9: "Field workers from Human Rights Watch interviewed CPTers for a report that will be presented to the U.N. The interviews focused on how CPTers are treated by Israeli settlers and soldiers."

41. See, for example, CPTnet, "HEBRON: Settler Security Officer killed in northern West Bank; Hebron area settlers retaliate," May 29, 2001. CPTnet, "HEBRON: CPT delegation witnesses settler attack in Beqa'a Valley," September 6, 2001.

42. CPTnet, "Hebron Update: October 22–29, 2001," November 23, 1001.

43. See CPTnet, "HEBRON: Israelis and Palestinians must stop killing each other," August 10, 2001; Barr, "'Aggressive pacifists' put their faith on the firing line,"12–13. Barr based this article on several visits to Hebron and interviews with the team. The old woman was the mother of Nisreen Abu Mayaleh's half-brother.

journalists and other visitors to Hebron sometimes made these visitors the target of attack instead of protecting them.

On one such occasion, British activist Angie Zelter (see above)[44] accompanied Dianne Roe, who was responding to a call about settler attacks on the vegetable market. As typically happened when the military lifted curfew, young settler women were assaulting vendors and trying to destroy their wares. One of the girls threw a rock at a seventy-five-year-old man, hitting him in the head. Zelter told the team later that she had been startled to see the man's white headscarf become uniformly red in a matter of seconds.

Roe accompanied the old man home while Zelter, wearing a red CPT cap and a black outfit, took pictures. In her statement to police, she wrote,

> I could see a group of around 15 or so, mainly female, settler children in their early/mid teens screaming and throwing rocks. I asked the soldiers to stop the violence and I tried to appeal to some of the kids to stop the violence. I then noticed an armed man in a white shirt with a long black beard and glasses . . . and asked him to try and stop the kids throwing rocks because people were getting hurt and tried to explain I had just witnessed an old man being badly hurt. He started screaming at me "You fascist whore," "f***ing Nazi," "Go home," the "Christians murdered the Jews". . . . I was trying to take photos of the violence going on all around and also asking him to try to stop it rather than letting it go on, he screamed that he had to suffer while the filthy Arabs took over his land and how he couldn't go certain places because of them, how they should all be killed. This may have taken only a couple of minutes but as he continued to scream at me more kids were gathering around and shouting out "Nazi, Nazi" and he got angrier and . . . One of his hands was clenched on his gun which was held slung in front of him and it was jerking up and down. He suddenly came at me "to teach me" and hit me on the right-hand side of the head . . . He grabbed my camera which was round my neck and which I held in my hands. I tried to keep hold of it but he wrested it out of my hands and over my ears and dashed it to the ground and stamped on it over and over again, screaming. By this time I was starting to cry . . . I just stood there with my hands open, looking at him

---

44. Zelter had come over under the auspices of the International Solidarity Movement (see below) and was exploring the possibility of setting up an all-woman team at some other location in the West Bank suffering from violent confrontations. She had been a member of the British Ploughshares movement and had been involved in actions against the Trident nuclear submarines and Hawk fighter planes the British government was selling to Indonesia while it was carrying out genocidal policies in East Timor.

with tears streaming down my face, trying to stop crying but not managing. Unfortunately my weakness seemed to make him and the kids even angrier. . . . Soldiers were looking on from their cars, like they had the whole time.

Roe returned at this point and saw the settler girls jeering at Zelter, "Boo hoo hoo. Boo hoo hoo. Jews never get hurt." When the police arrived, Zelter, whose late husband was Jewish, pointed to the globs of white spit all over her black blouse, the pieces of camera on the ground, and then the settler who was sitting on a chair, smiling as though nothing had happened. At her request, the police arrested him.

When Zelter said she wished to make a formal complaint, the police put her in their van with Roe and a Palestinian man whose keys settlers had stolen. Roe, Zelter, and the Palestinian man were left outside the station near the Il Ibrahimi mosque/Cave of Machpelah amidst a group of settlers. One of them, Baruch Marzel, took many pictures of the three at a close range.

At the police station, the police asked Roe if she had seen the attack. She said she had not, but when the Palestinian man said he had seen the attack, the police ignored him. He told Zelter later that the police had warned him against making a statement on her behalf. The case against the settler was later dropped by the Israeli police for lack of evidence, despite the fact that he was identified and arrested at the scene of the assault and despite the existence of numerous eyewitnesses, including Israeli soldiers and police.[45]

45. CPTnet, "HEBRON: Settler assaults guest of Hebron Team," September 1, 2001. On May 1, 2002, when Roe visited the families of men who had died when the Israeli military took over H-1, she learned that the elderly man who had been hit in the head by the rock had died in January 2002. The family told her that he had required frequent hospital treatments from the time of the attack until his death.

Zelter returned to Israel in autumn 2002 to testify against the man who had assaulted her. Dianne Roe missed the 2002 CPT full-timers' retreat so that she could also testify. In an August 7, 2004, e-mail to the author, she wrote,

> When the attorney for the defence saw me in the courtroom, they protested that they did not know there would be a witness. The court case was postponed so that I could give my statement to the police, and the defence could read it. The rescheduled date was December 31, 2002, but Angie was prevented from entering the country. In order to prevent Angie from using the court date to demand entrance, the defence pleaded guilty to a lesser charge (breaking the camera) and faced a minor sentence. Angie was deported.
> —Dianne

The outcome of Zelter's complaint is recorded in Palestinian Human Rights Monitoring Group, "SETTLER VIOLENCE HOTLINE ONE-YEAR REPORT."

Team members and their visitors often found this type of response from soldiers and police more distressing than the actual settler attacks. When settlers began pelting CPTers with rocks on several occasions, soldiers blamed CPTers for being present. "Don't you know they hate you?" one soldier asked them. "Why don't you leave and they won't throw stones at you."[46]

On July 19, 2001, soldiers watched and did nothing as settler youth jumped out of a car, pushed Rick Polhamus several times, and stole his CPT hat. Polhamus explained to the soldiers that settlers could plant the hat somewhere that would result in police investigating CPT. If the soldiers did not retrieve it, he said, he would file a complaint with the police. Settlers then gathered around Polhamus and Kawther Salam, whom Polhamus was accompanying, and began throwing eggs and garbage at them. One hit Polhamus on the head with a water bottle. They kicked Grace Boyer when she attempted to come to Polhamus and Salam's aid. Polhamus then called the police, and the soldiers, instead of stopping the settlers from attacking the CPTers, ordered the CPTers to wait in another location for the police.[47]

On September 6, 2001, two Ethiopian border policemen stood by and laughed as they made ineffectual attempts to stop about a dozen settler boys from attacking Kathleen Kern and Anne Montgomery with small stones, fistfuls of sand, and a water bottle. The two women had responded to a call from translator Zleekha Muhtasib saying that soldiers were detaining her brother, and a mob of settlers was about to attack him and her. The CPTers, when they arrived, evidently diverted the attention of the settler boys away from Muhtasib and her brother. When the soldiers did not call the police, Kern speed-dialed Israeli friend Neta Golan on the team's cell phone, who phoned the Hebron police. As soon as the boys saw the blue light of the police car, the two oldest ran into Avraham Avinu. (Police told team members they cannot detain Israeli children under the age of twelve.) The police put the two women in the van and began videotaping the boys

---

46. CPTnet, JoAnne Lingle, "Hebron: Let's Play 'Dodge Stones,'" December 29, 2001.

47. The three CPTers were taken to the police station around 2:15 PM and met three Palestinians who had been waiting there to lodge complaints since 8:00 PM When Polhamus suggested the police deal with the three Palestinians first, the police said they were "only Arabs." CPTnet, "HEBRON: Settlers attack CPTers on Shuhada Street," July 19, 2001.

who capered around the police, pushing them, kicking them, and trying to grab the video camera.[48]

Not all soldiers allowed the settlers to run roughshod over Palestinians and internationals. Members of the Nahal unit, for example, often made earnest attempts to keep settlers away from Palestinians as well as from CPT and TIPH observers. Settlers attacked one IDF officer when he tried to prevent them from shooting into Palestinian homes during one gun battle. He filed charges and the settlers insisted they had only "hugged" him because he was agitated.[49] Privately, many soldiers expressed disgust with the way the settlers behaved and told team members they felt they were protecting the wrong people. When Mary Lawrence and Claire Evans came across an old woman whom soldiers were preventing from walking to Shuhada Street from Beit Romano, where a crowd of settler boys had gathered, a soldier told them, "[S]he has every right to pass. Believe me, we appreciate the suffering this is causing. But it is for her own safety that we are stopping her."[50]

After several weeks of daily attacks on their persons, neighbors, and apartment, the team sent the following letter—accompanied by six photos showing settler attacks on May 29 and thirteen photos taken June 3 documenting damage settlers did to Palestinian crops—to the Commander of the Hebron Police Force, the National Police in Jerusalem, the State Comptroller and the Israeli Ministry of Justice:

> Dear Commander:
>
> We are seeking information concerning Israeli law and the enforcement of violations of the law by Israeli citizens.
>
> On Tuesday, 29 May 2000 [the team reported the 2001 date incorrectly] we witnessed the following incidents:
>
> In the area near Avraham Avinu settlement in Hebron, beginning at 10:00 a.m.:
> 1. Settler women and children smashing construction blocks belonging to Palestinians that had been stacked for repairing the shops settlers had blown up two months earlier.
> 2. Young settler women throwing stones at Palestinians.
>
> At the HaHarsina junction on Road 60 from about 5:00 p.m.:

---

48. CPTnet, "HEBRON: CPTers Anne Montgomery and Kathleen Kern attacked by mob of settler boys," September 8, 2001.
49. CPTnet, "Hebron Update: July 8–15, 2001," July 26, 2001.
50. CPTnet, "HEBRON UPDATE: November 5–11, 2001," November 26, 2001.

1. Three settler men, one of them clearly armed, trespassing on the property of Abdul Jawad Jaber. The settler in black threatened to plant a bomb in the home of Abdul Jawad Jaber.
2. Settlers pulling up and damaging rubber irrigation hoses belonging to Jowdi Jaber.

Israeli military and police were present at both sites. They appeared to be trying to restrain the settlers, but we saw no arrests being made.

We understand that settlers are citizens of Israel. Are we correct in assuming that damaging private property, throwing stones at people, trespassing on private property, and making violent threats to people are infringements of Israeli law, as they most assuredly are in most countries worldwide? If Israeli settlers are subject to Israeli law, why were no arrests made?

We will appreciate any information you will give us concerning these questions.

Sincerely,

Christian Peacemaker Team in Hebron[51]

Two months later the team took their exasperation up a notch when they put out the following urgent action release: "To the Israeli Civil Administration—What are you waiting for?":

Those of us who worked with CPT in 1995, the first summer and fall of the Hebron project, feel a strong sense of déjà vu these days. Once again, we see the grinning faces of the settler boys and girls as they throw stones and shout threats at our Palestinian neighbors and us. We see them swaggering down the street as though they know there is nothing that we, the police or anyone can do to stop them. We see the police apathy toward Palestinians who are calling while they are under attack. Wisam Abu Haikel, whom we accompanied to her kindergarten bus so settlers would not attack her, once again needs an escort to school, six years later.

Much of the overt settler violence ended in 1995 after Yigal Amir, who, according to the New York Times, used to organize the Saturday afternoon settler rampages in Hebron, assassinated Prime Minister Yitzhak Rabin. Suddenly, charges pressed against settlers in previous years became active again, and many of the settlers implicated in violent attacks against Palestinians, police officers, and internationals finally had to appear in court.

We are asking that our constituents write to the Israeli government and ask them whether they are waiting until someone assas-

---

51. CPTnet, "HEBRON: Are Settlers Above the Law?" June 11, 2001.

sinates another Israeli leader before they do something about the settler violence in Hebron and other parts of the West Bank.

Additionally note in your letters that

1. the attacks are often directed against Palestinians who are under curfew in their homes, but have also been directed against internationals living in Hebron.
2. settler young people committing most of the violence seem organized in their attacks
3. the stoning of homes with rocks and large chunks of concrete, the shooting of water tanks on top of the homes, the smashing of windows, and the destruction of Palestinian vehicles appears to be tolerated by both the police and the army in Hebron.
4. if Israel is going to veto the presence of international observers it is morally obligated to ensure the safety of Palestinians under its military occupation

Pictures taken by CPTers and others of settlers committing this violence are available at http://www.prairienet.org/cpt/urgent.php.

We encourage those writing to print the photos or attach them and send them to the American and Canadian embassies in Tel Aviv. Address your letters, faxes and e-mails to Dov Tzadekah, Israeli Civil Administration, care of the American or Canadian embassies. Attach a note to the letters addressed to your ambassador, saying that you are alarmed by the reports of settler violence directed against Palestinians, Americans, Canadians, and other internationals working in Hebron. Ask the ambassador to pass along your letter to the Israeli Civil Administration and investigate these reports by contacting CPT in Hebron.[52]

A few days later, the team put out a call for an end to verbal and physical attacks on the TIPH monitors. After a Hamas suicide bomber killed fifteen people at a Sbarro Pizzeria in Jerusalem on August 9, Israeli radio quoted senior Israeli army officers as saying that TIPH had supplied sensitive information to the Tanzim, a militant branch of the Fatah Party not implicated in the bombing. Brigadier General Amos Gilad, who coordinated activities in the Occupied Territories, said on August 13, 2001, that these charges were false, but settlers continued to attack TIPH monitors whenever they entered H-2. The special armored car TIPH observers drove began to look as though hundreds of people had beaten it with hammers. Because of the attacks, TIPH announced on August 20 that it would not send any patrols into H-2 until someone provided for their security.

52. CPTnet, "HEBRON URGENT ACTION: To the Israeli Civil Administration—What are you waiting for?" August 27, 2001.

The team noted in its release:

> We have ourselves been the targets of disinformation campaigns by the Hebron settlers. At various times in the last six years we have been accused of raising money for Hamas, making bombs for Hamas, shielding Palestinians who stab settlers, taking part in violent demonstrations, etc. We have been fortunate to have Israeli, Palestinian and international friends who encouraged us to continue our work in spite of the lies circulated about us.
>
> TIPH, because its mandate forces it to work under the restrictions of the Israeli Occupation authorities, has not been able to develop the close working relationships with Israelis and Palestinians that CPT has developed. We are therefore taking it upon ourselves to say we support TIPH's efforts in Hebron, and that the Israeli authorities should ensure they can safely carry out their mandate: documenting violence committed by both Israelis and Palestinians in Hebron.[53]

In September, after the assault on Kern and Montgomery, the team decided to try a more light-hearted approach and put out a release entitled, "The Difference between Nazis and CPTers":

> By now, getting called "Nazi" or saluted with "Heil Hitler," by the Hebron settlers and their sympathizers has become a daily event. Since 1995, we have not taken this slander seriously, because, well, we're not Nazis and no Israelis who have spent any time talking with us (as opposed to yelling at us) think of us in those terms.
>
> However, we also did not take seriously the threats to kill Yitzhak Rabin and Shimon Peres we heard on the streets of Hebron in the months leading up to Rabin's assassination. Recent attacks against our team in Hebron and members of the Temporary International Presence in Hebron have made us wonder whether

---

53. CPTnet, "HEBRON: CPT calls for end to verbal and physical attacks on TIPH," August 31, 2001. According to Rick Polhamus,

> The patrols restarted late in the summer or early fall of 2002. At first, it was only to very specific areas and usually in response to specific calls they had received. They were also limiting the amount of time in any particular area. At that time, there were some TIPH people who were very vocal to CPTers that if they didn't start doing the more regular patrols there wasn't any reason for them to be there. Some of these expressed interest in joining CPT so that they could continue working in Hebron. By winter the patrols were still slightly restricted but they were much more frequent.

February 9, 2005, e-mail to author. In a February 12, 2005, e-mail to the author, Dianne Roe wrote that TIPH were "in H-2 now, but in a very controlled way, and working closely in conjunction with the Israeli military."

we should respond to these efforts to demonize us by associating us with the Third Reich. So, in the interests of setting the record straight:

NAZIS were members of the National Socialist Party in Germany in the first half of the twentieth century.

CPTERS are Christians committed to nonviolence, who have, since 1992, provided violence deterring presences in Haiti, Gaza, the West Bank, Washington, DC, Richmond, VA, Bosnia, Chiapas, Mexico, Barrancabermeja, Colombia and with indigenous peoples in North America.

NAZIS worshipped themselves as the master race.

CPTERS worship God and believe God loves every human being on this planet equally.

NAZIS believed they had the right to dominate, exploit, and murder people whom they considered inferior.

CPTERS believe that no person has the right to dominate, exploit, or murder any other person.

NAZIS encouraged street hooliganism of party members and young people as they consolidated their hold on power in Germany.

CPTERS recognize that state toleration of street violence ultimately leads to massive abuses of human rights and genocide on the part of that state.

NAZIS brainwashed their children into believing it was acceptable to regard certain people as subhuman.

CPTERS believe that teaching children to hate others or regard others as subhuman is a form of child abuse.

NAZIS slandered Jews by recirculating the myths of the Protocols of the Elders of Zion and describing Jews as akin to vermin.

CPTERS report what they see and what they hear.

NAZIS: Right-wing

CPTERS: Not

We believe that referring to every person who does not agree with one's political or theological position as a Nazi hideously cheapens the tragedy of the Holocaust. We commit ourselves to fighting everything the Nazis stood for, wherever we encounter it.[54]

The reaction and discussion the team hoped the release would engender never materialized, because the team put it out on September 11, 2001, and world events overshadowed issues of petty harassment on the street.

Kern connected the issues of settler harassment and September 11 in an article for *Tikkun* Magazine, in which she described the toll that

---

54. CPTnet, "HEBRON: the difference between CPTers and Nazis," September 11, 2001.

months of settler violence had taken on her. Approached by boys in kipot (head coverings worn by observant Jewish men) at a bus stop in Jerusalem, she immediately assumed they wanted to hurt her when they only wanted to film her saying something positive about a cable access show they were launching. At the end of her article, she wrote:

> On a personal level, I wonder when I am going to regain my nerve. A couple days before I left the country, I saw a group of settler boys throwing stones at Palestinian shops while soldiers watched and laughed. A Palestinian family—father, mother and two small girls—walked past them on the street. The father's face registered little emotion beyond anger and disgust as the boys began throwing stones at them. As he strode past without turning his head—his daughters clung to his arms, one girl's eyes wide with fear, the other's face crumpled with incipient tears.
>
> They passed me without looking in my direction. I had not intervened, because I was afraid.[55]

NEW DIRECTIONS

The September 11, 2001, attacks by Al Qaeda on the World Trade Center and the Pentagon were just one of the aspects that set 2001 apart from the previous and subsequent months of the Intifada. The team also began to accompany students and teachers to school in a more systematic way in 2001 and saw the growth of several accompaniment movements that wanted to do what CPT was doing on a larger scale.

September 11, 2001

On the morning of September 11, 2001, Rick Polhamus called from Jerusalem and Gene Stoltzfus called from Chicago to tell the team that planes had flown into the World Trade Center and the Pentagon. The team began receiving dozens of calls from Palestinian friends who expressed condolences. Several times when team members said they had no television, their friends said some variation of, "It is better. No one should see these pictures." One friend told them, "As Palestinians, we know the tragedy that comes from innocent people being killed."[56]

---

55. "Settler Violence and September 11: A Report from the Mean Streets of Hebron," 30.

56. CPTnet, "HEBRON: Hebronites Send Condolences," September 12, 2001; CPTnet, "HEBRON UPDATE: September 7–15, 2001," September 24, 2001.

Because of footage showing Palestinians celebrating in East Jerusalem[57] and in Lebanese refugee camps, the team put out a two-paragraph news brief saying, "At no point in the course of the day, did team members witness anyone celebrating or even speaking with approval of the disasters."[58] In her *Tikkun* article Kern asked the rhetorical question, "How can I persuade people that it's much easier to film several hundred Palestinians celebrating the attacks than it is to show two million Palestinians grieving in front of their television sets?"

Soldiers, nevertheless, took their opportunity to express their rage by entering the team's neighbors' homes in the Old City. Kern wrote,

> When we asked them why they were screaming at the Palestinians living there and throwing their furniture around, they snarled, "Didn't you see these people dancing?"
>
> But we hadn't. At no time that week did I see a Palestinian dancing or hear one expressing approval for what the terrorists did to my fellow citizens in New York or Washington, DC. The Palestinians in Hebron know that my organization, Christian Peacemaker Teams, often criticizes U.S. foreign policy in the Middle East, and they had plenty of opportunity to express their own bitterness regarding U.S. policy to us. But they didn't. It seems that everyone knew at some level that grief was the only appropriate response in the days immediately following the bombings.[59]

The fact that the people who flew the planes that crashed into the World Trade Center, the Pentagon, and a rural Pennsylvania field were Arabs necessarily had repercussions for the Israeli-Palestinian conflict and hence the team's work in Hebron. Initially, the Bush administration seemed more willing to involve itself in the conflict as a result of the September 11 catastrophe. It pressured (unsuccessfully) Sharon to hold ceasefire talks with the Palestinians and announced on October 2, 2001, that the U.S. would back the creation of a Palestinian state. On October 5, 2001, the administration denounced as "unacceptable" statements of Sharon that compared U.S. coalition-building with Arab countries to the British appeasement of

---

57. A friend who had been in East Jerusalem and saw someone handing around sweets at Damascus Gate believed that event was staged. He said the boys mostly just wanted to eat sweets and be photographed. He noted that about twenty-five (out of hundreds of thousands of) Palestinians in East Jerusalem celebrated the catastrophe and thought it significant that the Israeli and international papers publicized those twenty-five.

58. CPTnet, "HEBRON: Hebronites Send Condolences."

59. "Settler violence and September 11," 28.

the Nazis in 1930.⁶⁰ But as time passed, Bush began to ally himself with Ariel Sharon, to the dismay of the Arab world and Israelis and Palestinians seeking justice and reconciliation.⁶¹

International Accompaniment Movements

A more significant part of the team's work in the summer of 2001 involved the role that *ad hoc* international groups began to play in the Israeli-Palestinian conflict. That summer, and in the ensuing months, groups seeking to do violence-deterring work in the Occupied Territories from France, Italy, Denmark, and Holland visited the team. More significantly, representatives from the World Council of Churches visited the team and later set up the Ecumenical Accompaniment Program in Palestine and Israel, based on the CPT model. WCC organizers chose Rebecca Johnson, a CPT reservist, to coordinate twelve EA (Ecumenical Accompaniers) teams in the West Bank and Gaza. Groups of international Jews wishing to do work similar to CPT's under the auspices of "Olive Tree Summer" also made connections with the team, sometimes putting its delegates to work with the team for days and weeks.

Members of the International Solidarity Movement (ISM) were by far the most famous group of internationals to pour into the Occupied Territories that summer. The organizers were familiar with CPT's work in Hebron and hoped to replicate on a massive scale in all the Occupied Territories some of the accompaniment work and public witness the Hebron team had undertaken.⁶²

---

60. Derek Brown, "Attack and Aftermath: a Glossary of Terms," September 27, 2001.

61. In April 2002, Bush referred to Sharon as "a man of peace," earning himself the permanent enmity of most Arabs and Muslims.

62. Not all the ISM organizers would have pointed to CPT as an "model" for ISM. When asked about CPT's influence on ISM, Huwaida Arraf wrote in a May 23, 2004, e-mail that she had been active in mobilizing internationals to support Palestinian nonviolent resistance long before she heard of CPT. She said further:

> We consider CPT amongst the founding members of the ISM. CPTers did the trainings for our first campaign and continued to help us out with trainings and be an active part of our organizing, especially LeAnne Clawson [*sic*] I would say the biggest influence the CPT had on the ISM was in the field of training. And of course, when the contact was a little stronger between CPT and ISM, the sharing of ideas, tactics, etc. made our efforts stronger, I believe.

Three young people most responsible for organizing the ISM volunteers—Neta Golan, George Rishmawi, and Huwaida Arraf[63]—had had extensive contacts with Hebron team members as they prepared to bring volunteers over. "Crazy George" Rishmawi had brought many international tour groups to visit the team in Hebron and had helped the Beit Jala team significantly as they set up the project there. He was also active in the Palestinian Center for Rapprochement, which had organized nonviolent demonstrations for years in which Hebron team members sometimes participated. Golan had responded to emergency pleas for help from the Hebron Team when the Jaber family had come under assault from Israeli settlers. She was also instrumental in placing CPT's first "Emergency" delegation in homes in Beit Jala on the night of July 31, 2001, when homes there suffered serious bombardment. (See n. 32 above for account of the Emergency Delegation in Beit Jala.)

The ISM organizers invited CPT to provide two-day trainings for the large groups of volunteers coming in. Two of the ISM volunteers in these trainings, Rachel Corrie and Tom Hurndall, would later die at the hands of Israeli forces in 2003.[64]

When logistically possible, members of the Hebron team began participating in ISM actions. Releases and updates from 2001 record team members traveling to ISM actions in Rantis, Nablus, Jerusalem, Bidya, Mashka, Bir Zeit, Ramallah, and Gaza.

During a June 15 witness at Al-Khader, whose lands the settlement of Efrat was trying to confiscate, Anita Fast and Neta Golan were both beaten and injured by the police. The Al-Khader villagers were retreating from the police, followed by Israeli and Internationals, when police began attacking them from behind.

Fast and Montgomery attempted to intervene when they saw police beating two older Palestinian women, kicking one hard in the behind as she retreated.

"There's no need to use violence," Fast said. She was then hit in the back of the head by a rubber-coated club or a fist—she could not tell.

---

63. Arraf, a Palestinian-American was engaged to and later married Adam Shapiro, a Jewish American, who was also a primary organizer of ISM.

64. Israeli forces crushed Corrie with a bulldozer as she tried to prevent the demolition of a Palestinian home and three weeks later shot Hurndall as he tried to move Palestinian children out of the line of fire. Hurndall lingered in a coma for months before his family removed life-support. The impact their deaths had on the team in 2003 will be discussed in the next chapter.

Police grabbed her and began alternately shoving her up the hill toward a police van and pulling her by the hair. "There's no need to be violent. I'm nonviolent. You're hurting me," Fast said repeatedly. One of the police officers manhandling her said, "You're crazy." Once she got to the van she was again hit in the back of the head and had her shirt ripped by the police.

Golan approached a policeman and asked, "What are you doing?" He started to beat her. Twisting her arm behind her back, he began to drag her up the hill. Golan did not resist, but walked with the policeman. At some point, he handed her over to a policewoman, who grabbed Golan by the hair and continued to drag her up the hill. Someone else took over the twisting of her arm behind her back, until she heard the crunch of her elbow breaking. Anne Montgomery ran behind Golan, calling for the police to stop twisting her arm and pulling her hair, but the police ignored her.

The six people arrested were charged with "refusing to obey a military order to leave" and "resisting detention." Fast's fingerprints, palm prints, and mug shot were taken. After they read her the charges, they asked for her statement. Fast said, "The police were very rough. They dragged me up the hill by my hair and I was nonviolent."

An army medic examined Golan and said she needed to go to the hospital, but the police continued a lengthy interrogation. They told her they would release her as soon as she signed a paper saying she agreed not to enter a "closed military zone" again. After she refused to sign it, they said, "If [your arm] really hurt you, you would sign." Four hours later, they let Fast, Golan, and the others they were detaining go, without anyone having signed the papers.[65]

SCHOOL PATROLS

When the Intifada started in September 2000, the education of thousands of Palestinian students was put on hold. Children living in the curfew areas of Hebron's Old City were particularly affected, as were children living near the settlements of Givat Ha Harsina and Kiryat Arba.

---

65. CPTnet, "BETHLEHEM DISTRICT: CPTer Anita Fast beaten by Israeli police at nonviolent witness," June 16, 2001. Bob Holmes, in a February 9, 2005, e-mail to the author, wrote that complaints that Golan and Fast filed along with photos of the incident he took appeared to have an effect on police behavior: ". . . [A] week later, in the same location, when arrests were made gently, we were kept in an air-conditioned room at the Efrat police station and even given lunch!"

The Hebron District Minister of Education told a November 2000 CPT delegation that of the 170 schools and 80,000 students in the Hebron district, thirty-two schools and 15,000 students were under curfew. Three schools had been turned into military camps, leading to impossible overcrowding in other schools.[66] Fariel Abu Haikel, headmistress of Qurtuba School across from the Israeli settlement of Beit Hadassah, told the same delegation that when the curfew ended, her students would study Arabic, English, and mathematics only. They would not receive any instruction in art, music, geography, or history for the next months, depending on when the curfew ended.[67]

To prevent the further interruption of Palestinian students' education, the Education ministry negotiated with the District Coordinating Office (DCO)[68] an agreement that stipulated children would be allowed to attend school even under curfew. For some reason, however, these orders often did not filter down to the soldiers in the street—even on September 1, 2001, the first day of school. Thus, a big part of the team's work for the rest of 2001 involved accompanying children on their morning and afternoon trips to school and convincing soldiers to relay news of this agreement to their commanding officer. Sometimes soldiers would then let the CPTers and students from H-2 pass, and sometimes they would not. On October 27, Anita Fast, Mary Lawrence, and JoAnne Lingle told soldiers who were not allowing children from the Old City to pass about the agreement. The soldiers told them they had new orders. Lawrence attempted to call the Israeli District Coordinating Office in Hebron to inquire about the new orders, but the DCO refused to talk with her.[69] This scenario, including the call to the DCO, was to be repeated several times over the next months. Even when the most persuasive CPTers were able to get children past the checkpoints, soldiers often went to the schools in H-2 and closed them

---

66. Just before the Intifada began, the Director of Education for the Hebron District told Gene Stoltzfus and Bob Holmes that thirty-four new schools were needed to accommodate the growing numbers of children in H-2 and area C and that the Israeli authorities refused to give permits for even one. CPTnet, Holmes, "HEBRON: Lessons learned . . . And not," April 10, 2001.

67. CPTnet, "HEBRON UPDATE: November 20–23, 2000," December 2, 2000. The Minister of Education also expressed concern about internationals believing that Palestinian parents deliberately put their children in harm's way.

68. Technically the DCO served as a liaison between Israeli and Palestinian Authority security forces, but by this time, the Palestinian Authority barely existed anymore due to Israel's assault on its infrastructure and police forces.

69. CPTnet, HEBRON UPDATE: October 22–28, 2001, November 23, 2001.

after students and teachers were already inside. CPTers then escorted the frightened students past the checkpoints on their way home.

In addition to the difficulties with the curfew, children in H-2 had to deal with attacks by settlers and soldiers on their way to school. School accompaniment was thus to remain a central part of CPT's work for the next years of the Intifada.

SEVEN

The Blood-Dimmed Tide
2002

By 2002, clashes had all but ended in Hebron and pitched battles between Palestinian gunmen and soldiers became rare, with some significant exceptions. The team continued to deal with land confiscation and home demolitions, curfews and closures, settler and soldier violence, and school patrols. They also became increasingly more involved with other international accompaniment organizations.

HOME DEMOLITIONS

In Hebron, on October 10, 2002, the Israeli military destroyed seven homes in the Al Sendas/Qilqis area and four homes in a neighborhood near Kiryat Arba. None of the homes had received official home demolition orders. An Israeli friend from Peace Now speculated that the demolitions had occurred in response to a bus bombing in Tel Aviv on the previous day. The military had also evacuated several settlement outposts on October 10, and the team noted, "In the past, the Israeli military has demolished Palestinian homes in conjunction with evacuating settlements to assuage Israeli settlers."[1]

---

1. CPTnet, Kennedy and Anderson, "HEBRON: Israeli Bulldozers Destroy Eleven Homes," October 11, 2002. The team also noted at the beginning of the report that "American-manufactured Caterpillar bulldozers" destroyed the homes. This specification reflected a growing movement among NGOs in Israel and Palestine to pressure Caterpillar into inquiring how the Israeli government was going to use its bulldozers before the corporation sold them the equipment. In July 2002, Cliff Kindy and Michael Goode had walked 193 miles from the Boeing headquarters in Chicago to the Caterpillar headquarters in Peoria, Illinois, to call attention to these corporations' contributions to the Israeli Palestinian conflict. Boeing sold Apache attack helicopters to Israel, used to carry out

The Blood-Dimmed Tide • 2002   161

A greater home demolition crisis began on November 15, 2002, when Palestinian gunmen opened fire on a group of Israeli settlers and soldiers who were walking from the Ibrahimi Mosque/Tomb of the Patriarchs to Kiryat Arba after Shabbat services. Nine Israeli soldiers and Border Police and three settler security people died as well as three of the gunmen who initiated the attack. Colonel Dror Weinberg, commander of the Israeli forces in Hebron, was one of the dead.

The next day, the team delivered the following letter to the military base next to the team apartment:

> Letter from CPT Hebron to the Israel Defense Force
>
> We, the Christian Peacemaker Team in Hebron, want to express our extreme sorrow and grief at this time. Our hearts are heavy with the losses of soldiers and civilians, and particularly Colonel Weinberg whom our team met on several occasions. We wish to extend our thoughts and prayers to the families and loved ones of those who died.
>
> May the God of all comfort give you strength and hope during this time.
>
> We condemn the violence that took so many lives yesterday and pray for peace and a better tomorrow. May you be surrounded by comfort from friends, families, and the God who sees our deepest needs.
>
> Again, we express our sincere condolences for your great loss, and will keep you in our thoughts and prayers.
>
> CPT Hebron
> Christian Peacemaker Team[2]

The military responded to the attack with several hours of firing into Palestinian areas. They also demolished two houses near the site of the shooting and gave other houses in the area demolition orders during the following week.

Prime Minister Ariel Sharon told *Ha'aretz* newspaper that the time had come to create a "zone" between the Old City of Hebron and Kiryat Arba exclusively for Jewish use, "An opportunity has been created and facts

---

assassinations. The action occurred about a month after the Israeli authorities denied Goode entrance into Israel (see n. 44).

2. CPTnet, Clausen, "Hebron: Fifteen Killed, More Wounded in Hebron Shooting Attack," November 16, 2002.

have to be created in the coming 48 hours," he said. These facts included the demolition of dozens of Palestinian homes along the corridor.³

Accordingly, the team put out an urgent action release on November 19, 2002, asking its constituency to fax or call immediately the Canadian and American ambassadors to Israel and the Israeli ambassadors to the U.S. and Canada. "Ask these officials to make urgent, strong and clear representation to the government of Israel opposing new settlements/settlement expansion in general and the Kiryat Arba/Hebron expansion in particular," the team wrote. The release also included a November 18, 2002, *Ha'aretz* article by Gideon Alon and Aluf Benn:

> According to the prime minister's proposal, the Jewish zone would extend from Kiryat Arba to Tel Rumeida and Beit Hadassah, and would include the ancient Karaite and Sephardi cemeteries. That would create contiguity between Kiryat Arba and the Tomb of the Patriarchs, through the eastern Casbah. Prayer arrangements under which Jews and Muslims share the Tomb would not be affected. The Jewish area would be surrounded by a wall. Those Palestinians remaining in the Jewish sector would be able to enter and leave through gates in the walls, but there would be no Arab commercial ventures inside the walled Jewish area, according to Sharon's plan.
>
> Sharon believes there's no reason for a large Palestinian presence in Hebron under Israeli control. The prime minister's proposal does not affect the ongoing IDF security operations in the city. He ordered the army to continue its security operations throughout the city, "according to security needs and without limitations."

Three days later, after more homes had received demolition orders, the team followed with another urgent action release, requesting that U.S. citizens fax Senator Richard Lugar of the U.S. Senate Foreign Relations committee, asking him to challenge the Israeli government's demolitions of these homes.

The team included a the following sample letter to Lugar in the release:

> Senator Lugar:
>
> I ask you to urgently challenge the government of Israel on their plans to demolish the home of the Mahmoud Jaber family. On November 21 the Jaber family was ordered to remove their possessions from their house on the east edge of Hebron, near the site of last Friday's gunbattle. There is absolutely no justification for making this family homeless.

3. Aluf Benn and Gideon Alon, "PM demands 'quick' changes in Hebron for Jewish control."

In the Israeli newspaper Ha'aretz for November 20, there was an article beginning with these lines:

> The one and only meaning to the creation of "territorial contiguity" from Kiryat Arba to the Tomb of the Patriarchs, is expulsion. The expulsion of thousands more Palestinian residents of Hebron, people who were unlucky enough to find that their homes, shops and gardens are in the area meant for "contiguity."
>
> The Jaber family is caught in this Israeli plan to build another indefensible settlement. Please do everything in your power to prevent this unwarranted attack on innocent civilians. Then please let me know what you have been able to do to prevent the demolition of the home of Mahmoud Jaber, his wife, and six children.[4]

Team members also spent several nights with families living in the Jabel Johar neighborhood to protect the homes.[5]

On December 12, Palestinian gunmen killed two Israeli soldiers near the Ibrahimi Mosque/Tomb of the Patriarchs. That night, the Israeli military demolished six houses from the surrounding neighborhood and two in northwest Hebron whose owners had abandoned them because of settler harassment. None of the thirty-seven people made homeless had any connection to the shootings. In their release about the incident, the team

---

4. CPTnet, "HEBRON URGENT ACTION: Next 48 hours critical. Tell Israel that more home demolitions are not the answer," November 19, 2002. CPTnet, "URGENT ACTION—Stop home demolitions in east Hebron," November 22, 2002.

5. In a memorial to Hebron team member Sue Rhodes, who died of liver cancer in 2003, Greg Rollins referred to a night that Rhodes had spent with the family in Jabal Johar:

> One night Sue and several others were sleeping in a house that had already had its kitchen destroyed by an Israeli bulldozer. There was a fear that the Israelis would return at any moment to destroy the rest of the place. Sue had trouble sleeping so she got out of bed and stared out the window. Not far away from the house, the Israeli army was bulldozing the land. Sue stood and watched as the bulldozer tore up an old olive tree. As the bulldozer tore the tree's roots from the earth, Sue heard the tree scream.
>
> The next morning Sue told her hosts what had happened during the night. How she watched the tree torn out of the earth and how she heard it scream. The family fell silent. One of them then told Sue that when their ancestors had planted that olive tree years and years ago, they said that if that tree were ever pulled from the earth, it would scream. After that, the family called Sue The Women who Heard the Tree Scream.

CPTnet, "HEBRON: Remembering Sue Rhodes, The Woman Who Heard the Tree Scream," December 3, 2003.

noted that twenty-two Palestinian homes along the route from the Old City to Kiryat Arba had now received demolition orders.[6]

More "conventional" demolitions took place on December 22 and 23, 2002, when the Israeli military destroyed several homes in the Beqa'a Valley. One of these homes belonged to Atta Jaber's brother, Jowedi and was attached to the home of their father Abdel Jawad Jaber. The team connected the demolitions with the restraining order the Israeli High court extended on December 18 that prevented the demolition of homes on the Kiryat Arba/Old City corridor. They also thought the military's removal of an outpost settlement that settlers had put up at the site of the November 15 shooting had something to do with the demolitions. Rich Meyer, Palestine Project Support coordinator from 2002–2007, wrote,

---

6. CPTnet, Yoder, "HEBRON: Two Soldiers Killed, Six Palestinian Houses Demolished in Response," December 26, 2002. When asked about how many of those homes were eventually demolished, CSD coordinator Rich Meyer wrote in a February 12, 2005, e-mail, "I think that the number 22 was reduced to 13 or 14 and finally to 3 by the courts. I think two were at least partially demolished, and one, belonging to Ayoub Jabber, has had a new bridge built THROUGH it. I haven't seen this, just heard it from Dianne and others."

John Lynes (see below, under "Internationals 2002" and n. 54), in a February 13, 2005, e-mail wrote

> The demolition order for dwellings along Worshippers' Way was appealed to the Israeli Supreme Court, which ruled, in February or March 2003, that the demolition order should not go ahead. Their ruling is not binding on the IDF. The Court suggested two alternatives: a new route parallel to Worshippers' Way, and a reinforced military presence especially on Shabbat. Also, to my delight, they warned the IDF to consider the "international repercussions" if they demolished houses along Worshippers' Way.
>
> The CPT team allowed me to play a small part in this outcome. I love Worshippers' Way (before joining CPT I was a lecturer in architecture) so when the demolition orders were issued I sent pictures to every archaeological group I could trace, urging them to protest. Eventually UNESCO intervened. Obviously, my own contribution was tiny, but I recall it every time I feel totally ineffectual, and now claim my small part in saving Worshippers' Way. Nice to be an "international repercussion"!
>
> Last year the IDF covered Worshippers' Way with tarmac and changed some of the levels. This can easily be reversed, so I don't feel angry about it. Also last July or August the IDF demolished two or three dwellings at the summit of Worshippers' Way. They were environmentally peripheral, but there were substantial protests at the time. I was in Chicago doing the CPT training, so was not directly involved.

(Note: "Worshipper's Way" is settler terminology for the path connecting Hebron's Old City with Kiryat Arba. Palestinians do not have a name for that path, but instead refer to the hill and valley it runs through: Haret iJaber and Wadi Nasara. Not surprisingly, most internationals in Hebron find using the English name more convenient.)

> Usually when the government acts against the will of the settlers, within a few days the government tries to mollify them by providing them with something that is in their interest. This process stops the settler protests and keeps them from becoming persistent opponents of the government. This pattern is predictable enough that when the settlement was removed on Thursday, I asked the CPT team in Hebron what they thought the "other shoe" would be this time. It would appear that the "other shoe" is Abdel Jawad's home, highly visible to settlers, right across from the Harsina settlement gas station—and the homes of others.[7]

On December 30, 2002, the year's final home demolitions in the Hebron District took place in Beit Ummar, approximately a month after the Beit Ummar team had closed the project (see below). In the late afternoon, hundreds of soldiers, along with five or six dogs and two bulldozers, arrived and ordered two families to vacate their houses. The soldiers did not allow family members to retrieve personal belongings before they began the demolition, during which process they killed two sheep. JoAnne Lingle and David Janzen, who documented the demolition the next day, called the Red Cross, which said its workers would bring tents, blankets, and other goods for the family.[8]

LAND CONFISCATION

The team's first urgent action release for 2002 described Israeli bulldozers plowing a road that totally encircled the Beqa'a Valley. The excavations were more than two kilometers away from the boundaries of Kiryat Arba at that time. The team asked U.S. citizens to contact Secretary of State Colin Powell, asking him to affirm previous declarations that settlement expansion must stop, and to impose logical consequences, such as the withholding of U.S. aid to Israel. "Emphasize that the subsistence farmers of the Beqa'a Valley deserve security too," the team wrote.

In a release on the previous day, the team referred to the Sultan family (with the pseudonym, "Abu Mahmoud") noting that two years earlier the Israeli military said that they would protect the Sultan home only if

---

7. Meyer's name does not appear on the quotation, but he was the Hebron Team support person at the time. CPTnet, "HEBRON URGENT ACTION: Stop Wave of Hebron Demolitions," December 23, 2002. See also CPTnet, "HEBRON UPDATE: December 20–27, 2002," December 29, 2002.

8. CPTnet, "HEBRON UPDATE: December 27, 2002–January 2, 2003," January 11, 2003.

he no longer talked with journalists, CPT, Israelis or internationals. "Two years later, under the Sharon government, the military is taking the entire area," the team wrote.[9] When the team brought a U.S. consular representative out to the Beqa'a Valley on January 30, his driver parked the official diplomatic vehicle near a Palestinian home. Settlers showed contempt for his presence by moving rubble to the entrances of the dirt roads accessing Highway #60, thus blocking the vehicles of the representative and his security officer. On July 17, 2002, settler security personnel bulldozed orchards and vineyards near the Givat Ha Harsina settlement that provided the sole source of income for three families.[10]

The team put out a second urgent action release on March 23, asking people to send faxes, yet again, to stop the expulsion of the Palestinian cave dwellers near Yatta (see chapters 4 and 6). They did so at the request of Israeli groups who believed that Israel was about to use a recent spate of bombings and counterattacks as cover for the expulsion of the cave dwellers, expansion of settlements, and eventually the annexation of this land near the green line (Israel's border with the West Bank) to Israel proper.[11]

The Israeli confiscation of Palestinian land included spaces within the Old City as well. In March, soldiers installed concertina wire across the entrances into the market near the team apartment and reinforced the barricade at the entrance to Shuhada Street directly below the team's apartment. Stepping over the barbed concertina wire required the efforts of two people: one would hold the strands down with a foot, while the other crossed, and then the one who had crossed through would hold the wired down from the other side. Sometimes team members simply unhooked the wire from the wall to pass through. Usually soldiers let them—the team mostly ignored the ones who yelled at them to stop.

Bulldozers and other heavy machinery cleared away stalls and tables in the vegetable market on April 2, 2002. Given the life and death crises happening throughout the West Bank and Gaza, the team did not make

---

9. CPTnet, "HEBRON URGENT ACTION: Stop confiscation of Beqa'a Valley," January 26, 2002. CPTnet, Bender and Roe, "HEBRON: Further Land Confiscation in Hebron's Beqa'a Valley," January 25, 2002.

10. CPTnet, "HEBRON UPDATE: January 21–31, 2002," February 4, 2002. CPTnet, Le Anne Clausen, "HEBRON: Settler Security destroys Palestinian orchards in Harsina Settlement Expansion," July 20, 2002.

11. CPTnet, "HEBRON DISTRICT URGENT ACTION: Stop the expulsion of cave dwellers from South Hebron," March 23, 2002.

a special point of addressing what amounted to Israel's confiscation of the market, as they might have before the Intifada.[12]

CURFEWS AND CLOSURES

Curfews and closures continued in 2002 to accelerate the downward spiral of the Palestinian economy and the flight of Palestinians from the Old City. Many of the team's 2002 releases describe the team's efforts to challenge these curfews and closures.[13]

On March 8, after weeks of curfew and soldiers preventing children from going to school, Kathleen Kern called Amira Hass. Since an article she published in November 2000 had been instrumental in lifting a forty-day curfew, the team thought another article might have the same effect. Hass apologetically told Kern she was exhausted from a week of covering Israeli military incursions into Tulkarm, Jenin, Balata refugee camp, and Ramallah. She also said that since so many were dying, the curfew would not be of interest to most readers.[14]

During the summer and fall of 2002, the team's interventions switched to survival mode. Several updates record the team delivering food to people trapped in their houses by the curfew or accompanying representatives of the Red Cross and Doctors Without Borders as they tried (and often failed) to make these deliveries. After the shootings of the Israeli soldiers

---

12. CPTnet, "HEBRON UPDATE: March 12–17, 2002," April 2, 2002; "HEBRON UPDATE: March 22–25, 2002," April 4, 2002.

13. CPTnet, "HEBRON: Fear not! Pilgrimage of Faith," January 3, 2002. The team decided to do a parallel trek with Cliff Kindy, who walked from Goshen, Indiana, to Columbus, Ohio, between December 22 and January 5, 2002. Both walks were connected to the U.S. invasion of Afghanistan. (See also, CPT, "FEAR NOT: A Pilgrimage of Faith.") CPTnet, Kenney and Schneider, "HEBRON: Police detain CPT delegation for removing roadblock," February 28, 2002. In a letter to the Israeli Civil Administration, the delegates wrote,

> We the undersigned internationals have removed this roadblock in Beit Ummar in response to the call of the prophets for justice. Creating barriers on Palestinian roads, confiscating Palestinian land, and devastating the Palestinian economy violates both the laws of God and the international community. As long as the Occupation continues, violence will continue, and we profoundly desire that neither Palestinians nor Israelis will have to live and die in fear of this violence for another generation.

Caoimhe Butterly, an International Solidarity Movement volunteer mentioned below, also participated in this action.

14. CPTnet, "HEBRON UPDATE: March 7–12, 2002," March 21, 2002. See also Hass, "The Mirror Doesn't Lie."

on November 15 (see above, under Home Demolitions 2002), the curfew imposed was especially tight. Soldiers threatened to shoot representatives of the Hebron Municipality if they attempted to deliver food. The team noted in their update covering November 18, "According to the Fourth Geneva Convention, occupation forces must guarantee occupied populations access to food, medical aid and humanitarian aid."[15]

SOLDIER VIOLENCE

Reports on the Hebron team's interactions with soldiers during the first half of 2002 contain a surprising number of positive conversations. Soldiers frequently told team members they had no sympathy for the settlers and were appalled by the restrictions imposed on Palestinians in Hebron. Team updates record several instances of soldiers intervening to prevent settler children from attacking people. When members of the February delegation asked a soldier on the eve of 'Eid al Adha (one of the busiest shopping days of the Muslim calendar) how long curfew would be imposed, he told them he hoped it would be lifted soon. "I know tomorrow is a feast day," he said. "I have Arab friends in my village and they have told me about their feast. I know how important it is to them." He then explained the significance of the Muslim Feast of the Sacrifice to the delegates.[16] On April 8, Mark Frey saw soldiers marching three young Palestinian men wearing blindfolds to a checkpoint. He found out that the soldiers had come across two Palestinian men beating their younger brother and intervened to prevent the abuse. They asked Frey to escort the young boy home. The boy confirmed the soldiers' account of what had happened and pleaded with Frey to tell his brothers not to beat him.[17] On April 12, Mary Lawrence chatted with

---

15. CPTnet, "HEBRON UPDATE: November 13–22, 2002." See also CPTnet updates covering June 23–26, 2002; June 27–29, 2002; November 13–22, 2002; November 23–29, 2002; December 6–13, 2002; and December 13–19, 2002.

16. See CPTnet, "HEBRON UPDATE: February 19–22, 2002," March 12, 2002.

17. Frey concluded his piece,

I returned to the checkpoint just as David and Co. [the soldiers] were marching the two brothers back toward the residential area where they returned the ID's and let them go. One of the journalists asked me, "So it really was just a domestic?" I nodded. David returned and I said, "You're right, that boy was really scared." With an exasperated smile, David exclaimed, "I'm not lying to you! We want peace."

David and Co. are a good reminder that things here are seldom black and white. Using their combat training (as an occupying power) to deal with a police-type domestic violence situation, the young men of David and Co. were trying to

some soldiers about the meaning of Easter and Maundy Thursday, which coincided with the celebration of Passover/Pesach in 2002. The soldier ran up to his guard post and brought back matzo for the team to use during their Maundy Thursday communion and foot washing service.[18]

Probably the most exhilarating of these interactions happened when Janet Shoemaker and delegate Bret Davis attended a Peace Now rally in Jerusalem on March 2, 2002. A young soldier stationed in Hebron approached them and introduced himself as Yehuda, then introduced them to another friend who was conscientious objector Shabtai Gold. The CO told them the CPT website was "the best thing on the web." At the end of a two-hour conversation, Yehuda told Davis and Shoemaker that he dreaded going back to Hebron, because the settler presence made the treatment of Palestinians there worse than anywhere else in the West Bank. He said that he especially hated enforcing the curfew. In the coming months, Gold visited Hebron several times and offered the team useful advice—especially after the army imposed severe restrictions on the team's movement in May 2003 (see chapter 8).[19] Yehuda Shaul would go on to set up an exhibit and organization called "Breaking the Silence" that informed the Israeli public about the abuses that soldiers and settlers in Hebron perpetrated on Palestinian civilians.[20] In subsequent years, Shaul and other Israelis who had served in Hebron would conduct "Breaking the Silence" tours of Hebron

---

help. I have suspicions they might have made the situation worse, having publicly aired the family's dirty laundry, involving foreigners, and dishonouring the brothers. I pray for the brother's anger and the safety of the Hazem. David and Co. really were trying to help.

CPTnet, "HEBRON: Just a Domestic . . ." April 8, 2002.

18. CPTnet, "HEBRON: Sharing the Bread," April 12, 2002.

19. CPTnet, "HEBRON: Conversations with soldiers, C.O., at Peace Now Rally," March 20, 2002. Shoemaker told Kern that Gold, given the pseudonym "Arik" in the release, told her, as part of his praise for the CPT website, that it "kicked ass." Rick Polhamus and Kathy Kamphoefner remember Gold giving them advice, but in a July 4, 2004, e-mail to the author, Shabtai Gold said he did not remember giving this advice, writing,

About the order-, I don't consider myself a legal expert, and as such I don't give legal advice. However, I might have said that there is room to question an order given in a language that is not understood. It is like reading someone his/her rights in a language not understood. However, if the order is explained to the person there is little room for maneuvering.

Chris Brown told the author in a July 11, 2004, e-mail that the refusenik who gave them advice was Yo'av Hass.

20. CPTnet, "HEBRON/TEL AVIV: "Breaking the silence" about Israeli soldiers' experiences in Hebron," June 28 2004.

for interested Israelis (see chapter 9). These positive encounters may have been due partly to the fact that most of the soldiers belonged to the Nahal Brigade—a relatively dovish branch of the Israeli military. Perhaps another significant factor was the release of a petition in December 2001 in which reserve officers proclaimed their refusal to support the occupation. It read, in part, "We shall not continue to fight behind the 1967 borders in order to dominate, expel, starve and humiliate an entire people." The petition caused a storm of controversy as hundreds of reservists quickly added their own signatures to the original forty. The soldiers and subsequent conscientious objectors breathed new life into the Israeli peace movement. Many soldiers with whom the team spoke in Hebron told team members they supported the "refuseniks," as Israeli society called them. On June 7, 2002, the team put out an urgent action release asking its constituents to check the itinerary of refuseniks on speaking tours, hold a public vigil in support of Israeli COs, and send supportive postcards to the soldiers facing the consequences of speaking out. The team also encouraged people to fax Israeli officials asking them to stop imprisoning COs.[21]

Unfortunately, the team's 2002 releases still provide a thick dossier of routine soldier violence at checkpoints and during home raids in other parts of Hebron and the surrounding environs. (Most of the positive interactions with soldiers happened near the team's apartments.) The releases also record, particularly in the second half of 2002, conversations with soldiers who told CPTers that all Palestinians were terrorists and needed to be beaten and humiliated. One soldier told Kristin Anderson and Mary Yoder that by helping Palestinians under curfew get food, they were helping terrorists. "These people should all starve and you should go back to America," he said.[22] Several times, soldiers threatened to shoot CPTers if they continued to protect Palestinians or assist them as they entered and left a curfew area. On one such occasion, Rick Polhamus told the soldier, "Maybe you will, but ten others will take my place." On another occasion, a soldier referred to an incident in which CPTers Greg Rollins, CPT intern

---

21. CPTnet, "URGENT ACTION: Support Israeli Conscientious Objectors," June 7, 2002. For a full text of the letter see Courage to Refuse, "Combatants Letter." The team had considered in previous years asking historic peace churches to "adopt" Israeli conscientious objectors, but Ya'alah Cohen, a friend of the team, told Kern and Rich Meyer that since COs were already marginalized in Israeli society, having the support of outsiders might make their status worse. Courage to Refuse marked a shift in this attitude, because its organizers welcomed international support.

22. CPTnet, "HEBRON UPDATE: December 13–19, 2002," December 26, 2002.

Greg Wilkinson and a member of TIPH had intervened to stop a young woman from stabbing a soldier. They had pushed her against a wall, while soldiers wrested the knife from her grip. The soldier told Rollins, "If I'd have been there, I would have shot TIPH for trying to help a Palestinian." When Rollins told him he had also been involved with the incident, the soldier said, "I would have shot you, too."[23]

The worst abuses often happened after a suicide bombing had killed Israeli soldiers and civilians. In October 2002, suicide attacks killed civilians in Haifa, Tel Aviv, and the Ariel settlement, as well as civilians riding a bus from Kiryat Shmona to Tel Aviv. On November 4, 2002, three Israeli soldiers entered a shoe factory in Hebron, vandalized it, beat the manager, and then made the employees and manager sit in a row. They said, "Because these people consider those who bomb to be martyrs, we will make them all martyrs. We will start with the manager first, then finish them off one by one." The brother of the manager pretended he was mentally ill and began shouting, which made the other employees shout, "Allahu Akbar!" (God is greater.) Neighbors heard the shouting, opened the door to the factory and the soldiers ran away. One of them dropped a flashlight, which later made identifying them easy. When the brothers filed a complaint with the DCO, a commander told the brothers, "These are crazy soldiers. They did this by themselves and without orders." The soldiers tried to enter the factory again on November 5, but someone spotted them and the employees locked themselves inside. On the second visit, the soldiers questioned neighbors about the "crazy" man. "We are concerned if he is in the hospital and would like to visit him," they reportedly said.[24]

The winter and spring of 2002 saw dozens of attacks and retaliations by Palestinian militants and the Israeli military. The Israeli military continued to besiege Yasser Arafat in his Ramallah compound, and a debate raged within Israel about whether the IDF should enter and kill him. Soldiers also regularly raided the Gaza, Balata, and Jenin refugee camps to kill militants suspected of attacks on Israelis. They killed dozens of civilians as well.[25] Suicide bombings within Israel and near settlements also

23. CPTNet, "HEBRON UPDATE: August 8–10, 2002." CPTnet, "HEBRON UPDATE: December 20–27, 2002," December 29, 2004. CPTnet, "HEBRON UPDATE: August 22–24, 2002," September 13, 2002.

24. CPTnet, Yoder, "HEBRON: Acting on Their Own," November 27, 2002.

25. Roe and Kern visited the Al Aroub refugee camp, north of Hebron, on March 12, because of team concerns that the Israeli military might invade there as it had in other refugee camps. Residents of the camp told them that unlike the Balata and Deheishe

ratcheted up, killing dozens of Israeli civilians. On February 11, about 300 Palestinians stormed Hebron's prison, releasing Hamas activists that Arafat's people had rounded up after recent terrorist attacks, because people were afraid Israel would bomb the prison as they had other Palestinian Authority institutions.

In one particularly gruesome attack, a suicide bomber killed thirty Israelis at a Passover celebration in a Netanya hotel on March 27, 2002. Two days later, tanks and bulldozers attacked Arafat's compound as the first stage, according to Ariel Sharon, of a "long and complicated war that knows no borders."[26] Suicide bombers subsequently struck in Tel Aviv and Haifa the next two days.

Some West Bank cities experienced battles in their streets for the first time since 1967. One contact of the team told them that Ramallah looked like Beirut at the height of Israel's invasion of Lebanon. A friend of Le Anne Clausen in Bethlehem told her the family was out of food, water, and electricity; a tank had run over the family car, and the stench of bodies lying in Manger Square had become unbearable.

While Mark Frey was leading a CPT delegation to the Sabeel conference in Jerusalem, sketchy reports of a massacre in the Jenin refugee camp began to make the news. Israel refused to allow journalists or humanitarian workers into the camp to investigate. (Later, in May 2002, it would block United Nations teams from entering the camp and investigating what had really happened there.) After visiting Deir Yassin, where a notorious slaughter by Zionist paramilitaries had taken place in 1948, the delegation listened to seventy-four-year-old survivor, Umm Saleh, describe how the soldiers had given her the choice of being hanged, shot, or buried alive in her house. Frey wrote,

> Deir Yassin is not over. Palestinians continue to trace the symbolic massacre through other brutalities like the massacre in Lebanon's camp of Sabra and Shatila. Deir Yassin is being relived right now, in the mind of Imm Saleh and other survivors like her on and the destroyed streets of Jenin. Imm Saleh said, "What is happening today is worse than what happened to us." And, like Sabra and

---

refugee camps, Aroub was in Area C. It had never passed out of Israeli control, so there was no reason for the Israelis to invade. CPTnet, "HEBRON UPDATE: March 7–12, 2002," March 21, 2002.

26. Goldenberg, "Israel turns its fire on Arafat."

Shatila, then-General and now-Israeli Prime Minister Ariel Sharon is the architect. And the world, in large part, is doing very little.[27]

The team's Palestinian, Israeli, and international friends moved closer and closer to the verge of despair as the body count for both Israelis and Palestinians kept rising and began to include international journalists. "They have crossed all the red lines," Fariel Abu Haikel told the team when they met her for school patrol one morning. "Everyone is afraid."[28]

All of Hebron was shocked at the end of March 2002 when two TIPH observers, Catherine Berruex from Switzerland and Deputy Head of Operation Division Turtug Cengiz Toytunç, were killed near Halhoul as they were driving to Tel Aviv. They had stopped driving when they heard shooting, and a Palestinian gunman standing in the road shot the two in the front seat of the TIPH vehicle. A third observer in the back seat was injured and dragged Berreux, who was still breathing, out of the car and laid her on the ground. Because Israeli soldiers fired back after gunmen shot at the IDF armored vehicles that arrived to help the TIPH members, no one was certain whether Israelis or Palestinians killed Berreux, at first. But a later release on the TIPH website noted that she could not have survived her initial injuries, even if she had been hit later in the crossfire.

Internationals in Hebron and Palestinians who lived in the neighborhood of the TIPH headquarters felt the deaths especially keenly. "The CPT Hebron team is grief-stricken and angry over the senseless shooting and wonders how this will affect any real chances for peace," the team wrote in a release. "But they are more determined than ever to remain in Hebron to continue to work for the cause of justice and peace."[29]

In the next weeks, CPTers Kathleen Kern, Greg Rollins, and Mark Frey would have their own narrow escapes in firing zones. On April 9, Kathleen Kern and Greg Rollins traveled to the village of Dura, just west of

---

27. CPTnet, "HEBRON: Brief report on the current situation," April 2, 2002; CPTnet, "HEBRON UPDATE: April 7, 2002"; CPTnet, "JERUSALEM: Massacre in Jenin, Deir Yassin relived," April 15, 2002.

28. CPTnet, Dianne Roe, "HEBRON: RED LINES—A Reflection on Recent Events," March 15, 2002.

29. CPTnet, "HEBRON: TIPH Observers Killed Near Hebron," March 27, 2002. CPTers Mary Lawrence, a Methodist minister and Christine Caton, a Presbyterian minister provided pastoral care to other members of TIPH after the killings. See also, Temporary International Presence in Hebron, "Two TIPH members killed near Hebron"; "Funeral of Ms. Berreux and Major Toytunç"; "Six years since two TIPH observers were shot dead in Hebron."

Hebron when they heard the Israeli military had occupied it. The team had called journalist Khaled Amayreh, whom the CPT delegation currently in Palestine had met in Dura three days earlier. He reported that ten to twenty tanks were in the village and helicopter gunships were sending rockets into the village. Soldiers were shooting anything that moved in the streets.

Upon arriving in Dura, Rollins and Kern had shots fired over their head at the entrance into the village. They began walking around the perimeter and joined a band of journalists who had gone to the roof of a high building to observe the shooting. When they called Amayreh again, he told them a wounded man was lying in the street in front of the house and that soldiers had shot at ambulance personnel who had tried to help him. He also told them they would be shot if they entered the town.

A man approached the two CPTers and asked if they could try to get his wife, three children, and two grandchildren out of his married daughter's home, which soldiers had taken over. Kern and Rollins borrowed a white headscarf and returned to the home from which the warning shots had been fired earlier. After soldiers fired over her head again, Kern was able to talk to the disembodied voice of a soldier who spoke with an American accent.[30] He initially told her that no one was in the house, but backpedaled when Kern told him the father had just talked to them on his cell phone. He then told her he would only release them if she backed off fifty meters and became exasperated when she asked where he was from in the U.S. "Do you want me to release them or not?" he snapped. She backed off.

Just before the soldiers released the family, about eight military vehicles came over the hill from the entrance to Dura and headed into Hebron. The journalists, who had been recording the encounter—and were only at Dura because they were waiting for the invasion of Hebron—left to follow them, probably believing the invasion had begun. Once they were gone, the hostages scurried across the road with a stroller. They later told Rollins and Kern that one soldier inside had been very good to them, providing them with earplugs when the shooting became very loud and generally reassuring them.[31]

---

30. Rollins and Kern decided together that the soldiers were less likely to shoot a woman, so they agreed Kern should be the one to approach.

31. CPTnet, Don Mead, "HEBRON: A call to Dura under invasion," April 9, 2002; CPTnet, "HEBRON UPDATE: April 8–11, 2002," April 11, 2002. "Hebron: Release the Captives," 1–2. An acquaintance on Dubboya Street told Kern he had seen her walking with the white scarf toward the house on the news. "At first, I was not sure it was you," he said, "But then the soldier kept saying 'Kathy, Kathy, Kathy.'"

On April 17, returning from Jerusalem, Mark Frey saw a long line of cars waiting to cross the bridge over the bypass road that separates Hebron from Halhoul. Soldiers were shooting at any of the cars that crossed, and two people had already been injured, one seriously, as they attempted to race across the bridge.

Frey called the Hebron Brigade Commander, and a woman said she would talk to someone and that Frey and the others could cross in five minutes. After five minutes, Frey offered to cross the bridge on foot first to see if the others could safely do so.

Waving his red hat, he began walking on the bridge, pocked with patches ripped out by bullets. After a burst of gunfire, he yelled, "Do you speak English? Anyone? I'm just going to walk across. Your commander said it was okay." After hearing no response, he continued and halfway across the bridge a bullet hit the wall ten feet in front of him. He called the commander's office again. When he spoke with the same woman, describing the situation, she became distraught and said, "Sorry, I'm just a secretary."

After another shot whizzed by, he turned around and walked back to the congregated Palestinians. Three different people extended the invitation to spend the night in their homes.

Two days later, Rollins spoke to a soldier in Hebron, asking why the military had been shooting at cars on the bridge. The soldier told him he had participated in the shooting. His unit had received intelligence that someone was going to try to bring a car bomb into Hebron. When Rollins asked why they had shot at civilians walking across, the soldier said, "We'd never do that!" He looked dumbfounded when Rollins related Frey's experience.[32]

Two of the ways that CPT sought to respond to the violence did not appear on CPTnet, except obliquely. Hisham Sharabati arranged a meeting with the team after Ramallah and Bethlehem were invaded. He told the CPTers that in those cities, the Israeli military had destroyed radio stations and made it impossible for the wounded to get to hospitals. Accordingly, Sharabati, along with a committee of journalists and medical personnel, divided Hebron into sectors and arranged to have a makeshift clinic and radio transmitter in each sector. (A great deal of panic happened in other West Bank cities when the Israeli military took out the radio and television stations. With the Hebron settlers poised to take over uninhabited parts of

---

32. Mark Frey, "Hebron: Braving the Bridge," 2.

the Old City, Sharabati and the other organizers wanted to make sure that people stayed in their homes as long as they could safely do so.) Sharabati asked the team to talk with Doctors Without Borders to get their assistance and told team members to be ready to disperse to the various sectors of the city when they received a call, so that each sector would have international accompaniment.

The other event that did not appear on CPTnet was the team's attempt to enter the Church of the Nativity on April 12, 2002, and bring food and water to people trapped there since April 2. On that date, as the Israeli shelling of the city intensified, thirty Palestinian gunmen broke into the church compound and a hundred and seventy civilians soon joined them. In the previous invasions of the city during the Al-Aqsa Intifada, soldiers had gone door-to-door detaining any man between the ages of fourteen and forty. Many parents thus sent their sons to the church for safekeeping, because they believed the Israelis would not invade the church. Additionally, Palestinian policemen, who had become targets for the Israeli military in the most recent round of violence, fled into the church. The Israeli military put the church under siege for the next five weeks. Soldiers gave the priests and nuns inside the compound the option of leaving, but most of them stayed to protect the church and the civilians.

The team, after consulting with clergy in Jerusalem, decided to intervene in the standoff, calling the action, "Operation Baby Jesus." Anne Montgomery accompanied clergy from Jerusalem to a place near Bethlehem University. The Hebron team walked nearly ten miles via back roads to meet them. While Greg Rollins, Christine Caton, and Le Anne Clausen waited at the Star Hotel to deliver a press conference for which nobody showed up, Rick Polhamus, Peggy Gish, Kathleen Kern, and Anne Montgomery walked with Michael Thomas of the Redeemer Lutheran Church, Henry Carse from St. George's Anglican school, Clarence Musgrave, pastor of St. Andrew's Church of Scotland, and Donald Moore, of the Pontifical Biblical Institute, through the silent streets of Bethlehem toward Manger Square. The damage that tanks and shells had done to buildings, monuments, and cars had left rubble ankle-deep in places.

As they moved into Manger Square, a soldier in a jeep and several stationed in towers around the squares called for them to stop. A tank parked at one edge of the square swiveled its gun turret and aimed it at the group as they approached. Pastor Michael Thomas told the soldiers that the group wanted to bring supplies to people in the church and to pray there because it was "the birthplace of our Lord."

A soldier responded, "No, no food to the church. There are a hundred and fifty terrorists inside and they will shoot you." The group told the soldiers that they did not believe the Palestinians inside would kill them, but when Polhamus, whose job it was to monitor soldiers' reactions, heard the soldiers calling for backup, he decided that the group should withdraw.

The group knelt and prayed by the mosque in Manger Square, ending by singing "Ubi Caritas."[33] They distributed the food they brought to residents of Manger Square who had not been able to leave their homes for almost two weeks. The day concluded with a visit to Mitri Raheb, pastor of the Christmas Lutheran church a block away from Manger Square. He had pneumonia and had been unable to get medicine for it since the military had imposed the curfew.

When asked if he remembered why he had stopped the group and why a release about the action never appeared on CPTnet, Rick Polhamus wrote in 2004,

> I didn't say to pray until another jeep arrived and I thought there was getting to be too many soldiers there and that we were placing them in danger. You had walked up to the outside edge and my gut feeling said to just keep walking but because of the agreement we had with the non-CPTers I felt we had to stop at that point. I also thought that this was a test of how far we could push it and we (CPT) would push the issue again later. This was the reason I think we didn't write about it at the time. We didn't want to say anything until we did it again.[34]

---

33. Anonymous ninth-century text.
34. E-mail to author, June 3, 2004. Polhamus continued,

> I think there were a couple of important parts of that whole thing. One was that we invited the clergy to participate with us which to me represents CPT helping others to take action instead of being bystanders. Another was the good planning and prayer at the beginning so that people knew their roles. One question that still lingers is whether it was Father Maroun's [the priest at the school in Beit Jala who gave the CPTers milk and cheese to take into Bethlehem] blessing of invisibility or my ability to use Jedi mind control that enabled us as we went in to pass the group of soldiers at Christmas Church that the media had told us the day before was impossible to get past.

Perhaps another significant reason the release did not appear had to do with the generally frantic pace of the team's work. With daily crises in Hebron, writing up what happened sometimes fell to the end of a "to do" list. Kern was responsible for posting on CPTnet at the time and was gone for a week during the fast with Linda Livni described below. CPTnet was also posting many Colombia releases at the time, because of an upsurge of violent episodes in Barrancabermeja and the Opón.

Donald Moore would later write of the event and what happened afterwards, concluding,

> On the other side [of the Bethlehem checkpoint] Susan Thomas, Michael's wife [and co-pastor], met us and we all eleven somehow piled into their van. I arrived home to the news that a suicide bomber had hit the upper part of Jaffa Road just fifteen minutes earlier. First reports had at least four were killed (the number will grow) and a much larger number injured. Killing vs. killing, terror vs. terror, violence vs. violence—a "liturgy of death" it was termed at our evening Mass. But death cannot have the final word. We will again and again counter it somehow with our "liturgy of life."[35]

On May 2, members of the International Solidarity Movement (ISM) entered the church with food and subsequently reported on conditions there.[36]

The team also sought to respond to the invasions in more public ways. Kathleen Kern participated in a weeklong highly publicized fast—"We are starving for peace" —with Israeli peace activist Linda Livni on the grounds of Tantur, which straddled the border between Bethlehem and Jerusalem. Others of the Hebron team participated in the fast on various days. The team circulated a statement from Sabeel Liberation Theology Center in Jerusalem entitled, "Remember the value of human life," which upheld nonviolent methods of resisting the occupation. On April 6, 2002, the team put out a "Call for Christians to Pray, Preach and Pester for Peace," encouraging its constituents to light a new candle every day until Pentecost and put them in the most public windows of their homes, churches, and workplaces. It also called its constituents to observe a day of "Prayer and Faxing," contacting official decision-makers in the conflict. On Saturday, April 6, a CPT short-term delegation led by Mark Frey had a "prayerful confrontation" with a soldier who fired a warning shot in the air as they attempted to walk into Bethlehem. (They knelt in a semicircle, facing Bethlehem, lit a candle, sang, prayed, and returned to a checkpoint they had bypassed earlier.)

---

35. Donald Moore, "An Afternoon in Bethlehem." See also Kathleen Kern, "Breaking the Siege in Manger Square."

36. Nathan Musselman—a young man who had spent time with the team as part of an Eastern Mennonite University trip and had later spent several nights out Beqa'a as a violence deterring-presence—was a part of this ISM action. He ended up in Ramle prison awaiting deportation. CPTnet, "HEBRON UPDATE: May 18–24, 2002," June 3, 2002.

Most significantly, the team called for an emergency delegation of up to twenty people to come to the West Bank from April 15–29, 2002. If the invasion of Hebron happened at the time the delegation was there, the team wanted to use delegation members to implement the plan of Sharabati and other organizers for the city of Hebron. If the invasion did not happen, the delegates would travel to other places in the West Bank harder hit by the invasion.[37]

Weeks passed that spring, and Hebron became the only major Palestinian city that Israel had not invaded. The fifteen-member Emergency Delegation divided into three teams, each led by a Hebron CPTer. One tried and failed to enter Ramallah. Le Anne Clausen's group managed to sneak into Nablus via an outlying village and steep hill. They, along with members of the International Solidarity Movement, helped the Union of Palestinian Medical Relief committees load supplies donated by the World Council of Churches into ambulances. They also visited a mass grave that contained fifteen bodies. Sixty more corpses stored in a mosque and refrigerator trucks awaited burial, and Palestinians were exhuming bodies from temporary graves so they could be buried properly. A third team went to Dura and accompanied a crew repairing a water main punctured by an Israeli bulldozer. The groups led by Polhamus and Montgomery also spent time in Bethlehem, documenting the destruction and slaughter there.[38]

---

37. See CPTnet releases: "HEBRON: 'We are starving for peace'—CPTers to participate in interreligious fast during Holy Week," March 19, 2002; "JERUSALEM: 'Remember the value of human life,'" March 23, 2002; "BETHLEHEM: 'Fast for Peace' Begins in Bethlehem," March 27, 2002; Kern, "Bethlehem: Fasting Update, Day Four: Picking up the pieces," March 28, 2002; "HEBRON: Brief report on the current situation," April 2, 2002," April 2, 2002; "HEBRON UPDATE: March 26–April 3, 2002," April 4, 2002; "HEBRON/CHICAGO: Light a candle in the Dark. A call for Christians to Pray, Preach and Pester for peace," April 6, 2002; "HEBRON: EMERGENCY CPT DELEGATION CALLED April 15–19," April 8, 2003; Rhonda Brubacher, Jeanne Clark, Don Mead and the short term CPT Middle East delegation, "Bethlehem: A prayerful confrontation," April 10, 2002.

The team also put out a CPTnet, "Temporary increase in frequency of Hebron Updates," on April 4, which noted, "Because of the current demand for up-to-date eyewitness information from Israel/Palestine, Hebron Updates will appear more frequently on CPTnet. The team in Hebron hopes that we will soon be living in less interesting times here."

38. See CPTnet releases: "HEBRON: Emergency delegation update," April 20, 2003; Aaron Froelich, "NABLUS: CPT Delegation Distributes Aid and Documents Stories," April 22, 2002; "HEBRON: Delegation Update," April 23, 2002; "HEBRON UPDATE: April 19–24, 2002," April 27, 2002.

On April 29, at 4:00 AM, after several false starts,[39] Israeli forces entered the H-1 area of Hebron, bringing to an end the control of the Palestinian Authority in that part of the city. Compared to the bloodshed in Jenin, Nablus, and Bethlehem, the invasion of Hebron was relatively mild. The military killed eight Palestinians and wounded twenty-five. CPTers visited one family who reported that when they heard screaming coming from cars that had been hit by shells and appeals for assistance on the radio, brothers Faris and Ibrahim Shaheen and their cousin Nader ran to help. All three died from helicopter missile gunfire. Soldiers destroyed several buildings, including the local television station, and arrested suspected Palestinian militants.

As had happened in other locations, the Israeli military imposed a curfew on the whole city, but people were still able to get supplies by knocking on side entrances of shops that were ostensibly closed. When Greg Rollins and Anne Montgomery reached a hospital in the city center to offer accompaniment for ambulances, the hospital staff said that no wounded were coming, but they could use fifty kilos of bread. Tanks stopped the CPTers as they pushed the supplies in an old shopping cart, but then allowed them to proceed. Rollins and Clausen spent the night at Al Mazan hospital at the request of the hospital administrator, but nothing happened. The next day, Polhamus and Rollins monitored the treatment of about one hundred and fifty handcuffed and blindfolded Palestinians at the DCO—some of whom had been arrested twice. An Israeli soldier admitted to Polhamus that sometimes soldiers did not check the papers of detainees that verified they had already been detained, investigated, and released.[40]

Over the next weeks, the team visited various locations in the outlying portions of Hebron that had sustained damage from shelling and soldier raids, including Harit iSheik, Abu Sneineh, Beit Ummar, and Shuyoukh (where the military blew up the communications center, causing considerable damage to surrounding homes and buildings).[41] Particularly hard hit

---

39. Rumors that Hebron was about to be invaded had been circulating since March. See CPTnet, "HEBRON NEWS BRIEF: Invaded or not invaded," April 4, 2002; CPTnet, "HEBRON UPDATE: April 7, 2002"; CPTnet, "HEBRON UPDATE: April 19–24, 2002," April 27, 2002.

40. CPTnet, "HEBRON: Israeli Military enters Hebron, imposes curfew on entire city," April 29, 2002; CPTnet, "HEBRON UPDATE: April 30, 2002," April 30, 2002.

41. See CPTnet releases: "Hebron Update: April 29–May 3, 2002," May 10, 2002; Mary Lawrence and JoAnne Lingle, "SHUYOUKH: Disneyland of the Hebron District," May 14, 2002; "HEBRON UPDATE: May 25–31, 2002," June 17, 2002; "HEBRON UPDATE: June 2–7, 2002," June 21, 2002.

was the Dweiban neighborhood, which Israeli tanks shelled on May 5, 2005, leaving ten families homeless. Soldiers also conducted room-to-room searches for militants, using a local blacksmith and the landlord's son as human shields to protect themselves from booby traps and gunmen. After hearing news of another suicide bombing, soldiers the following morning blasted open the gate of a textile factory, starting a fire that destroyed the factory and several residential apartments. The soldiers later claimed the factory had been making weapons.

Le Anne Clausen accompanied Hisham Sharabati and some international human rights lawyers to Dweiban on May 13, 2002, to take testimonies from the residents there. They told the investigators that the soldiers had not confiscated anything from inside the factory, as they presumably would have if they had found weapons.[42]

On June 26, 2002, the Israeli military struck the headquarters of the Palestinian Authority and security forces, as well as homes belonging to Yakoutib Sharabati—whom the military wanted for questioning—with tanks and helicopters. Three Palestinians died, and the military and civilian staff in the headquarters, which had served as the offices of both the British and Israeli occupation forces, were put under siege. The military then put the entire city under curfew.

Two days later, the Israeli military set off two large explosions in the headquarters, called "the Muqata" by Palestinians, and then leveled the remains with a bulldozer the next day. Team members visited families living nearby to document the extensive damage to their homes and to the nearby girl's school. A man who was visiting his family at the time told Diana Epp-Fransen and Kathy Kamphoefner, "This is all politics and business, and for us, it's been a very dirty game for thirty years. Poor people always pay the price for politicians."[43]

The team held a prayer vigil on the rubble of the Muqata on July 6, 2002, as tanks revved their engines and rotated their turrets to get their attention. The team ignored them and continued their worship. A release

---

42. CPTnet, "HEBRON UPDATE: May 11–17, 2002," May 31, 2002. No record exists of a suicide bombing occurring on May 6, but on May 7, a suicide bombing killed fifteen people at a billiard hall in the Israeli city of Rishon Letzion.

43. CPTnet, "Hebron: Israeli Military Re-Occupies Hebron," June 26, 2002. CPTnet, Kathy Kamphoefner and Jim Satterwhite, "HEBRON: Homes, school damaged by Muqata explosions," July 1, 2002. These releases have a problematic chronology. The first says the siege of the headquarters, the Muqata, began on June 26. The second says that the headquarters was finally destroyed on June 29, "after a five-day siege."

about the vigil noted that CPTers were beginning a walk from Chicago to Peoria, Illinois, to protest Boeing selling Apache Attack helicopters and Caterpillar selling bulldozers to Israel that it used to destroy the Muqata.[44]

SETTLER VIOLENCE

Settler violence continued with a similarly wearisome frequency in 2002, although assaults on team members themselves seemed to diminish. However, the team recorded more instances of settlers throwing rocks at their apartment. They also recorded bizarre Monty Pythonesque expostulations by settlers. For example, a settler male with a young son told Jerry Levin, "See, I spit at you CPT Christian killers. We will kill you! Our God will kill your God, because you have a bloody head" (referring to the red CPT cap Levin was wearing). Another told Dianne Roe and Janet Shoemaker—both U.S. citizens—in a series of drive-by shoutings, "Go back to Europe. Christians worship stones. We are the only true religion. We are Israel! We are Israel! You are Christian. You are the devil." In yet another reference to the red hats, another settler called out as he was driving by Bourke Kennedy and Jerry Stein, "Millions are being killed in Europe! Millions are being killed in Europe! No wonder your hats are red. There is blood on your hands." When delegate Bret Davis, who stayed on to help the Hebron team after his delegation ended, encountered a group of settlers near the Ibrahimi Mosque/Cave of Machpelah after a morning school patrol, one man called him a "f---ing Nazi," and shoved him with the butt of his gun. When Davis did not react, the settler began striking him and screaming further obscenities, ending with, "And you're sleeping with Palestinians!" Davis replied that he was not sleeping with Palestinians, but with Canadians and Americans, "Well, not SLEEPING with them exactly," he said. The settler responded, "Well, I'm not accusing you of adultery."[45]

For the residents of the Old City and those living near settlements outside of Hebron, harassment continued unabated. Settlers stoned and

---

44. CPTnet, "HEBRON: Instruments of Destruction," July 8, 2002. See n. 1 for further information on Kindy and Goode's walk between the Boeing and Caterpillar headquarters.

45. See CPTnet releases: "HEBRON UPDATE: March 22–25, 2002," April 4, 2002. "Hebron Update: June 9–16, 2002," June 28, 2002. "HEBRON UPDATE: July 7–16, 2002," July 31, 2002. HEBRON UPDATE: SEPTEMBER 4–10, 2002, September 20, 2002.

shot at their homes, threw trash in their courtyards, shouted death threats, killed their pets, stole their agricultural produce and household items, and cut their phone and electricity lines. They covered homes and shops with vicious graffiti like, "Watch out Fatima, we will rape all Arab women," "Exterminate the Muslims," "Die Arab sand-niggers," and "Mohammed was a pig."[46] They also destroyed Palestinian gardens and vineyards and cut down fruit and nut trees.

In the more rural areas of the Hebron district, settlers shot at and set dogs upon farmers trying to harvest their crops and punctured tires on their farm equipment so that they could not get their produce to the market. They also swam nude in Palestinian cisterns, thus polluting villagers' primary water supply.[47]

Sometimes soldiers intervened to stop settler harassment, and sometimes they ignored attacks taking place a few feet from their checkpoints. In one such case, a settler boy twice threw a rock at Kristin Anderson, then grabbed her hat and smacked her on the forehead. When she and an Ecumenical Accompanier from the World Council of Churches asked a soldier standing nearby why he had not stopped the attack, he replied, "They are children. What can I do?"[48]

Two notable settler rampages in 2002 happened after attacks on settlers and soldiers. The first occurred after a settler who had grown up in Hebron, Elazar Leibovitz, was killed in a Palestinian attack while on duty as an IDF sergeant in the southern Hebron District. The vigilante revenge attacks on Palestinians in the Old City shocked a minister's aide who was in Hebron for the funeral. The Israeli newspaper *Ha'aretz* covered the rampage as follows:

> Col. (res.) Moshe Givati, an adviser on settlement security for Public Security Minister Uzi Landau, yesterday termed the rioting that took place during the funeral of Elazar Leibovitz, "a pogrom against the Arabs of Hebron, with no provocation on the Palestinian side."
>
> Givati, who attended the funeral on Sunday, said he witnessed "brutal acts" and rejected absolutely explanations by the Jewish

---

46. CPTnet, "HEBRON UPDATE: April 29-May 3, 2002," May 10, 2002.

47. Most of the abuses listed occurred multiple times over the course of 2002 and may be found in the CPTnet 2002 archives.

48. CPTnet, "HEBRON UPDATE: August 15–17, 2002," August 31, 2002. Israeli soldiers rarely seemed to have this attitude toward Palestinian children throwing stones.

> Community of Hebron Council spokesmen who said they were acting in self-defense against Palestinian stone-throwing.
>
> Givati, who was commander of the Hebron brigade during the first intifada, has good relations with the settlement movement leadership. He was appointed six months ago by Landau to help smooth relations between the police and the settlement community . . .
>
> The violence began already on Saturday night, he says, when a group of Jewish youths invaded a Palestinian house in the city, and burned and vandalized the possessions inside . . .
>
> He said that "the Palestinians did not throw any rocks or boulders at the funeral procession . . . . I saw everything from very close range. There were long bursts of fire by the Israelis—into the air and at the houses."
>
> It was during that fire that 14-year-old Nibin Jamjum was killed by a bullet to her head, and a Palestinian boy was stabbed. IDF sources say that these two and the other wounded—15 Palestinians in all were reported wounded, and an equal number of police were hurt—were casualties of the Jewish violence. "Dozens of thugs, including youths from Hebron, burst into Arab houses for no reason. They broke windows, destroyed property and threw stones. These people were there for the purpose of making a pogrom," said Givati.
>
> Soldiers, police, and Border Patrol troops who arrived on the scene tried to arrest the rioters, but were attacked. "Police officers were beaten," Givati said. "I am an alumnus of the first intifada and I never saw anything like this. A dozen thugs knocked down a policeman and kicked at him."
>
> The police arrested some of the rioters, but the police car carrying them out was blocked by their friends, who damaged the police car. Boys and girls from Hebron kept up a stream of curses at the soldiers. They were called "Amalek's soldiers," and warned, "you're next."[49]

Since the team lived in the area where the settlers attacked, they responded to calls nonstop for most of the weekend. Settlers wrecked the Sharabati household around the corner from the team's apartment, throwing the family's water tanks into the street. Adel Samoh, a shoe store owner and longtime friend of the team who lived above Beit Hadassah, was hit in the head by a rock. When Palestinians in the market also began throwing back the stones that settlers had thrown at them, soldiers began shooting at the Palestinians.

---

49. Harel and Lis, "Minister's aide calls Hebron riots a 'pogrom.'" The Israeli human rights organization B'tselem took testimonies of people attacked by the settlers between July 26–28: "Standing Idly By." See also B'tselem, "Settlers attack Palestinians in Hebron, and kill Nivin Jamjum, age 14, July 2002."

While Le Anne Clausen, Greg Rollins, and Jim Satterwhite were with 'Adel Samoh, they received a call that settlers were in the market. Leaving Rollins to stay with the Samoh family, Clausen and Satterwhite went into the market, where people showed them the spent casings near the team apartment where settlers had shot into houses. Two men ran up to them and told them that settlers had entered their house, stabbed six-year-old Ahmed an-Natsche, and hit the boy and his aunt on their heads with stones. Satterwhite and Clausen arrived at the same time the soldiers did and followed the soldiers as they carried the little boy away, trying to stay in between the distraught father and uncle who were also following the soldiers. The two men relaxed when they saw the soldiers administering medical care. The team later learned that the settler who stabbed the little boy had missed his liver by 2.5 millimeters and that a settler had also lifted a younger brother by the ears, tearing one in the process, and slammed him to the floor.

Clausen and Shoemaker went to visit the Sharabati family (relatives of Hisham Sharabati) near their apartment on July 29, 2002, without realizing that settlers were still in the house and narrowly missed getting hit by a chunk of concrete. As they made their way back, they stopped at the home of another member of the extended Sharabati family and learned that the settlers had smashed everything in the house, including valuable antiques, and incinerated the library that had contained some books that were one thousand years old.

Although the primary rampage happened on the 27th and 28th, residual violence continued over the next week. On July 30, settler women and children invaded the old Market twice, destroying the wares of the vendors there, and settler boys threw stones at Palestinians in the chicken market. During the first invasion, Clausen stood between an elderly Palestinian man and two settler women who were trying to stone him. She then took a picture of the women trying to get past Jerry Levin, who was standing in the doorway of the team apartment. The women attacked Clausen, knocking her to the ground as she tried to protect her camera. They hit her with fists and stones and kicked her in the head until Levin crouched over her to protect her with his body. When soldiers came, the boys stopped throwing stones, but one of the settler women hit Clausen in the face with a chunk of asphalt. Although soldiers eventually arrived during both invasions to escort the women out, the team saw no arrests of settlers. One Palestinian man yelled at the soldiers when they escorted the settler women out for the second time, "Our God is watching this. And he will not let this happen." A soldier responded, very slowly, "He is our God, and He has saved us." The soldiers then declared curfew on the Old Market.

On August 1, the settler violence once again struck close to home when the team learned that Abdel Jawad Jaber (Atta Jaber's father) had broken his leg. Settlers had been throwing rocks from the wall above his house, and he rushed out to protect his granddaughter who was in the yard. Settlers hit him on the back with a rock and he slipped on the steps of the veranda, fracturing his left leg near the hip socket.[50] The attack would leave Jaber with a permanent limp.

The shooting that killed soldiers and settler guards on November 15, 2002 (see above, under Home Demolitions 2002), also resulted in settler rampages through the neighborhoods from which the Palestinian gunmen had fired. On November 16, *Ha'aretz* journalist Amira Hass went with the team to the location where the initial shooting had taken place. Observing settlers stoning Palestinian homes in the area, Hass told the police to stop them, which resulted in settlers shoving her, spitting on her, and stealing her notebook and glasses. Greg Rollins, Mary Lawrence, Jerry Levin, and Quaker peace activist John Lynes (who would later become a full-time CPTer) surrounded her, but no soldiers intervened to protect her until a reporter from Israeli TV came to escort Hass and the CPTers away from the mob. The next day, after the military had blown up five homes in the area, settlers broke the windshields of ten cars, destroyed the water tanks of two families, uprooted between fifteen and twenty olive trees, set the interior of one house on fire, and broke the windows of several other houses.[51]

---

50. CPTnet, K. R. Kamphoefner, "HEBRON: Settler rampage kills one, injures many," July 28, 2002; Jerry Levin, "HEBRON: Settler women attack CPTers, shop owners in Old Market," July 30, 2002. CPTnet, "HEBRON UPDATE: July 28–August 3, 2002," August 13, 2002.

In a June 8, 2004 e-mail message to the author regarding his and Clausen's response to the violence in the Market, Satterwhite wrote,

> What is interesting in all of this is that Le Anne and I almost went into the Old City originally in response to the call [to the Samoh house] via Beit Romano. Had we gone that way—instead of through the Chicken Market— we would have run head-on into the rampaging settlers, instead of being right on their heels. That was a sobering thought--and still is, when I think about it.

51. CPTnet, "HEBRON UPDATE: November 13–22, 2002," November 28, 2002; CPTnet, "HEBRON UPDATE: December 6–13, 2002," December 19, 2002; CPTnet, "HEBRON UPDATE: December 13–19, 2002."

A new settler violence trend in 2002 involved the looting of shops around settlements. While Palestinians were under curfew, settlers pried off locks and bars and stole chickens, peacocks, clothing, and other items. Settlers in Beit Romano broke a hole into an adjacent jewelry store and stole 50–60,000 dollars' worth of gold jewelry. On July 22, 2003, settlers broke into three more shops around Beit Romano, stole all the contents, and then barred the shops from the inside so their owners could not reenter. Greg Rollins wrote a release entitled "Legal Breaking and Entering," that addressed the thefts. Beginning with "I don't know about you, but where I come from, breaking and entering and stealing are illegal. If you are caught in the middle of the act, or sit in the place you have broken into and refuse to move, you will be arrested." Rollins noted that Israeli soldiers and police had prevented shop owners from entering their shops, but had done nothing to the settlers who refused to leave them. "It would have been impossible for the soldiers not to hear or see the settlers smash a hole in the cement wall," he wrote, referring to the shops next to Beit Romano. After settlers claim rights to a building, he wrote, courts rarely recognized a Palestinian's ownership of the property. "The Palestinians are left without a store, without a livelihood, without any compensation and without any justice."[52]

INTERNATIONAL ACCOMPANIERS

By 2002, the International Solidarity Movement (2002) began to make its influence felt in the portions of West Bank and Gaza most afflicted by soldier and settler violence. CPT continued to provide training for the waves of volunteers that came in and hosted volunteers in Hebron after their "tour of duty" with ISM was finished. In return, team and delegation members often participated in ISM-organized actions around the West Bank. CPTers also hosted/participated in other international delegations and accompaniment groups, including those sponsored by Rabbis for Human Rights, Global Exchange, Junity (a progressive Jewish group), the Christian Accompaniment Program (Denmark and Iceland), Civilians for

52. CPTnet, "HEBRON: Legal Breaking and Entering," August 10, 2002. Most of the updates from March–June, 2002, have some reference to settlers looting shops. For the case of shops invaded and looted near Beit Romano, see CPTnet, "HEBRON UPDATE: July 21–27, 2002," August 4, 2002; CPTnet, HEBRON UPDATE: August 25–30, 2002, September 17, 2002. In the update for August 26, one of the shop owners showed the team a copy of the complaint he had filed with the Civil Administration. The Israeli officer to whom he submitted the complaint had put no file number on the copy (the team assumed intentionally), which meant the shop owner would not be able to follow up on his complaint. As of February 2005, most of these looted shops remained closed.

Peace (the Netherlands), the Quaker Peace Team (United Kingdom), and the Fellowship of Reconciliation. In addition to training the ISMers, team members provided nonviolence training for Palestinian students and Fatah activists in Bethlehem, International Checkpoint Watch, the Quaker Peace Team, and the Service Civile International.

In August 2002, the Ecumenical Accompaniment Programme in Palestine and Israel began working in the Occupied Territories. Rick Polhamus attended the February 2002 organizational meetings for EAPPI in Geneva, which were focused on the "Draft Proposed Model . . . For Discussion":

> [World Council of Churches] WCC announced the official creation of Ecumenical Monitoring Programme in Palestine and Israel (EMPPI) on October 20, 2001, after the WCC Executive Committee meeting of September 11–14, 2001 unanimously called for the WCC to develop an accompaniment program that would include ecumenical presence similar to Christian Peacemaker Teams in Hebron and called on member churches to join in acts of nonviolent resistance, boycotts of settlement goods and prayer vigils to strengthen the chain of solidarity with the Palestinian people as part of a special focus of the Decade to Overcome Violence.

Following this announcement, WCC study groups visited Israel/Palestine and spent time with the Hebron team to see how CPT worked. Polhamus wrote,

> The most significant thing in my opinion that came from the meeting was the recognition that more than a monitoring presence was needed. I told them of Yusef Al-Atrash saying, "we don't need more people to come and tell me my son is being beaten and my home destroyed. We need people to come who will do something." This became a main theme in the discussions of what the EAPPI's role would be.[53]

---

53. June 10, 2004, e-mail to author. The "Draft Proposed Model," excerpt comes from Polhamus's e-mail, rather than from an official WCC press release.
Polhamus continued,

> I later attended some follow-up committee meetings in Jerusalem to address and fine-tune some of the issues that didn't get finished at the Geneva meetings. Later as the first group of EAPPI arrived and Rebecca Johnson (another CPT connection) was appointed to her role, there were other CPTers (Greg, Le Anne, possibly Jim Satterwhite) and maybe others that attended EAPPI meetings in Jerusalem during the time I was home.

Polhamus also noted that CPT was instrumental in calling for WCC volunteers to "accompany" rather than "monitor" (reflected in an original "EMPPI" designation.) The

Three ISM volunteers were to make significant contributions to the team's work in 2002.[54] Irish volunteer Caoimhe (pronounced "QUEE-vah") Butterly spent time with CPT and with their Palestinian contacts. In particular, she stayed in Beit Ummar for several nights—the evening of the February 22 action to remove a roadblock (see n. 13)—and temporarily managed to prevent a tank from entering Beit Ummar. She would later be one of the ISM members who infiltrated Yasser Arafat's Ramallah headquarters in March 2002 after Israeli tanks blew a hole in the side of the compound, and spend the rest of 2002 in the Jenin refugee camp where she was shot in the leg as she stood between a tank and three Palestinian children.[55]

Ramzi Kysia, a Muslim-American peace activist, also spent several weeks in Hebron with the team. He had previously worked in Iraq with Voices in the Wilderness, where he had met CPTer Anne Montgomery. In 2003, he would work with CPT's Iraq team prior to and during the initial invasion of U.S. forces.

Update covering December 5 notes that Polhamus and Anne Montgomery participated in an EAPPI organizational meeting in Jerusalem where participants affirmed that WCC volunteers needed to work on teams, like CPT did, rather than as individuals stationed with various organizations.

An August 26, 2002, WCC press release cited as an influence—in addition to CPT—a pilot Christian Accompaniment project carried by Danish and Icelandic church aid agencies that ran from March to July of 2002. World Council of Churches, "First group of ecumenical accompaniers begin work in Palestine and Israel." See also February 11, 2002, WCC releases, "Ecumenical solidarity and action promised in Palestinian-Israeli conflict" and "Ecumenical efforts towards peace in the Israeli-Palestinian conflict."

Updates mentioning the presence of EA's (Ecumenical Accompaniers) include CPTnet, "HEBRON UPDATE: March 18–30, 2003," April 9, 2003, and CPTnet, "HEBRON UPDATE: April 7–20, 2003," April 25, 2003. As of 2008, EAPPI was continuing its work in various locations around Israel and Palestine. See http://www.eappi.org.

54. John Lynes, of the Quaker Peace and Social Witness, UK, also spent significant time with the team in the fall of 2002 and winter 2003. He became a CPT full-timer in 2004.

55. CPTnet, "HEBRON UPDATE: February 14–18, 2002," March 9, 2004; CPTnet. "HEBRON UPDATE: February 19–22," March 12, 2004. See Barlow, "Courage under fire," for an account of the shooting that injured Butterly. Shortly after the Beit Ummar project started, the update covering April 10 noted that "Everywhere in Beit Ummar, children and adults ask about Caoimhe"—who was then in Arafat's compound. CPT Beit Ummar, "Beit Ummar Update: April 8–April 12, 2002." (This update never appeared on CPTnet.)

Interestingly, Palestinian friends of CPT who were very critical of Arafat and the Palestinian Authority —mostly because of their corrupt and undemocratic practices—still urged the Hebron team to go to Arafat's compound.

Sue Rhodes, a sixty-four-year-old British ISMer, came over in December 2001, went through the short training that CPT had begun providing for ISM volunteers, and participated in setting up a house for International Women's Peace Service in the Palestinian village of Hares, near Nablus, which was suffering from a high degree of soldier and settler violence. She visited the team in January 2002 and told them that she realized that she wanted to work with a faith-based, rather than secular organization. After joining the January Middle East delegation, she continued to work with the team and then went through the July 2002 training. Rhodes died of liver cancer in November 2003. A tribute on the CPT web site read as follows:

> She came most into her own when talking with Israeli soldiers while shepherding Palestinian children to school. We are fortunate to have some of these scenes recorded on videotape—the quality of interaction justifies their use as training films. And always, as a member of the team, Sue was taking care of her teammates.
>
> Sue Rhodes waited nearly forty years to work full-time for justice and peace in Israel/Palestine, and Christian Peacemaker Teams waited fifteen years for Sue Rhodes. We in CPT are grateful for the time we had together.[56]

The high-profile nonviolent interventions that ISM volunteers conducted in Ramallah, Bethlehem, and Nablus caused a crackdown by the Israeli government on many internationals entering the country and the deportation of others. In their update covering April 2, 2002, the team noted:

> Although the Israeli Minister of the Interior had issued orders to prevent "leftist extremists" from entering the country and issued deportation orders for dozens of French and Italian activists, the seven-member CPT delegation entered Israel at Ben Gurion airport without incident.[57]

Unfortunately, the Israeli Ministry of the Interior, which was scrutinizing internationals more closely, caught three CPTers—Michael Goode,

---

56. CPT Hebron, "Sue Rhodes." Kristin Anderson and Rich Meyer both spent time with Rhodes in England on their way to Hebron during her last days. See also Rollins' tribute to Sue Rhodes, CPTnet, "HEBRON: Remembering Sue Rhodes, The Woman Who Heard the Tree Scream," December 3, 2003.

57. CPTnet, "HEBRON UPDATE: March 26, April 3, 2004," April 4, 2002. CPT delegations during this period often plugged themselves into actions planned by ISM and other activist organizations.

Kurtis Unger, and Kathleen Kern—in its radar and denied them entry into Israel on June 23, August 30, and October 23, 2002, respectively.

None of them had ever been formally arrested—the ostensible cause for Wendy Lehman, Cliff Kindy, and Robert Naiman being barred from the country.[58] To address the issues of these deportations, CPT launched a fax campaign to Israeli consulates and embassies. The organization asked its constituents to tell the Israeli authorities they were monitoring the case and express concern about what it meant when the Israeli government denied entry to committed peace activists. The urgent action release included a portion of Kern's letter to Rafael Barak, Israel's Deputy Chief of Mission, whom the State Department told Kern to contact at the Israeli Embassy:

> Given that Christian Peacemaker Teams and I are absolutely committed to nonviolence, I am certain that we do not represent a security risk to the state of Israel. I believe that we actually enhance Israel's security, by connecting the Palestinians we work among with Israelis who care about their human rights . . . .
>
> It is in the best interests of the Israeli public that internationals trained in nonviolent theory and practice live among Palestinians in the territories and support Palestinian grassroots nonviolent resistance to the Occupation. It is in the best interests of the Israeli public for nonviolent activists to intervene when they see settlers and soldiers brutalizing Palestinians, because these interventions help decrease the feelings of helplessness and rage that can be channeled into violent resistance.
>
> If Palestinians believe their goal to end the Occupation can be accomplished nonviolently, there will be many fewer dead Israelis. And fewer dead Israelis and Palestinians is something that my coworkers and I truly yearn for."[59]

---

58. The Israeli government had also turned away Duane Ediger in 1993, when he went to join CPT's temporary presence in Gaza. (See Introduction.)

59. Although the fax campaign referred to Kern's deportation specifically—given her high profile as CPTnet editor and co-founder of the Hebron team—the campaign was meant to address the larger issue of deportations of peace activists as a whole. Kern met with Rafael Barak in November 2002, who told her that she should send him references of Israeli friends and that he would get back to her once he heard something from the Israeli Ministry of the Interior, which was on strike at the time. As of May 2004, the Interior Ministry had still not responded to Barak's query, according to a May 5 letter he wrote to Kern.

See CPTnet releases: "CHICAGO: CPTer Michael Goode refused entry to Israel," June 25, 2002; "CHICAGO/TORONTO: Unger denied entry into Israel," September 4, 2002; "CHRISTIAN PEACEMAKER DENIED ENTRY TO ISRAEL," October 24, 2002; "URGENT ACTION: Support CPTer Asking for Review of 'Entry Denied.'"

SCHOOL ACCOMPANIMENT

The school year of 2002–2003 was a particularly difficult one for the children of Hebron and consequently for the team. Team members repeatedly told soldiers about the agreement stipulating children could go to school, and soldiers repeatedly checked with their commanders who then acknowledged that there was such an agreement. However, these orders never seemed to carry over from day to day, leaving the impression that the Israeli military preferred not to allow children to go to school. One soldier told Dianne Roe and Kathleen Kern on March 5, 2002, that the orders to close Qurtuba School were coming "from very high up."[60] By the end of October, soldiers had closed the schools thirteen times. Between November 15 and December 11, the military allowed schools to open only twice.[61]

More disturbing than the refusal of soldiers to let children travel to school were actual attacks by soldiers on the schools—particularly the Ma'aref Boys' School and the adjoining Khadijaa Girls' school. These attacks were often responses to boys throwing stones,[62] but sometimes appeared to happen without provocation. Several times during the year, soldiers fired tear gas into the schools' courtyards. Lorne Friesen, a CPT reservist, describes soldiers' use of tear gas as "relatively frequent" for the six weeks he served in Hebron from mid-December 2002 to the end of January 2003. "On one day," he wrote, "the soldiers apparently fired five rounds of tear gas into the girls' school before anyone arrived in school."[63]

Other forms of harassment involved soldiers in jeeps "charging" at the hundreds of students walking to classes and injuring students and teachers by shooting them with rubber bullets.[64]

60. CPTnet, "HEBRON UPDATE: March 1–6, 2002," March 18, 2002.

61. CPTnet, "HEBRON UPDATE: October 28-November 15, 2002," November 21, 2002; CPTnet, "HEBRON UPDATE: December 6–13, 2002," December 19, 2002.

62. Sometimes the boys threw stones at the CPTers as well, while they mocked and harassed them. The update covering March 21, 2002, records Kathleen Kern and Mary Lawrence telling one of the headmasters that they would not continue patrolling the area if the adults did not stop the children from throwing stones. The update notes, "the headmaster of the Ibrahimi school took names of the boys so that he could speak with their parents later and seemed pleased that he could reciprocate the CPTers' protection. The stone throwers were generally not boys who attended school, and Palestinian teachers reassured team members by saying that sometimes the teachers got stoned too." CPTnet, "HEBRON UPDATE: March 18–21," April 4, 2002.

63. E-mail to author, June 14, 2004.

64. CPTnet, "HEBRON UPDATE: March 18–21," April 4, 2002; CPTnet, "HEBRON UPDATE: August 25–30," September 17, 2002.

The updates also frequently mention settler attacks on Palestinian school children and teachers, particularly the hard-pressed students and teachers at Qurtuba School opposite Beit Hadassah. These attacks included vandalizing of the school itself, e.g., breaking windows and spray-painting Hebrew insults on the walls—neither of which could have passed unobserved by soldiers.

NEW DIRECTIONS

As Israeli, Palestinian, and international nonviolent resistance to the occupation increasingly became a part of the Al-Aqsa Intifada throughout the West Bank and Gaza, the Hebron team began to explore setting up satellite projects. Eventually, it settled on locations in Beit Ummar and Jerusalem for these projects.

Beit Ummar

Beit Ummar is an agricultural village of about 12,000 people located in the northern part of the Hebron district. Despite the size of the village, the inhabitants have a more cosmopolitan attitude than most of the residents in Hebron. Many have studied overseas, and several families are the product of mixed Jewish-Palestinian marriages. Palestinian women can walk in the streets of Beit Ummar without their head covered more comfortably than women can in Hebron.

The Hebron team became involved in the lives of Beit Ummar's residents in 1997 after more than a dozen families received home demolition orders. Dianne Roe, in particular, developed a network of friendships in the village, and when the Campaign for Secure Dwellings began in 1997, Beit Ummar, along with the Beqa'a Valley and the Al Sendas/Qilqis area, became a focal point. Team members often brought Israeli and international Jewish visitors there, because they knew that the inhabitants of Beit Ummar would treat them with less suspicion or reserve than a family in Hebron might. The home of Edna Sabarneh, in particular became a place of hospitality for dozens of visitors.[65] Ghazi Brigith, an employee of the Beit Ummar Municipality was a member of the Bereaved Families Network—a joint Israeli and Palestinian group comprising those who had lost family members to violence—and as such also welcomed sympathetic Israelis.

---

65. Sabarneh was an Israeli of Iraqi-Kurdish descent who converted to Islam and became the second wife of her Palestinian husband.

Most of the families facing demolition lived along a stretch of road 60 (which also runs through the Beqa'a Valley), between Aroub refugee camp to the North and the turnoff for the settlement of Karmei Tzur to the south. While the home demolition policy affected at least twenty-three households, hundreds more were affected by the parallel issue of land confiscation, especially those families whose land lay adjacent to settlements. In the spring of 1998, the settlements of Karmei Tzur and Gush Etzion expanded onto Beit Ummar land from the south and north respectively. The proximity to settlements also led to attacks by settlers on Palestinians as they tried to harvest fruit from their orchards and vineyards (for which Beit Ummar is famous).

In 2002, Israeli soldiers began making almost nightly incursions into Beit Ummar. They shot up the village, vandalized cars, water tanks, and homes, conducted midnight raids into various homes, and rounded up men at random for questioning and beating.[66]

On April 8, 2002, Dianne Roe, Mary Lawrence, and JoAnne Lingle moved into an apartment in Beit Ummar shortly after the Israeli military had killed two young men from the community. The updates from Beit Ummar during this period record many visits to families with members who had been injured or killed by settlers and soldiers. Team members also traveled to the Aroub refugee camp and to smaller villages such as Shuyoukh, Jala, Surif, Beit Fajjar, and Al Jabah located near Beit Ummar.

Possibly the most significant help the Hebron and Beit Ummar teams provided to the residents of Beit Ummar and surrounding villages between April and November 2002 involved accompanying farmers as they harvested their crops—the main source of revenue for Beit Ummar residents. The previous summer, the Israeli military had prevented farmers getting their produce to the market, barricading the road between the market and Bypass Road 60 and shooting at farmers in the market. After the fruit was left to rot, Beit Ummar Mayor Rashid Awad estimated that farmers and the municipality had lost five million shekels.[67]

66. An incident relayed by ISMer Caoimhe Butterly (see above) testifies to the randomness of this violence. She spent a night in Beit Ummar with a family whose son soldiers had taken on the previous night. A daughter of the household who understood Hebrew learned from the soldiers' radio conversation that they realized they had entered the wrong house. Nevertheless, the soldiers began interrogating her brothers, and took one into custody. When she asked why, they told her, "Because we want to." When she implored them not to beat her brother, another soldier said, "We're not animals." CPTnet, "HEBRON UPDATE: February 14–18, 2002," March 9, 2002.

67. CPTnet, "BEIT UMMAR UPDATE: May 13–19, 2002," May 25, 2002.

On August 9, 2002, the Beit Ummar team put out an urgent action release asking constituents to write to Canadian and American legislators regarding Israel's refusal to allow the farmers of Beit Ummar to reach their land. In June, settlers from Karmei Tzur had expanded the settlement's borders by 300 meters (doubling the acreage of Karmei Tzur), built a road that destroyed dozens of fruit trees, and prevented farmers from harvesting their plums, which fell to the ground and spoiled.[68]

This land confiscation was one of several unfortunate events that occurred while the Beit Ummar project was on hiatus due to lack of personnel. Between May 22, 2002, when the project closed and July 13, 2002, when it reopened, soldiers conducted mass arrests, made most of the roads in and out of the village impassable, and refused to let farmers work in their fields.[69]

A May 27, 2002, roundup was especially brutal. The Israeli military went door-to-door in Beit Ummar, ordering eighty-five men between the ages of sixteen and seventy to report to the checkpoint and forced them to remain there all night. Soldiers beat many of them, including a mentally retarded man, and broke the arm of another man. They also shot up two homes. When the women of the village approached to check on their husbands, sons and fathers, the soldiers tear-gassed them. The mayor went to the checkpoint the next morning to intercede for the captives, and the soldiers forced him to stand in the sun for three hours, kicked him, and struck him with a gun butt. One of the team's Beit Ummar translators later told the team, "They spoke to us like we were insects. . . . There aren't enough words to express how disrespectful they were."[70]

A Palestinian gunmen killed two settlers and a soldier in Karmei Tzur on June 8, which may have precipitated the subsequent confiscation of Beit Ummar orchards.[71] The murders and CPT activities in Beit Ummar that had occurred shortly before led to some interesting rumor mongering

---

68. Ibid. See also CPTnet, "BEIT UMMAR URGENT ACTION: Allow Palestinian farmers to get to their land," August 9, 2002.

69. CPTnet, "HEBRON UPDATE: June 2–7, 2002," June 21, 2002. See also CPTnet, "HEBRON: Farmers, CPTers negotiate with Israeli military in fields of Halhoul," July 4, 2002.

70. CPTnet, "HEBRON DISTRICT: Israeli army rounds up eighty-five men in Beit Ummar," May 27, 2002.

71. Shragai and Harel, "Fences may not mean more security for settlers." CPTnet, "HEBRON UPDATE: June 9–16, 2002," June 28, 2002. CPTnet, "HEBRON UPDATE: June 30–July 6, 2002," July 15, 2002.

among partisans of Israel in 2004. On May 22, 2002, team members had photographed the confiscation of land from Halhoul, which also borders Karmei Tzur, where they had encountered settler guards and Israeli soldiers who exposed Kathy Kamphoefner's film and confiscated Bob Holmes's digital camera card. Holmes had fortunately slipped the card containing photos of the bulldozed land in a pocket.[72] In 2004, Johnathan Galt pointed to a website that linked the photos from May 22, a CPT nonviolence training with Fatah youth activists in Bethlehem and the June 8, 2002, settler deaths in Karmei Tzur:

> In late May, 2002, a settlement watch group organized by the "Christian Peace Makers Team" reported to its E-mail list that it had successfully photographed the fence surrounding the Carmei Tzur settlement. The CPT proudly reported that it had shown several breaches in the fence. The next day, the CSM (sic) met with the Fateh (Arafat's mainstream terror group) in Bethlehem. Two days later, late at night, armed members of the Fateh infiltrated the Carmei Tzur settlement at the precise breach that the CPT had photographed. The Fateh used that breach to murder a civilian couple in their bed. The wife was eight months pregnant.[73]

Rich Meyer sent the following E-mail to Johnathan Galt on May 24, 2004, under the subject heading," RE: allegations made against CPT on a Jewish website":

> Dear Johnathan,
>
> Thank you for contacting us about these serious but mistaken allegations. Please inform your sources of the following:
> 1. On May 22, 2002, members of Christian Peacemaker Teams went to Beit Ummar to document the bulldozing of three dunums (3/4 acre) of a Palestinian farmer's land by settlers from Karmei Tzur. They did this with photos of the damage done to the land, which was just outside the fence of the military base near Karmei Tzur. The fence surrounding the area was solid and continuous—so much so that the soldiers (inside the fence) had to drive out the gate and around the outside to meet the CPTers. There were no breaches in the fence.
> 2. The settlers who were killed on June 8, 2002 were in an expansion of Karmei Tzur that had no fence at all around it. In the Jerusalem Post reports of the killing (June 9), an IDF spokesper-

---

72. CPTnet, Holmes, "HEBRON DISTRICT: Angry Settlers," June 4, 2002.
73. http://www.israelbehindthenews.com/#research.

> son was asked by the reporter if a fence around the new settlement expansion would have helped, and the IDF spokesperson replied in the negative. The complete lack of fencing there makes the entire charge against CPT nonsense. The documentation by members of Christian Peacemaker Teams of the damage to the farmland outside the fence of the military base cannot have had any connection to the killing of settlers in an unfenced expansion of Karmei Tzur. Our participation in nonviolence training for a group of youth in Bethlehem later in June also cannot have had any connection to the killing of those settlers on June 8.
>
> Christian Peacemaker Teams is opposed to violence by any party against any party. Thanks for your inquiry, and I trust that you can ask the owners of the website making these false accusations to remove them.[74]

After CPT reopened the Beit Ummar project in July 2002, the updates record a more violent atmosphere than when the team was there in April and May. Indeed, the increase in violence was such that ISM organizers decided to open their own project in Beit Ummar.

The day after the CPT project reopened, soldiers shot out the village's telephone connections box, which cut all phone service between Beit Ummar and Hebron. They also detained thirty-two men from 10:00 PM to 3:00 AM and kept them standing in a 3x5 meter iron cage opposite the checkpoint on Road 60. They threatened the men with teargas and the arrest of their wives and children if they complained. Two days later, soldiers moved through the town shooting out the town's electrical transformer, streetlights, and water tanks on houses and the school. While the soldiers shot up another area of town, Dianne Roe and Greg Rollins provided accompaniment for a municipal employee while he fixed the transformer.[75] For the next weeks, the team recorded many incidents of apparently random shooting by soldiers in the village.

The Beit Ummar project closed for the winter because farmers no longer needed accompaniment to their fields, orchards, and vineyards. Additionally, the soldier brigade that replaced the brigade that had conducted the random shootings did not abuse the human rights of village residents as much. More importantly, Hebron was in crisis following the shootings of the soldiers and settler security guards on November 15, 2002

---

74. Meyer, e-mail to Johnathan Galt, May 24, 2004.

75. CPTnet, "HEBRON DISTRICT: Israeli military shoots up Beit Ummar," July 17, 2002.

(see above), and the Hebron team needed extra people. Although the team maintained the option of reopening the project when the weather got warmer, autumn 2002 marked the end of the Beit Ummar project.[76]

Rapid Response Team

The Rapid Response satellite project set up in Jerusalem on October 4, 2002, was less successful than the Beit Ummar satellite project. The original intent of the Rapid Response project was to have CPTers on hand as a violence-deterring presence in other cities hard hit by the Israeli military rather than just reacting to and documenting this violence after it happened. Because the International Solidarity Movement was already covering the northern West Bank, CPT began exploring possibilities for presences in Bethlehem, Beit Sahour, Jerusalem, and Gaza.

Team members eventually decided to base themselves in Jerusalem and respond as quickly as possible to scenes of bombings there. They hoped to provide a pastoral ministry to Israeli and Palestinian victims. A release announcing the beginning of the project quoted Rich Meyer as saying,

> Each Israeli helicopter missile shot into a Palestinian home and each Palestinian suicide bombing is another step up the ladder of escalating violence. We cannot predict these attacks in advance. The Rapid Response team will try to get to the scene as quickly as possible to offer a pastoral and compassionate presence.[77]

Only two releases about the Rapid Response team's work between October 2002 and February 2003 appeared on CPTnet—both of them letters written by British CPTer Sue Rhodes to her supporters. One of them detailed a vicious attack on the city of Khan Younis in Gaza. After Israeli tanks rolling through the streets had ceased shooting in all directions, people came out of their homes to check on neighbors and friends. An Apache attack helicopter fired a rocket into one crowd leaving dozens of dead, dying, and wounded people in the street. Nasser hospital, which was close to the attack, received seventy patients requiring emergency surgery. Sixteen people died. Rhodes noted that Israelis described the attack as "a successful operation."

Two days later, Rhodes wrote a letter from Nablus:

76. Bob Holmes, e-mail to author, June 15, 2004; Dianne Roe, e-mail to author, June 17, 2004; Greg Rollins, e-mail to author, June 18, 2004.

77. CPTnet, "JERUSALEM: CPT Rapid Response team begins work," October 4, 2004.

The sight of a home completely flattened with the children playing in the rubble, pulling at odd bits of material is sickening. Two kittens were fighting over a fragment of animal bone and neither had the strength to get a purchase on the morsel.

The owner of one home was screaming at us in agitation . . . His 3 storey home was just a heap of stone and dust and he had a family of six. "What you think we are going to do? No home no house no clothes no food no money and no work." He was banging his fist on the wall of his workshop where all his metal cutting, grinding and drilling equipment was broken by a bomb which had exploded inside . . . And I just feel so totally helpless in these situations, but when he screamed, "You take your pictures and you go home and you forget all this and you leave me here with nothing," it did "rattle my cage" a bit . . .[78]

CPTers in Jerusalem responded to one suicide attack there, but after hanging around the scene for thirty-five to forty-five minutes did not see much opportunity for them to help. Most often, CPTers in Jerusalem simply supplied bodies for organizations such as Rabbis for Human Rights when they needed workers to help Palestinians living near settlements pick olives or help with other activities. In February 2003, the team closed the apartment in Jerusalem, because the Hebron project needed the human and financial resources more.[79] The Hebron team would set up its next satellite project in September 2004, in the southern Hebron District, when CPTers began accompanying Palestinian schoolchildren from the village of Tuba to a central school in the village of At-Tuwani (see chapter 9).

---

78. CPTnet, "Gaza: 'A successful operation,' A letter from Sue Rhodes"; CPTnet, "NABLUS: Letter from Sue Rhodes," October 18, 2002.

79. Greg Rollins, e-mail to author, June 18, 2002. Anne Montgomery, e-mail to author June 20, 2004.

Part Four

Too Long a Sacrifice
The Intifada 2003–2005

Too long a sacrifice
Can make a stone of the heart.
O when may it suffice?

W. B. Yeats, "Easter 1916"

EIGHT

Resistance, Repression, and Restrictions
2003

BY 2003, MOST OBSERVERS of the Al-Aqsa Intifada had stopped looking for silver linings peeping behind ever-murkier, ever-more-toxic nimbuses of human suffering. A list of prayer requests the Hebron team sent out in early February 2003 set the tone for the year:

> The Christian Peacemaker Team in Hebron has been working long, busy days. These reflect the escalation of violence as both Israeli and Palestinian warmakers act to drive the lopsided, deadly conflict euphemistically known as the "situation" further into the abyss.
> Here are some of the crises that the team has been dealing with:
> - The closure of Hebron University by the Israeli military January 14. There are difficulties with keeping Palestinian schools at all levels open, and soldiers have teargassed CPTers and children on their way to school. (We may make a special appeal through our supporters at educational institutions for help to re-open Hebron University and other schools.)
> - Land confiscation in the Beqa'a valley. Israeli settlers have renewed their building of a network of roads on lands they are confiscating from Palestinians in the agriculturally rich valley. (The Hebron Team has conducted tours of this area for European and North American diplomats.)
> - The killing of Netanel Ozeri, an Israeli settler, in the Beqa'a on January 17. Two Palestinian gunmen killed him and injured his five-year-old daughter at the door of his home, an outpost settlement where he was attempting to confiscate more of the valley. The two gunmen were killed by Netanel's friends and Israeli soldiers, and then several thousand settlers went on a

rampage through the Beqa'a burning cars, smashing windows and beating Palestinians. Four or five Palestinians were taken to the hospital.
- The increasing brutality of the Israeli soldiers in Hebron. Many Israeli soldiers are targeting individuals and their families, seemingly at random. CPTers respond to calls for help following unprovoked soldier beatings, attempted rape or imprisonment without due process. Either military discipline is breaking down, or the Israeli soldiers are trying to make life for Palestinians in Hebron so miserable that they either leave or explode. (Following past patterns, the Israeli settlers can use either reaction to take more land.)
- House demolitions are increasing. There are fourteen families in Beit Mirsim and Al Burj who were given ten days notice of planned demolition on January 13. (Team members hope to bring embassy personnel to visit these villages.) On February 3, the Israeli military demolished twenty-two Palestinian structures in the Beqa'a Valley. The Israeli newspaper Ha'Aretz said the demolitions were likely in retaliation for the killings of Ozeri and several Israeli soldiers in Hebron.
- What Sharon may do if the U. S. attacks Iraq. Many Israelis and Palestinians fear that Sharon will use the fact that the world's attention is focused elsewhere to confiscate more Palestinian land and drive large numbers of Palestinians from their homes. Some Israeli peace activists believe that Sharon used the death of the Columbia astronauts as a cover for the demolitions on February 3.

CPT Hebron is trying to decide where we can be the most help with the most urgent need. Tonight we ask for your continued prayer, for these particular crises, and for the Palestinian and Israeli peoples in general.[1]

HOME DEMOLITIONS

As was the case in 2002, the Israeli military demolished homes in 2003 both to facilitate Israel's confiscation of Palestinian land and in reprisal for attacks by Palestinian militants.

In January, the villages of Beit Mirsim and El Buraj received demolition orders. Beit Mirsim had been switched to Area B from Area C after the Wye River negotiations in 1998, which meant that demolition orders on most of the homes in the village were revoked. Unilaterally moving the border,

1. CPTnet, "HEBRON: Prayer requests from the Hebron Team," February 6, 2003.

the Sharon government then claimed that seven homes were on the Israeli side of the green line.[2] The team put out an urgent action release to the CSD network (which did not appear on CPTnet) calling the CSD partners to send faxes to Colin Powell and Senator Richard Lugar. A second release went out on September 16, 2003, the day after the Israeli military destroyed nine buildings in the Beqa'a Valley and the southern edge of Hebron. Musa al-Rajabi, whose home had housed three families with thirty-one children, told the team, "Bush wants to win over Saddam and Sharon wants to win over Arafat. And who pays the price for all this? The poor."

These demolitions occurred at the time when the George W. Bush administration was touting its "Roadmap to Peace" plan for the Middle East, which stipulated Israel had to stop confiscating land and expanding settlements. The team's urgent action release quoted Jeff Halper, chair of the Israeli Committee Against House Demolitions, as saying, "Western countries tell Palestinians to use the political process rather than violence while the Israeli government demolishes homes. The countries sponsoring the Roadmap should insist these demolitions stop."[3]

Two other major demolition crises the team dealt with in 2003 fell into both avarice and reprisal categories: the homes involved were regarded both as security risks and conveniently situated on land that the settlement of Kiryat Arba wished to confiscate.

On February 3, 2003, the Israeli military demolished twenty-two structures in the Hebron area, including homes, garages, animal pens, and cisterns, all of which lay close to Israeli settlements. Israeli spokespersons gave as reasons for the demolitions, "security measures" and "standard enforcement of building rules." However, the Israeli paper *Ha'aretz* noted that the demolitions had occurred in reprisal for the killings of three soldiers and a settler the previous week in Hebron. The Israeli peace group, Gush Shalom, speculated that the authorities had also taken advantage of the death of Israeli astronaut Ilan Ramon, in the space shuttle disaster on February 1, 2003. The Gush Shalom activists believed that the fact the

---

2. CPTnet, "HEBRON UPDATE: January 13–23, 2003," January 31, 2003. Earlier team releases transliterated the village's name as "Beit Miersam."

3. The building that housed the families headed by the three al-Rajabi brothers had first received a demolition order in 1987. The brothers received the second demolition order on September 14, 2003, and their lawyer was appearing in court on the morning of the 15th, at the time soldiers were demolishing the homes, to contest the demolitions. CPTnet, "HEBRON: Israel demolishes nine buildings in Hebron Area," September 15, 2003; CPTnet, "HEBRON URGENT ACTION: Stop demolitions that leave families homeless," September 16, 2003.

media was covering Ramon's death "to the virtual exclusion of anything else," had provided cover for the demolitions.[4]

On March 7, 2003, two Palestinians from Hamas entered the Kiryat Arba settlement disguised as Orthodox Jews. They killed Rabbi Eliahu Horowitz and his wife Dina in their home and wounded eight others. According to the army, the assassins entered from the Jabel Johar neighborhood—where the team had spent so much time with the Shakir Dana family in 1995 and with their neighbors after the November 15, 2002, deadly ambush on soldiers and settlers (see chapter 7).

Following the murders, Israeli military bulldozers—along with six or seven settlers—razed nine dunams (about two acres of land) in Jabel Johar, destroying olive trees, grape vines, almond trees, and vegetables as well as four sheep pens. The Samia Dana family received a confiscation notice for the demolished land about a month later. Team members went out to Jabal Johar on March 9 and watched settlers and soldiers destroying crops. As William Payne began filming, a settler threatened to shoot him. Another threw rocks at Payne and tried to push a member of TIPH off a rock ledge.

About a month later, on April 5, 2003, a Hamas militant attacked Kiryat Arba, prompting a gun battle in which he was killed and another member of the Dana family, Yazid 'Imad Dana, was shot in the knee. Ambulance personnel waited for three hours before they received permission from the Israeli military to take him to the hospital. Shortly before midnight, the military flattened a plot of land with fruit trees on it and demolished an animal pen, a well, and a vacant house. Dozens of settlers began attacking homes in Jabel Johar, breaking windows. When soldiers summoned Samia Dana's father—who had had open-heart surgery a month earlier—to come out for interrogation, settlers began beating him and the soldiers told him to run back into the house. At 3:00 AM the army ordered the seventeen-member 'Abd al-Halim Dana family to evacuate and shelled their house.

The army put up a razor-wire fence on April 13, 2003, around the plot of land that formerly held the fruit trees, telling Samia Dana it was doing so for security reasons. When Kristin Anderson and Payne went out to observe, soldiers informed them that they could not document the fencing

---

4. CPTnet, "HEBRON: Israel demolishes twenty-two Palestinian buildings," February 3, 2003; CPTnet, "HEBRON UPDATE: January 30–February 4, 2003." The settler, Netanel Ozeri was killed on January 18, 2003, and the three soldiers killed on the evening of January 23, near the industrial zone at the southern edge of Hebron.

nor the bulldozing; they could not stay and observe, but at the same time were not allowed to leave the vicinity or Hebron. The two CPTers eventually left without the soldiers stopping them.

Three days later, the Civil Administration sent a letter saying Israel was confiscating the land in question and that the homes of Samia, Abd al-Halim, and Shakir Dana would be demolished. Although the letter stated that the families could raise objections within ninety-six hours, families received the letters two days into the Passover holiday, when all offices in Israel are closed for a week.[5]

The team learned on April 22, 2003, that eighteen internationals with the International Civilian Committee for the Protection of the Palestinian People (CCIPPP) had begun staying with the Danas in hopes of deterring the demolitions and nightly soldier harassment. The team put out an urgent action release on behalf of the Dana families on April 26, 2003, and began staying in the area along with the CCIPPP volunteers on April 25. On May 16, the team put out an urgent prayer request to its constituents, noting that the families' Israeli lawyer was able to get a stay on the demolition of the homes because no violence had ever been attributed to family members. "On the contrary," the request noted, "they have experienced considerable violence from Israeli settlers. These homes, and about fifteen other homes of Palestinian families, stand in the way of Kiryat Arba settlement expansion plans." The Israeli High Court ruled that the military had until May 21, 2003, to appeal the stay of demolition. For the next six days, CPTers stayed with the families at their request.[6]

Other homes in Hebron, most of which were not located near Israeli settlements, were clearly demolished in retaliation for attacks on Israelis.

---

5. B'tselem, "Hebron, Area H-2: Settlements Cause Mass Departure of Palestinians." In her April 23, 2003, CPTnet, reflection, "Passing Over," Hebron Team member Diane Janzen connected the threats to the Dana families and Exodus 12:26–27, which referred to the Lord passing over the houses of the Israelites at the time He "struck down the Egyptians."

For CPT involvement with the Jabel Johar families during this period, see CPTnet, "HEBRON UPDATE: February 28–March 10, 2004," March 22, 2003; CPTnet, Chris Brown, "HEBRON: The Almond Trees," March 10, 2003; CPTnet, "HEBRON UPDATE: April 7–20, 2003," April 25, 2003.

6. See CPTnet releases: "HEBRON URGENT ACTION: Stop demolition of homes near Kiryat Arba," April 26, 2003; Rollins, "HEBRON: The scenery around an expanding settlement," April 26, 2003; "HEBRON UPDATE: April 21–27, 2003," May 2, 2003; "HEBRON URGENT PRAYER REQUEST: Hold Dana families and their homes in prayer," May 16, 2003; "HEBRON UPDATE: May 5–18, 2003," June 3, 2003. According to a June 23, 2004 E-mail from Greg Rollins, the homes were still standing at the time he wrote.

On March 10, 2003, the team put out a release, "We Lament the Loss of Life," noting that hundreds of Israelis had attended the funeral of the Horowitzes—the middle-aged couple killed in Kiryat Arba—and hundreds of Palestinians had attended the funeral of the four young men who had carried out the attack. The release continued

> Yesterday morning three Palestinian homes in this city were demolished in retaliation for the local attacks and for a suicide-bombing attack in Haifa several days ago. Today, so many people here must grieve the loss of their loved ones. For some, they must face homelessness even as they grieve the loss of their sons. When will the cycle of pain, anger and suffering end?
>
> Christian Peacemaker Teams denounces all violence, especially lethal violence. We call on Israelis to remember that Palestinians are made in the image and likeness of God. We call on Palestinians to remember that Israelis are made in the image and likeness of God. We especially call on Christians, particularly those in North America, to remember that Jesus rejects all violence, all war. Our money is paying for so much death.[7]

On May 26, the Israeli military blew up two homes near Hebron University belonging to families of suicide bombers who had attacked Israeli buses in Jerusalem on May 18, 2003, killing twenty-three people and injuring a hundred and twenty-five. The families lived in apartment buildings, so more than eighty people had their homes destroyed or damaged after the military set off the dynamite in the apartment of the militants' families. A field worker for B'tselem told the team that the destruction of the building marked the first time that the military had imposed such measures on people who were not close relatives of the bombers.[8]

On June 9, soldiers blew up a home in the Old City where two gunmen involved in a shooting near the Ibrahimi Mosque were hiding. This demolition took place in an area of the Old City that the Hebron Rehabilitation Committee (HRC) was refurbishing with the help of donations from the European Union. The homes were almost ready for former owners and other Palestinians to inhabit. Early in the next month, the Rehabilitation Committee received a "Stop work" order from the Israeli military, which resulted in nearly four hundred builders and artisans losing their jobs and greatly increased demands on the Old City soup kitchen.

---

7. CPTnet, "HEBRON UPDATE: February 28–March 10, 2003," March 22, 2003; CPTnet, "HEBRON: We Lament the Loss of Life," March 10, 2003.

8. CPTnet, Brown, "HEBRON: Israeli military blows up two homes," May 29, 2003.

(In her release, "Hebron builders return to work," Sue Rhodes described the anxious faces of children watching to see if there was enough soup to go around.) A release that the team put out on its direct list, but never appeared on CPTnet, prompted calls from the donor countries to the Israeli government for more information, and the team sent a letter to UNESCO at the request of the HRC, regarding falling debris from bombed buildings. The team noted that this debris posed a significant danger to the curious children in the neighborhood, but the Israeli military refused to allow the HRC to come in to stabilize the building. On July 23, after international pressure, the Israeli military rescinded the "stop work" order and the men returned.

Four days after the June 9 destruction of the home in the Old City, the military blew up the home of an eighteen-year old suicide bomber who had killed seventeen and injured seventy Israelis in a Jerusalem bombing. He had been a student at Hebron's Polytechnic University.[9] Later in the month, on June 26, 2003, the military demolished a home on the southern edge of Hebron belonging to a man whose son was serving an eight-year jail sentence for his activities in Hamas.

In October, soldiers demolished the kitchen of a home at Tel Rumeida after soldiers killed a gunman who had shot and wounded two settlers near the settlement on October 22, 2003. The young militant had no connection with the family who lost their kitchen nor with the three families whose homes the Israeli military sealed after the shooting incident.[10]

The Israeli military destroyed several more homes in 2003 as a byproduct of assassinating militants. On August 15, they demolished a building with rockets and then forced the owner to go inside the remains and look for people there. Soldiers later found the body of Mohammed Sidar, an Islamic Jihad activist behind the building. On September 9, the military shelled a building in the neighborhood of Hebron University where two Hamas activists were hiding. The bombardments killed an eleven-year-old boy and

---

9. CPTnet, "HEBRON UPDATE: June 9–20, 2003," June 24, 2003. The Update notes that along with the Polytechnic student's house the "home of a previous bomber in Hebron" was also demolished, but does not say where.

See CPTnet releases: "HEBRON: Israeli military halts restoration in Old City," July 6, 2003; "HEBRON UPDATE: June 29–July 6, 2003," July 16, 2003; Pierce, "HEBRON: Bombed building poses danger to children in the Old City," July 20, 2003; Rhodes, "HEBRON: Hebron Builders Return to Work," August 1, 2003; "HEBRON UPDATE: July 7–23, 2003," August 6, 2003.

10. CPTnet, "HEBRON UPDATE: June 21–28, 2003," June 30, 2003. CPTnet, "HEBRON: Crime and Punishment," October 27, 2003.

gravely injured a thirteen-year-old girl and a young father. After soldiers killed the two militants, the building collapsed from the shelling, leaving twenty-six families homeless with their possessions buried beneath the ruins. On September 22, a Palestinian militant entered the home of a woman and her mentally handicapped son in the Haroos neighborhood, forcing them out of their house. Soldiers then destroyed the building with shells.[11]

LAND CONFISCATION

The Separation Barrier, Security Fence, Annexation Wall, Apartheid Wall (nomenclature indicates one's political leanings) that Israel began building in 2003 resulted in the confiscation of massive amounts of West Bank land and the destruction of hundreds of thousands of olive trees and other crops. According to the Sharon government, Israel built the wall to prevent terrorists from entering Israel. However, instead of building the wall along the 1967 border, Israel, beginning in the northern West Bank, constructed the wall so that it made deep incursions into Palestinian territory, sometimes encircling entire villages or even cities like Qalqilya.[12] Team members began participating in joint Israeli, Palestinian, and international demonstrations against the wall and tours of the wall's route as it cut through the northern West Bank.

They also began participating in strategy meetings with students and other local activists to prepare for the building of the wall in Hebron. According to Abdel Hadi Hantash, the chief cartographer of the Hebron District, the wall was slated to divide Hebron and connect Beit Hadassah, Beit Romano, Tel Rumeida, and Avraham Avinu to Kiryat Arba. Connecting the settlements would result in the confiscation of the entire Old City, along with the Ibrahimi Mosque/Cave of Machpelah. In an October report on the approaching wall, Kathy Kamphoefner noted that the Israeli army had fitted gates across all the eastern exits of the Old City, fenced off Shuhada Street, and restricted all access to it and the Old City via

---

11. See CPTnet releases: "HEBRON UPDATE: August 14–August 24, 2003," August 27, 2003; "HEBRON UPDATE: September 3–16, 2003," September 18, 2003; Williams, "HEBRON: CPT delegation documents human rights violations near destroyed building, September 23, 2003;" "HEBRON UPDATE: September 17–23, 2003," September 30, 2003.

12. See maps from the Applied Research Institute in Jerusalem (ARIJ), "Segregation Wall Path," and CPT Hebron bulletin insert, "Dividing Walls." Jaradat, "Hebron: Another Apartheid Wall in the Making." The initial plan for the barrier was approved by Ehud Barak's government in 2000.

Beit Romano. The military had also, by October 2003, forced hundreds of shops near the settlements to close—in some cases welding the doors shut. "In the big picture," Kamphoefner wrote, "the planned separation wall will encircle the entire Hebron district . . . Only a narrow gap will exist at the northern end of the district, shaped like a bottleneck, at the Gush Etzion checkpoint."[13]

The approaching wall thus began haunting the imaginations of Hebronites and CPTers. Several releases refer to people speculating that certain incidents had something to do with the wall. Residents near the settlement of Susia said that soldiers planted a landmine near their homes, detonated it, accused the residents of planting the mine, and set their houses on fire. A friend of the team told them he was sure that the soldiers' actions were part of a new campaign to get rid of Palestinians living in the path of the wall. In August, the Israeli military took over hilltops in Harit iSheikh and Abu Sneineh and built military camps in H-1, the area formerly ceded to Palestinian military control as part of the Oslo II agreement. Family members in Harit iSheikh whose land the military confiscated told Kathy Kamphoefner they believed the camps were meant to prepare for the wall dividing Hebron. In September 2003, the military put in two new roads and installed an enormous fence in Wadi Ghroos, site of the first demolition that CPT had witnessed and tried to prevent. The fence confiscated about one hundred acres of vineyards from their owners, most of whom already had demolition orders on their homes. Team members speculated in September and October releases that the Wadi Ghroos wall would eventually connect with the Annexation wall.[14]

As it turned out, the Wadi Ghroos wall probably had more to do with the Israeli decision to expand settlements by three hundred meters on all sides for security reasons.[15] Settlers doubled the size of Kiryat Arba and Givat Ha Harsina simply by erecting new fences outside the old,

---

13. CPTnet, "HEBRON: Wall slated to divide Hebron, take Abraham's Tomb," October 31, 2003.

14. See CPTnet releases: "HEBRON: New military camps go up Sunday night in H-1," August 21, 2003; "HEBRON UPDATE: September 3–16, 2003," September 18, 2003; "HEBRON: Israel fences in Wadi Ghroos, site of first home demolition CPT witnessed; soldier assaults children," September 12, 2003; "HEBRON UPDATE: October 1–7, 2003," October 18, 2003.

15. See Foundation for Middle East Peace, "Settlements Expand Security Perimeters," and CPTnet, "HEBRON UPDATE: January 13–23, 2003," January 31, 2003.

the way settlements had been expanding for years.[16] In other areas of the Hebron District, settlers also confiscated enormous amounts of land, seizures which, like the Wadi Ghroos confiscations, had little to do with the wall. Update after update records settlers bulldozing dozens of new roads and erecting fences that separated Palestinians from their fields, orchards, and vineyards—often the only source of income for the families living in these rural areas. Fences and roads also separated Palestinian villages and even neighbors from each other. Thousands of dunams were confiscated and razed, thousands of trees, grapevines, and other crops uprooted to make way for roads and fences connecting the settlements. As settlement construction crept nearer to Palestinian homes, the specter of new home demolitions arose.

Jerry Levin, in his August 2003 release "HEBRON: Catch-22," noted that the confiscation of farmland followed a basic pattern: settler security guards forbid Palestinians to enter their vineyards. Soldiers affirm the right of the Palestinians to work in their fields, but prevent farmers from entering "to protect them from the settlers." The Civil Administration, after the farmers complain, tells them they are in the right, but that it is the

---

16. In a June 25, 2004, e-mail to the author (responding to the question "Are the Wadi Ghroos, Harit iSheikh fences related to annexation wall?") Rich Meyer (coordinator of Campaign for Secure Dwellings and Hebron team support person) wrote,

> Currently the cabinet-approved Wall route does not include a finger up to Kiryat Arba. I think the fences in Wadi Ghroos and the Beqa'a are best described as standard leap-frogging-fence expansion of both KA and Harsina and a thickening of the connection between Kiryat Arba and Harsina. This does cut the Beqa'a off from Wadi Ghroos—at present only a few small breaks in the new fence allow pedestrians to pass.
>
> 1. Those military posts on Abu Sneineh and Haret es-Sheikh are just posts still, no "Wall" connects to them.
>
> 2. Ariel Sharon insists that Israel will keep Kiryat Arba and the Jewish community in Hebron. There are no developments that look like loosening the grip or shrinking the Israeli-only zone of downtown Hebron. The connection between KA and the in-town Israeli settlements is "Worshipers' Road" which is becoming more and more thoroughly off-limits to Palestinians. There is an effective separation now, and the Israeli-only areas keep expanding. I guess more Wall could go through anywhere, there where the military posts are or somewhere else.
>
> More home demolitions in the southern edge of the Hebron district seem related to placing the wall well north of the Green Line there. From past performance, I would say that at least as long as Sharon is in power, you can expect the Wall to come toward or to Hebron, eventually to surround KA, Harsina, and much of the center of H2.
>
> —Rich

soldiers' job to keep the settlers in line. After two to three years of preventing farmers from working in their fields, the Israeli government confiscates the fields, under the pretext that no one is working in them.[17]

As they had in 2002, the team gave tours of the Beqa'a Valley to European, American, and other international diplomats to show them the extent of the land-grabs by settlers, but these tours and the reports that resulted from them never seemed to have much of an effect.[18] Given the weaponry used by soldiers and settlers to oversee and maintain the confiscation of land, the residents of the Beqa'a and the Hebron team were almost literally fighting a losing battle.

CURFEWS AND CLOSURES

Curfew on the residents of the Old City and even the Bab iZawiyya area continued to intensify in 2003. The Israeli human rights organization, B'tselem, put out a report noting:

> In total, 169 families lived on the [main streets of the Old City] in September 2000, when the intifada began. Since then, seventy-three families—forty-three percent—have left their homes.
> Before the current intifada, Area H-2 was home to a wholesale market, a vegetable market, thousands of shops, and an industrial zone. Because of Israel's severe restriction on commercial activity in Area H-2, the city's commercial center has moved to Area H-1.
> Since the beginning of the intifada, 2,000 to 2,500 businesses have closed in the Casbah and Bab a-Zawiya.[19] There are five hundred shops on al-Casbah Street. Only fifteen of them are open for business; they open their doors once every few days for a few hours when the curfew is lifted. Of the ten bakeries and ten restaurants on the street that have closed, some have moved to Area H-1.
> The small al-Shalala Street contained 130 shops. All of them have

---

17. CPTnet, "Catch-22," August 2, 2003.

18. The team had given tours to representatives of the American consulate and diplomats from other countries since 1998 (these tours rarely made it into releases, at the request of the diplomats). In 2001, the team began planning a major information offensive, issuing invitations to representatives of the European community, who had heavily invested in aid and development projects in Palestine. These tours began in 2002. Sara Reschly, June 26, 2004, e-mail to author. Jamey Bouwmeester and Greg Rollins, June 27, 2004, e-mails to author.

19. The lower figure was provided by Khaled Qawasmi, of the Hebron Rehabilitation Committee. The higher figure was given by the Palestinian Chamber of Commerce, Hebron District.

closed. The shop owners do not have access to their shops, and, as mentioned, non-residents of the street are forbidden entry. On a-Shohada Street, all the shops have closed. Some of the shops have been broken into by settlers.

Another gauge of abandonment of the Casbah is the number of students who attend the Qordoba school, which is opposite Beit Romano. The size of the school's student body dropped from five hundred students before the intifada to 130 pupils at the end of this past school year. Khaled Qawasmi, of HRC, informed B'Tselem that, just prior to the intifada, there were eight hundred applications from Palestinians to move to the Casbah. That number now stands at ten.[20]

The team began to see the resulting flight of Palestinians from these areas as a policy of the Israeli military, rather than a byproduct of "security." A family living near the Ibrahimi Mosque/Cave of Machpelah reported to the team on January 8 that soldiers had invaded their home ten times in the previous twenty days. When the family complained to the local commander about soldiers abusing them during the raids, he said, "If you die, you die. If you live, you are lucky. You should move out of the Old City." In a January 16 release, Art Gish noted that extreme right-wingers had begun calling again for the transfer of Palestinians out of the West Bank. He then listed ways in which this transfer was effectively occurring in Hebron because of curfews, soldier raids, shop closings, and children falling behind in their education.[21] By February 22, the curfew had imprisoned residents of the Old City in their homes for one hundred days. In the update covering February 22, the team noted this statistic and broke from the normally dispassionate style of CPT updates by writing, "The usual celebrations for the [Ramadan] feast the previous week were impossible for them. Children had been able to go to school only when the commander has allowed it. Team members wondered how much longer their neighbors could endure this situation."

The ongoing curfew continued to devastate the Palestinian economy in the Old City as well. Art Gish referred in his population transfer release to the shop closures cited in the B'tselem report and noted that the vegetable market, site of the CPT "Oslo II" market witnesses, had become a settler parking lot. Soldiers began welding shops closed in areas around the

20. B'Tselem, "Hebron, Area H-2: Settlements Cause Mass Departure of Palestinians."

21. CPTnet, "HEBRON UPDATE: January 3–12, 2003," January 23, 2003; "HEBRON: Population Transfer," January 16, 2003.

settlements, and the team took on the task of intervening with soldiers on behalf of the shop owners who wanted to retrieve their merchandise before soldiers shut them out of their shops.[22]

In 2003, for the first time, the Israeli military ordered team members to abide by the same curfew that it had imposed on their neighbors for years. Shuhada Street became entirely off limits to the CPTers as well as Palestinians in contravention of the 1997 Hebron Protocol.[23] At first, these restrictions seemed to operate at the level of individual soldiers who told team members they could not pass through checkpoints into the Old City or could not accompany children to school during curfew.

On May 18, the restrictions became official. The day before, a suicide bomber dressed as a religious Jew blew himself up in front of Avraham Avinu, killing himself and a young couple, Gadi Levy and Dina Levy, who was pregnant. On the morning of May 18, at 6:00 AM, a Palestinian militant blew himself up on a bus in Jerusalem, killing seven people and wounding twenty.[24] When Mary Lawrence, Diane Janzen, Chris Brown, Germana Nijim, Harriet Taylor, and Greg Rollins attempted to do school patrol, soldiers refused to let them leave the Old City. Rollins, Brown, Lawrence, and Janzen then went through the tunnel network in the Old City to get

---

22. See CPTnet releases, "HEBRON UPDATE: February 28–March 10, 2003," March 22, 2003; Brown, "HEBRON: The Shopkeeper," March 27, 2003; "HEBRON UPDATE: March 18–30, 2003," April 9, 2003; "HEBRON UPDATE: October 16–22, 2003," November 1, 2003.

In an April 15, 2003, CPTnet release, "HEBRON: Planned by God," Greg Rollins described a shopkeepers' revolt after an Israeli officer had told them they could open their shops and soldiers had come by a couple hours later telling them to close down. The team had been on their way to put "This is Racism" banners on the rubble mounds that the Israeli military had erected at entrances to Hebron. The shop owners quickly borrowed the signs and set them up around the Old City. Twenty minutes later, the officer who had originally given them the permission to open their shops reissued the permission. When the team asked one of the shop owners who had organized their protest, he said, "We have no leader." One of their translators told them, "This action was planned by God." Rollins somewhat wistfully reflected that the shop owners' action testified to the power of nonviolence and might make a difference if such actions were incorporated by Palestinians on a wider level.

23. See CPTnet releases: "HEBRON UPDATE: February 28–March 10, 2003," March 22, 2003; "HEBRON UPDATE: April 7–20, 2003," April 25, 2003; "HEBRON UPDATE: May 5–18, 2003," June 3, 2003; "HEBRON: Turquoise awnings and the failure of the Hebron Protocol," July 22, 2003.

24. Diane Janzen, in a January 28, 2008, e-mail to the author said she believed the subsequent curfews, closures, and detentions in Hebron had more to do with the former act of terrorism than the latter.

to Bab iZawiyya. Seeing soldiers detaining about thirty Palestinian men at the Beit Hadassah checkpoint, Rollins and Brown went over to observe. Soldiers took Brown's passport and the ID of a Palestinian municipal observer. Unfortunately, Rollins had washed his passport in the laundry and was waiting to receive a new one from the Canadian Embassy. After three hours, the soldiers released Brown and most of the Palestinians. They took Rollins to the police station where the police put him under arrest. For the next two days, the team had no idea where the police had taken him; the Canadian consulate could only tell them they were looking for him. Jonathan Kuttab, a Palestinian lawyer and friend of the team's from Sabeel, presented a petition to the High Court asking it to block Rollins' deportation. The judge ruled that the Israeli government had seven days to respond. On May 22, Rollins called Kuttab, saying that he had been told to get his things together for his immediate departure. Kuttab contacted the office to seek an injunction against the deportation. Because she felt the government was showing contempt for the judge's ruling, the judge's assistant interrupted the judge in a meeting, and Rollins remained in prison.

On May 27, Rollins came before the Ramle District court, where his lawyers, Jonathan Kuttab and Sami Khoury, received a deportation order that contained no reason for Rollins's deportation. Since no charges had been filed, the judge declined to rule on the deportation. The Israeli High Court overturned the deportation order on May 29 and ruled that Rollins, from Surrey, BC, could remain in Israel until his petition challenging his arrest on May 18 was heard. The court gave the government until June 20 to respond to the petition.

Rollins was to remain in jail until June 4, 2003. On June 23, 2003, the Governor of the Hebron District held a reception to celebrate Greg Rollins' release from prison and to honor the work of CPT. Rollins spent the next six months in Hebron, because his appeal kept getting put off by the Israeli court. He left the country on December 22, 2003, under a ruling by the court stipulating that 1) there existed no restrictions on Rollins entering Israel, 2) that any past restrictions in Interior Ministry computers must be removed, and 3) that previous attempted deportation proceedings would not be held against him. However, when he attempted to enter the country on March 11, 2004, the Israeli government denied him entry. After the Israeli high court finally reviewed Rollins' case in June 2004, it decided not to lift his denial of entry into Israel based on a "top secret" file submitted by Israeli security. CPT decided against pursuing the case in a

Jerusalem court for reasons of cost and the likelihood that in the end the Israeli authorities would still deny him entry.

The day after Rollins's arrest, six Israeli soldiers searched the team's apartment. When the team asked why they had entered the house with guns, the soldiers told them that it was a "matter of life and death." (In her journal, CPTer Germana Nijim noted, "We are one step closer to being full-fledged Palestinians.") The next night, soldiers again entered the apartment. They examined the passports and visas of the CPTers present, photographed the apartment and individual team members, studied the maps and pictures on the wall, and scrutinized the contents of the filing cabinet.

The soldiers then verbally issued the following orders to the team:

- CPTers were not allowed in H-1—the area of Hebron formerly under Palestinian control. If Israeli troops caught CPTers in H-1, they would arrest and deport them.
- No internationals or Israelis were allowed in H-1 except those working for NGOs recognized by the Israeli government.
- CPTers were not to go anywhere near an Israeli settlement (all of which were in H-2).
- CPTers were not to accompany children to school in H-2.
- CPTers would not be allowed back into H-2 if they left (e.g., to go to Jerusalem).

On May 21, soldiers at the Beit Romano checkpoint gave team members information about where they could and could not go that contradicted the restrictions ordered on the 19th. Harriet Taylor phoned David Glass, the Israeli military liaison to Non-Governmental Organizations (NGOs), for written clarification of the orders in English. Glass told her that he did not have the authority to give her orders in English. After Taylor reminded him he had access to whoever could issue written orders, he agreed to follow up. The team continued to conduct their morning school patrols. On May 27, Glass met them at the locked gate recently installed in the alley where the team's apartment was located. Team members gave him a letter of condolence for the Israelis killed by a suicide bomber a few days previously that also reaffirmed the team's commitment to work peacefully in conflict zones. Through the bars, he showed them a paper in Hebrew, which he said barred them from H-1, the area of the city formerly controlled by the Palestinian authority. No one on the team read Hebrew, but the CPTers saw clearly the date "2001" written on the paper. Glass refused to give them a copy so they could have it translated.[25]

Although the team decided to continue CPT school patrols, they became more surreptitious about going to and from their apartment. Yoav Hass, an Israeli conscientious objector, buoyed their confidence when he told them that for these orders to be legal, the military would have to write them in English and give the team a copy. He also told them that showing people papers purportedly containing orders that they could not read was a standard tactic of the military.[26] Various updates record soldiers reminding the team that they should not be out during curfew,[27] but for the remainder of the year, no CPTers were detained or arrested because they were out during curfew.

---

25. Germana Nijim, "The Saga of Greg Rollins and the Christian Peace Teams," Journal entries from May 18–May 21, 2003. See also CPTnet releases: "HEBRON: Israel Cracks Down—CPTer Arrested; Office searched; Team Restricted," May 20, 2003; "HEBRON: Urgent Action and Update," May 21, 2003; "HEBRON Update on Deportation and Restrictions," May 22, 2003; "HEBRON: Update on restrictions that Israeli military has imposed on Hebron team," May 28, 2003; "HEBRON UPDATE: May 5–18, 2003," June 3, 2003. "HEBRON REFLECTION: Greg Rollins writes about his weeks in an Israeli prison," June 7, 2003. See also Eric Schiller, August 17, 2004, e-mail to author regarding meeting with David Glass.

CPTnet, "HEBRON URGENT ACTION: Greg Rollins denied entry," March 12, 2004; CPTnet, "HEBRON URGENT ACTION: Israeli Ministry of Interior still considering Greg Rollins' case; Faxes from churches, Israelis welcome," March 16, 2004. Greg Rollins, e-mail to author, August 16, 2004. See also CPTnet, "IRAQ: Can't enter Israel, can't leave Iraq—letters from Greg Rollins," August 21, 2004.

Some of the Hebron team and their supporters speculated that the arrest of Rollins and the restrictions on the team may have been related to the deaths of ISM volunteers Rachel Corrie and Tom Hurndall, in that the Israeli government seemed to increase its crackdowns on internationals in general after those incidents. See below under section "Internationals."

26. Greg Rollins, e-mail to author, June 2, 2004. Even before Hass told them the orders were invalid, the team suspected they were. Seeing a 2001 date on an order supposedly recently issued was only the first clue. When Kristin Anderson returned from visiting Tel Rumeida, a Border Policeman took her name and passport number, threatening her with arrest if she entered Area A again. "Hebron has no Area A," the writer of the CPTnet Hebron Update for June 9–20, 2002, noted (posted June 24, 2003). See also reference to Shabtai Gold in n. 19 of previous chapter.

27. In one such encounter, David Glass, CPT's contact with the DCO, introduced his replacement. Rich Meyer asked Glass to do something about opening the gate between the Old City and the mosque so that children could get to school in the morning. Glass then told Meyer, Jerry Levin, and EAPPI colleague Klaus Engle that the settlers had written an official letter of complaint about CPT to the Israeli Interior and Defense Ministers and then reminded them it was illegal for CPT to be in H-1. CPTnet, "HEBRON UPDATE: August 25–September 2, 2003," September 9, 2003.

The "virtual" closures imposed on the team were followed up by actual physical barriers in the Old City market area and areas leading from H-1 into H-2. In July, the military began installing a fence from the Ibrahimi Mosque to the gated entrance of the Old City market facing Shuhada Street. Jerry Levin noted in a release that when the gate was completed a soldier's key would trap the Palestinian residents of the Old City in a mini-ghetto—as the gates that the team helped take down in February 1996 had (see chapter 2). Subsequent updates record several instances of soldiers refusing to allow CPTers to enter and exit the Old City through these gates.

Barriers also went up on the road to Yatta leading out from the Market area—where settlers drove by Palestinian homes. In November, as Greg Rollins and Gary Brooks tried to walk out to the Beqa'a along the road settlers had designated as "Worshipper's Way," the soldiers told them CPT could no longer walk on that road. "It is for locals only," the soldier said.

"Local Palestinians?" Rollins asked.

"No," the soldier responded.

"Local settlers?"

"Yes."

In one particularly poignant incident on August 6, Dianne Roe and JoAnne Lingle were trying to escort a Jewish visitor into the Old City past a plastic blockade so that she could visit the mother of a Palestinian boy who lived in the same U.S. city as the visitor. The soldier refused to let them pass and said, "This plastic blockade must be sterilized of Palestinians." The woman began crying and told the soldier that her relatives had escaped the Holocaust. He listened to her tell him about the terrible treatment of Palestinians she had witnessed, but would not let them pass the blockade.[28]

Barriers and checkpoints continued to prevent Palestinians and CPTers from traveling between cities in 2003. On August 26, when Paul Pierce learned that his grandmother had died, he and his wife Kathy Kamphoefner tried to take the settler bus to Jerusalem, and a soldier told

---

28. See CPTnet releases, "HEBRON UPDATE: June 9–20, 2003," June 24, 2003; "HEBRON: Israeli army increases its chokehold on Hebron's Old City," July 8, 2003; "HEBRON UPDATE: June 29-July 6, 2003," July 19, 2003; "HEBRON UPDATE: July 30-August 13, 2003," August 18, 2003; "HEBRON UPDATE: November 13–21, 2003," December 1, 2003; "HEBRON UPDATE: November 22–23, 2003," December 6, 2003. Several updates also record helpful soldiers telling CPTers routes they could take where no soldiers would stop them.

them they did not have the authorization to ride with Israelis.[29] Trips out to the Beqa'a Valley—even on foot—became difficult. Curfews and closures began to apply to areas inside H-1 in 2003, not just the entrance and exit points to the city.

The Al-Manara market area (where the team had had its first apartment in the summer of 1995) was particularly hard hit. On January 30, the military put all of Hebron under curfew and leveled the vegetable stalls in Al-Manara with tanks and bulldozers. Art Gish, who was giving a tour to guests of the team, stood between soldiers (on foot and in tanks) and the Palestinian bystanders in the line of fire. On February 16, soldiers destroyed the Al-Manara market area a second time. In June, the army dug trenches into the five major roads that enter Al-Manara, thus effectively cutting off all traffic into Bab iZawiyya, Hebron's primary commercial district. They ordered the municipality not to repair the roads.[30]

Bab iZawiyya, which bordered H-2, also increasingly found itself under the same restrictions inflicted on Palestinians in H-2. Soldiers began imposing curfew and set up huge cement block barricades that essentially extended the border of H-2 to encompass the once-bustling market area.

"Not that anyone was surprised by this latest land grab," wrote Jerry Levin in July 2003.

29. CPTnet, "HEBRON UPDATE: August 25-September 2, 2003," September 9, 2003.

30. See CPTnet releases: Art Gish, "Terrorists among the apples," January 30, 2003; "HEBRON UPDATE: January 30-February 4, 2003," February 10, 2003; "HEBRON UPDATE: February 5–9, 2003," February 25, 2003. "HEBRON: Is this on the Road Map?" June 14, 2003; "HEBRON UPDATE: June 9–20, 2003," June 24, 2003.

When asked why the Israeli military had exerted control over Al-Manara, Greg Rollins wrote in a July 3, 2004, e-mail to the author:

> If I recall correctly, the IDF was pushing all the way to Al Manara for several reasons. One was the curfew, but there was not a curfew every day. Sometimes they did it because the settlers wanted to visit a shrine in H1 [of Othniel ben Kenaz, the first Judge of Israel (see Judges 3:9)] up the street from Osaid's parent's house [Osaid Rashid was a team translator.] Most of the time they did it without giving a reason. We believed it was to push the commerce away from Bab iZawiyya. Sometimes they told us it was to keep the settlers safe. If there was a funeral or holiday, they closed the area down. A member of TIPH told me once that according to the Hebron accords, the IDF was allowed to enter H1 up to Al Manara when they were chasing a suspected person. I don't know if that is true but this TIPHer said they had read that in the accords.

Art Gish, in an August 9, 2004, e-mail to the author said that soldiers told him they needed to clear the area of stalls so they could get tanks and other vehicles through the intersection.

The Israeli Army had been telegraphing its intentions fiercely and meanly for several weeks late last year. During the busiest part of the day, tanks would suddenly come tearing into the intersection, crushing or upsetting the portable stands, scattering goods and shoppers as they went. They would knock over and chase off not just those in the streets, but the ones on sidewalks, too. At other times, squads of Israeli soldiers would come dashing into the area, arbitrarily declaring curfew, gruffly shouting at shoppers to leave and ordering all businesses to shut down.[31]

To enforce curfew, soldiers shot percussion grenades into Bab iZawiyya, detained people at the Dubboya Street checkpoint, and charged into crowds with guns. On August 26, a soldier told Kristin Anderson and JoAnne Lingle that they were enforcing curfew, because Yom Kippur was approaching and many Israelis would be coming to pray and "atone for their sins." He then made a face suggesting that he understood the irony of the situation.[32]

SOLDIER VIOLENCE

As noted in the February release listing prayer concerns (see above), soldier violence in the first part of 2003 began to take on a nasty personal edge (as opposed to the routine abuses that occurred at checkpoints or during soldiers' home raids as they searched for militants).[33] During a follow-up visit to the area between Bab iZawiyya and Al Manara after the destruction of the fruit and vegetable stands, Sue Rhodes, Art Gish, Tracy Hughes, and Kathy Kapenga noticed an Israeli military jeep stopping to let a Palestinian man vomit. When the CPTers asked why the soldiers had detained the man, they did not answer, and the man, with tears in his eyes, shook his head. The soldiers drove around for another half hour, stopping occasionally and then released the man. He told a reporter that soldiers had beaten him for nearly two hours in the jeep.[34]

31. CPTnet, "HEBRON: While you were gone," July 26, 2003.
32. CPTnet, "HEBRON UPDATE: February 10–15, 2003," February 25, 2003; "HEBRON UPDATE: August 25-September 2, 2003," September 9, 2003; "HEBRON UPDATE: September 3–16, 2003," September 18, 2003.
33. Other noteworthy soldier interactions described in the team's 2003 releases included soldiers entering and searching the team's apartment much more often than in previous years and soldier attacks on journalists (most often Reuters journalist and nonviolence advocate Nayef Hashlomoun).
34. CPTnet, "The Things You Don't Want to Hear," January 2003 CPTnet archives. CPTnet, "HEBRON UPDATE: January 30-February 4, 2003," February 10, 2003.

The team did not know it at the time, but they had witnessed an incident that, among others, would lead to prosecution of the soldiers. On May 1, Israeli courts indicted four border police officers on charges of manslaughter in the death of 'Imran Abu Hamdiya, a seventeen-year-old youth from Hebron, whom they had thrown from a jeep. They were also charged with brutality, theft, and obstruction of justice.

B'tselem, the Israeli Human rights organization wrote,

> According to the indictment, the four border police officers set out on a journey of abuse and cruelty against residents of the city [Hebron], in which they misused their authority, by committing violent acts intended to cause bodily injury and damage to property and whose purpose was to humiliate and harass . . . During their travels throughout the city . . . the defendants put local residents whom they located by chance into the jeep and ordered them to jump from the jeep while it was moving. One of the local residents refused to jump while the jeep was moving at great speed, and the defendants pushed him out. He fell onto the road and struck his head, which led to his death. . . . In addition, the defendants abducted other local residents and beat them, at times with a club and rifle butt; robbed property, and also hurled tear-gas grenades and percussion grenades at local residents for no reason whatsoever.[35]

35. B'Tselem, "Border police Trial on Suspicion of Killing 'Imran Abu Hamdiya"; See also B'Tselem, "Hebron: Border Police officers beat 'Imran Abu Hamdia, age 17, to death, December 2002," and B'Tselem, "Hebron Area H-2: Settlements cause mass departure of Palestinians."
The report quoted in the text continues,

> On 6 July 2003, the state filed indictments against eleven more border police officers from the same company. The police officers are charged with harassing Hebron residents, damaging their property, looting stores, and beating passersby. An investigative commission appointed by the Border Police following an investigation by the Department for Investigation of Police recommended that the company be disbanded and its current commander and his predecessor be dismissed from command positions. The commission also recommended that a commander's remark be filed against the Border Police commander for Judea and Samaria, Big. Gen. Yiftach Avraham, and against the company's acting commander, Chief Superintendent Eldad Shusaf. The investigative commission submitted its recommendations to the Border Police commander and to the Police Commissioner, both of whom adopted the recommendations.

See also Dexter Filkins, "Hebron Residents Describe An Israeli Reign of Beatings."
Despite their title, Border Police function essentially as soldiers, rather than as Israeli civilian police. Israeli society tends to view Border police as units from the "dregs" of Israeli society, because they are not fit for service in more elite units. The team noticed over the years that they contained a high percentage of Israeli Druze and recent immigrants.

Other indignities imposed upon the Palestinian residents of Hebron by soldiers and Border Police included the vandalizing of homes and shops, strip searches of females, planting knives on Palestinians, then beating them for possessing the knives, and scaring schoolchildren for fun. The team recorded a soldier telling Diane Janzen, when she asked why they had confiscated a man's jacket and outer shirt and made him stand in the cold, "We haven't raped him yet." Another Border Policeman told Gary Brooks, an Arab-American CPT reservist, that all Arabs were animals and murderers.[36]

Two incidents of soldiers abusing their power were of particular concern, because they involved people with whom the team had had longstanding relationships. On February 8, Israeli soldiers attacked Zleekha Muhtasib, who had served as a team translator for years. Muhtasib frequently went out during curfew and told soldiers trying to stop her that her family had lived in Hebron for hundreds of years and thus had no obligation to follow the directives of various Israeli brigades cycling in and out. She would often breeze by settlers and soldiers who threatened to shoot her if she continued on her way. Muhtasib was also instrumental in setting up the school patrols in 2001. During the incident in question, a female soldier stopped Muhtasib, dug through her purse, and took out a freshly picked carnation. "Look at this rubbish," she told Muhtasib. "You carry rubbish because you are rubbish." Soldiers then began to kick her, hit her, and, once she was lying on the ground, beat her with rifle butts. They also pushed her against the wall, forced her to spread her legs (extremely shocking in Palestinian culture), and continued to beat her until their commanding officer heard her screams and stopped them. Referring to previous times soldiers had beaten her, she told Kristin Anderson and Kathy Kapenga, "Before it was okay, because I was always defending some-

---

However, team members found that some Border Police were amiable and sensitive, while members of "elite" units such as the paratroopers could be brutal.

36. See CPTnet releases: "HEBRON UPDATE: January 3–January 12, 2003," January 23, 2002; "HEBRON: Terrorists among the apples," January 30, 2003; "HEBRON UPDATE: January 24–29, 2003," February 5, 2003 ; "HEBRON: Prayer requests from the Hebron Team," February 6, 2003; "HEBRON UPDATE: January 30-February 4, 2003," February 10, 2003; "HEBRON UPDATE: February 5–9, 2003," February 25, 2003; "HEBRON UPDATE: February 10–15, 2003," February 25, 2003; "HEBRON UPDATE: February 18–27, 2003," March 3, 2003; "HEBRON UPDATE: October 30-November 5, 2003," November 17, 2003; "HEBRON UPDATE: November 22–23, 2003," December 6, 2003.

one. But this time was different. This time it was me they were after—me personally. This time they meant to destroy me."[37]

After Israel fenced in Wadi Ghroos (see above under "Land confiscation 2003"), soldiers assaulted two sons of the Zalloum family, whose home CPTers tried unsuccessfully to save in 1996. Soldiers picked up the eight-year-old by his head, lifted him high up in the air, and slammed him to the ground. Then they knocked the six-year-old boy down and kicked him. After their father, Wahed Zalloum, complained to the police, they asked the soldier why he had done it. According to Zalloum, the soldier said, "They will grow up to be terrorists, so it's better if we kill them now, while they're small."[38]

SCHOOL ACCOMPANIMENT

This casually cruel soldier violence extended to the school children whom the team accompanied on patrols. The updates for the first half of 2003 cite many incidents of abuse when soldiers enforced the curfew on the students. These abuses include the following:

- Soldiers using teargas and percussion grenades on students who were already returning home after soldiers told them they had to leave.
- Soldiers charging at children in their jeeps.
- Soldiers screaming at children and using obscene language as they closed down schools that had opened for the day—considered particularly deplorable when done in the presence of female students and teachers—and accusing children of being suicide bombers and terrorists.
- Soldiers kicking water from the gutter into the faces of schoolgirls.
- Soldiers aiming their rifles at young girls to scare them. In a February 17 incident, Art Gish stood between the soldiers and the girls at whom they were pointing their guns and said, "Aren't you ashamed of threatening little girls? Just let the girls go to school."

---

37. CPTnet, Kristin Anderson, "HEBRON: 'This Time They Meant to Destroy Me,'" February 14, 2003. See also CPTnet, "HEBRON UPDATE: February 5–9, 2003," February 25, 2003.

38. CPTnet, "HEBRON: Israel fences in Wadi el-Ghroos, site of first home demolition CPT witnessed; soldier assaults children," September 12, 2003.

- Soldiers shooting rubber bullets at the children. In one case, on February 19, they warned that CPTers would be shot if they tried to accompany the children.[39]

Despite these obstacles, school patrol continued to be a central focus of the team's work in Hebron for 2003. In May, after receiving the orders restricting their movement (see above) team members continued to accompany the children in the mornings and afternoons in defiance of these orders.

Team members repeatedly told soldiers who were stopping children from attending school about the agreement that allowed schools to remain open even during curfew. As had happened in the previous two years, sometimes the soldiers radioed their commanders to see if they could attend school and sometimes they did not.

Even when the military lifted curfew, CPTers walked with students past checkpoints to prevent harassment. Chris Brown, who served as school patrol coordinator for the 2002–2003 school year, told a reporter that on a good day, school patrol lasted about forty-five minutes between the time team members left the apartment and the time they returned. On a bad day, school patrol could last for five hours.[40]

Brown wrote a report in 2003 describing the trials of the 2002–2003 school year. At the beginning of the report, he noted that Israel is a signatory to the Fourth Geneva Convention. Article 50 of the convention reads as follows:

> In an occupied territory, the Occupying power must facilitate the proper working of all institutions devoted to care and education of children. It may not, under any circumstances, change their personal status or enlist them in formations or organizations subordinate to it. Should the local institutions be inadequate for the purpose, the Occupying Power shall make arrangements for the

---

39. See CPTnet releases: "HEBRON UPDATE: December 27, 2002–January 2, 2003," January 11, 2002; "HEBRON UPDATE: January 30–February 4, 2003," February 10, 2003; Art Gish, "HEBRON: No School Today," February 17, 2003; "HEBRON UPDATE: February 5–9, 2003," February 25, 2003; "HEBRON UPDATE: February 10–15, 2003," February 25, 2003; "HEBRON UPDATE: February 18–27, 2003," March 3, 2003; "HEBRON UPDATE: March 18–30, 2003," April 9, 2003; "HEBRON UPDATE: April 7–20, 2003," April 25, 2003.

The autumn 2003 releases record many fewer incidents of soldiers harassing students and the CPTers accompanying them, but see Kamphoefner, "HEBRON: Army teargasses children on their way to and from school," October 15, 2003; CPTnet, Brown, "HEBRON REFLECTION: The fire next time," November 4, 2003.

40. CPTnet, "HEBRON REFLECTION: The fire next time," November 4, 2003.

care and education of children who are orphaned or separated from their parents, if possible by persons of their nationality, language, and religion.

Brown's report included testimonies taken by fieldworkers for B'tselem and CPTers from students, teachers, and principals in Hebron. They described physical assaults by soldiers and settlers, the long roundabout routes to school students and teachers had to walk in order to avoid soldiers and settlers, declining enrollment because of the harassment, the vandalism of school buildings, and detentions of teachers while soldiers checked their ID's. Toward the end of the report, Brown listed sobering statistics: the military closed schools for 19 percent of February 2003, 22 percent of March 2003, and 80 percent in April 2003. During the 2002–2003 school year, soldiers arrested ten teachers and twenty-two students. From September 2002–March 2003 twenty-eight students and teachers filed complaints for injuries sustained at the hands of the Israeli military (most injuries went unreported). Of those injuries, twenty-seven happened to minors, one as young as eight.[41]

In addition to accompanying public school children in 2003, the team found itself once again supporting Hebron University and Polytechnic students after Israel shut down the institutions and confiscated their computers. On January 5, two militants from the Fatah Al-Aqsa Martyrs' Brigade blew themselves up in an immigrant neighborhood in Tel Aviv, killing twenty-three people and injuring a hundred and eight more. Despite the fact that no one associated with Hebron University or Hebron Polytechnic was implicated in the Tel Aviv bombing, the military closed the schools in

---

41. Chris Brown, untitled report, 2003. Brown's report includes a quotation from IDF press officer on February 2, 2003, regarding the imposition of curfew on students:

> Terrorism is illegal under international law and somehow something has to stop it. And you cannot remove a curfew because children have to go to school, because if you have information about the terrorists coming out of a city, the children inside Israel will die, okay? They won't just not go to school, they won't go anywhere anymore. So we have to make the decision, what's the primary thing in your mind. And of course its Israeli citizens, it's the safety and security of Israeli citizens, okay? And when you have information about terror infrastructure you will do everything in what's possible of course and everything in the, uh, in the legal point of view to try and stop this terror act and try and ensure the safety of Israeli citizens. Even if it's not allowing school day for a group of Palestinian youth.

Brown's report cited both that twenty-four school days in April were lost to the curfew and 11.5 percent of school days were lost. In a July 8, 2004, e-mail to the author, he said that the twenty-four days (or 80 percent) figure was correct.

retaliation. In a written statement, the army called the campuses "fertile ground for terror and a hothouse for terrorists and suicide bombers."

The nine-page document listed names of students from both universities who were accused of involvement in other deadly attacks on Israelis, including students from Polytechnic University said to have taken part in the November 15, 2002, ambush that killed twelve Israeli soldiers, border police, and security guards (see chapter 7). The statement also reported that Hamas had used a chemistry lab at Hebron University to train its members to prepare explosives—a charge vehemently denied by university officials.[42] The team found out later that the military had told officials that they could reopen if they informed the military about anti-Israel activities on campus. The administrators told the military that while they strongly condemned violence, their jobs did not include being policemen for Israel.

Students sawed through the Hebron University gates on June 4, partially because they had heard the rumor that the army was going to extend the closure for six months and partially because George W. Bush's "Roadmap to Peace" meetings were taking place in Aqaba, Jordan. The students thought participants in the meetings would show support for their right to education. Soldiers welded the main gate shut the next day. A suicide bomber who had attended Hebron's Polytechnic University killed seventeen Israelis and injured a hundred in Jerusalem on June 12, which no doubt ensured the continuing closure, if the Israeli authorities had not made up their minds to prolong it already.

At the request of the Hebron University and Polytechnic students, the team sent George W. Bush the following letter after Bush had made a statement supporting Iranian university students' right to free speech:

> June 17, 2003
>
> Dear President Bush,
>
> We are pleased to know that you support the right of students to obtain a university education free from government constraints, and we applaud your support for students' freedom of expression. We hope that the comments you made this week about Iranian students apply equally to Palestinian students attending Hebron University.

---

42. CPTnet, "HEBRON: Education is Against the Law," January 28, 3004; CPTnet, "HEBRON: Prayer requests from the Hebron team," February 6, 2003.
 See also "Israelis close two Palestinian Universities." The *Sydney Morning Herald* article quotes Karim Tahboub, dean of the college of engineering and technology at Polytechnic University, as saying the institution should not be punished for the off-campus actions of some students. "They can arrest them, but why close the university?" he said.

> Since 1994, the Israeli government has imposed a variety of restrictions on students attending classes at Hebron University. The Israeli army have repeatedly sealed the main gates of the university and invaded the campus, using tear gas and live ammunition against unarmed students.
>
> Recently, the military forced the university to close for six months and students are now required to attend classes in nearby schools, shops and homes instead of their own campus. They are prevented from using their library and technical laboratories, a situation clearly detrimental to the quality of their education.
>
> On June 4th, the students broke open the sealed gate of their campus, so they could attend classes. They did this during your visit to the Aqaba discussions of your Roadmap to Peace, in the hope that their initiative in seeking an open educational institution would be seen as a step toward peace. Their opening of the university was accomplished nonviolently.
>
> The students are determined to continue their education at Hebron University in an open atmosphere free from the fear, violence and restrictions of the Israeli military. The university administration has high praise for the students' use of nonviolent methods to continue their studies. They feel the right to an education is a basic one that should be available to all those who cherish knowledge and peace. . . .
>
> We know that you value the importance of a university education. As you pursue the Roadmap to Peace, we hope you will champion the right of students at Hebron University to pursue their studies, free from the fear, restrictions and violence that mars their efforts to achieve a quality education.
>
> Sincerely,
>
> Christian Peacemaker Teams
> Hebron, West Bank
> Cc: Secretary of State Colin Powell[43]

The Israeli military welded the gate of Hebron University shut again on July 10, chased students away with percussion grenades, and imposed a strict curfew on the surrounding neighborhood, which was once in H-1. On the following day, July 11, 2003, the Israeli military announced it was extending the closure on both the university and the Polytechnic by one month. The team accompanied Polytechnic students on July 14 as they broke into their building and cleaned the rooms, which had acquired a thick coat of dust during the previous six months. The next day, students

---

43. CPT Hebron, "An Open Letter to President George W. Bush From Christian Peacemaker Teams in Hebron, West Bank."

hoisted the Palestinian flag in front of journalists from Al Jazeera and held classes. Members of the Polytechnic administration then padlocked the front gate, to the dismay of the students, because they were afraid the Israeli military might enter and destroy their equipment or hurt the students.

On August 11, 2003, the Israeli military not only extended the closures of Hebron University and Polytechnic for another month, but refused to let graduation ceremonies take place. Polytechnic students dismantled the gates yet again the next day. On August 15, The Israeli Civil Administration told the presidents of both universities that they could open their schools.[44]

44. See CPTnet releases: "HEBRON: Education is Against the Law," January 28, 2003; "HEBRON: Prayer requests from the Hebron team," February 6, 2003;"HEBRON: Students reopen gates of Hebron University," June 5, 2003; "HEBRON: Israeli army welds Hebron University gate shut," June 10, 2003; "HEBRON UPDATE: June 9–20, 2003," June 24, 2003; Paul D. Pierce, "HEBRON: Palestinian students attempt to reopen University," July 15, 2003; Diego Scott [*aka* Greg Rollins, who was trying to keep a low profile before his court appearance (see above)], "HEBRON: Breaking open six months' closure," July 21, 2003; "HEBRON UPDATE: July 7–23, 2003," August 6, 2003; Rollins "HEBRON: Hebron University and Palestine Polytechnic University Re-opened," August 16, 2003; "HEBRON UPDATE: July 30–August 13, 2003," August 18, 2003.

For the Israeli government's spin on the closings, see Israeli Ministry of Foreign Affairs, "The Closure of the Polytechnic University and Islamic college in Hebron." (Note: although Hebron University has an Islamic college on campus, it also has colleges of Business, Sciences, Humanities, etc. Israeli and international media routinely refer to it as an Islamic college, however.) Israeli Ministry of Foreign Affairs, "Suicide Bombing of Egged Bus # 14A in Jerusalem," June 11, 2003.

Regarding the offer to re-open the Polytechnic, the Israeli government wrote:

April 3, 2003

Offer to Reopen Polytechnic University in Hebron
(Communicated by the IDF Spokesman)

As part of the IDF's ongoing battle against terrorism and its infrastructure, IDF forces closed the Polytechnic University in Hebron on the night of January 14, 2003.

Recently, in an effort to maintain the daily routine of innocent Palestinians and out of an understanding of the importance of regularly functioning educational institutions, an offer was made to the university's administration to reopen the school.

The re-opening was made conditional upon a halt in recruiting terrorists from the school's ranks, ceasing anti-Israel incitement, supervision over the student union, the prohibition of illegal activities, the removal of posters encouraging hostile activity against Israel, removing students involved in perpetrating terror, and establishing a mechanism that will ensure these conditions are upheld.

Although the offer was presented to the university's administration, they did not display an interest in cooperation nor in taking the necessary steps to distance terror from its doorsteps that would transform it into a proper academic institution.

SETTLER VIOLENCE

Fewer settler rampages occurred in 2003 than occurred in 2002, but Palestinians and international observers in Hebron continued to suffer from physical and verbal assaults on their persons, shops, and homes.

Palestinian militants killed five settlers in Hebron in the first half of 2003, setting off retaliatory cycles. On January 17, 2003, two Palestinian gunmen infiltrated a settlement outpost near the Sultan family home (see chapter 4), killing Netanel Ozeri and wounding several others. The settlers from the outpost had routinely attacked farmers in the area over the years, stolen farm equipment, animals, destroyed trees, and vineyards. Even though settlers and soldiers killed the two gunmen, on January 18 and 19, settlers attacked Palestinian homes and cars in the area, burning families' clothes and other personal possessions.

Dina and Rabbi Eliahu Horowitz (see above under "Home Demolitions") were the next Hebron area settlers to be murdered by Palestinian militants on March 7. Retaliations for their deaths were to hit the neighborhood of Jabel Johar. Ten days later, a suicide bomber killed Gadi Levy, Dina Levy, and her unborn child in front of Avraham Avinu (see above under "Curfews and Closures"). Beyond settlers banging on the doors of homes and shops, the murder of the Levys seemed to provoke no major attacks on Palestinians, possibly because most Palestinian homes and shops nearby had been abandoned or forcibly closed by this time.[45]

Therefore, the closure order against the Polytechnic University will remain in effect as originally decided, for a period of six months beginning January 12, 2003.

Since the beginning of the current conflict, academic institutions in general and the Polytechnic in particular have stood at the forefront, providing cover for extremist activity by terrorist organizations.

The terrorist organizations based a significant amount of their operational infrastructure on students by using the means available to them at the academic institutions. The activities included disseminating inciteful material, and the recruiting and training of hundreds of operatives.

Among the terrorists who came from the Polytechnic University was the terrorist that infiltrated Adura in April 2002 in which four were killed and seven injured, the terrorist who infiltrated Otniel in December 2002 in which four were killed and ten injured, and the three terrorists who perpetrated the shooting attack on "Worshippers Lane" in Hebron in which 12 Israelis were killed and 16 injured.

Israeli Ministry of Foreign Affairs, "Offer to Reopen Polytechnic University in Hebron."

45. See CPTnet releases, Gish, "HEBRON: Can anyone do something to stop this? Retaliation and Counter Retaliation," January 25, 2003; "HEBRON: Prayer requests from Hebron Team," February 6, 2003; "HEBRON: We Lament the Loss of Life," March 10, 2003; "HEBRON UPDATE: February 28–March 10, 2003," March 22, 2003; "HEBRON: Bomb kills two people near CPT apartment," May 18, 2003.

Several updates mention soldiers trying to prevent attacks by settlers on Palestinians. On January 25, a soldier prevented Fariel Abu Haikel, principal of Qurtuba School, from traveling her usual route to school because he said he did not want settlers to hurt her. When Abu Haikel asked if he could stop them, he told her, "No, they are crazy." When soldiers told shopkeepers near the Beit Romano checkpoint that they could reopen, they also told the merchants that they ought to install fences to protect themselves from the settlers. The update covering November 22 records an instance of soldiers protecting Palestinian schoolchildren from settler boys.[46]

The 2003 Hebron releases cover more incidents of settler attacks on Palestinians outside the city than inside. In March, settlers attacked the home of one family in the Beqa'a Valley and burned their cars. The Israeli army would not allow a fire truck through to extinguish the flames. When the family told the police which settlers had attacked them, the police responded, "What can we do?" Another family in the Beqa'a reported that settlers had prevented them from spraying their grapes, and that ten families depended on the income from that particular vineyard. Settlers kidnapped two farmers on tractors from Beit Ummar in April, eventually releasing the men but keeping the tractors. The team also recorded greater amounts of settler harassment in the southern Hebron District, which included assaults on schoolchildren, attacks on farmers working their land, bathing in cisterns that families used for drinking water, and stripping olives from their trees before farmers could get to the harvest.[47]

The 2003 updates also record a substantial number of minor settler attacks (physical and verbal) on team members. Usually soldiers intervened to stop the settlers, most of whom were boys throwing rocks. In one instance, settler boys spat on CPT delegation member Virginia Belford's jacket and hair, and then an adult settler came by and yelled at Belford for provoking the boys. When Belford and another delegate Kathleen Gale

---

46. CPTnet, "Hebron Update: January 24–29, 2003," February 5, 2003; "HEBRON UPDATE: September 17–23," September 30, 2003; "HEBRON UPDATE: November 22–23, 2003," December 6, 2003.

47. See CPTnet releases: "HEBRON UPDATE: March 11–17, 2003," March 24, 2003; "HEBRON UPDATE: April 7–20, 2003," April 25, 2003; "HEBRON UPDATE: April 21–27, 2003," May 2, 2003. "HEBRON UPDATE: May 5–18, 2003," June 3, 2003; "HEBRON UPDATE: June 21–28, 2003," June 30, 2003; "HEBRON UPDATE: July 24–29, 2003," July 31, 2003. July 2003 CPTnet Archives. "HEBRON UPDATE: July 7–23, 2003," August 6, 2003; "HEBRON UPDATE: July 30–August 13, 2003," August 18, 2003; HEBRON UPDATE: August 14–24, 2003," August 27, 2003; Rollins, "HEBRON DISTRICT: Harvesting Olives in Palestine," October 25, 2003.

told a group of soldiers about the incident, one of the soldiers apologized and said that settler boys did the same thing to him.[48]

Mary Yoder and Lorne Friesen were to suffer more severe attacks by settlers. On January 8, Yoder, Art Gish, and Kathie Uhler were accompanying Abdel Hadi Hantash and representatives from the German and Egyptian consulates on a tour of confiscated portions of the Beqa'a Valley. Yoder took a picture of a settler clearing land with a bulldozer. He charged her in the bulldozer. After she jumped out of the way, the settler jumped from the machine, pushed her down, and grabbed her camera. He headed down Bypass Road 60 and another bulldozer blocked the group in by pushing a large earthen mound at the entrance to the road. Soldiers arrived, and after the German diplomat reprimanded one soldier for pointing a gun at his head, they took Yoder to the police station, where she waited several hours to file a complaint. A police officer returned the camera and asked her if she would be willing to drop the charges if the settler apologized.

Two weeks earlier, the settler told her, his twenty-six-year-old brother had been shot and was paralyzed from the waist down. "He probably will not get married which makes me so sad," the man told her. Yoder offered condolences and told him that she took care of many injured patients as a nurse. The next day Yoder wrote him a letter, giving him information on the Christopher Reeves foundation, which researches treatments for paralysis. She gave the letter to the officer who took care of her, asking him to give it to the man who attacked her. Yoder would require neck surgery in March 2004 because of the attack.[49]

Ten days after the attack on Yoder, on January 18, the team accompanied members of Ta'ayush, an Israeli peace group, to protect farmers as

---

48. See CPTnet releases: "HEBRON UPDATE: January 3–12, 2003," January 23, 2003; "HEBRON UPDATE: March 18–30, 2003," April 9, 2003; "HEBRON UPDATE: March 31-April 6, 2003," April 19, 2003; "HEBRON: Urgent Action and Update," May 21, 2003. "HEBRON UPDATE: September 24–30, 2003," October 11, 2003; "HEBRON UPDATE: October 23–28, 2003," November 7, 2003; "HEBRON UPDATE: November 24–30, 2003," December 9, 2003..

49. CPTnet, "HEBRON UPDATE: January 3–January 12, 2003," January 23. Yoder forwarded sections from her journal about the incident to the author in an August 17, 2004, e-mail. Her entry for July 16, 2003, read as follows:

> I never heard back from the man who assaulted me, but I was always glad I wrote that letter. When my neck problems deteriorated and eventually led to surgery, I had times of real resentment towards him. But I always remembered that he did apologize and that we had a good verbal exchange. I thought about his brother, when I returned to work and had a partially paralyzed patient.

they worked in their fields near the village of At-Tuwani. As the farmers started plowing, the settlers began shooting from an outpost overlooking the fields. Some of the settlers charged down the hill, shooting or throwing rocks from slingshots. When they saw CPTer Lorne Friesen taking a picture, they knocked him down, smashing his camera and destroying his film. They then punched him in the side of the head. Rollins came to Friesen's aid and a settler punch sent his (Rollins's) glasses flying. Settler security personnel arrived at the scene, arrested a Palestinian who had thrown stones at the settlers, shifted the tractors into neutral, and pushed them down the hill so they flipped over.[50]

Violence of another sort greeted CPTer Chris Brown one day when he observed fresh graffiti reading, "WHITE POWER KILL NIGGERS," on a green steel door opposite the Hebron Team's apartment. Brown, an African-American, wrote in a release about the incident,

> Settlers call us CPTers Nazis all the time. It's really nothing new. I always laugh when they call me that. It's so foreign to me. But not the message I saw on the green steel doors. That message is one I've dealt with all my life, and its one I'll deal with till the day I die.... It would be nice to walk over to those green doors and paint right over that note. But I know, as I've always known, that it's going to take a lot more than paint to make those feelings go away.

The same day that Brown's release appeared on CPTnet, Brown, Paul Pierce, also African-American, and his wife Kathy Kamphoefner headed for Jerusalem so they could attend church the next day. Despite his best attempt to avoid soldiers, their taxi driver was cornered by two military jeeps. The soldiers' behavior to Brown and Pierce was markedly more discourteous than their behavior to Kamphoefner, who is white. Pierce concluded his piece on the incident, "Being Black in America is bad enough. Being Palestinian in the West Bank is even worse."[51]

---

50. CPTnet, "HEBRON UPDATE: January 13–23, 2003," January 31, 2003. The Israelis from Ta'ayush attacked by the Ma'on settlers filed complaints with the police in Jerusalem. Friesen's account of the attack in an August 1, 2004, e-mail to the author clears up the confusion in the update about whether Rollins or Friesen lost his glasses.

51. CPTnet, "HEBRON: A settler greeting card," June 13, 2003; "HEBRON REFLECTION: It's no fun being black in Hebron," June 20, 2003. See also Pierce's, "HEBRON REFLECTION: Images of the Occupation," November 11, 2003.

People of color who have participated in CPT delegations or as members of the Hebron Team are invariably pulled aside for questioning when they enter Israel's Ben Gurion airport.

INTERNATIONALS

In 2003, a U.N. Office for the Coordination of Humanitarian Affairs (OCHA) opened in Hebron during the summer and began organizing monthly coordination meetings for all local and international organizations working in Hebron. These meetings providing a forum for the organizations to share about their specific work and offer suggestions on ways to coordinate efforts, which significantly enhanced the efforts of the various NGOs.[52]

CPT continued to develop working relationships with EAPPI and ISM—the two other accompaniment organizations in Hebron—but the deaths of ISM members Rachel Corrie and Tom Hurndall eclipsed these cooperative ventures.

On March 16, an Israeli military bulldozer crushed ISM activist Rachel Corrie as she was trying to prevent it from demolishing a Palestinian civilian home. Corrie, twenty-three, from Olympia, Washington, had been part of an ISM team in Rafah (Gaza Strip) for the previous two months. According to her teammates, early Sunday afternoon they went to a neighborhood where two Israeli military bulldozers and a tank were demolishing several Palestinian houses. The eight volunteers stood in front of the houses and used megaphones to call on the bulldozer drivers to stop. The military initially left the area, but returned at about 5:00 PM, heading for a Palestinian pharmacist's home. Corrie was standing between the bulldozer and the house.

Although witnesses observed Corrie and the soldier driving the bulldozer speaking with each other as the machine was approaching her, the Israeli military later claimed that the driver never saw her. As the bulldozer approached, she stepped backwards and stumbled; it buried her in sand and rubble before driving over her. The machine then dragged her ten to fifteen meters before it stopped and reversed, rolling over her a second time. When her coworkers dug her out of the sand she was still breathing, although the bulldozer had crushed her skull and chest. A Palestinian ambulance crew transported her to hospital where she died. Israeli soldiers on the scene did not attempt to stop the bulldozer, nor did they offer medical care after the incident.

> 52. Diane Janzen, e-mail to author, January 28, 2008. Janzen noted in the e-mail that CPTers Kathy Kamphoefner and Paul Pierce, who were working with the American Friends Service Committee in Jerusalem, started a similar forum in 2004 for international peace teams working in the area. The forum included monthly meetings, and an e-mail list for organizations to share about the work in their specific regions, as well as sharing personnel, in some cases.

On April 5, Israeli forces in Jenin shot American ISM volunteer Brian Avery in the face—as he stood with other ISMers in front of an Armoured Personnel Carrier—for which he required several reconstructive surgeries. Five days later, Israeli soldiers shot British ISM volunteer Tom Hurndall in the head. Hurndall had been shepherding a group of Palestinian children out of a narrow passage where they had been playing when shooting started. Soldiers opened fire from a tank-mounted machine gun. Hurndall had just taken the hand of a little girl when the bullet hit him in the head. He remained comatose until his family disconnected him from life support in January 2004. Corrie, Avery, and Hurndall were all wearing fluorescent orange or red vests identifying them as human rights accompaniers when the Israeli military killed or injured them.[53]

The attacks hit everyone who had worked on the Hebron team hard. Corrie, Avery, and Hurndall had all participated in the nonviolence trainings led by the Hebron team at the request of ISM organizers. Many Hebron team members, as well as their Israeli and Palestinian friends, had stood between bulldozers and their designated targets as a part of their work. Furthermore, after Hurndall was shot, Israeli forces raided the ISM office in Beit Sahour, confiscating the organization's computers, photographs, and CD's and arresting an American volunteer and a worker for Human Rights Watch. They then moved on to the Palestinian Center for Rapprochement and confiscated its computer as well. Eight days later, soldiers in Hebron arrested Greg Rollins and searched the team's apartment (see above), so the May arrest and restrictions on the Hebron team may have been part of a larger push on the part of the Israeli government to get rid of human rights and peace activists.

An urgent action release put out on April 12, quoted Le Anne Clausen as saying,

> It feels like open season on peace activists. It's been open season on Palestinians all along, now the lack of accountability in the Israeli military has reached a new level. For Palestinians, the threat of "transfer" (ethnic cleansing) looms large; the Israeli attacks on human rights workers accompanying them seem to be part of a move

---

53. Joe Carr, who went through CPT training in 2004, was an ISM volunteer who witnessed the deaths of both Corrie and Hurndall. His sequence of photos showing Corrie's death and trip to the hospital were widely circulated on the internet. Carr wrote a rap song about Corrie that was also widely circulated under the titles "A Dove's Last Song" and "A Dove's Last Stand."

by the Sharon administration in this direction. If the internationals can be chased away, what will happen to the Palestinian civilians?[54]

CONCLUSION

At the close of 2003, most of the positive advancements the team had seen take place in Hebron since 1995 had disappeared. The Israeli military had re-occupied H-1 and once again asserted its right to close Hebron University and the Palestinian Polytechnic. The Old City market, once the heart of Hebron's economy, had become a ghost town; even the team's upstairs neighbors who had doggedly remained in the Old City on principle (although they had the financial resources to move) left in March 2003. The military had reinstalled the gates to the market that the team had helped Palestinians remove in 1996. The vegetable market where the team had sold the Oslo II tomatoes had become a settler parking lot. The Dana family in Jabal Johar again began living with daily attacks by soldiers and settlers as did Palestinians who remained in the Old City. Home demolitions were once again a fearsome reality for residents living on the outskirts of settlements, as was the confiscation of their land. The "security barrier" was heading inexorably toward Hebron, promising the confiscation of even greater amounts of land, and the further diminution of civil rights for those trapped behind it. Perhaps the most heartbreaking change was the collapse of relationships between Israelis and Palestinians the team had helped develop, because most Israelis were too scared to visit Hebron and because anger at daily violence caused both Israelis and Palestinians to retreat behind a wall of resentment.

A poem, "I dream of rage," that Greg Rollins wrote for CPTnet captured the team's mood at the end of this turbulent time:

> I dream of rage
>
> of rage
>
> of rage

---

54. CPTnet, "URGENT ACTION: Hold Israeli government accountable for killing and injuring human rights workers," April 12, 2003. The team soon adopted the new ISM policy stipulating that they would always place at least three workers in front of a bulldozer in the future.
CPTnet, "HEBRON URGENT ACTION: Stop Israeli attempts to silence international human rights observers," May 10, 2003. For more information on Avery, Corrie, and Hurndall, see Brooks de Wetter-Smith, and Michael Brown, "Photostory: Injured ISM activist Brian Avery returns home"; "Rachel Corrie Memorial"; "The Tom Hurndall Foundation Archives."

I dream of God in the desert
I dream of vast and open pain
and the sun that beats down on the sorrow

I see the pain on every face
on birds of prey
the breath of martyrs
I see the loss that comes this way
and the anger and fear that it follows

I hear the cries for open space
where walls are cut
and wires crumbled
and freed are those who sat in strength
because they refused to let go of their conscience

I dream of those whose lives were razed
in the metal mouths of caterpillars
and those who died in the wake
of lost hope for belts of horror

I dream of two trees whose roots were laced
their branches crossed and their bodies bled
each leaf they shed was mourned with revenge
while the world stood back in silence

I dream of rage
of rage
of rage
I dream of tribes in the desert
I dream of the lines on every face
etched by the burden of sorrow[55]

---

55. CPTnet, "I dream of rage," December 5, 2003. The poem appeared on the team's direct list on November 25—five days before Sue Rhodes died. Knowing that she was on her deathbed undoubtedly added to the Hebron team's own "burden of sorrow."

NINE

New Project in At-Tuwani
2004–2005

THE TEAM IN HEBRON put out noticeably fewer releases between 2004 and 2005, possibly because their regular activities of previous years continued and did not merit extra comment. A creeping depression and sense of futility regarding the political situation may also have factored into the lack of communication, as well as internal team conflicts.[1] Nevertheless, the Hebron team tried to intervene when confronted with soldier and settler violence and to continue recording the entrenchment of the Israeli occupation.

LAND CONFISCATION

At the beginning of 2004, the team spent considerable time documenting the increase in the boundaries of Kiryat Arba and Givat Ha Harsina settlements.[2] With the exception of the urgent action releases put out on behalf of Greg Rollins's petitions to the Israeli high court and denial of

---

1. The opening of the At-Tuwani project was also a factor in the dearth of releases, according to John Lynes. Because the Israeli settlers and soldiers there created more of a crisis situation in that region, and because working there required speed and agility, the younger, "more dynamic" CPTers went there, while older, slower, or less agile CPTers remained in Hebron, to keep up the standard routines of the work there. E-mail to author, November 9, 2007. Kim Lamberty, in her comments on a draft of this chapter, wrote that the At-Tuwani project started because not much was happening in Hebron; the closing of Shuhada Street to the team rendered much of their previous work impossible.

2. Diane Janzen, January 28, 2008, e-mail to author. Janzen, who photographed the moving settlement boundaries, said the gathered information was used for a diplomatic tour of the area on March 4, 2004.

entry into Israel,[3] the urgent action releases the team posted during these years all related to the confiscation of land in the Hebron district for the expansion of settlements. People in Wadi Ghroos, between the settlements of Kiryat Arba and Givat Ha Harsina, and the Jaber family were especially affected.[4]

In April 2005, the settlement of Karmei Tzur annexed forty-five dunams of Beit Ummar's land for a "security fence," but the fence—which was not connected to the West Bank Separation Barrier/Annexation Wall— would enclose four hundred and forty-four dunams of prime agricultural land, increasing the size of the settlement threefold.

After putting out an urgent action release for the Karmei Tzur annexation in April, the team put out a second in July 2005, regarding the Israeli military issuing orders for the largest confiscation of land in the history of the Hebron District. The urgent action release noted that the confiscation —near the village of Tarqumia—seemed timed to coincide with the Israeli government's removal of settlers in Gaza.

> World attention is focused on settler removal from the Gaza Strip, allowing land confiscation by the Israeli government in the West Bank to move ahead, unchallenged. The Hebron team's prior urgent action release in April asked people to protest a military confiscation order for Beit Ummar farmland that went unchallenged by members of congress. Seventy-four families in Beit Ummar lost their land.

The people of Tarqumia would also lose their land to the Separation Barrier/ Annexation Wall (see previous chapter regarding nomenclature).[5]

3. CPTnet, "HEBRON URGENT ACTION: Greg Rollins denied entry," March 12, 2004; CPTnet, "HEBRON URGENT ACTION: Israeli Ministry of Interior still considering Greg Rollins' case; Faxes from churches, Israelis welcome," March 16, 2004.

4. See CPTnet releases: "HEBRON URGENT ACTION: Israeli settlements in Beqa'a doubling in size," March 2, 2004; Jerry Levin, "HEBRON: Creeping Annexation spreading East and West from Wadi al-Ghroos," January 9, 2004; Art Gish, "HEBRON: The cauliflower was too small," January 27, 2004; Gish, "HEBRON: On the wrong side of the fence," February 2, 2004; Levin, "HEBRON: The piece process," April 17, 2004. April 2004 CPTnet archives.

5. CPTnet, "URGENT ACTION, HEBRON DISTRICT: Stop Settlement Expansion Near Beit Ummar," April 14, 2005; CPTnet, "HEBRON URGENT ACTION: Largest tract of land ever confiscated in history of Hebron District to take place 19 July 2005," July 8, 2005.

Rich Meyer, after speaking with the author on January 16, 2008, called Abdel Hadi Hantash and confirmed that the Tarqumia land had indeed been confiscated and the Separation Barrier/Annexation Wall had been installed there.

Aside from posting the urgent action releases, the team and other NGOs working on land confiscation issues felt they could do little to prevent the loss of these lands. However, after finding out that Palestinians refer to the Israeli military "shaving the land" when it confiscated their dunums, three team and CPT delegation members cut off their hair, as Israeli soldiers watched, on top of a Beit Ummar home demolished in April 2004.[6] Nine members of the summer 2004 training group in Chicago also shaved their heads in front of the Israeli consulate and ceremonially presented their hair to the Israeli Consulate's PR representative who arranged to meet with them two days later.[7]

---

6. Interestingly, given the Hebron team's past involvement in home demolition issues, the team mentioned this demolition and the demolitions that occurred in August 2004 near the Old City in updates only, instead of devoting a special release to each incident, which may testify to the general malaise engulfing the team mentioned at the beginning of this chapter. See CPTnet, "HEBRON UPDATE: August 8–16, 2004," August 19, 2004 and CPTnet, "HEBRON UPDATE: April 27-May 4, 2004," May 10, 2004. The 2004 CPT "Year in Review" (Annual Report) noted,

> In another attempt to push Palestinians to abandon the Old City of Hebron, the Israeli military demolished several homes between the Israeli settlement of Kiryat Arba and the Cave of Machpelah.
>
> Two Palestinian partner families in CPT's Campaign for Secure Dwellings lost their homes to demolition in the Hebron District, one in the Old City and one in Beit Ummar.

In a January 16, 2008, phone interview with the author, Rich Meyer said that at the time of the Beit Ummar demolition the team had not been maintaining regular contact with CSD families in the village. Regarding the demolition of three houses on the road leading from the Old City to Kiryat Arba (Wadi Nasara), he said they were a byproduct of the November 15, 2002, ambush on settlers and soldiers walking back to Kiryat Arba after Shabbat services (see chapter 7). Initially, the Israeli military had said more than thirty of the homes along the route presented a security risk and should be demolished. When it finally demolished the three homes in 2004, the Israeli left made a point of noting that the courts had found that only three homes were indeed a risk to settlers and soldiers, indicating that the Israeli authorities' desire to demolish the others was meant to facilitate a land grab. Because the families in the three houses knew the demolitions were coming, Meyer said, they had had the time to remove possessions, so the scenario of the demolition was somewhat different from the gut-wrenching spectacles that occurred when demolitions happened unexpectedly.

7. CPTnet, "CHICAGO: CPTers shave heads to dramatize destruction and confiscation of Palestinian land," July 30, 2004; Brett Kincaid, "Hebron: The shaving of the land," August 11, 2004.

In June 2004, Hebron team members Mai'a Williams, Kristin Anderson, and Christy Bischoff had shaved their heads, mostly as a lark, Williams told the author when they were on a delegation to the Democratic Republic of Congo (see also "Hair ye, Hair ye," June 23, 2004, GITW archives). However, they used the Palestinian expression as justification

CLOSURES AND RESTRICTIONS ON MOVEMENT

In his project report for the spring 2004 CPT Steering Committee, Rich Meyer noted that violence between Israeli settlers and Palestinians had decreased dramatically because of "intricate apartheid geography on the smallest scale."[8] The Israeli military sealed most entrances to the Old City of Hebron with checkpoints, resulting in economic and social strangulation of the area—which expanded to include Old Shalala Street, one of the busiest shopping areas in Hebron. A 2005 map of Hebron's Old City put out by the U.N. Office for the Coordination of Humanitarian Affairs (OCHA) noted seventeen checkpoints in the H-2 area, seven inner-city gates, and seventy-six road blocks composed of iron fences and gates, concrete blocks, barrels, and earth mounds.[9] Increasingly soldiers began asking CPTers their religion and rerouting them from streets designated as "Jews only."[10]

The restrictions in the Old City and the entrances to Hebron became even more acute after Palestinian acts of violence, such as the August 31, 2004, suicide bombings of two buses in the Israeli city of Beersheva[11] and

---

for doing so. CPT as an organization took the action more seriously and it seemed to hit a chord with Palestinians. Brett Kincaid wrote, in the release mentioned above, "They reminded us that a woman's hair is her honor, and that sacrificing her hair sends a powerful message that there are people outside the region who care and who are working to raise awareness among their own people about the Palestinians' suffering."

Sara Reschly, in a November 14, 2007, e-mail to the author mentioned that the CPTers at the witness in Chicago wrote emergency phone numbers on their arms, which distressed one young Jewish woman, for whom the shaved heads and numbers evoked concentration camp imagery.

8. "Hebron project update–Steering Committee March 2004."

9. United Nations Office for the Coordination of Humanitarian Affairs (OCHA), "Special Focus: The closure of Hebron's Old City," July 2005.

10. See CPTnet releases: Levin, "HEBRON: Law and order Israeli style in Old Shalala Street," January 1, 2004; Jack, "HEBRON REFLECTION: A Palestinian's home is not his castle," January 13, 2004; Gish, "HEBRON: The fence beside our door," January 26, 2004; Jack, "HEBRON: A soggy day in Hebron Town," January 27, 2004.

11. Christina Gibb, a CPT reservist from New Zealand, wrote in her comments on a draft of this chapter sent to author on December 19, 2007,

> The IDF imposed a total closure on the whole city for a month immediately following the suicide bombings, until they captured the head of the Hamas cell in the city. The [service taxi] drivers still managed to get in and out of Hebron by driving through vineyards and over rough farm tracks, or by dragging vehicles over the earth mounds, their routes changing from day to day. Palestinians brought produce in and out of the city by throwing it from one vehicle to another, backed up on either side of a large rock barrier under a bridge.

the March 7, 2005, shooting of two Israeli Border police at the Ibrahimi mosque/Cave of Machpelah. "The violence of the jailer is well known, but rarely punished," wrote Kim Lamberty, "while the violence of the inmate results in severe punishment for the whole population. The only difference is that most people here never committed a crime. They landed in this jail due to geography, international politics, ethnic origin and bad luck."[12]

As was the case with the increasing land confiscation, Hebron team members could do little more than serve as spectators to the imprisonment of the Old City. In a release about an August 5, 2005, CPT delegation witness against the series of gates installed, delegate Eileen Hanson wrote,

> The psalmist says, "Open to me the gates of righteousness" (Ps 118), and Amos proclaims, "Hate evil and love good, and establish justice in the gate." (Amos 5:15) Justice and peace cannot come about through separation and confinement. The biblical conception of justice is to live in right relationship with the other, not simply to cut off contact with those we find difficult. But still around the world, from the Separation Wall in the West Bank, to the wall along the US/Mexico border, we build higher and higher walls that serve only to imprison people on both sides.
>
> On 5 August 2005, Our CPT delegation took this message to the recently installed gates in the Old City. We stood in vigil at each gate, and prayed together that these gates and the gates of all hearts might open.
>
> The Old City in Hebron used to be a bustling market, crowded with people and goods. Settler and soldier harassment have forced many shops to close and the streets are mostly empty now.
>
> On 4 August, the Israeli military installed five iron gates in the Old City. They can be locked any time, sealing off the Old City from the rest of Hebron. Their installation represents the real meaning of "disengagement." Like the walls around Gaza, the gates ensure continuing Israeli control of the space without any human engagement with those who live there. Disengagement is simply the removal of any human interaction between occupier and occupied.
>
> The only salient difference between the Old City and a prison is that, for now, the gates are open. But as Palestinian journalist Khalid Amayreh said, the important question is not whether or not it is a prison, but rather, who holds the key. The military check-

---

12. CPTnet, "HEBRON: Lockdown," September 7, 2004. See also CPTnet, Bischoff, "HEBRON: Old City locked down after shooting outside Ibrahimi Mosque," March 8, 2005; CPTnet, Bischoff, "HEBRON: Who is responsible?" March 12, 2005.

points at the entrances, and IDF outposts on rooftops all around the Old City, make clear who holds that key.

We hoped by our small public witness to encourage the people here, to say to them that their suffering is not invisible, and their imprisonment is not forgotten. We pray that the walls that separate people, in Hebron, in Gaza, between the US and Mexico, and all over the world might be brought down so that people can live together in justice and in peace.[13]

SOLDIER VIOLENCE

Beit Ummar was the site of soldier invasions in early 2004. On January 2, 2004, soldiers entered the village at 2:00 AM, demolished a home, tore up water and phone lines, damaged an ancient cemetery, arrested six people, and injured five. One family told the team that soldiers had stolen 6,000 shekels when they invaded their home. According to the soldiers, they were punishing the town because some Beit Ummar boys had thrown stones and Molotov cocktails at Israeli vehicles on bypass road 60. The military distributed leaflets saying that disturbances would be met with "an iron fist." In March, soldiers took away the son of a CSD family with whom the team had had a long and important relationship. Two days later, they conducted another raid, detaining fifteen youth. The residents of Beit Ummar connected the January and March raids to the coming of the Separation/

---

13. CPTnet, Hanson, "HEBRON: 'Establish justice in the gate.' CPT delegation witnesses against prison gates in Hebron's Old City," August 13, 2005. Hanson would go through training in January 2007.

Christina Gibb, in her comments on a draft of this chapter, wrote,

> By the beginning of 2006, Palestinians had surreptitiously managed to remove all five extra gates, which the IDF did not re-erect. Three other gates, however, which were installed or fortified in August 2005, have remained as a source of constant harassment of everyone who goes through them. The main gate from the south in the Old City out to the area of the Ibrahimi Mosque/Caves of Machpelah has been strengthened, and divided by a tall, fixed barrier down the centre separating those going in from those coming out. Three tall turnstiles, controlled by a soldier in a booth, and a metal detector arch, like those in airports, complete the installation. The other two gates take the form of cabins, with twin entrances exits and metal detectors, again all electronically controlled. These bar the ends of Shuhada Street, the former main thoroughfare of Hebron, and now the road linking the four extremist Israeli settlements to the Caves of Machpelah. Other fixed barricades channel Palestinians trying to move from one side of the city to the other, or to go to the Ibrahimi Mosque, so that they have to go through one or more of these metal detector gates which turn these streets into a cattle race.

Annexation Wall, which would cut off Beit Ummar from most the villagers' farmland. They told the Hebron team that the soldier harassment was designed to intimidate the villagers so they would not protest.[14]

Releases from 2004 also recorded numerous instances of soldiers humiliating Palestinians at checkpoints. To prove they were not armed, Palestinian men were forced by soldiers near the Beit Romano checkpoint to lift shirts and drop trousers. They also began pressuring Palestinian women to enter a small cement guard tower where female soldiers could search them, causing a great deal of shame in a culture that placed high value on modesty. Team releases recorded soldiers detaining a mentally handicapped man well known to them for three hours "to teach him to look after his ID" which had become crumpled, as well as shopkeepers who had stores in the area and were also well known to them.[15]

Because of this harassment, team members began monitoring the Beit Romano checkpoint more systematically. For two weeks in the fall of 2004, they took notes to quantify the numbers of Palestinians who passed through the checkpoint and the percentage of those whom Israeli soldiers detained. Joe Carr and Christina Gibb were recording these statistics on November 4 when soldiers frisked them, confiscated their logbooks, took their passports, and called the police to arrest them. The police released them that night without pressing charges.

Joe Carr later wrote about his experience at the station,

> There was an extraordinary cast of characters at the police station. My first police interrogator was your classic tough guy, who backed me up against the wall, his face inches from mine as he questioned me. Baby-faced soldiers would pass by, smile, and say, "What's up?"—confused about why I was there. One jovial police officer was from Texas. "Occupied territory," he said, "Why aren't you there defending Mexican rights?" We told him about CPT's project on the Arizona-Mexico border and briefly discussed the evils of colonialism. Our final police investigator was an older . . . Libyan Jew who was kind of sweet and had terrible English. It took him ten minutes just to tell me I didn't have to answer his questions and that anything I said could be used against me. He let us write our own statements in English, which Israeli authorities rarely allow.

---

14. CPTnet, "HEBRON: No candy if you are bad," January 10, 2004; CPTnet, Roe, "HEBRON DISTRICT: 'They've taken our son,'" March 20, 2004.

15. CPTnet, Janzen, "HEBRON: What is 'haram?'" June 2, 2004. CPTnet, Gibb, "HEBRON: Everyday life with soldiers," October 16, 2004.

Eventually he released us, but not before serving us coffee and chatting with us about his life story.

The police told the CPTers that the statistics to which the Israeli military took exception were those recording the numbers of soldiers at the checkpoint and particularly the number of army vehicles, so the team resumed their monitoring without recording these figures.[16]

In late 2005, team members experienced a resurgence of home invasions in their own neighborhood. Soldiers would sometimes break in, lock the families in a room, and steal their valuables. After team members intervened in and documented several of these invasions, soldiers invaded the team apartment on December 11 and December 29, 2005. On the former occasion, they told team members they were searching the team apartment because Kristin Anderson and Diane Janzen had videotaped them while they were invading a Palestinian home. In their release about the December 29 invasion, the team wrote,

> Walking around the apartment, the soldiers showed interest in a bowl of old sound grenades, used tear gas canisters, rubber-coated bullets and shells that CPTers picked up from the streets in the past. The soldiers passed these items around, and then one decided that the two or three dented cartridges constituted weapons. He explained that possession of weapons in this part of Hebron is prohibited, but when questioned by a CPTer the soldier corrected himself that Israelis are permitted to carry weapons in this part of Hebron. CPTers pointed out that it would be dangerous or impossible to place those bullets into a gun.

16. CPTnet, Klassen, "HEBRON: CPTers Carr and Gibb arrested for observing soldiers detain people at Beit Romano checkpoint," November 4, 2004; Klassen, "Carr and Gibb released from custody," November 5, 2004; Carr, "HEBRON REFLECTION: Overcoming fear while under arrest," November 6, 2004. Gibb, comments on a draft of this chapter.

A week later, a Russian soldier involved in Carr's and Gibb's detention stopped Carr as he passed the Beit Romano checkpoint. She had heard that he had been deported for terrorist activity. He wrote,

> The Israeli police arrived within five minutes of the soldier's call. When was the last time you called the police and they came within five minutes? I was glad to see a significant amount of Palestinians were passing by unhindered while the soldiers and police argued about what to do with me. I figure the police negated the rumor that I'd been deported, and refused to arrest me since they had no grounds, not even dubious ones. My passport was returned and I was released; it all took a little over a half hour.

CPTnet, "HEBRON: Detained in solidarity," November 24, 2004.

A second patrol of six Israeli soldiers, including the captain, arrived. The captain collected the passports of all five CPTers present, and called the Israeli police. The police collected the display casings, shells and bullets and arrested John Lynes, Sarah MacDonald, Rich Meyer, Grace Pleiman and Harriet Taylor.

Although the team members locked the door behind them, and the captain assured them that no one would enter the apartment in their absence, when Kathie Uhler and Art Gish arrived at the apartment later they found the street door unlocked, the door to the office apartment forced, and the team's cameras, computers, and cell phones stolen. (A Palestinian-American computer store owner later recovered one computer for the team, when a Palestinian man came in to hock it.) The police formally arrested Lynes, MacDonald, Meyer, Pleiman, and Taylor, drawing up the required paperwork and having them sign a statement saying they would appear in court if called to do so. Afterwards, the police released them on their own recognizance and never contacted them further regarding a court date.[17]

SETTLER VIOLENCE

Jerry Levin wrote a release in April 2004 that perhaps best illustrates the sense of futility the team and its partners felt regarding CPTers' abilities to address settler violence in Hebron and its environs during this period. On a social visit to Abdel Jawad Jaber's home, team members found out that ten days earlier, settlers, escorted by three jeep-loads of soldiers, had sawed down twenty-three grapevines, some of which were thirty years old. When team members asked Atta Jaber why no one had called them, he said, "This was bad, but you know, we have had even worse than this. And what good would it do, if you did know? Who will help us? And by the way," he continued, "six settlers with guns walked around my house yesterday.

---

17. CPTnet, "HEBRON: Israeli military invades CPT apartment, arrests team; team computers stolen," January 8, 2006; CPTnet, Jerry Levin, "HEBRON: Good Samaritan alive and well in Hebron," March 1, 2006. Rich Meyer, interview, February 5, 2008. See also CPTnet releases: "HEBRON: Israeli soldiers occupy homes, take belongings," September 14, 2005; Rich Meyer, "HEBRON: Say it with a home invasion," December 21, 2005; Dianne Roe and Sonia Robbins, "HEBRON: Soldiers or Settlers? Palestinian's Hebron home sustains severe damage," February 3, 2006. For an example of soldiers invading a home in a more considerate way, see, "HEBRON UPDATE: 6–12 August 2005," August 23, 2005.

Rodeina . . . was home alone. They just walked around it. But it made Rodeina frightened and sick. Today she is still not well."[18]

The great majority of releases relating to settler violence in 2005 had to do with attacks on Palestinian residents in Tel Rumeida. This attention was partially due to the founding of the Tel Rumeida Project (TRP) in April 2005, by former CPTer Luna Villota and a CPT intern, Chelli Stanley, who chafed at the constraints under which the Hebron Team operated. Eventually, the project became loosely affiliated with ISM. Despite the frictions that had led to team members leaving, the Hebron team was grateful that internationals had set up a regular violence-deterring, human rights monitoring presence there, because they knew how vulnerable the Palestinian residents of the area were.[19]

The worst of the attacks occurred in April and May of 2005. On May 4, a large group of settlers vandalized homes on Tel Rumeida. The following day, CPTers Bill Baldwin, Sally Britton, David Janzen, and Grace Pleiman joined a tour group led by the Hebron Rehabilitation Committee (HRC) of South African, French, Swiss, Irish, and U.K. diplomats. They were trying to visit the site of the proposed settler road that was to run through the Muslim graveyard, but soldiers turned the group back so they would not interact with a settler mob that appeared to be waiting for them. Eventually, the soldiers allowed the diplomats to pass, but prevented the internationals and Palestinians from doing so. When the diplomats returned to the Tel Rumeida area, Dr. Tayseer Zeahda joined them and told them that settlers, enabled by both Israeli soldiers and police, had broken his water pipe, cut his phone lines, and stoned his home for several hours that day. Soldiers would not allow CPTers to visit the home and document the damage. While TIPH was monitoring the soldiers' interactions with the diplomats, Palestinians and internationals, settler girls attacked Dianne Roe, Kathie Uhler, and EAPPI workers trying to accompany Qurtuba students past the Dubboya Street checkpoint. The settlers pushed, kicked, and spat on Roe and Uhler, while Israeli soldiers stood by and laughed. The soldiers then declared Dubboya Street a closed military zone and would not let the internationals accompany the girls. The next day, May 6, CPTers again

18. CPTnet, "HEBRON: Israeli soldiers guard settlers as they destroy Jaber family vineyard," April 7, 2004.

19. When the author contacted the Hebron team about the current status of the Tel Rumeida Project, Donna Hicks responded in a November 27, 2007, e-mail, "The people who are living there now haven't mentioned the Project, and self-identify as independents or ISM." Former CPTer Joe Carr also provided support to the Tel Rumeida Project.

tried to visit the Dr. Zeahda's home to document the damage, and soldiers again told them it was a closed military zone.[20]

Two weeks later, about a dozen settlers stoned Hani Abu Haikel's home, breaking windows in the room where his children were hiding. They also stoned CPTers and other international observers on their way to visit the Abu Haikel home. Instead of intercepting the settlers, soldiers detained and blindfolded Hani Abu Haikel as he rushed to protect his children and chased and arrested thirty-two of forty-two Israeli peace activists who had come to make solidarity visits to the Palestinian residents of Tel Rumeida (the remaining ten slipped inside with the assistance of Palestinian bystanders).[21]

That summer, Jamal Abu Haikel, Hani's father, who had befriended the Hebron team in the summer of 1995, died at his home on Tel Rumeida. Normally suspicious of foreigners, according to Hani, Jamal Abu Haikel had, for some reason, taken a liking to CPTers—affection which they returned. Over the years, he had refused millions of dollars and promises of passports to any country he chose from the settlers in exchange for his property and resisted with grim determination settler attacks intended to make him and his family leave.

Hani Abu Haikel told the team that his father had purchased graves at the top of the cemetery, overlooking the Old City. When Hani asked him why he had bought six graves, his father told him, "Eventually the settlers will kill us all."[22]

SCHOOL PATROL

For the winter and spring of 2004, the team decided to discontinue accompanying children to school except on Saturdays when the possibility for settler violence was high. EAPPI had taken over the accompaniment of

---

20. CPTnet, "HEBRON UPDATE: 5–11 May 2005," May 19, 2005. Dianne Roe, CPTnet, David Janzen, and Kathie Uhler, "HEBRON: Settler riots stop diplomatic tour; Army declares tour area closed military zone," May 6, 2005;

21. CPTnet, "HEBRON: Israeli settlers escalate violence against Palestinians at Tel Rumeida," May 11, 2005; CPTnet, "HEBRON: Thirty-two Israeli peace activists arrested while attempting to visit Palestinians on Tel Rumeida," May 23, 2005.

22. CPTnet, Lorin Peters, "HEBRON: Jamal Abu Haikel, his life and death," August 10, 2005. The day after he died, settlers threw a party celebrating his death and pelted Hani Abu Haikel with chocolates and bonbons. Hani, besieged by settlers in May 2005, referred to his family's situation as "the final battle." CPTnet, "HEBRON: Israeli settlers escalate violence against Palestinians at Tel Rumeida."

the girls and teachers at Qurtuba School, and at the other schools, children and teachers seemed to be getting there and back without incident. CPT patrols resumed with the start of the school year in fall 2004, at the request of some teachers.[23]

The gates that the Israeli military installed across roads leading into the Old City in the summer of 2005 (see above) would change the nature of school patrol.[24] Included among the gates were metal detectors at two points on the edge of the Old City. Initially, female teachers of child-bearing age and students refused to walk through the metal detectors, citing two concerns: 1) health risks from frequent exposure to the equipment, and 2) violation of modesty from being closed in a metal cabin with a male soldier and the mistaken impression that the device would make their bodies underneath their clothes visible to the soldiers. After days of protest and noncompliance, the Israeli military agreed to allow teachers with school ID and students to bypass the cabins.

Over the next months, as Israeli soldiers rotated in and out of Hebron, new troops frequently disregarded the agreement and attempted to force all pedestrians through the cabins. A November 2005 update records several instances of spirited resistance to this protocol on the part of children and teachers, including toppling plastic barricades around the cabins, carrying signs in Arabic and English proclaiming their right to reach their schools, and teachers giving lessons to children sitting in the street.[25]

23. See EAPPI releases: Neil, "Walking to School in Hebron"; Styrbjörn, "Going to School in Hebron."
Explanations of why and when school patrols stopped and started from e-mails to author by Rich Meyer, Maureen Jack, and John Lynes sent November–December 2007, and from comments Christina Gibb made on a draft of this chapter.

24. The OCHA report cited in n. 9 has a section describing how the closure affected schools and school children in or near the Old City.

25. CPTnet, "HEBRON UPDATE: 16–23 November 2005," December 13, 2005. In a November 30, 2007, e-mail to the author, Maureen Jack wrote,

> The soldiers put up plastic barricades and the kids pushed at them and the soldiers pushed back. Eventually a kid realised that the better option was to pull the barricade. This they did and the soldiers put up wire on top. One day a kind of small petrol bomb got thrown and one day the soldiers threw tear gas. The day after we were allowed to make the hostage crisis [see below] public knowledge there was specific filming with a view to showing CPT's work in Palestine. I think that was 30 November... My understanding was that the resistance lasted a few more days and then ended but I left team on 30 November. There's video footage of the Nov resistance on the CPT website. It was done by Diane J as part of the effort to get the [CPT hostages] released. I was sad when I was in Hebron this summer [2007] to hear that resistance has ended.

More serious than the metal-detector standoffs was the Israeli military's prohibition against ISM, CPT, EAPPI, and TRP members accompanying students in September 2005 near Qurtuba. TRP members were placed under virtual house arrest, and soldiers forbade the other accompaniment groups from standing in places where they could observe the girls and teachers at points where they were most vulnerable to settler and soldier harassment. They also prohibited Doctors Without Borders personnel from entering the area.[26]

Eventually, however, the military once again allowed internationals to accompany the Qurtuba girls. As of this writing in 2008, team accompaniment of children to and from school remains a daily task. At the Yatta Road checkpoint, teachers and students now pass through the metal detectors, because the principal of the Ibrahimiyye boys' school has instructed his students not to cause problems, and the Qurtuba students also pass through the metal detectors on Dubboya Street.[27]

INTERNATIONAL AND ISRAELI SOLIDARITY MOVEMENTS

When asked about the most notable change affecting the Hebron team in the 2004–2005 period, CPTer John Lynes wrote,

> My impression is that the most important development during that period was that, for the first time, EAPPI and ISM established a significant continuous presence in Hebron. This changed the character of our work. We were no longer the only game in town. ISM took over much of the publicity side. EAPPI looked after Cortuba School.[28]

From the beginning of CPT's project in Hebron, team members had known that many teams of human rights monitors could be put to good

26. See CPTnet releases: Levin, "HEBRON: Continuing settler harassment, security measures, and cultural fears mar the start of school in Hebron," September 8, 2005; Levin, "HEBRON A second day of confrontation, anger, doubt and fear at checkpoint," September 9, 2005; Gibb, "HEBRON: Internationals banned from streets in Tel Rumeida area; teachers protest metal detector checkpoint," September 12, 2005; Levin, "HEBRON: Israeli army turnabouts keep frustrated Palestinians guessing at checkpoint," September 15, 2005. CPT, "Year in Review FYE 2006."(CPT Annual Report.)

27. John Lynes, e-mail to author, December 1, 2007. Donna Hicks, e-mails to author December 6 and 7, 2007. Hicks noted in her December 6 e-mail, "I know the teachers go through the gate, because a soldier allegedly lost the key the other day and held up the teachers for an hour until it miraculously reappeared."

28. John Lynes, e-mail to author, November 9, 2007.

use in the city and its outlying areas. The contributions EAPPI, ISM, and the TRP made toward the work of nonviolence helped CPTers feel less anxious about not being able to be every place at once. Team members could feel better about taking time off to go to church on Sunday, because they knew other groups would cover school patrol, and they in turn provided breaks for EAPPI and ISM teams when they needed to meet or attend other functions.

The releases from 2004 and 2005 also record the Hebron team's ongoing work with Israeli groups, including participating in demonstrations against the Separation/Annexation wall and olive tree planting actions.[29]

More significantly, in 2004, Yehuda Shaul and some other soldiers from the Nahal brigade set up an exhibit in Tel Aviv they called "Breaking the Silence." The team in 2002 had had many conversations with Shaul and other Nahal members who were troubled by the military and settler trampling of human rights they witnessed in Hebron (see chapter 7). Their exhibit showed photos of these abuses. It also contained a display of keys soldiers had taken from Palestinian drivers to refute the assertion by official Israeli military spokespeople that soldiers did not confiscate keys. When CPTers visited the exhibit, reservists told them that many soldiers had brought their families to it, hoping they might understand better the demoralizing duties they undertook in Hebron.[30] Shaul, an observant Jew, would also later go on to work with Bnei Avraham (Sons of Abraham), a group that undertook solidarity work with Palestinians in Hebron and brought hundreds of Israelis to the city so they could see the effects of the military occupation there.[31]

---

29. See, for example, CPTnet, Fox, "HEBRON REFLECTION: Uprooted," January 7, 2007; CPTnet, Berquist and Schmidt, "WEST BANK: Demonstration at Biddu," April 29, 2004; "HEBRON: Planting olive trees on the other side of the border," January 20, 2005.

30. On June 22, 2004, three of the reservists who had organized the exhibit were questioned by military police for over six hours. Ostensibly, the police were investigating the three for having committed the abuses they were exposing. The reservists assumed that the police questioning was done for the purposes of intimidation and punishment. CPTnet, "HEBRON/TEL AVIV: 'Breaking the silence,' about Israeli soldiers' experiences in Hebron," June 25, 2004.

31. See McIntyre, "A rough guide to Hebron"; Avraham, "Bnei Avraham-English"; CPT Hebron, "Israeli martial law imposes further restrictions on Palestinians, CPTers, Israeli peace groups, regardless of Israeli court decision."

In CPT semi-annual project reports for 2004–2006, teams responded to the question of why the CPT presence was still needed by noting that local partners wanted them to stay, that they helped them do things that would be more dangerous without CPT support, and that "There is currently no substitute for the constituency education work that we do, which can directly affect our countries' foreign policies." In the 2006 report, the team gave as a reason, "The Occupation continues and in some ways its vice-like grip on the lives of Palestinians increases."[32] None of these criteria leaves an impression of dynamic, hopeful work having a major impact on the violence in Hebron.

At the end of Ramadan in 2004, normally a festive holiday, one Muslim friend told Art Gish, "How can we celebrate when we are crying? Every day, people are being killed, here, and in Iraq, in Afghanistan. We can only cry." Gish also wrote about having eaten the "last fruits" from the land of one Palestinian family. Settlers had erected a fence, effectively confiscating two and a half acres, where the family had grown olives, vegetables, and grapes—food served to Gish for lunch. "I was practically in tears as I ate that precious food," Gish wrote.

> An important part of my faith is to constantly look for first fruits, for signs of God's Spirit breaking into the systems of oppression around us. I don't know how to deal with the concept of "last fruits." Last fruits symbolize death, despair, hopelessness, finality. I want to look for beginnings.
>
> I then remembered Jesus' last supper. That also symbolized an end. It came before something horrible, before the end of his life, before his defeat. Yet, after that defeat came victory over oppression and death.
>
> I need to remember that victory as I face the hopelessness of walls, fences, separation, destruction, and loss. I do not see any hope, but maybe there is hope in those last fruits I ate for lunch.[33]

When the team began checking with local Palestinian partners in 2005 about what their goals should be in the midst of such a dismal situation, Hisham Sharabati told them he valued CPT's work, "because in the heat of the confrontation, when the sounds of the cannons and the shooting and rockets are going on, nobody hears the cries of children." CPT, he implied, did hear those cries. The phrase reminded Jerry Levin of a song he had heard

---

32. Rich Meyer, Hebron annual and semi-annual project reports for 2004–2006."

33. CPTnet, "HEBRON: The last fruits," February 14, 2004; CPTnet, Gish, "HEBRON: We can only cry," February 21, 2004.

when he worked with CNN in Lebanon during the worst of the civil war there in the 1980s:

> It was a lament featuring a young girl pleading with an indifferent world to "Give us a chance. Give us a chance." As the song faded out, one heard the audience applauding loudly and cheering almost hysterically.
>
> Twenty-one years later, the moving plea somberly applies in and around Hebron's Old City where not nearly enough people are giving today's young people a chance. Twenty-one years later I, along with CPT colleagues, am encountering a too-familiar indifference to the needs of today's children on both sides of the metal gates, padlocked fences and newly upgraded electromagnetic metal detecting checkpoints that continue to abet hostility, divisiveness and violence.
>
> When CPT first arrived in the Old City of Hebron ten years ago, many Palestinian children and young people with whom we work or the Israelis against whose hostility we try to intervene were not much younger or older than that girl in Lebanon. Clearly since then, neither those Palestinians nor their Israeli counterparts have had a chance to live the kind of violence-free, oppression-free lives for which she was begging back in 1984. And that, of course, applies to the Palestinian colleague mentioned above who has married since CPT came to Hebron in 1995 and is raising three children.
>
> So it's not surprising that he could state concretely the reason we in CPT are here. We are here to continue responding to the cries of the children and take part in the nonviolent struggle to give them all a chance.[34]

AT-TUWANI

In the southern West Bank, also referred to as the South Hebron Hills, is a string of ancient villages, most with populations under two hundred. Because they lie near the Green Line, Israeli governments over the years have sought to evacuate the villagers, so that they could unilaterally move

---

34. In October 2008, due to several ongoing personnel issues, CPT brought its thirteen years of work based in the Old City of Hebron to a close. During the winter of 2008-2009, a series of exploratory teams consisting of CPTers who had worked in Palestine investigated other areas around the West Bank where CPT might be able to work. This exploratory work and eight months of "re-focusing" meetings resulted in the opening of a new Al-Khaliil/Hebron project in May 2009. As of 2009, the Hebron and At-Tuwani teams are considered branches of one unified Palestine Project, and the Hebron team has a Palestinian advisory council that provides direction similar to the direction that the South Hebron Hills villagers provide for the At-Tuwani team.

the border in by several kilometers and use the area for military training. In addition to the official state-sponsored violence since 1984, the people in the region have had to deal with particularly vicious settler violence committed by residents of the settlements of Ma'on, Susia, Karmiel, and their outposts. Villagers from the hamlets of Khoruba and Sarura, just south of the Ma'on settlement, deserted their homes in 1997 because they could not take the stress anymore. In a reflection on the harassment that drove them away, CPTer Jerry Levin, raised in a Jewish family, wrote:

> There's nothing that makes an ardent militant, acquisitive Zionist see red more quickly than someone claiming that what has been happening in the Occupied Territories resembles the persecution of Jews in Europe. I will not get into that, because I don't want the argument to center around how many dead Palestinians compared to dead Jews does it take to make a holocaust. It would dishonor the murders of both to get involved in that kind of numbers game.
>
> However, I do know a pogrom when I see one.[35]

Israeli friends of the Hebron team had long felt anxious about the families living in these villages, because they were so isolated the Israeli military could drive them out with relative ease—as it had the villagers of Susiya in the summer and fall of 2001. Abdel Hadi Hantash, the chief cartographer of the Hebron District, shared this anxiety and was perhaps most instrumental in getting CPTers to the area before the At-Tuwani project started in 2004.

The team's first forays into the region began in 1996, when CPTers tried to assist Hebron University professor Musallem Shreateh, whose wheat field the settlers of Susia were bent on confiscating (see chapter 2). From then onward, the team continued to make sporadic trips out to the area, to rebuild walls and animal pens knocked down by the military, to remove fencing settlers had erected around Palestinian land, and sometimes just to document the devastation, such as happened when the Israeli military destroyed caves—some continuously inhabited as far back as four thousand years—in 2002.[36]

---

35. CPTnet, "AT-TUWANI: Havat Ma'on—a perfect cover for bullies," December 22, 2004.

36. See CPTnet releases: "The Wheat Harvest Near Hebron," May 13, 1996; "URGENT ACTION: Hebron CPTers Arrested," May 30, 1996; "Hebron: Plowing Musallem's Land," October 27, 1996; "Hebron: Correction to Wheatfield Arson story," July 1, 1998; "HEBRON: Yatta farmer loses Entire Wheat Crop to Arson," June 27, 1998; "Hebron: Correction to Wheatfield Arson story," July 1, 1998; "HEBRON URGENT ACTION:

In a media packet that CPTers developed during the first year of the At-Tuwani project, they included an incomplete chronology of other violent incidents that had occurred between 2001 and the time CPT accepted an invitation to set up a project in Tuwani:

2001:

Israeli settlers attack children from Tuba on a path that runs between Ma'on and Havat Ma'on with stones. Six-year-old Fatimah Zen is hit on the head and hospitalized because of bleeding, she never returns to school. Israeli settlers accost Zehira Abu Jundii and her three children as they travel home to Tuba. Settlers attempt to steal her donkey.

2002:

Israeli settlers attack Umm Jabriil, an At-Tuwani shepherd, with sticks.

Israeli settlers accost Omar from Tuba and steal the olives he had been carrying home.

Four Israeli settlers stop the car of Juma Rabai, who is traveling with his brothers from the hospital in Yatta back to At-Tuwani with their sick father. The settlers pull Juma, his brothers, and his father from the car, force them to the ground, and beat them.

Israeli settlers attack and shoot sixty-year-old Umm Hani Makhamra (woman from neighboring village of Khallet Athba) in the leg.

On three or four occasions, the Israeli military shoots out the wheels of At-Tuwani tractors (replacement wheels are 700 NIS each).

Israeli police confiscate Juma Rabai's tractor as he was plowing his fields. The police offer to return the tractor if Juma will sign a release giving his land to the settlers. Juma refuses and is obliged to pay a fine of 1000 shekels to retrieve his tractor.

Palestinian Farmers and Shepherds driven off their land," November 16, 1999; "HEBRON UPDATE: March 16–30, 2000," April 8, 2001; "Hebron: urgent action release Devastation In Yatta Area," July 6, 2001; David Cockburn, "HEBRON DISTRICT: Happy New Year, or Just Another Day?" September 22, 2001; "HEBRON DISTRICT URGENT ACTION: Stop the expulsion of cave dwellers from South Hebron Hills," March 23, 2002. See also B'tselem report, "Means of Expulsion: Violence, Harassment and Lawlessness against Palestinians in the Southern Hebron Hills." In early releases, the team incorrectly referred to the people in these villages as Bedouin, unwittingly playing into Israeli government propaganda that the cave dwellers were transient and had not lived in the area long.

2003:

CPTers and members of Ta'ayush, an Israeli peace group founded at the beginning of the Intifada,[37] accompany farmers as they worked in their fields. Settlers attack Lorne Friesen and Greg Rollins and push Palestinian tractors down the hill. [See previous chapter.]

Three times the settlers throw stones at Juma's house in the night. Each time, the settlers run back into Havat Ma'on. At-Tuwani villagers call the Israeli police and army, who do not respond. On the third night, villagers hide behind the rocks and olive trees near Juma's house and throw stones at the settlers when they arrive. After this, settlers stop coming to Juma's house and throwing stones . . .

Israeli settlers harass a child who is returning home to Tuba from secondary school in Karmil. They steal his school bag.

2004:

January:
Israeli military sprays herbicide on wheat and barley crops planted by villagers from Jinba

April:
Seven Israeli settlers attack Hafez Hereni, his seventy-four-year-old mother Fatima, and Israeli Ta'ayush activist Salumka. They beat Hafez's mother, shoot at them, and attempt to steal their sheep. The victims give the Israeli police a video of the attack, but the authorities do nothing.

The Israeli military demolishes the houses of Saber and Ghanum Hereni, allegedly due to lack of Israeli permit.

At night, Israeli settlers put dead chickens in one of the two At-Tuwani drinking water wells.

Israeli settlers burn the wheat, lentil, and barley harvests from the villages of Tuba and Mufakra.

Israeli settlers shoot the car of Faher Mohammed Abu Aram from Karmil and steal his belongings.

Israeli settlers attack the sheep of Ibrahim Hammad Abu Jindea, from Tuba, while his fifteen year-old son tended them. The settlers kill four sheep with knives.

June–Aug:
Israeli soldiers repeatedly enter and search houses in At-Tuwani in the middle of the night.[38]

37. See Ta'ayush, "Who we are."

38. CPT At-Tuwani, "At-Tuwani Media Packet." See also CPTnet, "HEBRON UPDATE: January 13–23, 2003," January 31, 2003; CPTnet, Maureen Jack, "HEBRON DISTRICT: Destruction of crops in and near Jinba," January 31, 2003.

Because settlers targeted schoolchildren, who had to walk past Ma'on settlement on their way to the central school in At-Tuwani, villagers in the area asked Ta'ayush if it could provide accompaniment for them, and Ta'ayush contacted CPT, asking CPTers to join Ta'ayush members for a weekend visit to the area. As was the case in Hebron, the worst settler attacks often happened on Saturdays, so CPTers went down to At-Tuwani a few weekends in the spring of 2003 to accompany the children.[39]

In August 2004, Operation Dove, an Italian peace group[40] that had closer connections to Ta'ayush, sent an exploratory team for visits to Susiya and Jinba with an eye toward setting up a South Hebron Hills Project, and concluded that projects in those villages were not viable. CPTer Mai'a Williams, CPT intern Anna Sophia Bachman,[41] and Dove Cristina Graziani then stayed in At-Tuwani for one week, accompanying the villagers as they started building a clinic by climbing to the top of a mountain and yelling to village men when they saw an Israeli military humvee.[42] Following this exploratory delegation, CPTer Kim Lamberty, Doves Graziani and Piergiorgio Rosetti, and Ezra Nawi from Ta'ayush met in Jerusalem, where Nawi told them that At-Tuwani would be interested in hosting a team.[43] After this meeting, Lamberty, CPTer Chris Brown, Rosetti, and Hisham Sharabati went down for an overnight stay with village leader Hafez Hereni (who had hosted the previous exploratory delegation), to make sure the village, and not primarily Ta'ayush, wanted a team of internationals there. At that meeting, the villagers told them they wanted the internationals to provide accompaniment for the building of a village clinic and for

---

39. The Palestinian school week runs from Sunday through Saturday.

40. See "Operation Dove: Nonviolent Peace Corps." Because Operation Dove did not have the number of people available to supply the Tuwani Project that CPT did, it initially requested that CPT not use the names of its workers in its At-Tuwani releases. For this chapter, Laura Ciaghi, a Dove and CPT reservist who went through CPT training in 2007, consulted with Doves who appear in the narrative below regarding use of their names. The author thus uses the full names of those Doves who gave permission and the first initial of Doves who wished to remain anonymous.

41. Bachman worked with an NGO in Iraq and had met CPT's Baghdad team. When her office moved to Amman, several members of the Iraq team stayed with her there as they traveled back and forth to Iraq. Diane Janzen, December 7, 2007, e-mail to author.

42. Mai'a Williams Carpenter, January 19, e-mail to the author.

43. In a January 18, 2008, e-mail to the author, Mai'a Williams wrote, "That meeting was in part so necessary and quick after our little week of accompaniment delegation, because Ezra and members of the village felt that they did not want women doing accompaniment."

children during their walk to school, because the most direct route to the school from the villages of Tuba and Maghayir Al-Abeed passed between the settlement of Ma'on and an outpost settlement, Hill 833 (called Havat Ma'on by the settlers).[44]

The official joint CPT/Operation Dove At-Tuwani team began its accompaniment on September 27, 2004. On September 29, 2004, masked settlers attacked the children and CPTers accompanying them. They threw rocks at the children, causing minor injuries, and left Kim Lamberty with a broken elbow and a knee injury that made walking impossible. The same masked attackers whipped Chris Brown with chains and baseball bats, kicking him when he fell, causing head injuries and a punctured lung.

Kim Lamberty later wrote a report about the incident:

> I was supposed to leave Tuwani on September 29 [2004]. The evening before, Chris asked who would do the school accompaniment with him, and I agreed to do it before I left. I got up before six, packed my backpack, woke up Chris, and we set off to escort the kids from Tuba to their school in Tuwani....
>
> We accompanied the children on Monday and Tuesday without incident. On Wednesday morning, I was feeling anxious, because I wanted to finish in time to catch a van to Yatta at 7:30. We were hoping that the kids would meet us halfway, because the settlement

---

44. If the villagers built a clinic, the Palestinian Authority (PA) said it would send a doctor periodically to staff it. Given that roadblocks had made it progressively more difficult for the villagers to reach Yatta for medical care, they felt a clinic had become necessary for the overall health of the village. In a December 10, 2007, e-mail to the author, Rosemary Willey-Al'Sanah, Humanitarian Affairs Officer, U.N. OCHA—Occupied Palestinian Territories, Southern West Bank Office, confirmed that the PA had made the commitment, and noted that the Palestinian Ministry of Health was currently providing a weekly doctor in partnership with Care International in the completed clinic.

In her comments on a draft of this chapter, sent to the author on December 21, 2007, Kim Lamberty wrote,

> It might be good to say here that the road to school passes between Ma'on and Havat Ma'on, and it was a road that the settlers wanted to control, and that was why the walk to school was dangerous. If they allowed Palestinians to use that road, they gave up control of it. The Palestinians also understood what the real stakes were, which is why they fought for use of it.

For more background on the history of Tuwani and the Tuwani project, see CPT At-Tuwani, "At-Tuwani Media Packet." Some information also supplied by Kim Lamberty, Mai'a Williams, and Diane Janzen after reading a draft of this chapter. Lamberty sent additional facts about pre-At-Tuwani project work in a December 1, 2007, supplemental e-mail, and Williams made some corrections to the media packet timeline in a January 18, 2008, e-mail to the author.

area is at the Tuwani end of the path. Although the path is only two kilometers long, it feels like much more in the desert heat and rough terrain, and I was anxious about being late. Chris and I both grumbled about the kids not coming out to meet us. . . .

We arrived in Tuba at 6:30 a.m. in plenty of time for my planned departure. However, the children were not yet ready to leave. Some parents offered us tea, which Chris politely accepted, but I refused. Chris made it very clear that we were in a hurry and needed to leave, and by ten of seven, I had waited long enough and (stupidly) set off on my own. . . . Shortly thereafter, Chris and the five children left Tuba.

Before long, the two girls were next to me and Chris was not far behind with the three boys. The girls . . . and I chatted as best we could with my practically nonexistent Arabic and their practically nonexistent English. I shared my water with them.

As we approached the settlement area, the girls and I were still 20 or 30 feet ahead of Chris and the boys. This did not worry us, because there had not been any problems the last couple of days. On the right side of the path is the settlement of Ma'on surrounded by a chain link fence with barbed wire. Inside the fence is the paved settlement perimeter road. On the left side of the dirt path is a grove of trees containing a settlement expansion outpost called Ma'on Ranch. Settlers live there in trailers and mobile homes. The Israeli army prevents Palestinians from entering this area, and none dare attempt to enter for fear of arrest, beatings, or worse. It is a strictly settler area; the children are the only exception so they can go to school.

A few minutes after we entered into the settlement area, the girls next to me started to scream. I looked up and saw a man dressed in black swinging a chain coming out of the trees about thirty feet ahead. He had on a black facemask that looked like two scarves, one over the bottom half of his face and one over his forehead, leaving a slit for his eyes. The girls immediately turned around and started running back toward Tuba, and I followed them. Just as we reached Chris and the boys, at least four other men emerged from the trees similarly dressed. The children continued to run toward Tuba, and Chris started yelling, "Don't hurt the children, don't hurt the children!" It seemed that Chris and I were their targets, because they headed straight for us and let the children go. I learned later that the men had thrown rocks at the children as they ran toward Tuba, but that they did make it back safely.

We tried to run off the path, away from the masked settler men, but it was hopeless. They were bigger, faster, and stronger. I tried to pull out my cell phone to call for help, but they were on top of me immediately, tripping me, throwing me to the ground and beating me. I don't remember much of the actual beating, or feeling any pain while it was happening. I remember thinking to myself that if I just lie very still and pretend that I am unconscious or dead, maybe they will go away. I also remember hearing Chris scream, realizing that he was taking a much worse beating, and knowing that there was nothing that I could do for him.

I can piece together what happened from my injuries. I must have fallen on my face, where I have cuts and bruises on my jaw and above my lip. I must have broken the fall with my left arm, which is fractured just below the elbow. They must have kicked or beat me on the left side of my right knee, where I have an enormous bruise, a lot of swelling and pain, and an undiagnosed injury. They also must have kicked or beat me on the top of my head and my left upper arm where I have bad bruises. I also have other minor cuts and bruises on my hands and other parts of my body. I don't know if they used their feet, rocks, or chains. I am relieved that they got my already-bad knee instead of ruining my good one.

When they finished beating Chris, they started to head back into the grove of trees. One of them said in English, "Take her phone," and someone came over and picked up my phone from where it had fallen. They also grabbed my fanny pack from around my waist. When I heard them walking away, I ventured a look up. I saw the group go back through the grove of trees and into Ma'on Ranch. One of them looked back at me and I quickly put my head back down.

After a few minutes, I sat up and Chris walked over to me. I do not remember exactly what we said to each other in that moment. Chris' face was streaked with blood and I felt some dripping off of mine. I couldn't walk. Chris pulled out the cell phone concealed in his pocket and called Diane Janzen and P. [Piergiorgio Rosetti] who were back in Tuwani. He told them that we had just been attacked "really bad" by settlers but the kids were okay. I cannot remember what else he said, but I know that Diane and P. said that they were coming out to join us, and that they would call the police immediately. I called Cal in the Hebron office and told him to call the U.S. consulate to report that my passport had been stolen. Looking back, I cannot believe this is what I was thinking about!

Chris and I sat alone for 10 or 15 minutes in the spot where we had been beaten. We were both really scared. I knew the attackers were still in the trees somewhere and I was afraid that they were going to come back and finish the job . . .

Maybe ten minutes after Diane and P. got to us, settler security drove up. . . . The man got out of his car and asked us what happened. We told him that people from his settlement attacked us. He did not offer us any assistance or first-aid, even though we were bleeding and obviously in pain. He said that they attacked us because we had upset the balance of power between the settlement and Palestinians. He understood immediately, as we did, that the perpetrators were settlers attacking us because of our presence in the area.

Five or ten minutes after settler security arrived, the police and army came, and shortly behind them an Israeli ambulance. In all it took about thirty minutes for help to arrive, even though the region is swarming with army and police. . . . The Israeli police or the army did not search the grove of trees for our assailants. By taking so long to get to us, they effectively let the perpetrators get away.

The police asked us to explain briefly what happened. They gave us a piece of paper summoning us to the Kiryat Arba police station that same day. . . . The paramedics checked us over, put me on a stretcher, and took Chris, who had a punctured lung, and me to Soroka hospital in Beersheva. . . .

Later that afternoon the police came to the hospital to take statements from us. The US consular officer was appalled that the police insisted we come visit them at another settlement and instead insisted that they visit us. I gave a statement, which the officer wrote out in Hebrew. I refused to sign it because I did not know what it said. I do not know what has happened to that statement. I heard later that the police had gone to the court for a search warrant for the settlement but they were denied. I do not know if Ma'on or Ma'on Ranch were ever properly searched.[45]

A CPTnet update on Lamberty and Brown that appeared later on the day of the attack noted that Israeli articles written about the incident made a point of saying that the CPTers "claimed" their attackers were settlers, but could not say for certain, since their attackers were masked—even though

---

45. Report on settler attack e-mailed to author on October 11, 2004. See also, CPTnet, "HEBRON DISTRICT: CPTers Kim Lamberty and Chris Brown badly injured by settlers in the south Hebron hills," September 29, 2004..

Diane Janzen, in her comments on a draft of chapter 6 of the general CPT history, *In Harm's Way*, noted that two of the children sustained bruises and cuts from the settlers stoning them as the children fled back to Tuba.

In her comments on a draft of this chapter, Kim Lamberty wrote,

> I continued to follow up on this with the US consulate, insisting that they pursue it with the Israeli government. I also know that it was raised by U.S. Senator Hagel at a meeting with the Israeli foreign minister. I was finally told by the consulate, in the spring, that they had closed the case for lack of evidence. We could not identify the attackers because they were masked, and they never did a proper search of the settlement to retrieve evidence. I pursued it as far as I could because I thought that if they were caught, it would be a deterrent to settler violence in the area.

Brown and Lamberty reported that their assailants came out of the Havat Maon/Hill 833 outpost.[46] "For some reason," the release continued, "the BBC internet news reported on the incident under the headline 'Jewish settlers "attack" US workers' and illustrated the article with a picture of a screaming settler woman lying on the ground with her baby." The police told the *Jerusalem Post* that they believed the attacks were a robbery, even though the settlers took nothing from Brown, and only took Lamberty's waist pack after she tried to call for help. The release also quoted Rabbi Arik Asherman, Director of Rabbis for Human rights telling the *Jerusalem Post*, "I don't know how many Palestinian baseball teams there are in that area. It is quite clear that the attackers were settlers."[47]

The next day, Mai'a Williams and Cal Carpenter took the places of Lamberty and Brown, and, along with Operation Dove members, accompanied the children to At-Tuwani, after receiving confirmation from the DCO that the children indeed had a right to use the road past the settlement. In the morning, an Israeli police jeep parked outside Ma'on to ensure the children's safe passage. However, an army patrol entered At-Tuwani and warned the villages that if the international accompaniment continued, "there will be violence." On October 3, the military blocked the path of the children near the Ma'on settlement, declaring it a Closed Military Zone, when they came to school. On the way home, they forced the children to take a ten-kilometer detour. An Israeli lieutenant told the CPTers that ten kilometers was not a long way to walk, saying, "They can take a tractor like everyone else. These people are used to it."[48]

On October 9, the settlers attacked again, with wooden clubs and slingshots. CPTers Diana Zimmerman, Diane Janzen, Dove Adriano Rossi, two adult residents of Tuba, one adult resident of At-Tuwani, and two Amnesty International researchers, Donatella Rovera and Maartje Houbrechts, were walking back from the village of Tuba, after dropping off the children there. As soon as they saw the masked settlers, they called

---

46. The Israeli groups B'tselem and Peace Now have encouraged the team to use the latter designation, possibly because using settler terminology would grant it a legitimacy it did not have, even under Israeli law. From comments Diane Janzen made on a draft of chapter 6 in *In Harm's Way*.

47. CPTnet, "HEBRON DISTRICT: Updates on Brown and Lamberty's injuries and al-Tuwani accompaniment project," September 29, 2004.

48. CPTnet, "HEBRON DISTRICT: School children threatened in south Hebron hills," September 30, 2004; "HEBRON DISTRICT: Israeli military and settler security interfere with children's journeys to and from school," October 5, 2004.

the police. Three of the settlers began flinging rocks at the Palestinians with slingshots. The other five hit the internationals with clubs and stole Rossi's video camera. He was not able to move his arm after the attack and collapsed on his way to the ambulance after it arrived. Medical personnel later diagnosed that he sustained a kidney injury from the assault. After that attack, the Israeli army informed the villagers that if internationals continued to accompany the children, the army would not protect them from the settlers. Two days later, Israeli settlers again chased the children, and the army did nothing to intervene.[49]

The attacks generated several positive consequences. CPT and Operation Dove were able to garner much Israeli and international press attention for the plight of the South Hebron Hills villagers; they were even able to persuade representatives of the U.S. Consulate to visit—remarkable, because the prohibition against U.S. government workers entering the occupied territories had been in effect since the beginning of the Intifada. Citing these attacks, the Israeli group Machsom (Checkpoint) Watch prompted the Israeli Knesset Committee on the Rights of the Child to hold hearings on November 2, 2004, about the situation of school children in the South Hebron Hills. Afterwards, the Committee declared that the children had the right to take the shortest route to school, which ran by the Ma'on settlement gate, and ordered Israeli military to protect the children as they walked to and from school.[50] More impressive to the villagers in the region was the October 31, 2004, meeting the Israeli Civil Administration held with them—the first such meeting any of them remembered. They presented a list of concerns:

- Water: the villagers wanted to tap in to the Ma'on settlement's water line, given that the small spring in the village only provided enough for

---

49. Amnesty International "Israel/Occupied Territories: Israeli settlers wage campaign of intimidation on Palestinians and internationals alike." See also CPTnet, Mai'a Williams, "HEBRON DISTRICT: Settlers again attack CPTers, Palestinians and other international accompaniment volunteers," October 9, 2004; CPTnet, "HEBRON URGENT ACTION: Tell Israeli government to stop settler attacks on Palestinian school children," October 9, 2004.

50. CPTnet, "AT-TUWANI UPDATE: October 26–November 3, 2003," November 15, 2004. Kim Lamberty, comments draft of chapter 6 in *In Harm's Way*, and comments on draft of this chapter.

Doug Pritchard wrote in a November 21, 2007, e-mail to the author, "I was struck at the time that they didn't order a stop to the settler activity or arrest of the perpetrators but rather ordered the much more expensive and time-consuming army accompaniment."

drinking and cooking. Rainwater trapped in cisterns provided a limited supply of water for washing.
- Clinic: The village wanted to finish building their clinic, upon which the Civil Administration had put stop-work order.
- Safe passage to the At-Tuwani primary school for the children of Tuba.
- Electricity: At-Tuwani got its power from a diesel generator the village could only afford to run for a few hours each evening. Villagers wanted to connect it to the same grid from which Ma'on got its power.
- Road access to Karmil: The villagers wanted the Israeli military to remove three dirt barricades blocking the road from At-Tuwani to the larger Palestinian population centers of Karmil, Yatta, and Hebron. These barricades prevented access to the hospital, secondary schools, and stores located there.
- Improvement of the road to al-Mufakara and villages to the south: Five years earlier, Israeli authorities denied villager requests to improve the path.

The official told the villagers that Israeli soldiers would accompany the children—provided that the international accompaniers did not; they should go ahead and build their clinic, and that questions about the road would be studied. A village leader told the At-Tuwani team,

> This meeting today didn't just happen. We have had these problems, and many attacks by settlers for years, but no one outside knew. Thank you for being here; you have brought us attention. Please thank all the people who have helped us—the media, the US consular officials who visited, and the Israeli and international peace groups. Your help made this visit happen.[51]

When tested, the verbal assurances of the commander fell apart almost immediately. On November 1, Israeli soldiers detained the At-Tuwani team and Palestinian men who had accompanied the children to school and told

---

51. CPTnet, "AT-TUWANI, HEBRON DISTRICT: Tuwani villagers meet for first time with senior Israeli occupation official," November 1, 2004.

Joe Carr in a December 7, 2007, e-mail to the author, wrote,

> Regarding the meeting where the Israeli authorities tried to get the villagers to ask us to leave, one thing I remember Hafez saying that . . . the fact that Israeli authorities wanted us to leave confirmed to Tuwani that our work was effective. They also said that they didn't say NO outright to the soldiers, but just insisted that we were their guests and that it would be against their culture to ask us to leave.

them that the children could not use the shortest route to school, which ran by the gate of the Ma'on Settlement and the Hill 833 outpost. When they took a longer, five kilometer, route home, the promised soldier escort did not arrive, and the children had to take the ten-kilometer route home after they passed some settlers. Joe Carr, watching the scene from a neighboring mountain, saw another settler, who came out after the children had passed, train his gun on him and show his young son how to look through the gun's scope at Carr. Reflecting on Matt 10:28, Carr said Jesus's words about not fearing those who could kill only the body made him less afraid. "But I still decided to take off my red hat and watch the settlers from behind a large rock," he wrote.[52] The next day, November 2, soldiers made local men stop working on the clinic.[53]

Over the next weeks, the experiences the children had with their soldier escorts were mixed. The updates and other releases record the escort coming late, and sometimes not coming at all. Sometimes the settlers harassed the children by pushing them, shouting and blowing horns at them even when soldiers and Israeli police were present. On two occasions, the Israeli police loaded the children into their vehicle when stick-wielding settlers attacked. The settlers then stoned the police vehicles as they drove past.[54]

Over the next years, the school accompaniment settled into a routine, with some of the soldiers taking their duty to protect the children seriously,

---

52. CPTnet, AT-TUWANI DIARY: "All this for five kids going to school," November 20, 2004.

53. CPTnet, "AT-TUWANI UPDATE: October 26-November 3, 2003," November 15, 2004.

54. See CPTnet releases: Lamberty, "AT-TUWANI, HEBRON DISTRICT: Settlers attack At-Tuwani man while Israeli soldiers look on," November 4, 2004; Lamberty, "AT-TUWANI, HEBRON DISTRICT: Israeli soldiers, police, and civil administration escort children to school," November 8, 2004; Lamberty, "AT-TUWANI, HEBRON DISTRICT: Settlers harass children on the way to school despite soldier escort," November 10, 2004; Carr, "AT-TUWANI DIARY: Watching children go to school," December 3, 2004; Carr, "AT-TUWANI DIARY: "Cold, wet and determined, those five awesome kids . . ."" December 5, 2004; Levin, "AT-TUWANI: Israeli police protect Palestinian children from Israeli settler attack," December 9, 2004; Carr, "AT-TUWANI DIARY: 'Today I was sad,'" December 18, 2004; Cal Carpenter, "AT-TUWANI: Armed Israeli settler attempts to prevent children from attending school," January 4, 2005.

In December 2004, settlers from the Hill 833 outpost threatened to kill members of an NBC news crew when they mistakenly drove into the outpost area on their way to interview the school children from Tuba. When they recognized the NBC van, they ceased their threats and told the crew, "We thought you were Arabs." CPTnet, "AT-TUWANI: Israeli settler death threats, attacks continue in the South Hebron Hills," January 3, 2005.

and others grudgingly.[55] Every morning and afternoon on school days, CPTers and Doves watched from the hillside as children from Tuba and Maghayir Al-Abeed waited for the escort to school in an area close to the settlement. If problems arose, team members called the parents and Israeli police. Other team members waited near At-Tuwani, and when the children arrived for school, the internationals asked them about the details of their trip (the escort is out of eyesight for about five minutes) and gave them water. When soldiers were consistently late, or failed to protect the children, the team notified Israeli contacts, who spoke to the current commander of units in the region. Team members also wrote down data about the escort, noting how many children participated, whether the soldiers walked beside them instead of riding in the jeep, and other information.[56] Every four weeks or so, the team summarized this information in a spreadsheet and submitted it to Ta'ayush, OCHA, and Machsom Watch who submitted it to the Israeli Knesset Committee on the Rights of the Child.[57]

55. In May 2006, settlers ambushed the escort several times, building a roadblock to prevent jeeps from following the children. The soldiers did not always intervene to protect the children, but in one case, a soldier fired into the air to scare them off after several children sustained injuries from settlers stoning, kicking, and punching them. Kathleen Kern later watched an interview with a Ma'on outpost female settler by a man claiming to be a journalist supportive of the settlers. The settler told him that the soldier had overreacted and that the children had used bandages to fake injuries for the media. She said the settlers had "only been screaming" at the children.

CPTer Heidi Schramm, who played the video of this interview for Kern, told her that she, along with Rich Meyer and Diane Janzen, had seen the children shortly after the attack, and verified the injuries were real. Ta'ayush arranged with the military to have several children transported to the hospital in Yatta. CPTnet, "AT-TUWANI: 'Are you afraid of the settlers too?'" May 6, 2007; CPTnet, "AT-TUWANI: Tuba children and soldier escort ambushed by Ma'on settlers," May 7, 2006; CPTnet, "AT-TUWANI: Despite Defence Ministry orders, Israeli soldiers continue to shirk responsibility for protect[ing] Palestinian school children," May 25, 2006. Diane Janzen, e-mail to author, November 11, 2007.

56. A complete list of data the team collected is available in CPT At-Tuwani and Operation Dove, "Report on the Israeli Military and Police Escort of Palestinian Children from Tuba and Maghayir Al-Abeed to and from School in At-Tuwani for the 2005–2006 School Year," November 10, 2006.

57. Diane Janzen, in a November 28, 2007, e-mail to author wrote,

I'm not sure if [submitting the information to the Knesset committee] continued past the first year of the escort. I wrote the report that's on the CPT website last year, cause I was still pissed about the attacks that had occurred in the spring of 2006 on the kids and we had all this data and the engineering part of me said we could analyze and summarize it in a way that makes it easier to understand (and OCHA and ACRI had been hinting at the usefulness of such a report—but I'm not sure if either organization used it or not).

Between 2005 and 2006, the accompaniment allowed between fifteen to twenty-nine children (numbers varied day to day) from Tuba and Maghayir Al-Abeed to attend school in At-Tuwani. As of this writing in 2009, monitoring the school escort continues to be the central activity of the At-Tuwani team.[58]

ACCOMPANIMENT OF SHEPHERDS

While the children were in school, and during school vacations, team members accompanied shepherds from the villages as they grazed their flocks near settlements in the region or planted and harvested food and fodder crops. Regaining their grazing land from which settlers had driven them, sometimes for years, became one of the key goals of the Nonviolent Direct Action campaign waged by the South Hebron Hills villagers.

As had happened with the school accompaniment, the settlers pushed back when the shepherds attempted to graze their flocks with international accompaniment. On February 16, 2005, settlers came out of the Havat Ma'on/Hill 833 outpost while Diana Zimmerman and a Dove, M., were accompanying the shepherds and trained a gun on the two internationals just before the Israeli army arrived. Soon afterwards, when CPTer Sally Hunsberger and Doves Piergiorgio Rosetti and J. came over the hill, the same settlers saw their video camera and attacked the Doves. J. received a karate kick to his head that broke his jaw, detached the retina in one eye, and caused short-term memory loss.[59]

According to the At-Tuwani team, as of 2008, they still send the reports to Ta'ayush and the United Nations Office for the Coordination of Humanitarian Affairs (OCHA). November 29, 2007, e-mail to the author from Donna Hicks, serving on the Hebron team, who called the At-Tuwani team for the author. (Because of At-Tuwani's lack of electricity, communication with the team there can be difficult.)

58. In a November 12, 2007 e-mail to the author, Diane Janzen wrote that the number of children being escorted for the 2007–2008 school year was down, because some of the children had graduated to secondary school.

59. CPTnet, Barbara Martens, "AT-TUWANI: Settlers Attack and Injure Two OD Members," February 16, 2005.

In a December 24, 2007, e-mail to the author, Diana Zimmerman wrote, "In reviewing the video that was shot during the incident, you can hear a signal whistle come from the trees (surrounding the Hill 833 outpost), moments before the army arrived. At the sound of the whistle, the two men pulled back and the one lowered his weapon. I have heard the same whistle on numerous occasions and it has always been during settler attacks or harassments."

A worse attack for the villagers occurred in March 2005, when settlers laid poison-covered barley around Ma'on, under bushes where sheep usually graze and near one of At-Tuwani's water sources. Since the villagers' flocks not only represented their main source of income, but a staple of their diet, the loss was catastrophic. At first the poison was identified as 2-Fluoracetamide, a rat poison banned in several nations because of its toxicity and because it remains for a long time in soil and water. Prospective buyers in Israel must get special authorization from the Israeli government. Later, in April, a second type of poison was found, which a representative from the United Nations Office for the Coordination of Humanitarian Affairs (OCHA) said was called Brodifaucum. Israeli groups and the At-Tuwani team assisted the Palestinians in picking up the tiny poison pellets, which sometimes—given their size, the vast expanse of the land they covered, and the attempts by Israeli settlers and soldiers to stop them—seemed like a futile effort.[60] For the next six weeks, shepherds continued to find poison throughout the hills and valleys around the Ma'on settlement.

After a brainstorming session, the village leadership and the At-Tuwani team decided to hold a press conference and public witness regarding the poisonings. Over forty villagers from At-Tuwani and Mufakara, joined by CPTers, Doves, and other internationals, went to Hebron District Governor's office on April 5, 2005, which provided them the venue for the conference. Afterwards, they marched to the Israeli Kiryat Arba police station with a bucket of the poison. The Israeli police refused to take the bucket, saying the poisonings were neither their responsibility nor in their jurisdiction.

Sheep, goats, as well as gazelles and other wild fauna continued to die; in the end, the villagers from At-Tuwani and Mufakara lost more than a hundred animals. Concluding an account of these poisoning in the At-Tuwani media packet, the team wrote that as of July 31, 2005, neither Israeli nor Palestinian laboratories had provided results from tests on the dead animals to the villagers of At-Tuwani and Mufakara, and none of the people from either village were tested for possible poison consumed when

---

60. Ezra Nawi, an Israeli from Ta'ayush who had developed warm relationships with the local villagers, came down to help pick up the poison pellets. After finding the body of a dead gazelle, he requested CPT accompaniment to the gates of the Ma'on settlement. Kim Lamberty went with him in his truck. He dumped the gazelle's body inside the settlement and got into a shouting match with the guard on the way out. From Kim Lamberty's comments on a draft of chapter 6 in *In Harm's Way.*

they ate meat or dairy products from their flocks. None of the villagers received compensation for their losses.[61]

Settler attacks on shepherds continue throughout 2005, although the releases show a tapering off of the violence in the summer and the fall. CPTers regularly accompanied shepherds to police stations to make complaints. These visits were often frustrating experiences. Barbara Martens wrote,

> Justice in Palestine operates by two standards. At the police station, the line of response to the death threat went like this: "Did you say there was only ONE youth? Did he take his gun (they are all allowed to be armed) and point it at you? No? He only held up a stone? Did he strike you with it? No? Well then, you weren't really hurt, were you? He's just a youngster. He probably meant no harm."
>
> We know of Palestinian youth who have been beaten and thrown into jail for throwing a stone at a settler, let alone uttering a death threat.[62]

SOLDIER HARASSMENT

Despite the assurances of the Israeli commander at the October 31, 2004, meeting, residents of the South Hebron Hills faced ongoing harassment from the Israeli military when they tried to make improvements on the roads connecting the scattered villages, build their clinic, replant olive trees that settlers and soldiers had uprooted, and graze their flocks on land for which they had deeds and which other military commanders had told them they could use.[63] In May 2005, the military demolished nine homes

---

61. CPT At-Tuwani, "A chronology of the poisonings during spring 2005." See also CPTnet, Claire Evans, "AT-TUWANI: Shepherds Confront Police with Poison that Kills their Sheep," April 7, 2005; CPTnet, Kristin Anderson, "AT-TUWANI: The little one and the Loss," June 9, 2005. Kim Lamberty, e-mail to author, November 9, 2007. Diane Janzen and Kim Lamberty provided additional information in their comments on a draft of this chapter.

62. CPTnet, "AT-TUWANI: Settler attacks shepherd, threatens volunteers; police not interested," February 4, 2005.

63. See CPTnet releases: "HEBRON/AT-TUWANI: Palestinians and internationals plant olive trees," December 7, 2004; Cal Carpenter, "AT-TUWANI: Israeli authorities halt road improvements in the south Hebron district," January 10, 2005; Art Gish, "AT-TUWANI: Two roads to At-Tuwani," January 19, 2005; Art Gish, "AT-TUWANI REFLECTION: A rocky road," February 3, 2005; AT-TUWANI: Israeli Soldiers Drive Shepherds from Their Land," February 24, 2005; Gish, "AT-TUWANI: Hard Day near the village," February 26, 2005; Gish, "AT-TUWANI REFLECTION: Hungry sheep and hungry people," March 4, 2005; Kim Lamberty, "AT-TUWANI: Israeli military

in three of the villages. During the same month, settlers destroyed wheat and lentil crops and stole livestock belonging to the villagers. Then the Civil Administration and police had the chutzpah to meet again with the villagers and ask that they tell the internationals to leave, promising that soldiers would be more helpful with the settler violence. The villagers told them they wished the internationals to remain.[64]

During this period, Ta'ayush was fostering relationships between the inhabitants of the South Hebron Hills and Israeli lawyers, including two who worked with Rabbis for Human Rights and the Association for Civil Rights in Israel (ACRI). The ACRI lawyer filed a petition in the Israeli courts, asserting Palestinian ownership of the land in the Khoruba Valley. In the fall of 2005, an Israeli judge ruled that the valley was indeed owned by Palestinians and the Israeli military could protect them from settler attacks when they worked there.[65]

Although the shepherds conscientiously notified the DCO every time they knew they would be doing major planting or harvesting work, the military often failed to show up or showed up late. However, the court's decision and the persistence of the shepherds to work in their fields, even when their phone calls to the military produced nothing, paid off. Settler attacks in the Khoruba Valley began diminishing and the villagers began strategizing grazing actions for the next valley over to the north.[66]

---

commander threatens At-Tuwani shepherds," March 11, 2005. Diana Zimmerman and Kim Lamberty, "AT-TUWANI: Ma'on settlers invade Palestinian land"; Kim Lamberty, "CPT Members Intervene in Settler Clash with Shepherds," April 7, 2005; Maureen Jack, "Sheep killed in Tuwani," April 28, 2005; "AT-TUWANI: Israeli military, police and settlers prevent Palestinians from grazing sheep and goats," May 24, 2005.

64. CPT At-Tuwani, "At-Tuwani Media Packet."

65. Diane Janzen, in a November 28, 2007, e-mail to the author, wrote, "from the spring of 2005 on-wards the At-Tuwani team began providing the lawyer with documentation about incidents that occurred on the land between the Palestinians and the settlers and soldiers."

66. Diane Janzen, e-mail to author, November 28, 2007. Another form of Israeli military harassment occurred in 2006, when the Israeli authorities began building a low concrete wall the length of Route 317 (an Israeli bypass road from the Green Line to Hebron) that would effectively cut off the entire South Hebron Hills region from jobs, schools, and hospitals in Hebron and Yatta. Efforts of the villagers to protest this wall with Nonviolent Direct Action and legal appeals would result in the dismantling of the wall in 2007. Christian Peacemaker Teams and Operation Dove, "Immanent Peril: The Impact of the Proposed Security Wall along Route 317"; CPTnet, "AT-TUWANI: Israelis and Palestinians arrested demonstrating against planned security wall," April 24, 2006; CPTnet, "AT-TUWANI URGENT ACTION: Tell Israeli government to halt construc-

As of 2009, the At-Tuwani team remains in place, and the villagers continue to initiate nonviolent direct actions to reclaim their land and dignity. Hundreds of Israelis and internationals come to support these initiatives, making the region one of the few places in Palestine where the transforming power of nonviolent resistance is evident in the eighth year of the Al-Aqsa Intifada. With the closure of the Hebron project in 2008 (see n. 34), At-Tuwani became CPT's flagship project in Palestine.[67]

---

tion of new wall in South Hebron Hills," April 26, 2006; "At-Tuwani: Parting the Wall"; CPTnet, "'Security' wall along Route 317 dismantled," August 20, 2007. See also, "HCJ Orders State to Dismantle Concrete Wall in Southern Hebron Hills."

Diane Janzen wrote, "the organization of resistance to [the low wall] was the start of the internal push among the villagers for a nonviolence committee among the South Hebron Hills villages—and the success of the various efforts in the removal was huge for the villagers in the area." E-mail to author, November 28, 2007.

67. Diane Janzen, in her November 28, 2007, e-mail commenting on what the author had written regarding At-Tuwani in the CPT history, *In Harm's Way*, noted that another significant part of the At-Tuwani work was documenting the additions to settlements and outposts in the area, which violated both the Road Map to Peace and stated Israeli government policies. She continued,

> I would make more emphasis . . . on the cooperation that exists between the different parties working to support the Palestinian non-violent resistance in the south Hebron hills (of course there are times of frustration and mis-communication, but for the most part the cooperation has been quite remarkable and has produced some results—like the removal of the low wall). These results are perhaps not that evident in the writings that come from the team as the writings are generally more based on a specific incident and don't always include the history that led up to the incident (sometimes because the knowledge of the history is lacking and sometimes because there isn't space to put it all in a release!). In general I would sum it up as something like:
>
> "The internationals living in At-Tuwani provide daily accompaniment to the Palestinians shepherds and farmers in the area. Several Israeli peace groups support the work of the internationals and the non-violent resistance of the Palestinians by joining them on occasion in the accompaniment or in solidarity actions. The Israeli peace groups also have made connections with Israeli lawyers willing to take on cases in the area (sometimes the Israeli peace groups arrange the funding necessary for the lawyers) and the internationals have provided valuable documentation of incidents of attacks or harassment and property damage done by Israeli settlers or soldiers. . . . We've provided video and pictures to lawyers working in the area (i.e., the report on the barrier was something that ACRI asked if we could provide for them to use as evidence in the court case—and ACRI has a lot of our video and pictures), to OCHA, to B'Tselem, to Machsom Watch, to Peace Now and to Ta'ayush (for their own reports, lobbying the Israeli government and to try and get it to the Israeli media). I think the naming of more Israeli peace groups working in the area is important—it's not just all Ta'ayush and us (CPT and the Doves)."

RESPONSES TO THE HOSTAGE CRISIS

In November 2005, CPT's Iraq team was hosting a small delegation led by CPT Canada co-coordinator Jim Loney. Norman Kember from the United Kingdom and Harmeet Singh Sooden, a Canadian citizen and resident of New Zealand,[68] were the only other delegates. Team member Tom Fox accompanied the three men to an afternoon meeting at the Muslim Scholars' Association on November 26, 2005.[69] They, their translator, and driver had just left the office of the Muslim Scholars Association—a Sunni organization—when two cars pulled up in front of and behind theirs. Gunmen forced the driver and translator out of the van, took their phones, and then drove away with the delegation. Thus began a four-month odyssey of fear, anguish, and grace as CPT traveled in unfamiliar waters to seek release of the four hostages.

The Hebron and At-Tuwani teams, having many Arabic-speaking friends and colleagues, were the teams in the best position to intervene during the crisis. After the first video of the four hostages appeared on Al-Jazeera, along with a note accusing them of spying, numerous Palestinian friends called to offer help. For the next ten days, the teams in Palestine did little else but focus on ways they could win the release of Kember, Loney, Fox, and Singh Sooden.

The team's lawyer, Jonathan Kuttab, began submitting stories about the work of the team in Hebron to Arabic-language media, and as he had for the previous ten years of the Hebron team's existence, Hisham Sharabati jumped in to help them with the crisis. He and Hamed Qawasmeh from the Hebron District Governor's office began contacting all of the Palestinian political parties, and late on the night the video appeared, they had gathered signatures from eight groups on a statement appealing for the release of the hostages, which was read at a press conference the next morning. Westerners probably did not appreciate the dramatic symbolism of Fatah, Hamas, the Popular Front for the Liberation of Palestine, and the other Palestinian political parties usually at odds with each other appearing on the same platform to call for the release of the hostages. Also speaking at the press conference were Fariel Abu Haikal of Qurtuba Girl's school, Naim Daour from Hebron University, and Campaign for Secure Dwellings participant, Jamal Miqbal. At the press conference, one of the

---

68. Singh Sooden was born and raised in Zambia to Sikh parents originally from Kashmir.

69. Greg Rollins, e-mail to author, May 29, 2007.

political leaders in Hebron offered to go to Baghdad if the team thought it would help. Later in the day, a Palestinian Authority official issued the following statement from the Ramallah offices:

> November 30, 2005
>
> A Plea to the Iraqi People
>
> From Palestine we call upon you to release the four from the Christian Peacemaker Teams who were kidnapped from Baghdad. This is an organization that has helped and continues to help our people living under Israeli occupation in the city of Hebron and in other regions throughout our occupied homeland. They expose themselves to danger in order to provide protection to our women and children in front of Israeli military checkpoints.
>
> We urge you in the name of humanity and in the name of all peoples that have tasted bitter wars, violence and occupation . . . we urge you to release Tom Fox (American citizenship), Norman Kember (British citizenship), James Loney and Harmeet Singh Sooden (Canadian citizenship), all of whom insisted on helping our family in Iraq and living with our Iraqi brothers and sisters through the war and destruction, believing in the message that every human being has the right to live in freedom and with dignity and that occupation is wrong and must end.
>
> We have faith that you will find that this group is among those working for peace and against occupation and that you will release them immediately, god willing.
>
> Coordinator of the National Committee to Resist the Wall
> Qadura Fares[70]

Qawasmeh lost his job at the Hebron District Governor's office for complying with the team's request to hold the press conference in a place of Islamic religious significance. However, whenever the team tried to thank him or other Palestinians for their help, the uniform response was, "No, don't thank us, we have to do this; it is our duty."

The International Solidarity Movement also eagerly offered assistance. Its members organized press conferences and demonstrations, for which they produced expensive photo banners of the captives, and obtained statements from Muslim clerics and spokespeople from villages where Singh Sooden and Fox had worked or participated in demonstrations.

These initial actions, covered by the Arabic and other international media outlets, rapidly inspired other Arabs and Muslims around the world

---

70. International Solidarity Movement, "Statement by the National Committee to Resist Settlement and the Wall on the CPT Hostages in Iraq."

to speak out for the captive CPTers. The large banner of Fox holding a sign, saying "Stop the Wall" in particular seemed to produce a response. Local Palestinian friends called whenever they saw something about the hostages in the media and translated the team's releases into Arabic. Palestinian journalists went out of their way to publicize the press conferences, demonstrations, and calls from the Arab world to release the hostages. By the end of December 2005, the Palestine project had added more than three hundred contacts to its e-mail list of Arabic language media.

After the Palestinian Prisoners' Society[71] organized a demonstration that connected the CPT hostages to the administrative detention of Palestinian prisoners, the team thought of another angle to try. The kidnappers had called for the release of Iraqi detainees before they released the hostages: the very work that captives and CPTers in Iraq, Palestine, and Canada had been addressing. A photo of Loney calling for the release of post-9/11 Arab detainees in Canada began circulating. The Hebron team also decided that whenever they talked of Kember, Loney, Singh Sooden, and Fox, to the media, they would use the opportunity to highlight the situation of Iraqis detained by Coalition Forces.[72]

In At-Tuwani, the villagers' predominant reaction to the kidnappings was one of outrage. They remembered Tom Fox, who had worked in At-Tuwani for a few days. On November 30, 2005, the head of the village, Hafez Hereni, borrowed the team's video camera and took testimonies of local villagers. Speaking directly to "Iraqi brothers and sisters" who might be viewing them, the villagers described what their lives had been like before CPT came to live in At-Tuwani and how they had changed once CPT began providing regular escorts for their children. Hereni assured Kristin Anderson that when the kidnappers knew CPT, they would set the hostages free.

Anderson found out later that Hereni had not gone to work for a week. Knowing that his meager wages were supporting his five children, wife, and mother, and that he had shouldered additional burdens as the nonviolence

---

71. The Hebron chapter of the Palestinian Prisoners' Society had provided considerable assistance to the team during its 1997 Fast for Rebuilding (see chapter 3). In 2004, after the prisoners went on a three-week hunger strike, demanding better living conditions and more contact with their families, the Hebron team also spent considerable time with families of these prisoners in a fasting solidarity tent. See CPTnet, Roynon, "HEBRON REFLECTION: Fences, walls and the Palestinian prisoners' hunger strike," September 3, 2004; CPTnet, Cal Carpenter, "HEBRON: Prisoners are still an issue," September 16, 2004.

72. Rich Meyer, "With a Lot of Help from Our Friends: The Call from Palestine for the Release of the Peacemakers," 63–70.

coordinator of the southern Hebron district villages, Anderson tried to ask about a recent Israeli high court case regarding the village's land. Hereni interrupted her, saying, "Really Kristin, I cannot think about anything else right now. Right now everything I am doing is for them."[73]

On December 2, the people of At-Tuwani held a demonstration calling for the release of the hostages at their school. The children held photos of the four men, or had these photos taped to their chests.[74] Mothers and grandmothers held handwritten signs, and young men held banners professionally made in Yatta. More than a hundred people gathered. One was a shepherd who came from Jinba village, even though that day his lawyers and the Israeli authorities were meeting at his house to discuss land confiscation orders and plans for the construction of the Separation Wall on Jinba's lands. After marching the short distance between the village school and health clinic, the village held a press conference. The speakers told of the sacrifices that CPT had made for Palestinians and Iraqis, and said that with all the injustices faced by Palestinians and Iraqis, they should not be unjust toward those who were trying to help them.

When the people of the South Hebron Hills heard about the demonstration in Hebron organized by the Palestinian Prisoners' Society, almost a hundred people, including half of the village of At-Tuwani, came to march. Some of them had never come to Hebron before.

In the intervening period between the demonstrations in December 2005 and Fox's death in March 2006, Anderson had dinner with Hafez Hereni and his family. His mother stood up and said the hostages had been held for too long, and that she was going to Iraq to get them, at which point she left the room. Amidst the laughter, Hafez Hereni translated for the team and added, "Really, she says she'll go." "We joined the laughter," Anderson wrote in a letter to the captives, "knowing that if anyone could march into Iraq to get the four of you, it would be Fatima."[75]

After Fox was murdered on March 9, 2006, the village descended on the team's one room dwelling in At-Tuwani to mourn with them, and assure them that those who had killed him were not true Muslims. Fatima Hereni, who had never before come to the team's house, said she would

73. Kristin G. Anderson-Rosetti, "Excerpts from Letters to Tom, Norman, Harmeet and Jim: Written from the village of At-Tuwani, West Bank, Palestine," 53–56.

74. A photo of the At-Tuwani children displaying these pictures became the cover for CPT's book about the kidnappings, *118 Days: Christian Peacemaker Teams Held Hostage in Iraq*.

75. Anderson-Rosetti, "Excerpts from Letters," 59

plant an olive tree after the forty-day Muslim mourning period and care for it as if it were one of her children.

On March 26, 2006, Anderson wrote a letter addressed to all four captives at the time of Loney's, Singh Sooden's, and Kember's release:

> In between settlers killing two goats, settlers assaulting a young boy with spray resulting in temporary vision loss, settlers beating that boy's father, police arresting two shepherds, the death of this year's bee crop, other lost crops, and a worsening water shortage, the village celebrated your freedom.
>
> Though I wasn't there, others told me our neighbor family cooked a big meal the night they heard you were freed. Kiefa prepared the meal and Nasser encouraged overindulgence saying, "Eat, eat, this is a celebration!" Others offered thanks, and through wide smiles, conveyed their happiness. One man told a CPTer that he hoped the three of you would someday visit At-Tuwani.
>
> Days later, at a village meeting, the people again expressed their joy at your freedom, and their sadness over Tom's death. They spoke of the deepening trust between the village and CPT and saturated the room with "ilhumdulla's" ("thanks be to Allah").[76]

Anderson closed her final letter with the story of Fatima and three grandchildren planting the olive tree at the end of the mourning period. "Before me, the hands of the Hereni family move in and through the earth," she wrote. "I watch closely because in these hands, I see what has taken root."[77] Rich Meyer, referring to Fatima Hereni at the end of his chapter on what the CPT Palestine teams did during the hostage crisis, wrote, "I hope that someday Jim, Norman and Harmeet can meet her on their 'Thank you, Palestine' tour."[78]

---

76. Ibid., 60–61.

77. Ibid., 61.

78. "Rich Meyer, "With a Lot of Help from Our Friends: The Call from Palestine for the Release of the Peacemakers," 70.

When Loney returned to Canada after his ordeal, he spoke of a "a great hand of solidarity . . . that included the hands of Palestinian children holding pictures of us, and the hands of the British soldier who cut our chains with a bolt cutter. That great hand was able to deliver three of us from the shadow of death. I am grateful in a way that can never be adequately expressed in words." CPTnet, "TORONTO: Statement by Jim Loney on his arrival home," March 27, 2006.

TEN

On the Education of Aliens:

Issues Arising from CPT's Work in the West Bank

EVERY NEW PROJECT IN CPT raises issues with which both team members and the wider CPT organization have to struggle. Because CPT has worked in Palestine longer than it has on any other project location, and because of the high profile the region has in both secular and religious media, the issues that have arisen out of the West Bank work have significantly shaped the entire CPT culture.[1] Following is a discussion of some of these issues.

CULPABILITY OF THE UNITED STATES IN THE ISRAELI-PALESTINIAN CONFLICT

In the first months of the Al-Aqsa Intifada, Dianne Roe and Kathleen Kern were hurrying to the neighborhood of Harit iSheikh so they could spend the night with a family there whose home had been hit by shells and bullets (see chapter 5). After he saw Roe pick up a bullet as they walked down Shuhada Street, a soldier demanded that she give it to him, as well as others she had collected earlier. Roe wrote that she wished she had said,

---

1. One could argue, however, that CPT's work in Colombia made more dramatic changes to the CPT culture and philosophy. In the Colombia project, for the first time, team meetings were held in Spanish, and Colombian Nationals went through training and joined the team. These changes, in turn, caused CPT to re-evaluate the "effective racism" component of accompaniment—that those whose lives the world deems more valuable could provide protection for those whose lives the world deems less valuable. See chapter 10 in *In Harm's Way*.

"Excuse me sir, but I think those are mine. You see I come from the United States. It is my country that has paid for your army. It is my country that vetoed U.N. resolutions and thus enabled your country to carry on this brutal occupation. It was my congressman who joined over 400 other congressmen in supporting your country's assault on the people in these neighborhoods."

I could have said, "These bullets are mine. They were paid for with my taxes. I want to return them to their rightful owner." But I did not need to argue with him. There are hundreds more on the street. I will see to it that some of them are returned to their rightful owners in Washington, DC, wrapped in a photo of one of the children who received it as a gift from America.[2]

The principal grievance in the Arab/Muslim world toward the United States is its default and overt support of Israel. Although the U.S. State Department and an array of U.S. presidents have given lip service to the principle that Israeli settlement expansion is detrimental to peace, the government has continued to send massive amounts of aid to Israel, which has enabled it to continue building settlements and confiscating land. When Arabs see U.S.-built Apache and Blackhawk helicopters killing Palestinian civilians and U.S.-built Caterpillar bulldozers demolishing Palestinian homes, U.S. advocacy for "peace" negotiations rings hollow. Similarly, the lip service the U.S. pays to "democracy" seemed hypocritical in later years of the Intifada, when the U.S. boycotted the democratically elected Hamas government. The boycott confirmed what Palestinians suspected—that "democracy" to the U.S. means that Palestinians should vote for the candidates the U.S. supported.[3]

Jeff Halper, the director of the Israeli Committee Against House Demolitions, has told several CPT delegations that the U.S. Congress is the institution most responsible for keeping the Israeli occupation of the West Bank and Gaza in place. U.S. presidents, the State Department, and many Israeli politicians have understood that Israeli settlements are the primary obstacle to peace in the region. More than half of the Israeli electorate thinks that Israel should get out of the West Bank and Gaza. However, the political power of the right-wing partisans of Israel is enormous. Congressional representatives who have dared to criticize Israel for

2. CPTnet, "HEBRON: WHOSE BULLET IS THIS?" November 16, 2000.

3. The consequences of the boycott on team friend Abdel Hadi Hantash and other Palestinians working in the public sector were detailed in CPTnet, "HEBRON URGENT ACTION: Tell U.S. Senate to stop punishing Abu Muneer," June 22, 2006.

its abuses of human rights or ask that it abide by U.N. resolutions and pull out of the occupied territories have lost their seats due to the power of the Israeli lobby—primarily represented by AIPAC (American Israel Public Affairs Committee).[4]

Hebron team members have watched, with increasing discouragement the American participation in the 1995 Oslo II accords, the 1997 Hebron Protocol, the 1998 Wye River Memorandum, the 1999 Sharm el-Sheikh Memorandum, the 2000 Camp David II negotiations, the 2001 Taba talks and Mitchell Report, the 2002 "Roadmap to Peace" proposed by the "Quartet" of the European Union, Russia, the U.S., and the U.N., and the 2007 Annapolis conference. None of these meetings ever really addressed Israel's resolve to hold onto parts of the West Bank and keep Palestinians from attaining anything resembling self-determination. Neither did they show the U.S. maintaining even the pretense of evenhandedness in how it related to Israelis and Palestinians.

The 1997 USAID project in Hebron that was an outgrowth of the Hebron Protocol illustrates futility of American attempts to "help" both Israelis and Palestinians in a balanced way. When the team first came to Hebron, the Israeli military kept Shuhada Street closed to Palestinian drivers most of the time. The Hebron Protocols stipulated that Shuhada Street must be opened to Palestinian traffic, so USAID sent engineer David Muirhead to lay new water, electricity, and sewer lines that would serve both the Hebron settlers and Palestinians in the Old City. His crew also installed turquoise awnings and streetlights, covered up and sandblasted off hateful settler graffiti, and put non-native palm trees requiring irrigation in the middle of the street to create a boulevard.

Muirhead began the project with the cheerful plan of hosting a barbecue for both the Jewish and Palestinian residents of Hebron once he finished the renovations. With the frequent closures the Israeli military imposed on the West Bank and settler attacks on his Palestinian workers

---

4. The defeat of Georgia Congresswoman Cynthia McKinney in the 2002 election is an example of how partisans of Israel control congress. Israeli peace activist Uri Avnery wrote at the time that McKinney "had dared to criticize the Sharon government, to support the Palestinian cause, and (worst of all from the Jewish establishment's standpoint) she had gained the support of Israeli and Jewish peace groups," "Manufacturing Anti-Semites."

See also Tivnan, *Lobby*. For other sources on the U.S. political relationship with Israel, see Bookbinder and Abourzek, *Through Different Eyes*. Chomsky, *The Fateful Triangle*. Green, *Living by the Sword*. Novick, *The Holocaust in American Life*. Quandt, *Peace Process*. Rubenberg, *Israel and the American National Interest*. Findley, *Deliberate Deceptions*. Ball and Ball, *Passionate Attachment*.

and construction equipment, he soon had a different perspective on the situation. The project ended up with a 200 percent cost overrun. In their update covering September 2, 1997, the team wrote,

> Tuesday, September 2
>
> At about 8:00 a.m. settlers threw chunks of concrete from the roof of Beit Hadassah down at one of the Palestinian engineers working on Shuhada Street. Other workers on the road said that the soldiers and police present did nothing to find the perpetrator but maintained a presence on the street afterwards.
>
> Local settler Anat Cohen demanded that the police arrest one of the workers who had a small Palestinian flag sticking out of his pocket. The police told him to put the flag inside his pocket and he refused.
>
> An hour or so later, settlers shot out the window of a bulldozer with a pellet gun. When the Palestinian driver kicked broken glass from the window in the direction of an Israeli police officer, he was arrested.
>
> David Muirhead, the American engineer in charge of the U.S. AID funded road renovation, attempted to intervene and was himself arrested by the Israeli police.
>
> "I was arrested for holding up the police in arresting the driver," Muirhead later told an Associated Press reporter.

Kathy Reilly of the U.S. Consulate in East Jerusalem phoned members of the team and asked them to talk with workers on Shuhada street, which runs near the CPT apartment, to get the details that led up to Muirhead's arrest, because she was not able to get anyone from the Israeli government to respond to her.

By 2004, the Shuhada Street awnings were covered with more settler graffiti, grillwork and streetlights had been thoroughly vandalized, and neither Palestinians nor CPTers were allowed to walk, let alone drive, on Shuhada Street. The Hebron Protocol, which had stipulated that the Old City vegetable market be opened as well, was null and void, all without apparent protest from the U.S., which had been a signatory to the Protocol.[5]

U.S. culpability in the Palestinian Israeli conflict also has ramifications for how the organization communicates issues that arise from its West Bank work to its non-U.S. constituency. Since the majority of CPTers serving

---

5. See CPTnet, "Hebron Update: August 29–September 2, 1997," September 8, 1997. CPTnet, Dianne Roe, "HEBRON: Turquoise awnings and the failure of the Hebron Protocol," July 22, 2003. See chapter 5 for a description of how Muirhead intervened when settlers sabotaged a water pipe during the first months of the Intifada.

in Hebron have been Americans, the U.S. support of Israel has been the prime target for much of the Hebron Team's advocacy work. The fact that the U.S. government has been culpable in the Israeli-Palestinian conflict in a way that the Canadian government has not has led to some difficulty when the team has sent out urgent action releases. With increasing numbers of CPTers from the United Kingdom joining the Palestine teams, the United Kingdom's culpability in the conflict is also an issue.[6]

6. In January 2008, the author posted a question on the intra-CPT discussion group GITW to Canadian and U.K. CPTers: "Is there a lobby [with the power of AIPAC] in Canada and the U.K.? Would you describe your governments as generally pro-Israel (as opposed to marching in lockstep behind Israel)?"
Diane Janzen responded in a January 28, 2008, e-mail,

> I would say that the Canadian government's position in the Middle East has shifted in the last several years to be more aligned with the US. Prior to [Stephen] Harper being the [Conservative Party Prime Minister], the government tried to walk the middle line and not stir the waters too much (I do remember I think a 2003 report by Canadian MP's who visited Palestine after the 2002 incursions . . . Sabeel was selling the report books—I think MP's were shocked). Since Harper has come to power there has been a much more public shift in support of Israel . . . like:
> 1. Canada being the first country after the Jan 2006 [Palestinian] elections to refuse to "deal with" the new Hamas government (even before the US) . . . however the Canadian officials from Ramallah were quick to point out that Canada never really did give much money to the Palestinian government directly . . . it was given via development organizations, and there would be no change in that (however this wasn't reported in the media)
> 2. Canada was the first country to support Israel in their attack on Hezbollah in 2006, spent considerable sums of money to evacuate the rather large Lebanese-Canadian population, however didn't make any public statements or pressure on Israel to stop the attacks on Lebanon
> 3. Canadian Conservative MP's snubbed visit to Canada by Mustafa Barghouti in spring of 2007 . . . one thing of amusement was the recent sending of "Happy Hanukkah" cards by Harper's office to Canadian citizens whom they deemed were Jewish (the mistakes that were made in the determination of who was Jewish made it a news item). Didn't hear any similar issues of "Happy Ramadan" cards.
> 4. Janzen also cited an article describing the development of the Canadian Jewish Political Affairs Committee (CJPAC) in 2005, which appeared to have emerged under the guidance of AIPAC: Dan Freeman-Maloy, "AIPAC North."

U.K. CPTer John Lynes responded to the question in a January 22, e-mail,

> Up to about 1950 the bias in the British parliament was mildly anti-Zionist, largely as a result of Zionist attacks on British troops and targets in Palestine in the 1940s; the explosion at the King David Hotel in Jerusalem remains to this day the biggest "terrorist" attack in that region. Between 1950 and 1967 the bias swung the other way for various reasons.

Canadians, in particular, however, are too used to Americans behaving as though Canada were a U.S. protectorate and should simply adopt U.S. policies. CPT has a large Canadian constituency and on principle, tries to include in its urgent action releases contact information for Canadian governing bodies. These have included the Canadian Minister of Foreign Affairs and the Canadian Ambassador to Israel, and the Israeli Ambassador to Canada. However, most people involved in the Hebron project know that the U.S. President, State Department, and Congress are the agencies

> In the past 20 years the Zionist lobby has become more sophisticated, and a vigorous pro-Palestinian lobby has emerged. The latter probably owes more to anti-imperialism, Muslim immigration, old-fashioned antisemitism (stronger here than in the US?), the occupation of Gaza and the West Bank, and sympathy with the underdog, than to a well-organised pressure group.
>
> One hears reference to "the Jewish vote" in constituencies, for example in North London, with a conspicuous concentration of Jewish voters. I doubt if a Jewish vote actually exists in the UK. Jews disagree among themselves about politics and about everything else. It is interesting that the MPs with the strongest anti-Zionist credentials—George Galloway, Jeremy Corbyn, Gerald Kaufman and, among Euro-MPs, Caroline Lucas—all hold seats with higher-than-average numbers of Jewish voters.
>
> At meetings in the UK in support of CPT I encounter both lobbies. The Zionist lobby tends to be articulate, well-informed and well-coached. Their spokesmen (yes, usually male!) invariably trot out their eye-witness accounts of a suicide bombing. It's hard to believe all those accounts can be first-hand. Pro-Palestinians are more numerous, more enthusiastic, and embarrassingly grateful for CPT.
>
> So, in answer to Kathy's first question: No, we don't have an AIPAC in the UK. As for her second question about our government, words fail me. Maybe they aren't in lockstep behind Israel, but they are certainly in lockstep behind George W Bush, and that can amount to the same thing. Sometimes I despair!

U.K. CPTer Maureen Jack added in a January 25 response on GITW,

> My own view has been for some time that the problem with the UK government is that they try to maintain a balanced view on Israel/Palestine. The problem with that is that the situation is not balanced and so it's not appropriate to have a balanced view. I agree with John that it is important to our successive governments not to stray too far from the US position. I'm not aware of anything equivalent to AIPAC, but I do know from BBC contacts that there are always objections (in what seems a coordinated way) when anything that presents Israel in a less than wholly positive way is broadcast; from this I think we would have to assume that actions/comments from the UK government would bring forth the same kind of response.

However, Jack went on to note in her posting that she had received a response from the Foreign Secretary to a letter she had written expressing concern about the settlements. It strongly reiterated the position that all Israeli settlements, including the ones around Jerusalem, were illegal under international law, and that the Separation Barrier had to be moved to the Green Line.

that really have the power to make positive or negative contributions to the conflict. Some necessary actions applied uniquely to U.S. citizens, such as the response called for in 2002, after the U.S. House Republican Majority Leader essentially called for the ethnic cleansing of Palestinians from the Occupied Territories.[7] Still, as of 2008, the Hebron team usually tries to include Canadian and U.K. contacts in most of their urgent action releases.[8]

The presence of new CPTers from New Zealand, Colombia, Italy, and Germany, in recent years, as well as from the United Kingdom and Canada helps deflect the justifiable anger Palestinians feel toward the U.S. (and by extension, U.S. citizens) away from the team. The growing international diversity has other benefits as well. Scottish CPTer Maureen Jack, wrote, "I think one of the strengths of the Palestine team is that it is becoming more international and that perhaps of all of the areas in which CPT operates this is the one which is most likely to attract people from different countries . . . and so could be a catalyst for growing CPT."[9]

PARTISANSHIP ISSUES—"BALANCE"

Related to the U.S.-culpability in the Israeli-Palestinian conflict is the issue of "balance" in the discourse about the Israeli-Palestinian conflict. In the U.S. (and to a lesser extent in other Western nations), any remark remotely construed as sympathetic to Palestinians must be "balanced" by the Israeli view or by the views of Israel's partisans. The "Israeli" view does not include the opinions of Israelis who are ardent foes of the occupation and care about the human rights of Palestinians. It subscribes instead to the doctrine that Israel has a right to do whatever it wants to Palestinians. When pro-Israel views are widely discussed in the mainstream U.S. media, opposite, "balancing" views that express what Palestinians suffer do not need to appear.

CPT does not claim to be neutral in any conflict with which it is involved. Teams live with people whom the powers that be oppress and exploit. Rather than neutrality, the model is more "guests in the house of the disenfranchised." Within that role, CPTers find themselves better able than

---

7. CPTnet, "CHICAGO/HEBRON URGENT ACTION: Demand Dick Armey Retract Call for Ethnic Cleansing of Palestinians," May 4, 2002.

8. In At-Tuwani, because of the language differences, the Italian members of Operation Dove and CPTers send out urgent action releases separately, although they consult each other on wording.

9. Jack, e-mail to author, January 19, 2008.

their hosts to greet the oppressors at the door. Using active nonviolence as a means of communication, they confront and engage those in power, making it clear that they will A) tell the truth about what CPTers see them doing; B) physically lay down their lives to prevent their harming CPT's hosts; and C) treat them—the oppressors—with the respect and love to which they are entitled as children of God.[10]

These tenets, applied to CPT's work in Haiti, Washington DC, Chiapas, and Colombia, have not provoked much controversy. When applied to Israel and Palestine, however, they only enrage Israel's partisans, particularly when CPTers speak in U.S. communities with significant Jewish populations. Although as of 2009, greater access to alternative views in the media has made speaking about the Israeli occupation of the West Bank and Gaza less controversial, CPTers, when they write or speak about the conflict, continue to face accusations that their presentations are unbalanced or pro-Palestinian.

INTERACTIONS WITH ISRAELI SOLDIERS

As it has on several different project locations, the question of how to interact with soldiers in Hebron has caused considerable disagreement within the Hebron team over the years. Most Palestinian contacts of the team would prefer that CPTers not talk to soldiers at all, unless they are intervening to help a Palestinian. This factor has given rise to many arguments over whether CPT is more than a Palestinian solidarity group.

Most Israeli citizens, with the exceptions of Palestinian citizens of Israel and Ultra-orthodox Jews, go into the army for two to three years and remain on call as reservists until they are in their fifties. Since the majority of Israeli Jews serve in the armed forces, the soldiers that CPTers encountered in Hebron expressed a wide variety of political opinion—although the most dovish soldiers usually managed to avoid getting stationed in the West Bank and Gaza.

---

10. Kern, "From Haiti to Hebron: The CPT Experiment," 199–200. This model, as of 2008–2009, is in the process of changing. CPT has been trying to rethink aspects of its work that have paternalistic or colonial undertones. Its experience in At-Tuwani—where it has provided support for villagers who have organized their own acts of nonviolent resistance, and who have directed the work of the team—has influenced the entire organization. The model, in effect, is becoming more a case of the disenfranchised people meeting their oppressors at the door and asserting their rights, while CPTers serve as a visible presence, documenting what happens.

The team's first relationship with an Israeli soldier began when a young border police named Meron approached members of the team as they were doing morning worship in 1995. Across the strap of his automatic weapon, he had written "R.E.M." —an American alternative rock group—and the title of one of its biggest hits, "Losing My Religion." He revered American music and wanted to talk with the team about his favorite groups. Meron, obviously ill-suited to military life, would continue talking with the CPTers even after his commanding officer had shouted orders for him to stop. He expressed appreciation for the work of the team and hatred of the Hebron settlers, one of whom had called him a Nazi when he refused to let her park in front of the Ibrahimi Mosque. Coming from a mixed Arab/Jewish neighborhood in Tel Aviv, he said he saw no reason why Palestinians and Israelis could not live together.

One day a Palestinian friend of the team who worked in a pottery shop adjacent to the grounds of the Ibrahimi Mosque told the team that the soldier he had seen the team talking to the other day had shoved him and verbally abused him. When the team mentioned this to Meron, he looked ashamed and said that if he did not hassle the Palestinians the other border police in his unit made life miserable for him.

This relationship with Meron characterizes the difficulty the Hebron team has had coming to consensus about the "right" way to interact with soldiers. Israeli soldiers in Hebron are mostly young and unhappy to be working there; they are anxious for contact with civilians, especially women.[11] Relating to them on a friendly basis arouses suspicion or causes pain for Palestinian friends and acquaintances of the team. On the other hand, CPTers have also helped humanize soldiers for Palestinian contacts, especially when these soldiers believe that the settlers should be removed from Hebron and that Palestinians should have the same civil rights that Israelis do (as many who have served in the Nahal Brigade believe). Soldiers have stopped CPTers accompanying Palestinians at checkpoints, and in the ensuing conversation these Palestinians have found that these soldiers would prefer to relate to them as equals rather than as a conquered people. And conversely, CPT interventions sometimes humanized Palestinians in the

---

11. Interestingly, age does not seem to make a difference for women. Some Hebron team members have theorized that young male soldiers miss their girlfriends, sisters, mothers, and grandmothers. Thus female CPTers can serve as substitutes for each of these roles. Rich Meyer, Palestine Team Support Coordinator from 2002–2007, speaks of "the grandmother effect" when older female CPTers make Israeli soldiers think about whether they would do what they are doing if their grandmothers were around.

soldiers' eyes too. When CPTers saw soldiers with whom they had had friendly contact abusing Palestinians, the prior relationship sometimes shamed the soldiers into behaving better. Such scenarios were not the norm but did happen multiple times in the team's history.

As of this writing, CPT has been in Hebron thirteen years, and team members still have not achieved consensus regarding the "correct" way to relate to soldiers. Sara Reschly sparked a lively debate around this issue in 2002 on the GITW (Getting in the Way) discussion group for full-timers and reservists.

> I have some reflections on a paragraph from a recent Hebron update (Sep. 18–24). I'm a bit hesitant to make them, because I don't want them to be received as critical. I began thinking about the dynamics of power that exist in the larger context in which this incident takes place and thought I'd share it with y'all to see what you think.
>
> The incident reported in the Heb update:
>
> "On school patrol, Ken Near, a delegation member, asked soldiers enjoying a breakfast of bread and cheese at the Kiryat Arba checkpoint if he could take their pictures. About fifteen minutes later, CPTers noticed an elderly Palestinian man walking down the street with cheese and bread shared by the soldiers."
>
> This incident reminded me of a similar incident that took place a few years ago— I did not see the sharing of bread as a positive thing. I saw two soldiers punch a Palestinian teenager in the face several times. I confronted the soldiers. They said they were detaining the teenager because he didn't have an id and had a knife on him. They showed me a pocketknife. Soon a few older Palestinians gathered. One had a cell phone called the Palestinian teenager's house and got someone to bring his id. The ID was brought. By this time the Israeli police arrived and declared the Palestinian teenager could go on his way. I asked the two soldiers why they were beating the Palestinian. They denied it.
>
> As we were talking, two Palestinian boys walked past us (me and the soldiers). The soldiers called them over and offered them a loaf of bread and leftover peanut butter and jelly. The boys took it from the soldiers and began walking down the street. The older Palestinian man who had negotiated the release of the teenager told the boys to return the bread.
>
> I thought this a brilliant move on the older Palestinian's part. Why? Offering leftover bread is not a gesture of peace, but rather an alleviation of guilt. I would rather see soldiers stop beating Palestinians and offer no bread, than to beat them and then toss a few crumbs at children. Even greater would be for the Israeli military to

terminate curfews and closures, thus allowing Palestinians a chance to work and buy their own bread and cheese.

What does it mean if soldiers give bread and cheese to an old man meanwhile enforcing a curfew/closure that impoverishes Palestinians. Although not directly mentioned in the update, some readers may infer that the "sharing bread incident" was a "good" deed. I do not read it that way. Rather, I find it similar to the analogy of an abusive husband who opens the car door for his wife, yet refuses to allow her to go anywhere without his accompaniment or worse yet, beats her up once they're in the car.

Peace,
Sara[12]

The responses that followed retraced the years of discussion over the motivations of soldiers, serving as nonviolent witnesses to these soldiers, stereotyping soldiers, loving the enemy, and acknowledging the system as evil rather than individual soldiers as evil. The debate continues.

INTERACTIONS WITH SETTLERS

In November 2005, Scottish CPTer Maureen Jack wrote a reflection describing the breathtaking effect that the malice of Hebron settlers and their supporters can have on CPTers working in Hebron:

> I'd not met him before. He was perhaps slightly older than I, and he was wearing a green cap, not unlike my red CPT one. By his accent I could clearly tell he was clearly originally from London, though he now lives in a settlement. I said hello. "Fuck you. Screw you," he said.
>
> We were standing across the street from an entrance to the Israeli settlement of Beit Hadassah in Hebron. I was there with Anne and John (both in their late seventies) and some other internationals on school patrol at the foot of steps leading up to Qurtuba School, a school for Palestinian girls. We were waiting for the girls to come down on their way home. He was there with a group from Women in Green, an organization that supports Israeli settlements. They were also there waiting for the schoolgirls.
>
> The girls and female teachers started to make their way nervously down the crumbled steps. The Israeli visitors pushed forward taking photos. We got between them as best we could. I didn't document at all. I took no photos. I had no idea of what went on around me. All I could see was the fear on the faces of the women

---

12. GITW archives, October 16, 2002.

and girls. All I could feel was the tremor in their hands as I helped them down. All I could hear was my faltering Arabic as I tried to find something reassuring to say.

And then it was over. The girls and the teachers were all on their way home. But the Israeli ex Londoner was not finished. "Have you got cancer yet? I hope so," he said to me.

"Please don't say that. My husband died of cancer six years ago," I replied.

"I am happy about that," he said.

What has this man's life been like that he has such hatred? How is he feeling now? Is he thinking of me, as I am thinking of him? Is he weeping now, as I am? And am I weeping for myself, or for him?[13]

When Jeff Heie, Kathleen Kern, Cliff Kindy, and Wendy Lehman set up the Hebron project in 1995, they knew that having dialogue with the settlers there would be risky and possibly harmful to the development of close working relationships with Palestinians in Hebron (and for that matter, progressive Israelis). They also believed that the team should seek out chances for this dialogue in a low-profile way.

What they did not understand at the time was the comfort that some of the Hebron settlers felt with spreading enormous lies. After team members learned about the rumors accusing Cliff Kindy of being a Hamas activist, raising money to kill Jews (see chapter 1),[14] Kindy talked with a settler, Eli, who had previously spoken in a non-hostile way with CPTers on the street. The rumors continued. Kindy and Art Gish then spoke with Hebron settler spokesperson Noam Arnon in the winter of 1996 about the work of CPT and the pacifist beliefs of Mennonites and Church of the Brethren. They also gave him a copy of Kathleen Kern's *We Are the Pharisees* book, which deals, in part, with the history of anti-Semitism in Christianity. Still, the lies continued, and the team largely gave up trying to relate to the Hebron settlers, choosing instead to chat with settlers from outside of Hebron who occasionally visited the city to show support for the Hebron settlers. (The Hebron settlers were often less likely to attack people on the street when these outside visitors were present.)

In 1997, the team also established a relationship with a young couple in Kiryat Arba to whom they would bring subsequent CPT delegations to put a human face on "settlers." The couple, who asked that the Hebron

13. CPTnet, "HEBRON REFLECTION: On hatred," November 25, 2005.

14. The threats against Kindy were the impetus for CPT's first Statement of Conviction.

team not use their names in a public forum, even invited Kathleen Kern and Rich Meyer to their Passover meal in 1998. Eventually, however, the couple separated; the team believed the split had something to do with their political differences (the husband had served in the Peace Corps and told the team he'd prefer to live in Jerusalem rather than in Kiryat Arba, but the rent in Kiryat Arba was much cheaper). The team never again found local settlers who could present a similarly humanizing perspective to delegations.

In 1998, settlers went on the verbal offensive to get CPT removed from Hebron, by putting out the following release:

> Date: Mon, 4 May, 1998 6:12 AM EDT
> Hebron-Past, Present and Forever
> By David Wilder
> The Jewish Community of Hebron
> CPT—Squalor on the Face of the Earth[15]
> May 3, 1998
> CPT is the abbreviated name of Christian Peacekeeping Teams. This primarily Mennonite group ends each of its internet postings with the following signature:
>
> 'CPT Hebron has maintained a violence reduction presence in Hebron since June of 1995 at the invitation of the Hebron Municipality.'
>
> Hebron Municipality = Arab Mayor Mustepha Natsche
>
> What does CPT really stand for? On February 18, they posted the following: "CPT calls on Christians committed to stop hostility towards Iraqi people to wear ribbons with the words FOOD NOT MISSILES inscribed on them. The ribbons will signify our faith that food for people in Iraq rather than missiles represents the deepest will of God."
>
> Blatant, official support for Saddam Hussein.
> Members of CPT have been arrested and imprisoned in the United States following violent and illegal demonstrations.
>
> These people preach peace and non-violence. In fact, they implement the exact opposite.
>
> Fact: Art Gish from Athens, Ohio was detained in Hebron for attempting to aid a Palestinian terrorist who had just stabbed a 14 year old Jewish girl. According to eye witnesses, he stepped on the knife used in the attack in order to hide the evidence from the IDF.

---

15. A multilingual Israeli friend of the team, Ya'alah Cohen, was visiting at the time they received the release. She frowned as she read it and then said, "I think he meant to say 'filth.'"

Fact: A number of CPT members have been deported and/or denied entry into Israel. Others have been arrested for participating in violent confrontations with the Israeli Defense Forces and other Israeli security forces.

How impartial is CPT? Last June, CPT member Kathleen Kern was interviewed by IMRA's Aaron Lerner. An excerpt:

IMRA: Do the current disturbances, with rock, firebomb, and bomb throwing, fall into this category (of supporting non-violent protests)? Kern: No. There is not a lot we can do but watch. IMRA: What are you doing to stop this violence? Kern: We are not set up to deal with the sort of things that have been happening in the market. It is much easier to work on STRUCTURAL VIOLENCE like land confiscation and the demolition of houses. IMRA: Have you thought of trying to influence the local population?

Kern: It would be patronizing for us to come in and say "we want to develop you. The roots of violence, what is happening in the market place, reflects the underlying symptoms."

What do these people spend their days doing? Adorned in red baseball hats, they walk the streets of Hebron, looking for trouble. They have even begun giving "tours" of Hebron to unsuspecting Christian groups, spreading their venomous duplicity. History takes a back seat to falsehood—Jewish property is "occupied Arab land."

On April 18, 1998, THE DAY BEFORE Dov Dribin was murdered, CPT members visited Arabs living in the vicinity of Maon. They posted an article specifically mentioning and vilifying Dov Dribin.

On April 26 they posted:

"Another visitor in the hospital room shared some of the following details. Ahmed, a Palestinian from Yatta was traveling near the area last Sunday. He reported that he left the car and walked along the rocky goat paths of the grazing land. Driben and the other injured settler had already been lifted by helicopter and taken to a hospital in Beersheba. Dabadseh was lying motionless on the ground and bleeding from bullet wounds to his chest, below his right shoulder, and in his right arm. Israeli soldiers, police and settler security paid no attention to Dabadseh. Ahmed picked up the injured Dabadseh and put him on one of the many donkeys that were nearby. As he put it, "I stole him from the soldiers so I could take him to the hospital."

On May 1, they posted the following:

Hebron: A Short Concise Background

"Since the early 1980s, this quiet land of shepherds has become dotted with Israeli settlements. These settlements are built and subsidized by

the government of Israel in arrogant disregard for international law, under which they are illegal. They are built on Palestinian land confiscated by the Israeli Defense Force (IDF, the army). Recently 100 families in the area were given eviction notices by the IDF to make room for more settlements. Israelis living in these settlements that look more like military camps than residential communities are well armed and given free reign by the IDF to terrorize the local Palestinians. For years, the most infamous of these settlers has been Dov Dribin. We have heard countless first hand accounts of Dov's brutality, including two execution style murders in which he tied the hands of his victims before shooting them. Dov and the other settlers in this area have romantic visions of themselves as cowboys, claiming the land for Israel and exterminating the "savages" who inhabit it.

On April 19, Dov and several others blocked a group of unarmed Palestinians who were trying to get to their fields. According to eye witness accounts, Dov and one of the Palestinian farmers began to struggle. Dov yelled to one of his settler friends, "Shoot him! Shoot him!" The settler shot, missed the Palestinian and killed Dov."

Of course, the libelous allegations in these reports are pure, unadulterated lies.

1. Dov Dribin never killed anyone—he was never investigated, indicted, or tried for murder.

2. Dov Dribin was shot at least five times in the chest and once in the head. He was not shot by one of his friends. He was murdered by an Arab who grabbed a weapon from one of Dov's friends. Dov was unarmed and was known not to carry a weapon.

3. Eye witnesses at the scene of the murder have given detailed accounts of what actually happened. No Arab was left lying, bleeding, in the field. All the Arabs involved fled, including those who claim to have been shot.

4. The community of Maon was legally established by the Israeli government over a decade ago. The small farm being developed by Dov Dribin and his friends is located on land officially belonging to the State of Israel. Dov and his friends were never asked, or ordered to evacuate the farm.

5. In the vicinity of the murder, there are not any "Arab fields."

6. International law disallows the use of murder and terrorism, the likes of which have been perpetrated against Israelis by Arabs in all parts of the country, including Judea and Samaria. CPT seems to have forgotten this.

7. International law does not prohibit Jews from living on their own land in Eretz Yisrael.

Under a guise of "violence reduction presence," this group of anti-Semitic Israel-haters continues to incite Arabs in Hebron, and

> in the Hebron area, against Israelis living here. This incitement may very well have been instrumental in Dov Dribin's murder. Those responsible should be arrested and imprisoned. As for the others, it is time for Israeli security and legal forces to take all measures necessary to evict this squalor from Hebron and from Israel before they do any more damage.
>
> In the mean time, anyone desiring to express opinions directly to CPT is invited to write to them at: cpt@igc.apc.org (Christian Peacemaker Teams, Chicago, IL).[16]

The Chicago office was not inundated with hate mail, as the team feared it would be, after the release. An aide to Senator Joseph Lieberman did request a response to the accusations.[17] Below is a draft of that reply (italics added for clarity) written by members of the Hebron team, both in the field and those at home:

> On May 3rd, David Wilder of Hebron's settler community widely distributed a release that contained some serious accusations against our organization, Christian Peacemaker Teams (CPT). We have written the following for our supporters and interested observers who have asked for clarification regarding these accusations. Because David Wilder's article, "CPT—Squalor on the Face of the Earth" was lengthy we have excerpted portions for the sake of brevity. People who wish to check out the full article may check the Hebron settlers' website at http://www.hebron.org.il.
>
> *DW:* "'*CPT Hebron has maintained a violence reduction presence in Hebron since June of 1995 at the invitation of the Hebron Municipality.*'
>
> *Hebron Municipality = Arab Mayor Mustapha Natsche*"
>
> CPT: Yes, we were invited by the mayor of Hebron, and yes, his name is Mustapha Natsche. [The final draft read "Yes, he is Arab."] As the project has developed, we have also established relationships with other groups. Presently, as part of our Campaign for Secure Dwellings, we work most closely with The Israeli Committee Against House Demolitions and The Palestinian Land Defence Committee.
>
> *DW: "What does CPT really stand for? On February 18, they posted the following: to wear ribbons with the words FOOD NOT MISSILES*

---

16. Wilder, "CPT-Squalor on the Face of the Earth."

17. Kern would meet the aide in 1999 at a conference. No longer working for Senator Lieberman, he gave her his card and asked her to give it to the team, in case they needed assistance in the future.

inscribed on them. The ribbons will signify our faith that food for people in Iraq rather than missiles represents the deepest will of God."

CPT: Yes, we believe that food for the people of Iraq is more conducive to peace than bombing is.

DW: Blatant, official support for Saddam Hussein.

CPT: No, we do not support Saddam Hussein; we just don't want the Iraqi people to starve. We also wish to point out that Saddam Hussein's actions against Iranians, Kurds, and other Iraqis were just as vile when the U.S. considered him an ally.

DW: "Members of CPT have been arrested and imprisoned in the United States following violent and illegal demonstrations."

CPT: Members of CPT have indeed been arrested for participating in demonstrations at the U.S. Navy's ELF facility in northern Wisconsin, a giant antenna for signaling Trident submarines in a first strike capacity. CPTer Anne Herman, a 64 year old grandmother, is serving a six month sentence in Danbury Federal Correctional Institute because she trespassed on to the School of the Americas property to protest the SOA's training of Latin American soldiers to torture, kill and generally abuse the human rights of people in their home countries.

In the witnesses at both ELF and the SOA, the demonstrations were strictly nonviolent. Because both institutions generate the possibility or reality of enormous violence against innocent people, CPTers felt that it was worth getting arrested in the course of demonstrations there. We believe this puts us in good company with Gandhi, King, and other nameless heroes who have committed their lives to nonviolent social change.

DW: "Fact: Art Gish from Athens, Ohio was detained in Hebron for attempting to aid a Palestinian terrorist who had just stabbed a 14 year old Jewish girl. According to eye witnesses, he stepped on the knife used in the attack in order to hide the evidence from the IDF."

CPT: Gish came upon the scene of a stabbing and stood between angry settlers and innocent shopkeepers, thus preventing an escalation of the violence. The police took him away for his own protection, because they were afraid settlers would kill him.[18]

18. Regarding the rumor about Art Gish and the knife, he wrote in an August 23, 2004, e-mail to the author:

> I first heard the story about the knife when I returned to Hebron a year later. I then went to Noam [Arnon] and told him that the story was not true. He acted like he knew nothing about it, but said that he would check with others about the story. I am not sure, but I think we never talked about that again.

DW: *"Fact: A number of CPT members have been deported and/or denied entry into Israel. Others have been arrested for participating in violent confrontations with the Israeli Defense Forces and other Israeli security forces."*

CPT: No one has been deported. Two have been denied entry into Israel. Several have been arrested for being present at violent confrontations and refusing to leave when asked to.

By "other Israeli security forces," Wilder may be referring to the private armed settler security personnel. In May 1996 when CPT members accompanied a Palestinian landowner to harvest his wheat, armed settler security at Susia settlement threatened to shoot them if they did not leave the land. CPT members have never responded violently to these or any other threats.

DW: *"How impartial is CPT? Last June, CPT member Kathleen Kern was interviewed by IMRA's Aaron Lerner. An excerpt: IMRA: "Do the current disturbances, with rock, firebomb, and bomb throwing fall into this category (of supporting non-violent protests)? Kern: No. There is not a lot we can do but watch."*

CPT: Wilder leaves out the context of those comments, which were as follows:

"IMRA: I understand that your goal is to 'support local nonviolent efforts.' What activities in Hebron today fall under that category?

Kern: Grass roots organizers who are working to prevent home demolition. We were there with the university students when they had their nonviolent witnesses.

We are pacifists ourselves. To use a nonviolent strategy doesn't mean to be a pacifist yourself. . . . As long as people are not using physical violence, we are interested in supporting them.

IMRA: Do the current disturbances, with rock, firebomb, and bomb throwing, fall into this category?

Kern: No. . . ."

Lerner himself edited out Kern's comments indicating that CPT viewed the rock and Molotov throwing as both extremely counterproductive, and antithetical to the philosophy of nonviolence:

I have no memory of meeting David Wilder the first few years I went to Hebron. About 4 years ago I approached him on the street and he spewed out a lot of anger toward CPT. I listened. He brought up the knife story. I said I was the person who was accused and told him it was not true, and that the Torah forbids making false accusations against others . . .

The subject keeps coming up. Occasionally soldiers still repeat the story to me. Shalom, Art

"We found that our small four person team just could not be effective in dealing with this type of violence."

Kern further commented to Lerner that if the team had at least fifty people, it might be able to stand between the soldiers and rock throwers. People who wish to have the text for the IMRA interview may contact the Chicago office.

Our frustration at our inability to intervene in the clashes was compounded by the fact that the media ignored simultaneous structural violence such as home demolitions and land confiscations while the focus of the world was on two blocks of street violence.

DW: "What do these people spend their days doing? Adorned in red baseball hats, they walk the streets of Hebron, looking for trouble. They have even begun giving 'tours' of Hebron to unsuspecting Christian groups, spreading their venomous duplicity. History takes a back seat to falsehood—Jewish property is 'occupied Arab land.'"

CPT: There is occupation all around us. And yes, we are often asked to give tours to international groups and introduce visitors to Palestinian families. We take them to families like the Al Atrashes who had their home demolished by the Israeli military on March 3, 1998. They meet other children who have been made homeless by Israel's home demolition policy. This is not "venomous duplicity"; this is painful truth.

DW: "On April 18, 1998, THE DAY BEFORE Dov Dribin was murdered, CPT members visited Arabs living in the vicinity of Maon. They posted an article specifically mentioning and vilifying Dov Dribin."

CPT: It is a tragedy when anyone dies whether it be in military conflict, paramilitary activity, "friendly fire" or in normal everyday life activities. On April 18th, we talked with families whom Dov had threatened to kill. While we were there, Dov released his horses into the families' wheat fields. We reported that in our release. Several Israeli and Palestinian organizations who are better equipped to do so have offered to assemble various records and affidavits testifying to Driben's history of harassing his Palestinian neighbors. We would be happy to share those when they become available.[19]

---

19. Much to the team's chagrin, they found out later that they had reported false information regarding Driben's murder. In a November 23, 2004, e-mail to the author, Mark Frey wrote,

> This is what I remember: Dov was killed by a Palestinian. [A journalist] told us she interviewed people involved and while she wrote something along the lines of what CPT reported, she said she made it up because she didn't want to write that Palestinians killed him. So much for journalistic integrity. She was probably our main source for the release we put out. We were shocked when she told us.

> DW: "Under a guise of 'violence reduction presence' this group of anti-Semitic Israel-haters continues to incite Arabs in Hebron, and in the Hebron area, against Israelis living here. This incitement may very well have been instrumental in Dov Dribin's murder. Those responsible should be arrested and imprisoned. As for the others, it is time for Israeli security and legal forces to take all measures necessary to evict this squalor from Hebron and from Israel before they do any more damage."
>
> CPT: We would suggest that those who are concerned about these accusations contact Israelis who have worked with us and know us personally for their opinion.[20]

As CPT became more established in Hebron, team members were better able to ignore the hostility of the settlers or to find humor in some of their bizarre comments (see chapter 7). But their capacity to inflict pain still was evident at times, as demonstrated by a 2006 poem written by British CPTer, John Lynes, who had been raised in a Jewish family:

> Shabbat patrol
> The young have no time for miracles.
> You must forgive an old man. Today I pray for a miracle.
> Miracles? Why not?
> Apartheid ended without bloodshed;
> the Berlin Wall fell;
> Leningrad became St Petersburg;
> the IRA gave up their arms.
>
> A Jewish child, I hid my eyes
> from the pictured corpses of Belsen and Buchenwald.
> There but for the grace of God—
> Resurrection was not a word I knew.
> How could I believe I would live to see
> children and grandchildren of the Holocaust
> crossing the fields of the Promised Land
> to synagogue on Shabbat?
> Could there be a more heavenly vision?
> But surely not for this world?
> Yet two by two, there they walk as I write,
> not to any old shul:
> to synagogue on the very spot where Abraham, Isaac and Jacob,
> Leah, Rebecca and Sarah, lie buried.
> "Shabbat shalom," I greet the worshippers.
> Some have learned to recognise my red hat
> the mark of a Christian Peacemaker in Hebron,

---

20. CPT Hebron, "Response to David Wilder's 'Squalor on the Face of the Earth.'"

and they spit at me
and they curse me as a Nazi. And it hurts.
It hurts.
You must forgive an old man—old enough to recall real Nazis.
Today I pray for a miracle.
I long to be part of that miracle, whatever the cost.
Will you pray with me?
"Lead us from death to life, from falsehood to truth,
lead us from despair to hope, from fear to trust,
lead us from hate to love, from war to peace.
Let peace fill our hearts, our world, our universe."[21]

CHARGES OF ANTI-SEMITISM

The last week of December 1996 closed with Christian Peacemaker Congress in Washington DC issuing a call for Christians to sign the "Pledge by Christians to our Jewish Neighbors." The pledge developed as a way to deal with charges of anti-Semitism leveled at CPT because of its work in Hebron. Those who signed promised not to allow contempt for Jews and Judaism to go unchallenged. "However," concluded the pledge,

> Because of our concern for human rights, inspired by the Jewish prophets and a Jewish carpenter from Nazareth, we cannot pay the price exacted by some people for meaningful Jewish-Christian dialogue—that of silence regarding Israel's human rights abuses. We believe that silence makes us complicit in the injustices at work in Israel and Palestine.
>
> We realize our intention to confront Israeli abuses of power may mean that we cannot have harmonious relationships with some of our Jewish friends. We will mourn the loss of these relationships. We will also pray for the eventual restoration of these relationships as we pray for a just peace between Israelis and Palestinians. And until such time as the restoration of these relationships occurs, we will celebrate those Palestinians and Israelis, Jews, Christians and Muslims who have worked diligently and self-sacrificially for justice in the Holy Land.[22]

---

21. CPTnet, "HEBRON POEM: Shabbat Patrol," January 21, 2006.

22. Christian Peacemaker Teams, "A Pledge by Christians to our Jewish Neighbors." See also the CPT Steering Committee's "A letter to our churches about anti-Semitism," April 27, 1999. In the end, the Pledge was not considered an entirely successful effort, because actual incidents of anti-Semitism, such as attacks on synagogues were relatively rare in North America.

In the next several months of 1997, approximately a hundred and fifty people requested the pledge and signed it. Charges of anti-Semitism, however, would continue to plague the Hebron team. In later years, team members would have an easier time dealing with these charges because of their close working relationship with groups like The Israeli Committee Against Home Demolitions, Bat Shalom, Rabbis for Human Rights, and Ta'ayush. A large percentage (relative to the number of Jews in the world) of International Solidarity Movement volunteers (see chapters 6–9) were Jewish, and many of them made their way to Hebron to visit or work with the team. When confronting charges of anti-Semitism, team members thus could simply refer people to the Israeli and Jewish friends with whom they had worked, celebrated, and mourned over the years.[23]

More difficult than dealing with anti-Semitism charges against themselves was dealing with Palestinian friends and acquaintances who used anti-Jewish rhetoric. When the team's landlord stopped by to pick up rent, he invariably launched into a monologue about how Jews controlled the world. As some Palestinians explored why settlers, soldiers, and the Israeli public regarded them with contempt, why they destroyed their homes and confiscated their land, rhetoric from the Protocols of the Elders of Zion began to make sense to them. In one notable example, Mark Frey listened to a man in the Beqa'a Valley whose cistern had been demolished and land confiscated lecture Yehudit Keshet, an Israeli woman from Bat Shalom, about Jewish avarice throughout history while Keshet graciously listened.

23. On November 22, 2004, the author posted a query on GITW asking non-North American CPTers who had worked in Hebron whether they had had similar experiences in their own countries. British citizen John Lynes wrote,

> I don't suppose my reply is worth much because I always declare "Hebron is where one of my ancestors was buried: his name was Abraham." I was born a Jew, so am unlikely to attract accusations of anti-Semitism. My (Jewish) cousins understandably disapprove of my Christian/Quaker position, and working with CPT in Hebron has confirmed their worst misgivings. (Too bad, but it's fun being in the same position as the authors of the Gospels and Acts.) Hebron settlers have called me a Nazi, but I can't take this seriously, being old enough (76) to remember real Nazis.
>
> In reply to your specific question, I have never been accused of anti-Semitism in the UK. The only formal complaints (including one from the Israeli Embassy!) came from people who were not actually present at my talks.
>
> Right now I'm teaching for a month in Nova Scotia. I've experienced just one vehement attack over here on me and CPT, and have met several fellow-Quakers in Canada who have been accused, grotesquely, of anti-Semitism. So I'm inclined to suspect that charges of anti-Semitism are more likely to be met in North America than in the UK. That's sad.

When the team challenged Palestinians about their anti-Jewish rhetoric, citing Israelis and other Jews who genuinely cared about their human rights, Palestinians often would say, "Of course, some are good," but maintained that in general, Jews were greedy and did not care about human rights.

As the Al-Aqsa Intifada escalated, so did the anti-Jewish rhetoric. How-ever, many Palestinians suffering in Hebron seized on examples of Jews intervening on the behalf of Palestinians, when they heard about them, as though the anti-Jewish rhetoric did not sit all that comfortably in their souls. During the Israeli siege of Arafat's compound in Ramallah, a neighbor of the team whose business curfews and closures had decimated his business, greeted Kathleen Kern in the market on April 3, 2002. His face was alight as he described the Jewish International Solidarity Movement (ISM) volunteers entering the compound and serving as human shields. Referring to Adam Shapiro, a Jewish organizer of ISM, speaking at a press conference, the shop owner told Kern, with great earnestness, "And he said many, many good things."[24]

CHRISTIAN/MUSLIM ISSUES

Many CPTers experienced both meaningful Christian-Jewish dialogue and Christian-Muslim dialogue for the first time as part of their work in Hebron.[25] Since Islam, like Christianity, is a proselytizing religion, their friends, acquaintances, and sometimes strangers on the street tried to convert them. Ahlam Muhtasib, the public relations director for the Hebron Municipality in 1995, told Wendy Lehman and Kathleen Kern, as they talked about setting up a project in Hebron, "Wouldn't it be wonderful if you became Muslims!" Others in the course of the next twelve years would approach CPTers on the street, assure them they cared about them, and then tell them how sad they would be if the CPTers died that night and did not make it to Paradise.

---

24. CPTnet, "HEBRON UPDATE: March 26–April 3, 2002," April 4, 2002. The team took several months in 1995 figuring out that "the Jewish" meant soldiers and settlers in Hebron, not Jews and Israelis in general.

25. "Meaningful" Christian-Jewish dialogue happened more easily in Israel than it did in North America. Progressive Israeli Jews were seeing the same things that the team in Hebron was seeing and thus did not immediately negate team members' observations or make sure they were aware of the history of anti-Semitism. Marc Ellis, a Jewish theologian, once told the author that he refuses to participate in Christian-Jewish dialogue groups because they are thinly veiled attempts to keep Christians from criticizing Israel.

Demystifying the Western bogeyman of Islamic fundamentalism was a positive outcome of these encounters. (In general, Hebron CPTers encounter much more anti-Muslim rhetoric in their home countries than anti-Jewish rhetoric.) The team found out through their work in Hebron that Islamic fundamentalists were not that different from Christian fundamentalists. They also gained Muslim friends who were serious about their faith but valued the Christian faith that undergirded the work of the team in Hebron. From these friends, they learned about Islam's commitment to hospitality, mercy, and caring for the poor—values that the Western media rarely mentions. Team members were "rescued" from difficult situations numerous times in the first years of the Hebron project by Muslim strangers who saw them looking bewildered on the street or in crowds and helped them as an expression of their Islamic faith.

CHRISTIAN ZIONISM

The murders of Muslims and Jews through crusades and inquisitions are a permanent stain on the history of Christianity. On their way to "the Holy Land," European crusaders killed most of the Jews living in the Rhineland. After they reached Jerusalem, a monk, Fulk of Chartres, wrote that Frankish crusaders

> joyfully rushed into the city to pursue and kill the nefarious enemies, as their comrades were already doing. Some Saracens, Arabs, and Ethiopians took refuge in the tower of David, others fled to the temples of the Lord and of Solomon. A great fight took place in the court and porch of the temples, where they were unable to escape from our gladiators. Many fled to the roof of the temple of Solomon, and were shot with arrows, so that they fell to the ground dead. In this temple almost ten thousand were killed. Indeed, if you had been there you would have seen our feet colored to our ankles with the blood of the slain. But what more shall I relate? None of them were left alive; neither women nor children were spared.[26]

Working in Hebron required an awareness of this history of persecution, and members of the Hebron team often did not feel free to criticize aspects of Judaism and Islam that contributed to the violence they meant to deter.

Christian Zionists, however, were another matter. Very generally speaking, Christians Zionists believe that in order for Jesus to return all

---

26. Fulk (or Fulcher) of Chartres, *Gesta Francorum Jerusalem Expugnantium*, 109–15.

Jews must return to Israel, where two thirds will die in Armageddon, and the remaining third will convert to Christianity (see Zech 13:7–9). Rather than condemning this philosophy as fundamentally anti-Semitic, the Israeli government and the Israeli settler movement have gladly received Christian Zionist financial and political support.

Hebron CPTers have felt free to criticize Christian Zionism and make their church constituency aware of the threat they believed it posed for prospects of peace in the Middle East. Kathleen Kern, in particular, did significant amounts of writing on the topic between 1995 and 1997,[27] quoting material she picked up at the Third Christian Zionist Congress in 1996:

> Some selections from literature picked up at the Third Christian Zionist Congress:
>
> From Gary Cooperburg's *Project Shofar* brochure:
>
> The shofar blast is a symbolic warning that we must all stand up to the challenge and fight the attempt to thwart the Divine Process of Redemption. Christian Zionists can work together with observant Jews in this effort. It is a holy effort which brings Divine grace upon those who involve themselves with it.
>
> Project Shofar salutes the participants of the Third Christian Zionist Congress taking place under the auspices of the international Christian Embassy in Jerusalem. We welcome your recognition that the only peace plan is the one which G-d promised to the Jewish People through our father Abraham.
>
> From Cooperburg's brochure, *What's a nice Jewish boy doing in a place like this?*
>
> The Christian Embassy, which established itself as an embassy in Jerusalem for the express purpose of showing the nations of the world that Jerusalem is the exclusive, eternal capital of the Jewish State has put the Israeli government to shame. It has consistently spoken out against our rejection of the countless miracles performed for us which they recognize and our leaders fail to see. They call for a "not one inch" peace plan. They spoke out against the infamous "Oslo" underground sellout of the Jewish State. They have reached into their pockets to help bring Jews home from the former Soviet

---

27. Kern, "Ambassadors for the End Times: The International Christian Embassy Jerusalem"; "Crossing the Weirdness Threshold: Christian Zionism in Jerusalem"; "Undercover with Christian Zionists at Kiryat Arba." See also, CPTnet, "BLESSING ISRAEL?" October 28, 1997. CPTnet. "Blessing Israel? Christian Embassy Responds, Kern Replies" November 2, 1997.

Union. They cry out to the Jewish government to act like Jews and maintain their Jewish integrity. They have initiated an annual feast of tabernacles convention which, among other things, seeks to comfort the Jewish people and remind us that we are still G-d's Chosen. And now, just as the leadership of the Jewish people is seeking peace at the expense of Zionism, we see the Christian Embassy sponsoring the third Christian Zionist Congress in Jerusalem.

From Cooperburg's brochure, *God's word is our guarantee*:

The cunning Arab squatters, whose ancient historical connection with the Land of Israel spans nearly 100 years, include among their slander of the Jewish people, their complaint that Jews have come from other countries and taken away what is rightfully theirs. If one would but trace the history of these fraudulent Arab migrants and thieves, he would discover an abundant lack of authentic history, or legal acquisition of the land upon which they live. But rather than waste time on trivial mundane pursuits, one has but to open his Bible to clearly see what is taking place in the Promised Land today. . . .

From Richard A. Hellman's *The Vision of CIPAC* (Christians' Israel Public Action Campaign):

. . . Judea and Samaria, the biblical names for the so-called occupied territories of the West Bank are the heart of biblical Israel. Israel obtained them by legal right and has no need to give these lands over to anyone. . . .

. . . Biblically speaking, I don't believe that Israel should concede land for peace. I believe that Israel and the Jewish people have been given this land, have been restored in their land, and that this should be in perpetuity. However, the nations of the world in the United Nations and even America have brought pressure upon Israel to concede land for peace . . . But the way I read the Bible, Israel has title deed from Dan to Beersheva, from the River of Egypt to the Euphrates River, from the Mediterranean Sea virtually to Saudi Arabia, including present day Jordan.

From Ramon and Zipporah Bennett's *Arm of Salvation* newsletter Vol. 5, No. 4:

Continue to pray for complete success with the ARROW antimissile system and for the production of large numbers of missiles and launchers.

Continue to pray for a revelation of the TRUTH about JESUS and for Israeli hearts to be open and receptive.

> Pray for protection and a HEDGE OF FIRE to be all around Ramon for having written *Philistine*.
>
> From "The Five Lies of Islam," *Middle East Intelligence Digest*, vol. 7 #3:
>
> #1 Allah is God
>
> Islam's big lie, which underpins all the falsehoods upon which it stands, holds that the source of revelation imparted to Muhammad is the God of the Bible worshipped by Christians and Jews.
>
> In fact, Allah was the name of the pagan moon-god to whom temples were built across the Middle East. . . .
>
> To deceive non-Muslims, Muslims back up the claim that they worship God by pointing out that the word, "Allah," appears in the Arabic language Bible. But while the noun "allah" does mean "god," as a proper noun it has no connection to the Name of the God of Israel, the One who calls Himself YHWH. [Author's note: You mean like the English word, "god?"][28]

Possibly at the behest of Hebron settlers and their supporters, CPT has received quantities of hate mail from Christian Zionists over the years. Following are some examples the organization received between April and July 1998, some months after Hebron settler David Wilder's "Squalor on the Face of the Earth" appeared (see above).

> Subject: CPT in Israel
>
> To whom it may concern,
>
> I was sorry to see what appears to be "Christian" discouragement of the people of the people of Israel—discouragement designed to hinder God's chosen people, Israel, from living in all the land the God of Israel and the God of Messiah Jesus has given to them—forever.
>
> Please understand, Arabs may live in Israel, but they must do so with a full recognition that Israel, and no illegal (from a scriptural perspective) Palestinian regime, is sovereign. In truth, Arabs fair much better under Israeli sovereignty than they might dare to imagine living under despots such as Arafat, Assad etc. God spoke clearly to Abraham—a blessing to those who bless you and a curse to those who curse you. I do not desire that anyone should be cursed of God; yet, His word will accomplish its purpose.
>
> In His love,
>
> JH

---

28. These excerpts appeared, among other places, in Kern's satirical novel about working in Hebron, *Where Such Unmaking Reigns*, 66–68.

Subject: (none)

why don't you send christians to defend arab christians against the real threarts and murderous behavior of the animuslims . . . when christians wke up and begin to do the rigth thing then maybe jesus will return to help out. In the meantime your insane programs do nothing to help the cause of peace which is an oxymoron for arabs who live in dreaded fear because of the horriffic backward and animalistic docrine called Islam. Read the warning signs. . . . just listen to arab rhetoric and wake up= and stop your sick behavior and dumb propaganda.

Doctors for real peace.

Subject: What are you attempting to prove??

What exactly is your organization trying to prove by supporting the enemies (Palestinians) of the Chosen People, the Jews. My advice to you is to get out of our land. You seem to support the blatant murders of the Jewish people. You claim to be Christians when in fact you are proving to be the tools of Satan and the False Messiah (Anti-Christ). There are a lot of Jewish believers in the Messiah and as believers we hold to the entirety of the word of G-d, not the doctrines of the catholic sponsored and written doctrines. We will soon completely remove you as well as your Palestinian allies from our home land. You Christians are Anti-Judaism, anti-Semite groups of vile hatred and have no inheritance with the Chosen People of G-d. You place yourselves in a place of dictatorial rule and force your demonic beliefs upon those who follow the ENTIRETY OF THE LAW OF G-D. We hold NOT to the Pagan ways of the Christians instead we do as was commanded by G-d to our fore-fathers. We were intrusted with His Holy Word because we were the only ones found to be responsible enough to ensure that it not be perverted. So how dare you enter into our homeland and try to convert us into paganism.

Remember the Messiah Yeshua will return and destroy those who try to pervert His fellow Jews and His Holy Land Yisrael

Subject: (none)

My name is Marcel and I'm from Orlando, Fla. I'm not surprised by your anti-Israel bias, but to call yourself Christians that's a tall one. You seem more concerned about International law than the Kingdom of God. From your actions its clear that you don't really believe the Bible. A more accurate description would be arrogant humanistic feel good world system fixers. [Only Jesus will fix it] Your pride has deceived you. Do you believe Amos 9:14–15? Hahaha,

Allah is a lie and thats why the Moslem world cannot tolerate Israel. Their living on land once under Dar al Islam makes Allah look dead, false or just plain weak. Your allegiance to this false god is clear, and your anti-God of Israel stand is clear. I'm going to do the best I can to let true Christians wake up to false brethren in their midst.

Marcel

Subject: I wish you would kindly drop . . . .

the word "Christian" from your name. No way could you be one, and do what you have done in Israel, especially in the Hebron area. I personally would like to see judgment done against your group for the complicity in the incitement of murder against an innocent man due to your violence and hatred against the Jews.

Jon

Subject: stop your bullshit

I recently sent you mail and yet you continue your nonsense . . . when Christ returns you all will burn forever in the living hell you deserve for your lies . . . its really that simple.

Subj: Re: Upcoming CPT Delegations

I sent your recent postings to a good friend of mine in Jerusalem and this was her reply for you to ponder.

WK

About CPT.
Yes I know of course. I know. I know about all the slander and all the tales that were spread about the Jews ever since Abraham our Father and Founder whom we buried in Chewron. I know the tales and who told them. The Protocols and the blood in the Pesach-matsa, the murder of the Christian Annointed and the stealing of Palestine (as the enemy always calls the Jewish Homeland). I know it all.

Although to-day Israel has many very real friends in the Christian world (and I want to mention the Christians for Israel), Christian hatred, based on a completely false interpretation of the basics of that religion, is still very much in evidence as is being proved again by the e-mail I received through you. There are still Christians who want to promote a state they call Palestine, although they must realise that this biblical land belongs to the Jews. If they do not realise this than they are not Christians. This is my Jewish statement.

On the political and practical level I must state that one needs a building permit in Israel for building even an extension like e.g. a porch to one's home. If one cannot put such a permit on the table one's porch, one's home (illegally built) is being demolished and it does not make any difference whether one is a Jew or anything else, e.g., a Moslim. The law is blind. Religion blind. And colour blind. Total equallity.

Emotionally speaking I want to ask how many Jewish homes are being built in the Moslim world??? But let me not get carried away by emotions. I might go on than, saying that the Moslim presence in the Land of Israel should not be pictured as an innocent presence because it is not innocent. It is directed towards annihilation of the Jewish presence. But we, the Jews do not answer in kind. We are a democracy and every citizen is a citizen. CPT does not look very knowledgeable to me. The name of the township they misspelled as Betinjan (not an Arab sound) is really Betunya and it is a very dangerous place for Jews. Even driving through it makes my blood-pressure go up. I remember all the stones thrown, all the Molotovs exploding, the killings and near killing of Jews just driving past this place: Betunya. Where CPT works so tirelessly. But not for peace. In any case not for peace with the people of Israel, the nation of the Bible, the Owners of the Land G'd promised them.

As far as disruptive effects are concerned, terrorist acts against the Jews had and have an extremely disruptive effect on the Jews. We the Jewish people will need generations in order to get over the damage that was done to our souls by the hatred, the constant war, the murder of even little children, babies in their cribs, by the Arabs of our region. What it did to us (and the whole world -almost- stood besides them as once it stood besides the Nazi's of Europe) can only be compared to the trauma's we suffer from the fourties of this century. What can I say to defend my people that do not need any defense Wim? Only this really: "ma towu ohale-cha Ja'acov, mishkanotecha Yisra'el," How good are your tents oh Ya'acov, your dwellings oh Israel.

The G'd of Israel will bless the ones that bless His people, curse the ones that curse Israel.

WL

Subj: Re: HEBRON: PROVOCATION, VIOLENCE, SECURITY [a release written by Sara Reschly, posted May 30, 1998 on CPTnet]

Dear misguided CPT's,

Why don't you publish the whole truth and nothing but the truth (see enclosure about the Atrash family, who's house you helped to rebuild)? Or are you indeed completely blinded by the view points of Amelek, Martin Luther, Adolf Hitler and Ahmed Shukary? It is one thing to be engaged (and to associate) with a particular side in a conflict (even as fanatics who are looking for a remote cause, because they can harvest "respect and honor" afterwards)), but it is quite an other thing to greedily engage in lashon rah (that is the Hebrew equivalent for slander against persons) against Jews who have legal titles to their own possessions and who—as long as they are not pushed around—harm nobody while living in their own premises. Are 500 Jews a danger to 130 thousand Arabs plus Arafat's army, TIPH and you guys? You must be bloody joking! It's the Jews who need protection from you and your allies, like they would have needed protection in WWII from your spiritual ancestors in the German and German occupied areas of Europe!

Think about it: will G'd appreciate what you are doing against His people, or will He commit you to hell for being on the side of evil incarnate? You misguided sods really have no idea what you are doing.[29]

In May 1998, a small CPT delegation attended the Christian Zionist celebration of Israel's fiftieth birthday in Orlando, Florida. Delegation members wanted to provide an alternative Christian witness to what was happening in Palestine/Israel. Probably the most encouraging news coming out of the delegation was that less than half of the expected participants attended, and they had to move into a smaller hall for the main assemblies. Christian Zionism is still a factor, however, in American policy-making. As many American Jews have become more detached from Israel, or have become increasingly vocal in their condemnation of Israel's human rights abuses, the Israeli government and Israelis in general increasingly have come to regard the U.S. Christian Right as reliable allies.[30]

REACTING TO THE BIZARRE

In the concluding chapter of *In Harm's Way*, which chronicles CPT's entire history from 1986 to 2006, one of the issues discussed is the role of team dynamics in the work of the team:

> The best-functioning teams often have significant spiritual undergirding and find fresh approaches to their work from times of

---

29. *Where Such Unmaking Reigns*, 186–91.

30. See, for example Zev Chafets's cynical, *A Match Made in Heaven: American Jews, Christian Zionists, and One Man's Exploration of the Weird and Wonderful Judeo-Evangelical Alliance.*

prayer, worship, and Bible study. They also tend to have people with good senses of humor, which may be a spiritual discipline itself, in that it tends to acknowledge human frailty and shine light on the absurd actions and philosophies that Powers and Principalities have put in place.

In no other project is the level of the absurd quite as pronounced as it is in Palestine, as witnessed by some of above the statements by settlers and Christian Zionists.[31] Other CPTers from the various projects have funny stories to tell of the work in those locations, but most of them relate to CPTers developing interesting diseases, making cultural *faux pas,* or encountering strange critters—animals and human—while camping. Also, the level of tragedy, the exponentially greater loss of human life in places like Iraq and Colombia, possibly dampens the potential for humor.[32]

Perhaps the fact that Israel claims to be the only democracy in the Middle East, and has denounced the sort of racism that sent eleven to twelve million people—Jews and other targeted groups—to death camps, while at the same time treating Palestinians as inferior beings, fosters the bizarre. Perhaps some of Israel's foundational myths—that the land was empty when the Jews came, that no such thing as Palestinians existed, that somehow Israel was blameless for the Palestinian refugee crisis—also contributed to the atmosphere of the absurd. After the 1967 war, more outrageous myths took root, such as settlements only taking "state land" over which Palestinians had no claim. Out of such myths, catch-22 situations developed, such as the military prohibiting Palestinians from ac-

---

31. At a CPT Support Team retreat in June 2007, Mark Frey and Kathleen Kern, long-term Hebron workers, were sharing some stories with other staff members, who had worked in Colombia, Iraq, Chiapas, and most other CPT projects, hoping to garner examples of other bizarre stories, but in the end, other staff admitted, the context of the Israeli Occupation of Palestine lent itself to a certain weirdness that did not apply to other projects.

32. However, CPT Iraq team member Allan Slater, after reading this section, submitted the following anecdote he wrote on November 9, 2003, in Baghdad.

> Last night, around mid-night, we were all wakened to serious gun-fire on our street. It was obvious that automatic weapons were being fired. There was no sign of American armoured vehicles so we thought it could be looters or some tribal feud being played out. We huddled in a back room of our apartment. We were putting walls between us and the flying bullets. We discussed what we should do if people carrying guns entered the apartment. This morning all seemed normal on the street. Our landlord knew that Iraq had won a football game . . . YIKES! [In many Arab cultures, shooting into the air often happens at celebrations, such as weddings.]

cessing their land and then confiscating it because no one was using it. (Currently, in the South Hebron Hills, Palestinian shepherds and subsistence farmers plow the ground in their olive groves, even though doing so is detrimental to the trees—according to what one villager told members of the At-Tuwani team—since otherwise their land might be confiscated because they are not tilling it.)

Whatever the reasons for the climate of absurdity caused by the Israeli occupation of the West Bank and Gaza, funny stories from the Palestine teams could fill a book. Below are some examples:

In the summer of 1995, a journalist friend told the team that the IDF had confiscated a cow from a family living south of Hebron, because the soldiers said it was too nice a cow for Palestinians to own; they must have stolen it. "Now they have a cow at police headquarters and they don't know what to do with it," she said.

When Kathleen Kern and Anne Montgomery were doing their night Patrol route to the Ibrahimi Mosque/Cave of Machpelah, a soldier stopped them from throwing their trash into the dumpster that the Hebron team generally deposited their garbage. He told them that it was for Jews only. Seeing that they looked confused, he pointed to the dumpster in question, and then a dumpster across the street, repeating, "Jews, non-Jews; Jews, non-Jews."

On their way back from the patrol, Kern pointed out to the soldier who had issued the order that the Jews-only dumpster was next to a Palestinian shop and about one hundred yards away from the Israeli settlement of Avraham Avinu. His comrade then said, "Put your trash wherever you want."

The young soldier became plaintive, "No!" he said, "Really! My-my-" he tapped his upper arm with two fingers.

"Your Commanding Officer?" Kern asked

"Yes!" he said, relieved and grateful to Kern, "My officer told me I had to keep non-Jews from putting their trash in here."

Mark Frey wrote, in 1997, about an incident in which the team intervened to stop soldiers from abusing young Palestinian men outside the team apartment. After kicking one of the men in the backside, the soldiers told the CPTers that they had NOT seen them kicking anyone.

"We found this in the car trunk," the soldier said, holding out nunchucks, a weapon used in martial arts—the team found out later that the boys were returning from a karate class. "But it was in the trunk," Frey said to the soldier, and it's a piece of chain." The soldier said, "What if it had been a gun?"

"'Ah,' we thought," wrote Frey. "But it isn't; it is a chain, and it was in the trunk."

Frey concluded the piece, "During the incident, which took over one-and-a-half hours, I saw three groups of 6–8 settler men walk by, with two men in each group carrying automatic weapons. And these soldiers were angered about a length of chain."[33]

When the author put out a request for humorous stories on GITW, the intra-CPT discussion group, Diana Zimmerman responded:

> Art Gish has a funny story about when a settler said something like fuck you to him. He replied by asking if the man wanted to have sex with him and kind of took it from there. The soldiers had to put down their guns they were laughing so hard and all the while it distracted the usual tableau and allowed the Palestinians some time to graze their sheep.
>
> Honestly, I think the things that struck me as the most funny are really not funny to those who haven't been in the situation. Death and threats of violence from the settlement security guard toward me cause no end of humor to those of us who were on team at the time. A lot of people probably wouldn't see the humor in "God forbid I should pull out my gun and shoot you dead" or "Go to your Rais [Head or Leader] in Ramallah and tell him that you are the problem, you being here is causing all the violence." or pointing to [Matt Chandler] and saying, "You . . . you are nothing," and then turning to me and saying "and she . . . she is worse than nothing."

---

33. Although Kern evidently used Frey's piece for an article, "Humor and the Occupation," in the Mennonite Literary Magazine, *Rhubarb* (Fall 1998), no record of the posting is currently in the CPTnet archive. The previous stories were taken from the same article.

Frey is noted within CPT for a dry sense of humor that manifests itself in various releases. See n. 23 in chapter 5.

Granted he had no physical bullets but I always took it along the lines of, if they are shooting at you, you must be doing something right.

And sometimes I laugh because I really don't know how to cry.[34]

Greg Rollins also responded with the following account:

> I once made friends with a soldier who told me one day that soldiers always made jokes about life in Hebron. He refused to tell me any on the account that he didn't want to come off as cruel or insensitive. I finally managed to convince him to tell me some and lo and be hold, they turned out to be the same ones we told, like Palestinians breaking the curfew and when they get caught, acting confused: "There is a curfew? Are you sure? So that is why the streets are so empty." Stuff like that. Another time Wissam from Abu Sneineh came over. He was very angry. He had just been searched at a check point. He vented to Rick and I about soldiers always checking him for weapons. "Why don't you come to the checkpoint naked?" I suggested. "What difference would that make?" Wissam argued. "The soldiers would just stick their flashlights in my ears and up my nose."[35]

Elayne McClanen also wrote of an interaction with a soldier:

> A conversation I had with a young Israeli soldier at our apartment corner behind the sandbags. . . . his gun always pointing at my head as I passed by . . . I asked him one day if, as a child, his mother ever told him, never to point a gun at someone. He said, "Yes, she did."
>
> "Your mother should be prime minister," I said.
>
> "Yes, she should," he replied.[36]

34. Zimmerman, January 18, 2008, e-mail to author. Art Gish, in a follow-up January 23, 2008, e-mail wrote that he had told the settler, "You mean you want to have sex with me? You really want to have sex with me? Really?"

35. Rollins, January 19, 2008, e-mail to author.

36. McClanen, January 19, 2008, e-mail to author.

Diane Janzen wrote that the central importance of videotaping on the At-Tuwani has led to some of the humorous aspects of the job being saved for the record—which included the settler telling Zimmerman and Chandler they were nothing and worse than nothing. Some other of Janzen's favorites included

- Christy & I (me taping again) on Khoruba hill doing school patrol, 2 settler guys on horse back with a colt free behind them come gently riding out of Havot Ma'on, Christy calls our other teammates to tell them that there are settlers in the area but no problems, and just when that phone call end the settlers start galloping straight towards us, I say "shit call them back" and stuff the camera (still running into my bag). The settlers ride up to us and stop, Christy and I say "hello how are you doing?" several times. . . . the settlers don't say anything. So I say, "that's a nice little horse you have there" I was just glad afterwards that I used horse instead of horsey. The settlers continue riding by and we are facing away from Tuwani when all of a sudden, we turn around and there is this truck full of men shouting. It took us a couple of seconds to calm our hearts down and notice that a man on the back of the truck is swinging around a kafiyya. Tuwani men had been working on Ezra's house near the school and one of them had noticed the settlers riding to Khoruba hill (where they knew we were) and the men convinced Ezra to drive them out to us to see if we were okay. . . .

- Piergiorgio from the Doves video taping from Khoruba hill, zooming in on what he thinks is settlers sitting and [saying], "oh, no, only rocks. Stupid Italian"

- Settler youth being arrested by the police after they had stolen wheat and he gets away from the police several times running around a wheat field with his hands handcuffed behind his back and an elderly out of shape police man running after him.[37]

In the conclusion to an article about humorous aspects of CPT's work in Hebron, Kathleen Kern wrote,

> [Given] the enormous effort by propagandists to prove that the Israeli occupation of the West Bank and Gaza is benign . . . the

---

37. Janzen, e-mail to author, January 28, 2008.

subversiveness of humor makes it the weapon of choice for puncturing these deceits.

Telling humorous stories conveys more about the absurd evil of the Occupation to laypeople than earnest human rights reports, citing statistics of people killed, houses demolished, olive groves bulldozed—the depressing list goes on and on.

C.S. Lewis once said that he Devil cannot stand to be laughed at. One could argue then, that humor is not only beneficial, but *mandatory* for Christians doing human rights work. Indeed, sometimes a good laugh is all that stands between our getting the work done and becoming paralyzed by the dreary, thudding reality of the oppression we see around us.[38]

GENDER ISSUES

Traditional Arab culture observes strict gender segregation. Boys and girls attend separate public schools, and at large gatherings men usually go into one room and the women and children into another. These realities made life difficult for the initial work of the team in the summer of 1995, since Cliff Kindy and Jeff Heie would occasionally talk about work strategies for the team with the men, and Wendy Lehman and Kathleen Kern had to hear about these strategies second-hand. As time passed, however, and their Arabic language skills improved, women on the Hebron team found that socializing with the women and children was actually more interesting than remaining with the men. Palestinian women tended to hold actual conversations, while men on the team found themselves being lectured, often in Arabic, which became frustrating.

The team also found that the fact that both male and female team members lived in the same apartment in their first year was disturbing to many of their neighbors. Dr. Deborah "Misty" Gerner gave the team some money to rent an upstairs apartment for the women after these neighbors moved out, and the team found that this separation made their neighbors feel more comfortable.[39] Unfortunately, the amenities of the upstairs

---

38. "Humor and the Occupation," 14. The role of Hisham Sharabati, CPT's first contact in Hebron, in fostering a humorous perspective on life in Palestine should also not be underestimated. In their initial 1995 meetings with him, Wendy Lehman and Kathleen Kern learned quite a few jokes about the Occupation from him. He also recommended Emile Habiby's satirical novel about the 1948 and 1967 wars, *Secret Life of Saeed*, which served as an inspiration for Kern's satirical, *Where Such Unmaking Reigns*.

39. In Spring of 1996, Marge Argelyn and Kathleen Kern were walking in the market when an old man grabbed each of them by the arm. "You, you sleep together, yes?"

apartment were nicer than the original apartment, and the original apartment also contained the office, so the men on the team did not have the "retreat" that the women did.

On the other hand, the men were rarely sexually harassed. Young women on the team were almost inevitably sexually harassed in Hebron or Jerusalem by a minority of Palestinian men who considered them fair game for groping in taxis or on the street. As time passed, they began to follow the lead of Palestinian women and take precautions not to sit next to men, when at all possible. Some women on the team also began to consider slapping someone's hand and loudly calling attention to the groping of a Palestinian male an acceptable form of nonviolent resistance.

PALESTINIAN VIOLENCE

One of the iconic images of the Al-Aqsa Intifada was a little boy in Gaza standing in front of a tank, winding up his arm to sling a rock at it. Team members saw the poster in many shops in Hebron and throughout the West Bank. For most Palestinians, the picture symbolizes bravery in the face of overwhelming odds. Indeed, most Palestinians view throwing rocks at Israeli soldiers and settlers as nonviolent resistance, since they do not expect to kill the people at whom they throw rocks and bottles.

CPTers, Israelis, and most of the world do not perceive stone throwing as nonviolent. For CPTers, the rock throwing is emotionally painful, because they see the excuse it gives for soldiers and settlers to shoot Palestinians—some of whom are not even participating in the clashes. (Soldiers shot the little boy in the picture who threw a rock at the tank shortly after a photographer turned him into a symbol.)

In the summer of 1995, CPTers made a few futile attempts to stand between stone throwers and soldiers, but found these attempts ineffective for a small group of people. (See above, under "Interactions with Settlers.")

Interestingly, Hebron team updates did not often record *why* a clash was happening, although team members usually knew the reason, e.g., the signing of agreements detrimental to the residents of Hebron, or the circulation of a poster depicting Mohammed as a pig writing the Quran. At times, the clashes seemed like a force of nature, the product of two storm fronts colliding.

---

he asked sternly. Both women nodded vigorously, understanding immediately what he needed to hear.

Still more painful for the team was the lethal violence Palestinian militants committed—especially against Israeli civilians. After the team rode the #18 bus in 1996 (see chapter 2), no more incidents of "predictable" terrorism occurred. The best the team could do was publicly condemn the violence, but such condemnations seemed paltry in the face of hideous injuries and loss of life. Sometimes the best answer team members could give for how they prevented violence against Israelis was that by diminishing the systemic brutal violence against Palestinians, they were diminishing the rage that led young men to turn themselves in to human explosives.[40]

Palestinian leaders who advocated violence did not help matters when the team was trying to convey to the CPT constituency the exponentially greater amounts of violence committed against Palestinians by Israeli forces. During the Al-Aqsa Intifada, certain Palestinian officials would describe the brave struggle between Palestinian forces and the Israeli military as though their militant groups were somehow on par with one of the largest, best-trained militaries in the world—which in turn made Israelis feel their vicious attacks that killed primarily Palestinian civilians were justified.

Kathleen Kern accompanied a South African diplomat to a meeting with Abbas Zaki, Arafat's man in Hebron (see chapter 3), shortly after the outbreak of the Al-Aqsa Intifada. When she asked him how much longer he thought the Intifada would continue, he told her that he did not think it would last much longer. Noting that six million Palestinians lived all over the world, he said that they would begin bombing Israeli and U.S. targets, which would cause Israel to begin negotiating in good faith. Stunned, the diplomat said, "Your Excellency, did you just say you were planning for Palestinians to begin attacking Israelis and Americans all around the world?" Backpedaling, the Zaki said, "No, no, just with knives, not bombs."

This incident illustrates the disconnect between the Palestinian leaders promoting violence and ordinary Palestinians bearing the brunt of the Intifada's violence. Regardless of their political beliefs, the Palestinian subsistence farmers, shepherds, schoolteachers, etc. with whom CPT had relationships would have understood that Zaki's comments were shockingly ill

---

40. One of several examples of the team trying to connect and condemn both Israeli and Palestinian violence appeared in a release put out after Palestinian militants killed two soldiers, and the military demolished six Palestinian homes in response: "The Christian Peacemaker Team in Hebron strongly condemns the evening of violence, along with the violence of home demolitions, and calls for both sides to end the cycle of revenge," CPTnet, Yoder, "HEBRON: Two Soldiers Killed, Six Palestinian Houses Demolished in Response," December 16, 2002.

advised and could only bring harm to the Palestinian people. Additionally, Palestinians at a grassroots level often understood that nonviolent resistance worked better than violent resistance, but once they began to organize a broader movement, they would find their efforts dismissed and even stymied by the leadership of the Palestinian Authority.[41]

In 2004, Mai'a Williams wrote a poem after Palestinian militants bombed two buses in Beersheva, which touches on the helplessness team members felt when seeking to respond to acts of Palestinian terror:

> After the suicide bombing in Beersheva, my senses have become more acute.
>
> The men sitting in plastic lawn chairs in front of tea shops gave me the sketchy details about the bombing. They pressed their ears against transistor radios—their eyes and mouths wide, their faces paralyzed in horror, anger, grief, distress.
>
> The next day, I discovered that the bombers had come from well-known families in Hebron. They were relatives of people I know and with whom I work.
>
> There are charred bodies in Beersheva, in Chechnya. Palestinian prisoners are starving themselves in prisons across Israel. There is a prison in Beersheva. There are melted buses in Beersheva.
>
> Hamed Qawasme was the assistant to the governor's office this spring. He is bright, tactful, with graceful hands. His mother, Nowraz, took us to the house of one of the suicide bombers, the day after the Beersheva bombing. The charred basement smelled of smoke and ash. The bomber's

---

41. Hisham Sharabati, who does not consider himself a pacifist, has told Hebron team members that he prefers nonviolent resistance because it is more broad-based. During the first Intifada, he said, most Palestinians participated in boycotts, demonstrations, strikes, and other forms of nonviolent resistance. When terrorism became part of the movement, many Palestinians stopped taking responsibility for their own resistance, and instead supported charismatic leaders who were committing or planning the attacks.

While the Palestinian leadership bears some responsibility for rejecting creative, nonviolent actions as a preferred form of resistance, one must never overlook the role that the Israeli government has played in stymieing this sort of resistance. Harry Huebner, who had worked in the MCC Jerusalem office in the 1980s, told the author that when the Israeli Civil Administration had asked him for a list of MCC's activities, he had included "Teaching nonviolence." The head of the Civil Administration called him in and said MCC was not allowed to teach the subject. "We know what to do when the Arabs are violent," he told Huebner. "We don't know what to do when they are nonviolent."

grandmother, Amira, around 100 years old, clasped my hand on the veranda

as I gave my condolences. Her eyes were the color of the sun's corona.

We followed Nowraz as she went upstairs to the women's mourning room.

The bomber's mother was laying down, surrounded by thirty women relatives, crying. I was too paralyzed to cry. I drank tea and looked out the window onto the quiet streets of Hebron. Contrary to the newspaper reports from the day before, I did not see anyone dancing in the streets.

What can I say to the mother, to the three Qawasme brothers of the bomber arrested by the Israeli military early that morning? Were they their brother's keeper? Am I?

All I can say is what a principal of one of the Hebron schools said to me: suicide bombing has a lot more to do with suicide than with bombing.

All I can say is today I heard a story about one of my favorite little boys in Palestine, Majd. He went to Jerusalem with his aunt. Along the way an Israeli soldier stopped them at a checkpoint near a convent. Majd asked the soldier for his gun. He said he would bring the soldier another gun when he returned from Jerusalem. The soldier laughed.

His aunt bought him a toy gun, taller than him, in Jerusalem. Every time

Majd hears that is aunt is going to Jerusalem, he asks her to bring him the gun from the convent soldier. He does not want a toy gun, he wants a real one.

I do not know why Palestinian men blow apart themselves and Israeli citizens apart. All I can say is that peace is more than the difference between a toy gun and a real one . . .[42]

WASTA

Much of traditional Palestinian society operates on the principle of "wasta." That is, people from humbler stations in life appeal to people with more

---

42. CPTnet, "HEBRON POEM: After the suicide bombing in Beersheva, my senses have become more acute," September 20, 2004.

influence, or "wasta" to get something done, and those with *wasta* are supposed to have a sense of *noblesse oblige* regarding these requests. Part of CPT's accompaniment ministry bears similarity to this system. CPTers often have the ability to intercede with soldiers or other Israeli authorities more effectively than Palestinians do. On the other hand, CPT's guidelines also prohibit CPTers from becoming involved with aid and development work, so Hebron team members have experienced some painful moments telling Palestinian friends they do not have the *wasta* to procure funds for them.

Particularly in the case of the Campaign for Secure Dwellings families, CPTers found that their *wasta* only extended so far. The Al Atrash and the Jaber families (see chapter 3) had hundreds of people visiting them, advocating for them and donating money toward the rebuilding of the homes through the Israeli Committee Against Home Demolitions. Their high profile brought with it extra persecution from the Israeli Civil Administration, and in 1998 they asked the Hebron team not to put their names in any more releases or urgent action releases. By that time, both families were also deeply in debt. The Israeli Committee Against Home Demolitions (ICAHD) had decided the Palestine Land Defense Committee (LDC) would allocate funds to families participating in the Campaign for Secure Dwellings and ICAHD. The LDC felt that the Al Atrashes and Jabers had already received the lion's share of the funding and wanted to distribute monies more evenly to other families. Although ICAHD and CPT pointed out that the Al Atrashes and Jabers had also suffered more than other families, they had to respect the wishes of the LDC organizers. They thus demonstrated to these families that CPT had no *wasta* even with their friends and co-workers.

COLLABORATING WITH OTHER NGOs

When Wendy Lehman and Kathleen Kern first proposed that CPT set up a project in Hebron, they anticipated they would be working most with the activists in the Hebron Solidarity Committee, who had told them that the mainstream Israeli Peace Now movement was "lame." Over the next few years, the Hebron Solidarity committee disbanded, with most of its membership emigrating back to North America, and the Rehovot Peace Now group became actively involved in the issue of home demolitions. As of this writing, CPT Palestine works closely with several groups that did not exist at the turn of the century.

Deciding which groups would make appropriate allies, and which might harm their work, has been an issue for Hebron team members for the entire life of the project. Many Israelis, Palestinians, and internationals working for Non-Governmental Organizations (NGOs) in the region take a jaundiced view of starry-eyed activists who waltz in with the intention of getting everybody to "kiss and make up," and the CPT Palestine teams have adopted some of this caution. Idealists do not last long in Palestine and Israel, unless they acquire some humility along the way. Additionally, as was the case with the Hebron Solidarity Committee, conflict has a way of wearing out even sober and practical activists. However, in general, the team has erred on the side of openness when contemplating alliances, possibly because more experienced inhabitants of the region once viewed CPT-Hebron as a group of starry-eyed activists.

Working with the International Solidarity Movement (see chapters 6–9) caused special concerns. On one hand, the team had wished for years to have hundreds of people coming to the region to do mass nonviolent direct action. On the other hand, many of the volunteers that initially flooded in were loose cannons with a poor opinion of any kind of authority—even the authority of the ISM organizers. As time passed, however, the ISM became more selective and set up methods of keeping volunteers from doing too much damage. CPT began working more closely with the ISM, helping to lead trainings and participating in public ISM witnesses. After the deaths of ISM activists Rachel Corrie and Thomas Hurndall in 2003, current and former team members felt that they had lost their own people.

Certain ongoing difficulties existed, however, with ISM. ISM volunteers were told to lie about their intentions when they entered Israel to avoid the authorities denying them entry.[43] ISM as an organization also refused to condemn Palestinian violence against Israelis, viewing it as part of a liberation struggle. Although the organizers insisted that international ISM volunteers make an absolute commitment to nonviolent resistance, because of their stance on the Palestinian struggle, the Israeli authorities unjustly accused them of inciting violence and routinely referred to the ISM as a "pro-Palestinian" group rather than a peace group. Still, they filled

---

43. It should be noted that, within CPT, workers have not come to consensus on lying to illegitimate authority. Since truth telling was an important part of Gandhian and Kingian nonviolent movements, many CPTers believe that telling falsehoods runs counter that tradition. On the other hand, most CPTers have learned not to volunteer information, either, that could be used to deport them, deny them entry, or make life more difficult for the people among whom they work.

a nonviolent niche that CPT could not fill, and as of this writing most people on CPT's Palestine teams and most Palestinians appreciate deeply their presence in the West Bank and Gaza.

CPT's relationship with Operation Dove in At-Tuwani was a new experience for CPT as an organization. It did not work "with" the Doves, as CPT would say it worked "with" ISM or Ta'ayush. Rather, Operation Dove was as much a part of the At-Tuwani team as CPT was. In general, relationships between CPTers and Doves have been positive and warm, but subject to the same vagaries of personality, commitment, and maturity that teams on all of CPT's project locations experience. Lack of a common language has also sometimes been a handicap—although as is the case with most Europeans working in Palestine/Israel, Doves have had more acquaintance with English than CPTers have had with the Doves' first language, Italian.

Reflecting on the experience, Matthew Chandler wrote:

> On the side of organizational differences, while CPT and Operation Dove are VERY similar in their missions and methods, they are not the same. CPTers tend to have a more envelope-pushing, or even revolutionary, outlook, while Doves tend to have a more conciliatory outlook. That has on occasion led to disagreements when planning the work of the team in Tuwani. Also, Operation Dove has a somewhat more hierarchical structure than CPT, such that the Dove directors in Italy sometimes have specific mandates for the work of the team, while the CPT support staff tend to leave the vast majority of decisions up to the team on the ground. This disjunct in authority has also led to team conflict.[44]

44. Chandler, November 16, 2007, e-mail to author. Kim Lamberty, after reading Chandler's comments, wrote in a January 22, 2008, e-mail:

> I would just adjust use of the word "conciliatory" in Matt's comments. As I understand it, integral to OD's mission is to try and facilitate processes of reconciliation (which is different than being "conciliatory" in English) between divided groups. While that was mostly not what the mission in Tuwani was about, it was what they were about in Abboud. I would say that at times their focus on reconciliation would have led to a different emphasis in a given situation than CPT's, because reconciliation is not really part of CPT's stated mission. Reconciliation is a key component of Catholic theology, and OD is a Catholic organization.

Chandler then responded on January 24, 2008:

> I have no problem with changing my use of the word "conciliatory" to "reconciling" or something along those lines . . . However, I did deliberately use the word "conciliatory" in my original phrasing because I was describing my impression of the outlook of most individual doves in sort of a typo-

However, it has also been the case that Doves and CPTers in At-Tuwani have, on some issues, presented a united position, challenging the positions of their staffs in Italy and North America. Despite the occasional friction between CPTers and Operation Dove, the world is not so full of people committed to Christian nonviolence and willing to live in the rugged conditions of At-Tuwani that either CPTers or Doves can afford to treat each other's contribution to the work lightly.

WHEN A PROJECT NEVER ENDS

As Lehman and Kern prepared to leave for Palestine/Israel in 1995, CPT Director Gene Stoltzfus told Lehman, who was twenty-three at the time, "You're so young; I hate to see you get involved with this," referring to the intractable nature of the Israeli-Palestinian conflict, and the emotional toll it takes on people who become preoccupied with it. As mentioned earlier in this chapter, when Kern and Lehman wrote their proposal for the Hebron project in 1995, they thought the project would last for five months. The "short-term" mentality of the earliest Hebron team workers meant that they did not make a serious effort to learn Arabic and risked arrest more often.

By 1997, Hebron team members began applying themselves to learning Arabic and taking more precautions, because the elimination of the CPT presence in the Old City would have had serious consequences for their neighbors.

The institutionalization of CPT's work in Palestine has had positive results. The efforts of the team garnered wide respect and support from peace and human rights organizations. The Hebron Team is even listed in the *Lonely Planet* tour guide to Israel and the Occupied Territories. But as of 2008, no end to the violence in Palestine/Israel appears to be in sight, and CPT as an organization continues to struggle with the question, "What should CPT do when crisis is chronic?"[45]

---

logical comparison to most individual CPTers, rather than the theological foundations of either organization, which is especially important when we recognize that not all members of Operation Dove ascribe to Catholic theology, and not all CPTers adhere to Peace Church doctrine.

45. As of this writing in January 2008, the question also applies to CPT's work in Colombia and Iraq. See n. 34 in chapter 9 regarding the discontinuation of the Hebron project in 2008.

Perhaps it is unfortunate that this history concludes at a time when the Israeli Occupation of the West Bank and Gaza has become even more entrenched, the Palestinian economy devastated, and one sees a dearth of leaders in Israel, Palestine, and the U.S. who have the moral vision to find a path that will lead to peace, reconciliation, and justice between Israelis and Palestinians.

However, in South Africa during the 1980s most observers predicted that a blood bath would occur when Apartheid fell. Instead, Nelson Mandela, F. W. de Klerk, and thousands of unsung activists made the largely nonviolent transition from Apartheid to democracy possible, bringing about not only majority rule, but also even the beginnings of reconciliation between warring parties. Just because CPTers and all those who are emotionally involved with Palestine and Israel cannot see a just peace on the horizon does not mean that this peace is not there. The author opened the chapter on CPT's first year in Hebron with a quotation from Zoughbi Zoughbi. She will conclude this chapter with another of his quotations that addresses the shred of hope to which people of faith can cling: "It is the Holy Land. Miracles have been known to happen here."

And until a miracle of reconciliation comes to pass, CPTers, as resident aliens, will continue standing with Palestinians and Israelis who care more about justice than nationality.

Bibliography

Unless otherwise indicated, all unpublished documents are stored with the Christian Peacemaker Teams Collection, Mennonite Church USA Archives-Goshen, 1700 South Main St., Goshen, Indiana 46526. E-mails and other digital files cited in this manuscript are also stored at the Mennonite Church USA Archives. Web site of the archives: http://www.mcusa-archives.org/.

Reports, evaluations, CPTnet releases, and other documents, in keeping with a tradition of viewing CPT's work as a collective effort, have often not been attributed to individuals over the course of CPT's history. The author has thus attributed documents that came out of the various teams to "CPT Haiti," "CPT At-Tuwani," "CPT Iraq," etc. Documents coming out of CPT as an organization, or the exploratory work that led to the development of teams, are attributed to "Christian Peacemaker Teams."

CPTnet

CPTnet releases 1998–2008, Christian Peacemaker Teams Archives. Online: http://www.cpt.org/news/archives.

CPTnet releases from 1993–1997 are stored in Christian Peacemaker Teams Chicago Office Digital archives and at the Mennonite Church USA Archives in Goshen, IN.

OTHER DOCUMENTS

118 Days: Christian Peacemaker Teams Held Hostage in Iraq. Ed., Tricia Gates Brown. Chicago/Toronto: Christian Peacemaker Teams, 2008.

Abu-Sharif, Bassam, and Uzi Mahnaimi. *The Best of Enemies: The Memoirs of Bassam Abu-Sharif & Uzi Mahnaimi.* Boston: Little, Brown and Company, 1995.

Abunimah, Ali. E-mail to Kathleen Kern, December 5, 2005.

Adalah Legal Center for Arab Minority Rights in Israel. "Summary Report to the United Nations Human Rights Commission Emergency Session on Israel/Palestine, 17–18 October 2000." Submitted on October 16, 2000. Online: http://www.adalah.org/eng/intladvocacy/unhrces.htm.

Al-Aqsa Martyrs Brigade. "Statement by the Al-Aqsa Martyrs Brigades Palestine on the CPT Hostages in Iraq." December 6th, 2005, International Solidarity Movement. Online: http://www.palsolidarity.org/main/2005/12/06/statement-by-the-al-aqsa-martyrs-brigades-palestine-on-the-cpt-hostages-in-iraq.

Amnesty International. "Israel and the Occupied Territories: Demolition and dispossession: the destruction of Palestinian homes." Amnesty International, December 8, 1999. Online: http://web.amnesty.org/library/Index/engMDE150591999.

———. "Israel and the Occupied Territories: Imported arms used in Israel and the Occupied Territories with excessive force resulting in unlawful killings and unwarranted injuries." November 17, 2000. Online: http://www.amnesty.org/en/library/info/MDE15/065/2000.

———. "Israel/Occupied Territories: Israeli settlers wage campaign of intimidation on Palestinians and internationals alike." Online: http://www.amnesty.org/en/library/info/MDE15/099/2004.

Anderson-Rosetti, Kristin. "Excerpts from Letters to Tom, Norman, Harmeet and Jim: Written from the village of At-Tuwani, West Bank, Palestine." Chapter 5 in *118 Days: Christian Peacemaker Teams Held Hostage in Iraq*, ed. Tricia Gates Brown. Chicago: Christian Peacemaker Teams, 2008. Earlier draft of chapter available in Mennonite Church USA Archives.

Anonymous ninth-century text ("Where charity and love are, God is there"). Set to music by Jacques Berthier. Copyright Les Presses de Taizé (France.) Used in *Hymnal: A Worship Book*, 452. Scottdale, PA: Mennonite Publishing House, 1992.

Apartheid in Hebron: the True Face of Oslo. Booklet. Jerusalem: Hebron Solidarity Committee, 1995. Mennonite Church USA Archives.

Applied Research Institute in Jerusalem (ARIJ). "The Jahalin vs. Ma'ale Adumim: Case History." Online: http://www.arij.org/index.php?Itemid=26&id=273&lang=en&option=com_content&task=view.

———. "People of the caves targeted by the Israeli occupation forces." June 22, 2004. Online: http://www.poica.org/editor/case_studies/view.php?recordID=405.

———. "The Segregation Wall Path." June 16, 2003. Online: http://www.poica.org/editor/case_studies/view.php?recordID=271.

———. "Segregation Zone." Online: http://www.arij.org/images/DownloadedFiles/Segregation%20Wall%20Path.pdf.

"Arabic Materials-Links." CPT. Online: http://www.cpt.org/iraq/response/arabicresources.htm.

Arraf, Huwaida. E-mail to Kathleen Kern, May 23, 2004.

Ashrawi, Hanan. *This Side of Peace*. New York: Simon & Schuster, 1995.

Association for Civil Rights in Israel (ACRI). "HCJ Orders State to Dismantle Concrete Wall in Southern Hebron Hills." Online: http://www.acri.org.il/eng/story.aspx?id=346.

"At-Tuwani: Parting the Wall." *Signs of the Times* 16:3 (2006) 4.

Avissar, Oded. *Sefer Hevron*. Jerusalem: Keter 1970.

Avnery, Uri. "Manufacturing Anti-Semites." Counterpunch website, October 2, 2002. Online: http://www.counterpunch.org/avnery1002.html.

Avnery, Uri. *My Friend, the Enemy*. Westport, CT: Lawrence Hill, 1986.

B'tselem. The Israeli Information Center for Human Rights in the Occupied Territories. "Border police Trial on Suspicion of Killing 'Imran Abu Hamdiya." Archived in Internet Archive Wayback Machine. Online: http://web.archive.org/web/20030622104419/http://www.btselem.org.

———. "Hebron, Area H-2: Settlements Cause Mass Departure of Palestinians." Status Report, August 2003. Online: http://www.btselem.org/English/Publications/Summaries/200308_Hebron_Area_H2.asp.

———. Impossible Coexistence: Human Rights in Hebron since the Massacre at the Cave of the Patriarchs." Information Sheet, September 1995. Online: www.btselem.org/Download/199509_Impossible_Coexistence_Eng.doc.

———. "Means of Expulsion: Violence, Harassment and Lawlessness against Palestinians in the Southern Hebron Hills." Online: http://www.btselem.org/English/Publications/Summaries/200507_South_Hebron.asp.

———. "Settlers attack Palestinians in Hebron, and kill Nivin Jamjum, age 14, July 2002." Testimonies 2002. Online: http://www.btselem.org/english/Testimonies/index.asp?YF=2002&image.x=18&image.y=9.

———. "Standing Idly By: Non-enforcement of the Law on Settlers: Hebron, 26–28 July 2002." Case Study No. 15, August 2002. Online: http://www.btselem.org/english/publications/Index.asp?TF=05.

Ball, George W., and Douglas B. Ball. *The Passionate Attachment: America's Involvement with Israel, 1947 to the Present*. New York: Norton, 1992.

Barak, Rafael. Letter to Kathleen Kern, May 5, 2003.

Barlow, Katie. "Courage under fire." *The Guardian Unlimited*, November 27, 2002. Online: http://www.guardian.co.uk/israel/Story/0,2763,848521,00.html.

Barr, Cameron W. "'Aggressive pacifists' put their faith on the firing line." *Christian Science Monitor*, February 13, 2002.

BBC News. "Concern grows for Iraq hostages." *BBC News*, December 10, 2005. Online: http://news.bbc.co.uk/1/hi/world/middle_east/4515814.stm.

Benn, Aluf, and Gideon Alon. "PM demands 'quick' changes in Hebron for Jewish control." *Ha'aretz*, November 18, 2002.

Benvenisti, Meron. *Conflicts and Contradictions*. New York: Random House, 1986.

———. *Intimate Enemies: Jews and Arabs in a Shared Land*. Berkeley: University of California Press, 1995.

———. *Sacred Landscape: The Buried History of the Holy Land Since 1948*. Berkeley: University of California Press, 2000.

Benzimann, Uzi. *Sharon: An Israeli Caesar*. New York: Adama, 1985.

B'nei Avraham. "Bnei Avraham-English." Google Groups. Online: http://groups.google.com/group/bnei-avraham/web/cover-page--english.

Bookbinder, Hyman, and James G. Abourzek. *Through Different Eyes: Two Leading Americans, A Jew and an Arab, Debate U.S. Policy in the Middle East*. Bethesda, MD: Adler & Adler, 1987.

Bouwmeester, Jamey. E-mail to Kathleen Kern, June 27, 2004.

———. "Hebron: Building, Birthdays, and the Occupation." *Signs of the Times* 9:2 (1999) 2–3.

———. "In Harm's Way." *Signs of the Times* 9:4 (1999) 2–3.

Brown, Chris. E-mail to Kathleen Kern, July 8, 2004.

———. Untitled report on school accompaniment in Hebron 2002–2003. Unpublished. Mennonite Church USA Archives (digital copy).

Carr, Joe. "A Dove's Last Song." Online: http://lovinrevolution.org/beta/?q=olivebranch#dove.

———. E-mail to Kathleen Kern, December 7, 2007.

———. E-mail to Kathleen Kern, January 16, 2008.

———. E-mail to Kathleen Kern, January 17, 2008.

———. Reflection and eyewitness account of Rachel Corrie's murder. Online: http://lovinrevolution.org/rachel_writings.htm.
Center for Economic and Social Rights. "The Right to Water in Palestine: A Background." Fact Sheet #1. Online: http://cesr.org/node/451.
———. "The Right to Water in Palestine: Crisis in Gaza." Fact Sheet #2. Online: http://cesr.org/node/452.
Chacour, Elias. *Blood Brothers*. Tarrytown, NY: Chosen, 1984.
Chafets, Zev. *A Match Made in Heaven: American Jews, Christian Zionists, and One Man's Exploration of the Weird and Wonderful Judeo-Evangelical Alliance*. New York: Harper Collins, 2007.
Chandler, Matthew. E-mail to Kathleen Kern, November 16, 2007.
———. E-mail to Kathleen Kern, January 24, 2008, 3:34 p.m.
———. E-mail to Kathleen Kern, January 24, 2008, 3:43 p.m.
"Chicago Center for Urban Life and Culture." Online: http://www.chicagocenter.org/.
"Chicago to Peoria Peace Walk." *Signs of the Times* 12:3 (2002) 12.
Chomsky, Noam. *The Fateful Triangle: The United States, Israel and the Palestinians*. Boston: South End, 1983.
———. "The New War Against Terror." Speech delivered at the Massachusetts Institute of Technology, October 18, 2001. Online: http://www.chomsky.info/talks/20011018.htm.
———. *World Orders Old and New*. New York: Columbia University Press, 1994.
Christian Peacemaker Teams. "A Brief History Of CPT's Work." Flier, December 12, 2000.
———. "Christian Peacemaker Teams activities 1984–2000." Online: http://www.cpt.org/publications/chronology.php.
———. "Christian Peacemaker Teams 2000 Annual Report." Mennonite Church USA Archives.
———. "Considerations for CPT Decision Making Entering into Crisis Situations," October 10, 1993. Mennonite Church USA Archives.
———. "CPT Sunday, October 27, 1996." A collection of materials for use in worship. Mennonite Church USA Archives.
———. CPTers Freed." March 23, 2006, CPT. Online: http://www.cpt.org/iraq/response/06-23-03statement.htm.
———. "Discussion Points for Middle East Peacemaking Hebron Ibrahimi Mosque Massacre." March 1994. Mennonite Church USA Archives.
———. "FEAR NOT: A Pilgrimage of Faith In support of the Christian Peacemaker Teams delegation now in Pakistan en route to Afghanistan." CPT. Online: http://www.cpt.org/afghanistan/afganohiowalk.php.
———. "LITURGY AT THE TWIN TOWERS: for the CPT Delegation to Afghanistan." Written by, but unattributed to Jane Pritchard, December 16, 2001. CPT. Online: http://www.cpt.org/afghanistan/afghantwintowersliturgy.php.
———. Notes from Support Team Call on Feb. 13, 2007. Sent as e-mail to GITW by Doug Pritchard on February 21, 2007.
———. Notes from Support Team call on Sep 11, 2007. Sent as e-mail to GITW by Doug Pritchard on September 26, 2007.
———. "A Pledge by Christians to our Jewish Neighbors." Brochure, written by but not attributed to Kathleen Kern. Mennonite Church USA archives.
———. "REPORT OF FORCED RETURN OF CPT PERSON FROM ISRAEL." July 6, 1993. Mennonite Church USA Archives.
———. "Some Evaluation/Reflections on the Fast for Rebuilding." Gene Stoltzfus, with a response from Mark Frey, April 16, 2007. Mennonite Church USA Archives.

———. Steering Committee Minutes, April 6–8, 2000, sent by Mark Frey to Kathleen Kern as an e-mail attachment, October 18, 2007. Mennonite Church USA Archives.

———. Year in Review, 2004: February 1, 2004–January 31, 2005. CPT. Online: http://web.archive.org/web/20051222063218/www.cpt.org/annreport/2004/YearinReview2004.php.

———. "Year in Review FYE 2006—Getting in the Way: February 1, 2005–January 31, 2006." (CPT Annual Report.) CPT. Online: http://www.cpt.org/annreport/2005/YearinReviewFYE2006.php.

"Christian Peacemaker Teams: Presented for discussion by Council of Moderators and Secretaries." Flier, January 1986. Mennonite Church USA Archives.

"Christian Peacemaker Teams: A Study Document." February 1986 Akron, Booklet. Mennonite Historical Library. Mennonite Church USA Archives.

Churches for Middle East Peace, Documents and Resources. "Text Of The Mitchell Report: Report Of The Sharm El-Sheikh Fact-Finding Committee." Online: http://www.cmep.org/documents/MitchellReport.htm.

Ciaghi, Laura. E-mail to Kathleen Kern, December 5, 2007.

———. E-mail to Kathleen Kern, December 6, 2007.

———. E-mail to Kathleen Kern, December 7, 2007, 2:54 a.m.

———. E-mail to Kathleen Kern, December 7, 2007, 7:14 a.m.

———. E-mail to Kathleen Kern, December 20, 2007.

———. E-mail to Kathleen Kern, January 4, 2008.

Cohen, Aharon. *Israel and the Arab World*. New York: Funk & Wagnalls, 1970.

"Collective Punishment: Closures, Curfews and House Demolitions." *Signs of the Times* 6:2 (1996) 1–2.

"Confiscation Protest." *The Other Israel*, 72 (April–May 1996) 14–15. Online: http://israelipalestinianpeace.org/issues/72toi.htm#THE.

Contreras, Joseph. "Radicals in the Ranks: A Soldier's Rampage Undercuts Mideast Peacemaking." *Newsweek* 129:2 (January 13, 1997) 40–42.

Cook, Jonathan. "'Democratic' Racism." *Al-Ahram Weekly On-line*, July 8–14, 2004. Online: http://weekly.ahram.org.eg/2004/698/op11.htm.

Courage to Refuse. "Combatants Letter." Online: http://www.seruv.org.il/defaulteng.asp.

CPT At-Tuwani. "At-Tuwani Media Packet." CPT. Online: http://www.cpt.org/hebron/documents/Tuwani_media_packet.htm.

———. "A chronology of the poisonings during spring 2005." *At-Tuwani Media Packet*, CPT. Online: http://www.cpt.org/hebron/documents/Tuwani_media_packet.htm.

"At-Tuwani: Parting the Wall." *Signs of the Times* 16:3 (2006) 4

CPT At-Tuwani and Operation Dove. "Immanent Peril: The Impact of the Proposed Security Wall along Route 317." February 7, 2006. CPT. Online: http://www.cpt.org/palestine/at-tuwani/documents/CPT_OD_317_security_wall_report.htm#proposed.

———. "Report on the Israeli Military and Police Escort of Palestinian Children from Tuba and Maghayir Al-Abeed to and from School in At-Tuwani for the 2005–2006 School Year." November 10, 2006, CPT. Online: http://www.cpt.org/palestine/at-tuwani/documents/CPT_OD_2005_2006_school_patrol_report.htm.

CPT Beit Ummar. "Beit Ummar Update: April 8-April 12, 2002." CPT Hebron Yahoo groups newslist. Online: http://groups.yahoo.com/group/cpthebron/message/138.

"CPTers Defy Death Threat, Stay in Hebron." *Mennonite Weekly Review*, January 22, 1998.

"CPTers Imprisoned, Released and Resuming Work in Hebron." *Signs of the Times* 6:3 (1996) 1–3.

CPT Hebron. "Atta Jaber Family." Write-up for Campaign for Secure Dwellings. CPT Hebron Office.
———. "Chronology, 1995–2003." CPT. Online: http://www.cpt.org/work/palestine/hebron/chronology.
———. "CSD—Sample Urgent Action appeal." CPT. Online: http://www.cpt.org/csd/csdsampleua.php.
———. "CSD URGENT ACTION: Revenge demolitions and arrests." July 2001. Printout in Mennonite Church USA Archives.
———. "Dividing Walls." Bulletin insert, CPT. Online: http://www.cpt.org/hebron/wall_bulletin.pdf.
———. E-mail to direct newslist, January 2, 2001. Mennonite Church USA archives.
———. E-mail to Joseph Lieberman's office in response to David Wilder's "CPT-Squalor on the Face of the Earth." Date uncertain. Printout of penultimate draft, not the final copy that went to Lieberman's office, available in the Mennonite Church USA archives.
———. E-mail to Kathleen Kern, November 18, 2007.
———. Explanation for why team had not put out releases, January 2, 2001. CPT Hebron direct newslist. Printout in Mennonite Church USA Archives.
———. "General Background on the Beqa'a Valley and the Story of Atta Jaber (in his words)." Mennonite Church USA Archives.
———. "Getting in the Way of Guns." Report on 10 January 1999 intervention, March 1, 1999. Mennonite Church USA Archives.
———. "Israeli Martial Law Imposes Further Restrictions on Palestinians, CPTers, Israeli Peace Groups, Regardless of Israeli Court Decision." CPT Hebron Yahoo groups newslist. Online: http://groups.yahoo.com/group/cpthebron/message/1142.
———. "An Open Letter to President George W. Bush From Christian Peacemaker Teams in Hebron, West Bank." June 17 2003, e-mailed to Kathleen Kern by Paul Pierce, July 10, 2004. Printout at Mennonite Church Historical Archives.
———. "PROPOSAL FOR CONTINUED CPT PRESENCE IN HEBRON, PALESTINE." February 28, 1997. Mennonite Church USA Archives.
———. Response to David Wilder's 'Squalor on the Face of the Earth." Penultimate draft in Mennonite Church USA Archives.
———. "Sue Rhodes." CPT. Online: http://www.cpt.org/hebron/suerhodes.php.
———. "Urgent Action Appeal." November 9, 1995. Longer version of CPTnet release, "HEBRON ACTION ALERT." November 13, 1995. E-mail printout. Mennonite Church USA Archives.
CPT Iraq. "CPT in Iraq Statement of Conviction." CPT. Online: http://www.cpt.org/iraq/response/iraq_team_statement_of_conviction.htm.
"Demolition Season Reopened." *The Other Israel* 91:14 (November 1999). Online: http://www.Israelipalestinianpeace.org/issues/91toi.htm.
Drake, Laura. "A Netanyahu Primer." *Journal of Palestine Studies* 26 (1996) 58–69.
Ecumenical Accompaniment Programme in Palestine and Israel (EAPPI). Inger Styrbjörn, "Going to School in Hebron." Online: http://www.eappi.org/en/news-events/ea-reports/r/browse/18/article/4837/going-to-school-in-hebron.html.
———. Neil from the United Kingdom (author), "Walking to School in Hebron, Online: http://www.eappi.org/ru/news-events/ea-reports/r/browse/30/article/4837/walking-to-school-in-hebr.html.

Electronic Intifada. "SIGN THE URGENT APPEAL: PLEASE RELEASE OUR FRIENDS IN IRAQ." December 2, 2008, Nigel Parry News Archives. Online: http://lists.electronic intifada.net/mail.cgi?flavor=archive;list=nigelparrynews;id=20051202133506.

Electronic Intifada representative, e-mail correspondence with Rich Meyer, March–April 2006, forwarded by Meyer to Kathleen Kern, August 8, 2007.

Elon, Amos. *A Blood-Dimmed Tide: Dispatches from the Middle East.* New York: Columbia University Press, 1997.

Filkins, Dexter. "Hebron Residents Describe An Israeli Reign of Beatings." *New York Times,* January 2, 2003.

Finch-Dürichen, Pauline. "Hebron peace workers take precautions but opt to stay: Waterloo man among seven church-sponsored volunteers." *Kitchener-Waterloo Record,* January 23, 1998.

———. "K-W man on peace team threatened with death." *Kitchener-Waterloo Record,* January 22, 1998.

———. "Waterloo peace worker shares first-hand view of life in Hebron." *Kitchener-Waterloo Record,* March 20, 1998

Findley, Paul. *Deliberate Deceptions: Facing the Facts about the US-Israeli Relationship.* New York: Lawrence Hill, 1993

Finkelstein, Norman G. *Image and reality of the Israel-Palestine Conflict.* New York: Verso, 1995.

Flapan, Simha. *The Birth of Israel: Myths and Realities.* New York: Pantheon, 1987.

Foundation for Middle East Peace. "Settlements Expand Security Perimeters." *Report on Israeli Settlement in the Occupied Territories* 13:2 (March–April 2003). Online: http://www.fmep.org/reports/archive/vol.-13/no.-2.

Freeman-Maloy, Dan. "AIPAC North—'Israel Advocacy' in Canada." Znet. Online: http://www.zmag.org/content/showarticle.cfm?ItemID=10485.

Frey, Mark. E-mail to Kathleen Kern, November 23, 2004.

———. E-mail to Kathleen Kern, November 19, 2007.

———. E-mail to Kathleen Kern, January 24, 2008.

———. "Hebron: Braving the Bridge." *Signs of the Times* 12:2 (2002) 2.

Friedman, Robert I. *Zealots for Zion: Inside Israel's West Bank Settlement Movement.* New York: Random House, 1992.

Friesen, Lorne. E-mail to Kathleen Kern, June 14, 2004.

———. E-mail to Kathleen Kern, August 1, 2004.

Fulk (or Fulcher) of Chartres. *Gesta Francorum Jerusalem Expugnantium [The Deeds of the Franks Who Attacked Jerusalem].* In *Parallel Source Problems in Medieval History,* edited by Frederick Duncan and August C. Krey, 109–15. New York: Harper & Brothers, 1912.

Gibb, Christina. Comments on draft of chapter 9 sent as e-mail attachment, December 19, 2007.

———. E-mail to Kathleen Kern, January 17, 2008.

Gil, Moshe. *A History of Palestine, 634–1099.* Cambridge: Cambridge University Press, 1992.

Gish, Art. E-mail to Kathleen Kern, August 9, 2004.

———. E-mail to Kathleen Kern, August 23, 2004.

———. E-mail to Kathleen Kern, January 23, 2008, subject heading: Re: [GITW] Different types of humor in Palestine and other project locations (or, "Kathy making gross generalizations again").

———. E-mail to Kathleen Kern, January 23, 2008, subject heading: Funny story you were a part of.

———. *Hebron Journal*. Scottdale, PA: Herald, 2001.

———. "Hebron: Opening Gates to Freedom." *Signs of the Times* 6:1 (1996), 1–2.

———. "Love overcomes fear in Hebron." *Signs of the Times* 10:1 (2000) 4–5.

GITW (Getting in the Way internal CPT discussion group). April–June 2005 (not archived).

———. Kathleen Kern, posting, October 8, 2004. Christian Peacemaker Teams Chicago Office.

———. Maia Williams, posting, June 23, 2004. Christian Peacemaker Teams Chicago Office. Printout in Mennonite Church USA Archives.

———. James Loney, posting, June 27, 2005. Christian Peacemaker Teams Chicago Office.

———. William Payne, posting, October 8, 2004. Christian Peacemaker Teams Chicago Office Archives.

———. Sara Reschly posting, October 12, 2004. Christian Peacemaker Teams Chicago Office.

———. Matt Schaaf, posting May 25, 2005. Christian Peacemaker Teams Chicago Office.

Goldenberg, Suzanne. "Israel turns its fire on Arafat." *The Guardian*, March 30 2002. Online: http://www.guardian.co.uk/world/2002/mar/30/israel5.

Green, Stephen. *Living by the Sword: America and Israel in the Middle East 1968–87*. Brattleboro, VT: Amana, 1988.

Gush Shalom. "Barak's 'Generous' Offer." Online: http://www.gush-shalom.org/generous/generous.html.

———. "Who Is violating Oslo?" *PS: The Intelligent Guide to Jewish Affairs* 105, May 13, 1998.

———. "Who Is violating the Agreements?: A Gush Shalom, research paper, January 28, 1998." Online: http://gush-shalom.org/archives/oslo.html.

Habiby, Emile. *The Secret Life of Saeed the Ill-fated Pessoptimist*. Northampton, MA: Interlink, 2001.

Halper, Jeff. (Under the auspices of the Israeli Committee Against House Demolitions-ICAHD.) E-mail to British Ambassador to Israel, David Manning, March 23, 1998, ICAHD e-mail newslist. Printout in Mennonite Church USA Archives.

———. "A Most UnGenerous Offer." *The Link* 35:4 (September–October 2002). Online: http://www.ameu.org/page.asp?iid=191&aid=233&pg=2.

Harel, Amos, and Jonathan Lis. "Minister's aide calls Hebron riots a 'pogrom,'" *Ha'aretz*, July 31, 2002.

Hass, Amira. "The Mirror Doesn't Lie." *Ha'aretz*, November 1, 2000.

Hauser, Christine. "U.S. Nun plays witness to Israeli-Palestinian strife." *USA Today*, December 7, 2000.

"Hebron Hooligans." *Ha'aretz*, January 16, 2006.

"Hebron: Release the Captives." *Signs of the Times* 12:2 (2002) 1–2.

Hebron Solidarity Committee. "Second Anniversary of Oslo: Hebron Settlers Incite Riots at Palestinian Girls' School." September 13, 1995. E-mail newslist printout. Mennonite Church USA Archives.

Hicks, Donna. E-mail to Kathleen Kern (while Hicks was serving on Hebron Team), November 7, 2008, subject heading: "Use of Al Atrash and Jaber Family Names in CPT West Bank History."

———. E-mail to Kathleen Kern (while Hicks was serving on Hebron Team), November 7, 2008.

———. E-mail to Kathleen Kern (while Hicks was serving on Hebron Team), November 9, 2008.

———. E-mail to Kathleen Kern (while Hicks was serving on Hebron Team), November 27, 2007.

———. E-mail to Kathleen Kern (while Hicks was serving on Hebron Team), November 29, 2007, subject heading: "Re: Please respond ASAP Do the stats from the Tuwani school escorts still go to Ta'ayush, Machsom Watch and then to the Knesset Committee on the rights of the child?"

———. E-mail to Kathleen Kern (while Hicks was serving on Hebron Team), November 29, 2007, subject heading: Re: Dr. at Tel Rumeida."

———. E-mail to Kathleen Kern (while Hicks was serving on Hebron Team), December 6, 2007.

———. E-mail to Kathleen Kern (while Hicks was serving on Hebron Team), December 7, 2007.

———. E-mail to Kathleen Kern, December 13, 2007.

———. E-mail to Kathleen Kern, February 2, 2008, subject heading: Re: [GITW] Palestine Project People please peruse these paragraphs perceptively.

———. E-mail to Kathleen Kern, February 2, 2008, subject heading: Resident Aliens.

Holmes, Bob. E-mail to Kathleen Kern, June 15, 2004.

HonestReporting, "The Dishonest Reporter 'Award' 2001." Online: http://www.honest reporting.com/a/dishonest.asp?p=6.

Hull (Arendt), Cole. "Weed and Seed." Sermon preached July 21, 1996, at Seattle Mennonite Church. Mennonite Church USA Archives.

———. "*Signs of the Times* in Hebron." *Signs of the Times* 6:1 (1996) 3.

Human Rights Watch. "Israel/Palestine: Armed Attacks on Civilians Condemned." February 21, 2001. Online: http://www.hrw.org/press/2001/02/isr-pa-0221.htm.

———. "SECOND CLASS: Discrimination Against Palestinian Arab Children in Israel's Schools." September 2001. Online: http://www.hrw.org/reports/2001/israel2/ISRAEL 0901.pdf.

Hunsberger, Sally. E-mail to Kathleen Kern, December 20, 2007.

International Solidarity Movement. "Statement by the National Committee to Resist Settlement and the Wall on the CPT Hostages in Iraq." December 6, 2005. Online: http://www.palsolidarity.org/main/2005/12/06/statement-by-the-nationalcommittee-to-resist-settlement-and-the-wall-on-the-cpt-hostages-in-iraq.

Israeli Committee Against House Demolitions. "Frequently Asked Questions." Israeli Committee Against House Demolitions. Online: http://www.icahd.org/eng/faq.asp?menu =9&submenu=1.

Israeli Ministry of Foreign Affairs. "The Closure of the Polytechnic University and Islamic college in Hebron." January 15, 2003. Israel Ministry of Foreign Affairs. Online: http://www.mfa.gov.il/MFA/MFAArchive/2000_2009/2003/1/The%20Closure%20 of%20the%20Polytechnic%20University%20and%20the.

———. "Offer to Reopen Polytechnic University in Hebron." April 3, 2008. Israel Ministry of Foreign Affairs. Online: http://mfa.gov.il/mfa/go.asp?MFAH0n940.

———. "Suicide Bombing of Egged Bus # 14A in Jerusalem." June 11, 2003, Israeli Ministry of Foreign Affairs Web site: http://www.mfa.gov.il/MFA/MFAArchive/2000 _2009/2003/6/Suicide%20bombing%20of%20Egged%20bus%20No%2014A%20 in%20Jerusalem%20.

Israeli-Palestinian Interim Agreement on the West Bank and the Gaza Strip. Signed in Washington DC, September 28, 1995. Jerusalem: Ministry of Foreign Affairs.

"Israelis close two Palestinian Universities." *Sydney Morning Herald*, January 17, 2003. Online: http://www.smh.com.au/articles/2003/01/16/1042520725582.html?oneclick=true.

"It could have been worse." Sidebar, *Signs of the Times* 6:3 (1996) 3.

Jack, Maureen. E-mail to Kathleen Kern, August 1, 2004.

———. E-mail to Kathleen Kern, August 4, 2007.

———. E-mail to Kathleen Kern, November 16, 2007.

———. E-mail to Kathleen Kern, November 30, 2007.

———. E-mail to Kathleen Kern, January 19, 2008.

———. E-mail to Kathleen Kern, January 25, 2008, subject heading: funny things.

———. E-mail to Kathleen Kern, January 25, 2008, subject heading: [GITW] In reply to Kathy Kern's enquiry re UK government's position.

———. E-mail to Kathleen Kern, February 19, 2008, subject heading: A few more.

———. E-mail to Kathleen Kern, February 19, 2008, subject heading: Issues chapter.

———. E-mail to Kathleen Kern, February 20, 2008.

———. E-mail to Kathleen Kern, February 21, 2008.

Janzen, Diane, comments on a draft of chapter 6, of *In Harm's Way* sent as e-mail attachment to Kathleen Kern, October 25, 2007.

———. Comments on draft of chapter 9 (formerly 10) of this book, sent as e-mail attachment to Kathleen Kern, December 20, 2007.

———. E-mail to Kathleen Kern, September, September 1, 2004.

———. E-mail to Kathleen Kern, September 19, 2004.

———. E-mail to Kathleen Kern, November 11, 2007.

———. E-mail to Kathleen Kern, November 12, 2007.

———. E-mail to Kathleen Kern, November 28, 2007.

———. E-mail to Kathleen Kern, December 7, 2007, subject heading: Re: Who was Anna Sophia Bachman?

———. E-mail to Kathleen Kern, December 7, 2007, subject heading: Re: question about clinic.

———. E-mail to Kathleen Kern, January 28, 2008, subject heading: "Re: [GITW] Chapters 7, 8, 9 of _As Resident Aliens: CPT's work in the West Bank now available for reading."

———. E-mail to Kathleen Kern, January 28, 2008, subject heading: Re: [GITW] Question for U.S. and U.K. CPTers (SORRY I MEANT CANADIAN AND UK CPTERS.

———. E-mail to Kathleen Kern, January 28, 2008, subject heading: Re Who says the Occupation isn't funny?

Jaradat, Ahmad. "Hebron: Another Apartheid Wall in the Making." June 21, 2004, The Alternative Information Center website, archived in Internet Archive Wayback Machine. Online: http://web.archive.org/web/20040624085030/http://www.alterna-tivenews.org.

Jewish Community of Hebron. "The Jewish Community of Hebron condemns the murder of Prime Minister Yitzhak Rabin." E-mail newslist Hebron Today, November 5, 1995. Printout in Mennonite Church USA Archives.

Johns, Loren. E-mail to Al Shekhtman, subject heading: "FW: Your religion." January 21, 1998. Printout in Mennonite Church USA Archives.

———. E-mail to Al Shekhtman, subject heading: "Your threatening message." January 21, 1998. Printout in Mennonite Church USA Archives.

Judd, Terry. "Abu Qatada appeals for release of the hostages." *The Independent*, December 8, 2005. Online: http://www.independent.co.uk/news/world/middle-east/abu-qatada-appeals-for-release-of-hostages-518582.html.ece.

Kember, Norman. "Christianity is a Radical Call to Peacemaking." *Daily Telegraph*, December 12, 2007.

Kern, Esther. E-mail to Kathleen Kern, January 22, 2008.

Kern, Kathleen. "Ambassadors for the End Times: The International Christian Embassy Jerusalem." *The Door* 42 (July/August 1995) 23–24.

———. "Breaking the Siege in Manger Square." April 15, 2002, CPT Hebron Yahoo groups newslist. Online: http://groups.yahoo.com/group/cpthebron/message/140.

———. "Christian Peacemaker Teams." Chapter 9 in *Nonviolent Intervention Across Borders: A Recurrent Vision*, edited by Yeshua Moser-Puangsuan and Thomas Weber. Honolulu: University of Hawaii Press, 2000.

———. "A clash of views at the Canadian border." *The Buffalo News*, April 6, 2003.

———. "Crossing the Weirdness Threshold: Christian Zionism in Jerusalem." *Mennonot* 6 (Winter 1995) 11–12.

———. E-mail response to Rabbi Moshe Yehudai-Rimmer appearing in the "Dialogue" section of *Signs of the Times* 11:1 (2001) 8.

———. E-mail to Al Shekhtman, January 18, 1998. Printout in Mennonite Church USA Archives.

———. "From Haiti to Hebron with a Brief Stop in Washington DC: the CPT Experiment." In *From the Ground Up: Mennonite Contributions to International Peacebuilding*, edited by John Paul Lederach and Cynthia Sampson. New York: Oxford University Press, 2000.

———. "Hebron—H-2: The Necklace of Umm Yusef." *Challenge Magazine* 65 (January–February 2001).

———. "Hebron's Theater of the Absurd." *The Link* 29:1 (1996).

———. "Humor and the Occupation." *Rhubarb: a publication of the Mennonite Literary Society* 1:1 (1998) 13–14.

———. *In Harm's Way: A History of Christian Peacemaker Teams*. Eugene, OR: Cascade, 2008.

———. "Interventions of Truth in Hebron." *Signs of the Times* 5:4 (1995) 3.

———. "BETHLEHEM: O Come all Ye Faithful." Hebron/Beit Jala teams' direct newslist, December 26, 2000. Printout in Mennonite Church USA Archives.

———. "Rage Rocks Hebron." *Signs of the Times* 10:4 (2000) 1–2.

———. "The rest of the story." *The Mennonite* 7:4 (February 17, 2004) 16–17.

———. "Settler Violence and September 11: A Report from the Mean Streets of Hebron." *Tikkun* 16:6 (November/December 2001) 29–30.

———. "Sobbing on the Stairs." *Buffalo News*, April 8, 2001.

———. *Where Such Unmaking Reigns*. Philadelphia, PA: Xlibris, 2003.

———. "Under-cover with Christian Zionists at Kiryat Arba." *Bridge: A Forum on Christian-Muslim Relations*, January 1998, 9–11. (A version of this article also appeared on the CPT discussion group, menno.org.cpt.d@mennolink.org, on November 4, 1997, CPT Chicago Office Digital Archives.)

Kern, Kathleen, and Wendy Lehman. "Teaching Nonviolence in Hebron: Christian Peacemaker Team's Experiences with Palestinian High School and University Students." *The Acorn: Journal of the Gandhi-King Society* 9:1 0(1997) 37–43.

Kern, Marilyn Rayle. E-mail to Kathleen Kern, January 28, 2008.

———. E-mail to Kathleen Kern, January 29, 2008, subject heading: more corrections.

———. E-mail to Kathleen Kern, January 29, 2008, subject heading: Re: ger and toshav.
———. E-mail to Kathleen Kern, February 7, 2008.
———. E-mail to Kathleen Kern, February 9, 2008, subject heading: MORE on rewritten footnote.
———. E-mail to Kathleen Kern, February 9, 2008, subject heading: Re: Rewritten footnote not in a confusing attachment.
———. E-mail to Kathleen Kern, February 11, 2008.
———. E-mail to Kathleen Kern, February 12, 2008.
———. E-mail to Kathleen Kern, February 13, 2008.
Khalidi, Rashid, *Palestinian Identity: the Construction of Modern Nation Consciousness*. New York: Columbia University Press, 1997.
Kifner, John. "The Zeal of Rabin's Assassin springs from Rabbis of Religious Right." *New York Times International Edition*, November 12, 1995.
Cliff Kindy. E-mail to Kathleen Kern, August 23, 2007.
———. "Indiana Peacemaker Softens Israeli Raid on Palestinian home." August 2, 1993, unpublished. Mennonite Church USA Archives.
Kortenoevan, Wim, and Irene. E-mail to Doug Pritchard, January 23, 1998. Printout in Mennonite Church USA Archives.
Krahn, Natasha. "Now I Lay Me Down to Sleep." *Signs of the Times* 10:2 (2000) 8.
Lamberty, Kim. Comments on draft of chapter 6 in *In Harm's Way*, sent as e-mail attachment on November 28, 2007.
———. Comments on draft of chapter 9 (formerly 10) of this book, sent to Kathleen Kern as e-mail attachment, December 21, 2007.
———. E-mail to Kathleen Kern, October 11, 2004.
———. E-mail to Kathleen Kern, November 7, 2007.
———. E-mail to Kathleen Kern, November 9, 2007.
———. E-mail to Kathleen Kern, November 13, 2007.
———. E-mail to Kathleen Kern, November 18, 2007.
———. E-mail to Kathleen Kern, November 27, 2007.
———. E-mail to Kathleen Kern, November 28, 2007.
———. E-mail to Kathleen Kern, December 1, 2007.
———. E-mail to Kathleen Kern, December 7, 2007.
———. E-mail to Kathleen Kern, December 21, 2007.
———. E-mail to Kathleen Kern, January 23, 2008.
Lancaster, John. "Hebron Daunting for Ex-DC Activist: Advocate's Efforts Result in Israeli Detention." *The Washington Post*, July 15, 1995.
Lehman, Wendy. "Arrest Report." July 25, 1995. Mennonite Church USA Archives.
———. "Christian Peacemaker Team Lays Foundation in Hebron." June 27, 1995. Unpublished. Mennonite Church USA Archives.
———. "Christian Peacemaker Team Report by Wendy Lehman and Duane Ediger, following their exploratory visit to Chiapas August 21–September 3, 1997." Undated, Mennonite Church USA Archives.
———. E-mail to Kathleen Kern, November 12, 1995.
———. E-mail to Kathleen Kern, March 2, 2005.
———. E-mail to Kathleen Kern, November 30, 2007.
———. E-mail to Kathleen Kern, January 18, 2008.
———. "Hebron Team Confronts Violence." *Signs of the Times* 5:3 (1995) 1
———. "Israeli settler and soldiers assault Palestinians, one killed." July 1, 1995. Unpublished. Mennonite Church USA Archives.

———. "Israeli Settlers Assault CPTers." *Signs of the Times* 5:4 (1995) 1–2.
———. "Israeli Soldier Opens Fire on Palestinian Marketplace." *Signs of the Times* 7:1 (1997) 3.
———. "Military Detains Two American Members of Christian Peacemaker Teams." July 12, 1995. Unpublished press release. Mennonite Church USA Archives.
———. "Prepared to die, but not to kill." *Signs of the Times* 8:1 (1998) 5.
———. "Uncle of slain Palestinian teenager talks about attack." July 3, 1995. Unpublished. Mennonite Church USA Archives.
"Letters." *Signs of the Times* 12:1 (2002) 14–15.
Levin, Sis. *Beirut Diary: A Husband Held Hostage and a Wife Determined to Set Him Free.* Downers Grove, IL: InterVarsity, 1989.
Levine, Mark. E-mail to Al Shekhtman, January 20, 1998. Printout in Mennonite Church USA Archives.
Levy, Gideon. "All in order." *Ha'aretz Magazine,* March 27, 1998, 3.
Lingle, JoAnne. E-mail to Kathleen Kern, January 31, 1998. Printout in Mennonite Church USA Archives.
Lis, Jonathan, and Ofra Edelman. "Border policeman convicted in brutal killing of Hebron teen jailed for 6 years." *Ha'aretz,* April 29, 2008.
"Lives in Jeopardy: Hebron Team Threatened." *Signs of the Times* 8:1 (1998) 1–2.
Loney, James. "No Greater Love." Chapter 22 in *118 Days: Christian Peacemaker Teams Held Hostage in Iraq,* edited by Tricia Gates Brown. Chicago/Toronto: Christian Peacemaker Teams, 2008. Earlier draft of chapter in Mennonite Church USA Archives.
"The Loosing of the Hounds." *The Other Israel* 72 (April–May 1996) 1–4. Also available online: http://israelipalestinianpeace.org/issues/72toi.htm#THE.
Lynes, John. E-mail to Kathleen Kern, November 22, 2004.
———. E-mail to Kathleen Kern, November 9, 2007.
———. E-mail to Kathleen Kern, November 14, 2007, subject heading: Re: [GITW] 2004 GITW comments on head shaving.
———. E-mail to Kathleen Kern, November 14, 2007, subject heading: Re: Question about home demolitions in 2004.
———. E-mail to Kathleen Kern, November 15, 2007.
———. E-mail to Kathleen Kern, December 1, 2007.
———. E-mail to Kathleen Kern, January 22, 2008.
———. E-mail to Kathleen Kern, January 27, 2008.
———. E-mail to Kathleen Kern, February 3, 2008.
Lynfield, Ben. "In Mideast, Crossfire More Careless." *Christian Science Monitor,* May 22, 2001.
Machsom Watch: Women against the Occupation and for Human Rights. Online: http://www.machsomwatch.org/en.
Mahoney, Liam, and Luis Enrique Eguren. *Unarmed Bodyguards: International Accompaniment for the Protection of Human Rights.* West Hartford, CT: Kumarian, 1997.
McIntyre, Donald. "A rough guide to Hebron: The world's strangest guided tour highlights the abuse of Palestinians." *The Independent,* January 26, 2008. Online: http://www.independent.co.uk/news/world/middle-east/a-rough-guide-to-hebron-the-worlds-strangest-guided-tour-highlights-the-abuse-of-palestinians-773018.html.
McClanen, Elayne. E-mail to Kathleen Kern, January 19, 2008.
Meyer, Rich. "Bulldozers and Steamrollers." *Signs of the Times* 9:4 (1999) 2.
———. E-mail to Johnathan Galt, May 24, 2004. Printout in Mennonite Church USA Archives.

———. E-mail to Kathleen Kern, June 25, 2004.
———. E-mail to Kathleen Kern,, March 9, 2005.
———. E-mail to Kathleen Kern, February 12, 2005.
———. E-mail to Kathleen Kern, March 24, 2007.
———. E-mail to Kathleen Kern, subject heading, "Correspondence with [N] from EI, August 8, 2007.
———. E-mail to Kathleen Kern, subject heading, " Re: [GITW] Role of Electronic Intifada during hostage crisis." August 8, 2007.
———. E-mail to Kathleen Kern, November 8, 2007 (while Meyer was serving on the Hebron Team).
———. E-mail to Kathleen Kern, November 15, 2007, subject heading: Re: Question on school patrol 2004–2005 in Hebron.
———. E-mail to Kathleen Kern, November 15, 2007, subject heading: Re: Soliciting advice about whether I should include encounter with Abbas Zaki in CPT West Bank history.
———. E-mail to Kathleen Kern, December 18, 2007.
———. Hebron Project annual and semi-annual reports and updates for 2004–2006, sent as e-mail attachments to Kathleen Kern, October 24, 2007. Mennonite Church USA Archives.
———. "Hebron project update—Steering Committee March 2004." sent as e-mail attachment to Kathleen Kern, October 24, 2007, Mennonite Church USA Archives.
———. Telephone interview with Kathleen Kern, January 18, 2005.
———. Telephone interview with Kathleen Kern, February 12, 2005.
———. Telephone interview with Kathleen Kern, March 25, 2007.
———. Telephone interview with Kathleen Kern, January 16, 2008.
———. Telephone interview with Kathleen Kern, February 5, 2008.
———. "With a Lot of Help From Our Friends." Chapter 6 in *118 Days: Christian Peacemaker Teams Held Hostage in Iraq*, edited by Tricia Gates Brown. Chicago/Toronto: Christian Peacemaker Teams, 2008. Earlier draft of chapter in Mennonite Church USA Archive
Milgrom, Rabbi Jeremy. E-mail to Kathleen Kern, November 8, 2007.
———. E-mail to Kathleen Kern [or publisher], October 21, 2009.
Montgomery, Anne. E-mail to Kathleen Kern, June 20, 2004.
———. E-mail to Kathleen Kern, July 14, 2007.
———. E-mail to Kathleen Kern, August 23, 2007.
———. E-mail to Kathleen Kern, January 29, 2008.
Moore, Donald. "An Afternoon in Bethlehem." *Olive Branch from Jerusalem: News, articles and documents from the Holy Land Issue* 146 (April 16, 2002). Online: www.lpj.org/Nonviolence/Raed/Olive/Branch160402.htm.
Morey, Melyssa. "A Tale of Two Killings: Observations of Media Bias in Reports of Palestinian and Israeli Deaths." Cited in James Zogby, AAIUSA WASHINGTON WATCH, June 18, 2001, "The Media War We Are Losing But Can Win." Online: http://www.aaiusa.org/washington-watch/1561/w061801.
Morris, Benny. *1948 and After: Israel and the Palestinians*. Oxford: Clarendon, 1994.
———. *The Birth of the Palestinian Refugee Problem, 1947–49*. Cambridge: Cambridge University Press, 1989.
Mortellito, Nicole. "West Bank: Under Fire in Beit Jala." *Signs of the Times* 11:4 (2001) 11–12.

Nafziger, Tim and Simon Barrows. "Writing Peace out of the Script." Chapter 15 in *118 Days: Christian Peacemaker Teams Held Hostage in Iraq*, edited by Tricia Gates Brown. Chicago/Toronto: Christian Peacemaker Teams, 2008. Earlier draft of chapter in Mennonite Church USA Archives.

Natshe, Mustafa. Fax to Chicago Office, April 3, 1995. Mennonite Church USA Archives.

Nijim, Germana. "The Saga of Greg Rollins and the Christian Peace Teams." Journal entries from May 18–May 21, 2003, American Perspectives on the Middle East. Online: http://www.apomie.com/greg.htm.

Nir, Ori. "Anti-Arab Policy bias worsens." *Ha'aretz*, June 24, 2002.

Novick, Peter. *The Holocaust in American Life*. New York: Houghton Mifflin, 1999.

Orme, William J. "Jerusalem Christians Now Back Palestinian Sovereignty." *New York Times*, December 24, 2000.

"Operation Dove: Nonviolent Peace Corps." Online: http://www.operationdove.org.

Palestinian Centre for Human Rights. "Uprooting Palestinian trees and leveling agricultural land, 1 Jul 2002–31 Mar 2003." Reliefweb: http://www.reliefweb.int/rw/rwb.nsf/db900SID/OCHA-64BSU5?OpenDocument.

Palestinian Human Rights Monitoring Group. "Criminal Negligence? Settler Violence and State Inaction during the Al-Aqsa Intifada." *Palestinian Human Rights Monitor* 5:2 (March 2001). Online: http://www.phrmg.org/monitor2001/apr2001.

———. "SETTLER VIOLENCE HOTLINE ONE-YEAR REPORT." *Palestinian Human Rights Monitor* 6:5 (2002). Online: http://www.phrmg.org/monitor2002/Dec2002-4.htm.

"Peacemakers Fast for 700 Hours." *Signs of the Times* 7:2 (1997) 1–2.

Polhamus, Rick. E-mail to Kathleen Kern, January 16, 2004.

———. E-mail to Kathleen Kern, May 10, 2004.

———. E-mail to Kathleen Kern, June 3, 2004.

———. E-mail to Kathleen Kern, June 10, 2004.

———. E-mail to Kathleen Kern, January 27, 2005.

———. E-mail to Kathleen Kern, February 9, 2005.

———. E-mail to Kathleen Kern, January 25, 2008.

"Police launch 'zero tolerance' policy for Hebron rioters." *Ha'aretz*, January 16, 2006.

Pritchard, Doug. E-mail to Kathleen Kern, November 15, 2007.

———. E-mail to Kathleen Kern, January 21, 2008.

———. E-mail to Kathleen Kern, January 26, 2008.

———. E-mail to Kathleen Kern, January 27, 2008.

———. E-mail to Kathleen Kern, September 19, 2008.

Quandt, William B. *Peace Process: American Diplomacy and the Arab-Israeli Conflict Since 1967*. Washington, DC: Brookings Institute, 1993.

"Rachel Corrie Memorial, 1979–2003." Online: http://www.criticalconcern.com/rachelcorrie.html.

Rehm, Paul. Letter to Kathleen Kern, February 19, 2008.

Rempel, Terry. "Redeployment and Division of Hebron." *Signs of the Times* 7:1 (1997) 1–2.

Reschly, Sara. Comments on draft of chapter 4, Hebron, sent as e-mail attachment, to Kathleen Kern, May 4, 2004.

———. E-mail to Kathleen Kern, November 14, 2007.

Rubenberg, Cheryl A. *Israel and the American National Interest: A Critical Examination*. Urbana/Chicago: University of Illinois Press, 1986.

Rubinstein, Danny. "Slouching toward Jerusalem." *Ha'aretz*, February 28, 2001.

Bibliography

———. "Things Fall Apart." *Ha'aretz*, January 30, 2004.
Reuters news brief. "Hundreds of settlers rampage in Hebron." *New York Times*, October 1, 1995.
Rich, Adrienne. *Dream of a Common Language: Poems: 1974–77.* New York: Norton, 1978.
Roe, Dianne. E-mail to Kathleen Kern, November 22, 2003.
———. E-mail to Kathleen Kern, June 17, 2004.
———. E-mail to Kathleen Kern, August 7, 2004.
———. E-mail to Kathleen Kern, February 12, 2005.
———. E-mail to Kathleen Kern, February 14, 2007.
———. E-mail to Kathleen Kern, February 15, 2007.
———. E-mail to Kathleen Kern, August 23, 2007.
Rokach, Livia. *Israel's Sacred Terrorism: A Study Based on Moshe Sharett's Personal Diary and Other Documents.* Belmont, MA: Association of Arab-American University Graduates, 1986.
Rollins, Greg. E-mail to Kathleen Kern, July 3, 2003.
———. E-mail to Kathleen Kern, June 2, 2004.
———. E-mail to Kathleen Kern, June 19, 2004.
———. E-mail to Kathleen Kern, June 27, 2004.
———. E-mail to Kathleen Kern, July 6, 2004 (while Rollins was serving on the Iraq team).
———. E-mail to Kathleen Kern, August 16, 2004.
———. E-mail to Kathleen Kern, January 19, 2008.
———. "The Response from Baghdad." In *118 Days: Christian Peacemaker Teams Held Hostage in Iraq*, edited by Tricia Gates Brown. Chicago/Toronto: Christian Peacemaker Teams, 2008. Earlier draft of chapter in Mennonite Church USA Archives.
Rose, Carol. E-mail to Kathleen Kern, March 7, 2007.
———. E-mail to Kathleen Kern, November 14, 2007.
Ruether, Rosemary Radford. "The Faith and Fratricide Discussion: Old Problems and New Dimensions." Chapter 13 in *Anti-Semitism and the Foundation of Christianity*, ed. Alan Davies. New York: Paulist, 1979.
Ruether, Rosemary Radford, and Herman J. Ruether. *The Wrath of Jonah: Crisis of Religious Nationalism in the Israeli Palestinian Conflict.* New York: Harper & Row, 1989.
Said, Edward. *The Politics of Dispossession: The Struggle for Palestinian Self Determination 1969–1994.* New York: Pantheon, 1994.
———. *The Question of Palestine.* New York: Random House, 1980.
Said, Edward, and Christopher Hitchens, editors. *Blaming the Victims: Spurious Scholarship and the Palestinian Question.* London, NY: Verso, 1988.
Satterwhite, Jim. E-mail to Kathleen Kern, June 8, 2004.
Savir, Uri. *The Process: 1,100 Days that Changed the Middle East.* New York: Random House, 1998.
Schiller, Eric. E-mail to Kathleen Kern, August 17, 2004.
Segev, Tom. *1949: The First Israelis.* New York: Free, 1986.
———. *One Palestine, Complete: Jews and Arabs Under the British Mandate.* Second edition. New York: Owl, 2001.
———. *The Seventh Million: Israel and the Holocaust.* New York: Hill & Wang, 1993.
"Settlers complete Hebron wholesale market eviction." *Ha'aretz*, January 31, 2006.
Shantz, Pierre. E-mail to Kathleen Kern, April 19, 2005.

"Sharm el-Sheikh Memorandum on Implementation Timeline of Outstanding Commitments of Agreements Signed and the Resumption of Permanent Status Negotiations." September 4, 1999, Israeli Ministry of Foreign Affairs. Online: http://www.mfa.gov.il/MFA/MFAArchive/1990_1999/1999/9/Sharm+el-Sheikh+Memorandum+on+Implementation+Timel.htm.

Shragai, Nadav, and Amos Harel. "Fences may not mean more security for settlers." *Ha'aretz*, June 16, 2004.

Shekhtman, Al. E-mail to CPT Chicago Office that bounced to Kathleen Kern, January 17, 1998. Printout in Mennonite Church USA Archives.

———. E-mail to CPT Chicago Office that bounced to Kathleen Kern, January 18, 1998. Printout in Mennonite Church USA Archives.

———. E-mail to CPT Chicago Office that bounced to Gene Stoltzfus's addresss, January 19, 1998. Printout in Mennonite Church USA Archives

———. E-mail to EJERALEIGH@(domain withheld), January 24, 1998. Printout in Mennonite Church USA Archives.

———. E-mail to gillham@(domain withheld), January 28, 1998.

———. E-mail to Kathleen Kern, January 19, 1998. Printout in Mennonite Church USA Archives.

———. E-mail to Kathleen Kern, January 22, 1998. Printout in Mennonite Church USA Archives.

———. E-mail to Loren Johns, January 21, 1998. Printout in Mennonite Church USA Archives.

———. E-mail to Mark Levine, January 19, 1998. Printout in Mennonite Church USA Archives.

Shlaim, Avi. *The Iron Wall: Israel and the Arab World*. New York: Norton, 2000.

Sidebar, *Signs of the Times* [no volume or issue number specified] (November 1994) 1.

Sider, Ronald J. "God's People Reconciling." CPT. Online: http://www.cpt.org/resources/writings/sider.

———. *Nonviolence: The Invincible Weapon?* Dallas: Word, 1989.

———. *Rich Christians in an Age of Hunger: Moving from Affluence to Generosity*. Nashville: Thomas Nelson, 2005.

Slater, Allan. E-mail to Kathleen Kern, January 25, 2008.

Stein, Janice Gross. *The Widening Gyre of Negotiation: From Management to Resolution in the Arab-Israeli Conflict*. Hebrew University Press, 1999.

Stein, Jerry. E-mail to Kathleen Kern, March 4, 2005.

———. E-mail to Kathleen Kern, August 5, 2007.

Steiner, Mary Pannabecker. "History Prof held, released from Hebron Jail." *Bluffton College Scope*, November 1998, 3.

Stoesz, Donald B. "The Conquest of Canaan as an Oppressive Event." *The Conrad Grebel Review* 9 (1991) 153–68.

Stoltzfus, Gene. E-mail to Kathleen Kern, July 31, 2007.

———. E-mail to Kathleen Kern, subject heading: "More on Gaza piece." August 27, 2007.

———. E-mail to Kathleen Kern, subject heading: "some thoughts ref. Gaza." August 27, 2007.

———. E-mail to Kathleen Kern, October 30, 2007.

———. E-mail to Kathleen Kern, December 1, 2007.

———. "PROPOSAL TO PLACE A FIVE PERSON TEAM IN GAZA FOR THE PERIOD OF TWO MONTHS." April 30, 1993. Mennonite Church USA Archives.

Ta'ayush, "Who we are." Online: http://www.taayush.org/new/we.html.
"Techny Call." MCC Peace Section Newsletter/July–August 1987. (No volume or issue specified.) Distributed by Mennonite Central Committee.
Temporary International Presence in Hebron (TIPH). "Funeral of Ms. Berreux and Major Toytunç." April 2, 2002. Online: http://www.tiph.org/en/News/?module=Articles;action=Article.publicShow;ID=1578;_t=238.
———. "Six years since two TIPH observers were shot dead in Hebron." Online: http://www.tiph.org/en/News/?module=Articles;action=Article.publicShow;ID=1652;_t=238.
———. "Two TIPH members killed near Hebron." Online: http://www.tiph.org/en/News/?module=Articles;action=Article.publicShow;ID=1579;_t=238.
"Tent for Lent 2000: Prayer, Fasting and Public Witness Around the Globe." *Signs of the Times* 10:2 (2000) 8.
Tivnan, Edward. *The Lobby: Jewish Political Power and American Foreign Policy*. New York: Simon & Schuster, 1987.
Tolan, Sandy. "Mideast Water Series: Collision in Gaza." Online: http://www.loe.org/shows/segments.htm?programID=98-P13–00010&segmentID=6.
———. "Mideast Water Series: The Politics of Mideast Water." Online: http://www.loe.org/shows/segments.htm?programID=98-P13–00011&segmentID=5.
The Tom Hurndall Foundation Archives. Online: http://www.tomhurndall.co.uk/media.asp.
Turki, Fawaz. *The Disinherited*. New York: Monthly Review, 1972.
"Under One Tree- Tent for Lent Worship Resources Available." *Signs of the Times* 10:1 (2000) 5.
UNICEF. "Iraq surveys show 'humanitarian emergency,'" August 12, 1999. Online: http://www.unicef.org/newsline/99pr29.htm.
United Nations General Assembly, "Report of the Special Committee to Investigate Israeli Practices Affecting the Human Rights of the Palestinian People and Other Arabs of the Occupied Territories." Online: http://domino.un.org/UNISPAL.NSF/c25aba03f1e079db85256cf40073bfe6/a20e3bd823298ba58525611500646c28!OpenDocument.
United Nations Office for the Coordination of Humanitarian Affairs (OCHA). "Special Focus, the Closure of Hebron's Old City." July 2005. Humanitarian Update: Occupied Palestinian Territory. Online: http://www.humanitarianinfo.org/opt/docs/UN/OCHA/ochaHU0705_En.pdf. The map of the closures is on the last page of the report.
Weaver, David. "CPT/CPC: What is our purpose in Gaza?" August 14, 1993. Mennonite Church USA Archives.
———. Fax to CPT Chicago Office, July 6, 1993. Mennonite Church USA Archives.
———. Fax to CPT Chicago Office, July 11, 1993. Mennonite Church USA Archives.
———. "Gaza Team Applauds Peace Efforts, Reports Deep Suspicions." September 1, 1993, unpublished. Mennonite Church USA Archives.
De Wetter-Smith, Brooks, and Michael Brown. "Photostory: Injured ISM activist Brian Avery returns home." June 16, 2003, Electronic Intifada. Online: http://electronicintifada.net/v2/article1607.shtml.
Wilder, David. "CPT-Squalor on the Face of the Earth." May 4, 1998, Hebron-Past, Present and Forever e-mail newslist. E-mail printout in Mennonite Church USA Archives. Also available on David Wilder's blog: http://davidwilder.blogspot.com/1998_07_01_archive.html.
Willey-Al'Sanah, Rosemary. E-mail to Kathleen Kern, December 10, 2007.

Williams Carpenter, Maia. E-mail to Kathleen Kern January 18, 2008.
———. E-mail to Kathleen Kern, January 19, 2008.
Winslow, Philip C. *Victory for Us Is to See You Suffer: In the West Bank with the Palestinians and the Israelis.* Boston: Beacon 2007.
World Council of Churches. "Ecumenical efforts towards peace in the Israeli-Palestinian conflict." February 11, 2002. Online: http://www2.wcc-coe.org/pressreleasesen.nsf/index/pu-02-02.html.
———. "Ecumenical solidarity and action promised in Palestinian-Israeli conflict." February 11, 2002. Online: http://www2.wcc-coe.org/pressreleasesen.nsf/index/pr-02-06.html.
———. "First group of ecumenical accompaniers begin work in Palestine and Israel." August 26, 2002. Online: http://www2.wcc-coe.org/PressReleases_ge.nsf/index/pu-02-25.htm.
Worrell, John. "Iraq: Why Don't They Hate Us?" *Signs of the Times* 12:4 (2002) 10–11.
Yehudai-Rimmer, Moshe. E-mail to Christian Peacemaker Teams, cited in *Signs of the Times* 11:1 (2001) 8
Yoder, Mary. E-mail to Kathleen Kern, August 17, 2004.
Zimmerman, Diana. E-mail to Kathleen Kern, November 12, 2007.
———. E-mail to Kathleen Kern, November 28, 2007.
———. E-mail to Kathleen Kern, December 24, 2007.
———. E-mail to Kathleen Kern, January 18, 2008.
Zuercher, Melanie. "Forum: Anabaptist at heart." *Context: Bethel College Alumni Magazine,* April 2006. Online: http://www.bethelks.edu/bc/news_publications/context/archives02-06/archives/002338.php?presentation=normal&issue=April2006.

Index

As was noted in the Foreword of this book, systems for transliterating Arabic and Hebrew words are not exact, and CPTers writing from Palestine over the years did not consistently spell certain names the same way. This index preserves the variant spellings by putting the most commonly used version first, followed by the variations, e.g., "Jaber/Jabber family."

Abboud 320
Abd al Asem Zaatari, Mamdoh 66
Abourzek, James G. 279
Abraham, biblical patriarch 16, 211, 251 296, 298, 301, 303, 305
Abu Aram, Fahed Mohammed 256
Abu Hadwan, Moath Ahmad 137–38
Abu Haikel/Heikel family 25–27, 43, 144
Abu Haikel, Fariel 32–33, 158, 173, 231
Abu Haikel, Hani 26, 28, 39, 106, 115–16, 248
Abu Haikel, Jamal 248
Abu Haikel, Wisam 149
Abu Hamdiye (Hamdia), 'Imran 222
Abu Jindea (Jendia), Ibrahim Hammad 113–14, 256
Abu Jundii, Zehira 255
Abu Kabeer prison 22
Abu Mayaleh, Nisreen 118, 138, 144
Abu Mayaleh family 138–44
Abu-Sharif, Bassam 116
Abu Sneineh, Abdel Aziz 117
Abu Sneineh neighborhood 114, 117–20, 122, 129, 132, 148–41, 180, 211–12, 311
Abu Turki, Ibrahim 115–16
Abu Turki, Nabil 115

Abuata, Tarek 9
Accompaniment: In Beit Ummar 194, 197; In Dura 179; In Hebron 21, 24, 26, 197, 145, 147, 149, 167, 180–81, 285; In At-Tuwani/South Hebron Hills 199, 256–58, 262–71, 294, 312; of farmers 194, 197 ; of neighborhoods 120, 127, 176; of students in Hebron 32, 39, 52, 55, 58, 109, 153, 157–60, 173, 182 197, 215, 217–18, 223–29, 247–51, 257, 271, 286–87; principle of 153, 155, 277, 318
ACRI (Association for Civil Rights in Israel) 266, 270–71
Adalah Legal Center 104
Adas, Jane xiii, 79, 85, 94, 139
Administrative detention of Palestinians 43, 85, 274
Adura 230
Advocacy 5, 82 95, 195–96, 281, 318
Afghanistan 130, 142, 167, 252
Africa 1, 3, 67
Ahmad, Mansour Saied 116
AIC. *See* Alternative Information Center
Aida Refugee Camp 123
Al Andalus Mall, Hebron 16, 115
Al-Aqsa compound 16, 115

Al-Aqsa Intifada 18, 26, 43, 45, 64, 101–237, 271, 277, 299, 314–15
Al-Aqsa Martyrs' Brigade 226
Al-Alameh, Ibrahim 117
Al Aroub Refugee Camp 171–72, 194
Al-Atrash family xi, 74–79, 90, 92, 188, 295, 306, 318
Al-Atrash , Hussam 78
Al-Atrash , Manaal 78
Al-Atrash , Wila' 78–79
Al-Atrash, Yussef/Yussuf 75–76, 78, 188
Al-Atrash, Yussef/Yussuf
Al-Atrash, Zuhoor 75–78
al-Balbisi, Bassam 118
al-Bayed, Mahmoud 39
Al Burj/El Buraj 204
Al-Dura, Mohammad 117
al-Fawwar/Fawar Refugee Camp 54, 116
Al-Jabah 194
Al-Jabali, Ahlam 137–38
Al-Jabali, Areeg/Arij 137–38
Al-Jazeera 229, 272
Al-Khader 115, 156
Al-Khaliil. *See* Hebron
Al-Manara 220–21
Al-Mazan Hospital 180
Al-Natshe/Natsche, Mayor Mustafa/Mustapha/Mustepha 19, 289, 292
Al-Qaeda 153
Al-Qawasme, Arit 137
Al-Qemari, Fayez Mohammad 117
Al-Rajabi, Musa 205
Al-Sendas 92, 115, 132, 160, 193
Al-Wawi, Shadi 116
Albright, Madeleine 81
Alia Hospital 116, 139
Alien (biblical term). *See* Ger
Alleman, Nait 98
Alon, Gideon 162
Alrai, Majdaleen 139
Alternative Information Center (AIC) 22, 86
Amalek/Amelek 72, 184, 307
Amayreh, Khalid/Khaled 174, 242
Amir, Yigal 39, 41–43, 149
Amman, Jordan 257
Amnesty International 64, 121–22, 262–63

Amos, biblical prophet 108, 242, 304
Anabaptism 2, 5, 69, 73
Anderson-Rosetti, Kristin 160, 170, 183, 190, 206, 218, 221, 223–24, 240, 245, 269, 274–76
Annapolis Conference 279
An-Natsche, Ahmed 185
Annexation of Palestinian land, *See* "Confiscation of Palestinian land"
Anti-Semitism 1, 72, 282, 288, 291, 296–99, 301
Apache attack helicopters 160, 182, 198, 278
Apartheid, characteristics applied to Israeli Occupation 15, 143, 210, 241
Apartheid, South African 296–322
Applied Research Institute Jerusalem (ARIJ) 56, 95, 210
Aqaba, Jordan 227–28
Aquifer, West Bank. *See* "water issues"
Arab countries 54, 154
Arabic language study 77, 121, 313, 321
Arabs 2, 16, 17, 20, 35–38, 47, 50, 54,154–55, 223, 265, 273–78, 290 291, 295–96, 303–4, 307–16
Arafat, Yasser/Yassar/Yassir 21, 28, 46, 58, 66, 68, 89, 96–97, 104, 107, 110, 117, 124, 142, 171–72, 189, 196, 205, 299, 303, 307, 315
Areas A, B, C designated in Oslo Accords 64, 75, 204, 158, 172, 218, 220
Arendt, Cole, *See* Hull, Cole
Argelyn, Marge 313
ARIJ. *See* Applied Research Institute, Jerusalem
Armageddon 301
Armey, Congressman Dick 283
Arnon, Noam 288, 293
Arraf, Huwaida 155–56
Arutz-Sheva 43
Ascherman/Asherman, Rabbi Arik 66–67, 262
Ashkelon 47, 49, 53, 56
Ashrawi, Hanan 14
al-Assad, Hafez 303
Assassinations 21, 24, 38, 40–44, 47, 54, 58, 64, 110, 140, 142, 149, 151, 161, 206, 209

Ateek, Naim 5, 13, 67, 105
Athens, Ohio 289, 293
At-Tuwani x, 15, 94, 199, 233, 253–71, 274–76, 283–84, 309, 312, 320–21
Aukerman, Dale 14
Avery, Brian 235–36
Avi (Border Policeman) 84, 131
Avissar, Oded 17
Avnery, Uri 16–279
Avraham Avinu (Hebron settlement of) 30, 46–47, 63, 98, 112, 115, 138–39, 144, 147–48, 210, 215, 230, 309
Avraham, Brigadier General Yiftach
Awad, Rashid 194
Awad, Selwa 77, 121
Ayyash, Yahye 47–48, 54

Baatsch family 144
Bab izawiyya/izawiyye/a-zawiya 116, 239, 213, 216, 220–21
Bachman, Anna Sophia 257
Badil 63
Baghdad 30, 257, 273, 308
Balata Refugee Camp 167, 171
Baldwin, Bill 247
Ball, Douglas B. 279
Ball, George W. 279
Bani Naim 112–13
Bar Ilan University 54, 58
Barak, Ehud 89–90, 92–93, 96–97, 107, 130
Barak, Hillel 22
Barak, Rafael ix, 191
Barghouti, Mustafa 281
Barlow, Katie 189
Barr, Cameron 144
Barrancabermeja, Colombia 152, 177
Bat Shalom 86, 105, 298
BBC 49, 88, 262, 282
Bedouin 56, 255
Beersheba/Beersheva 241–61
Beirut 140–41, 172
Beit Fajjar 194
Beit Hadassah (Hebron settlement of) 18, 23, 32–33, 36–40, 43, 73, 98, 111, 134, 143, 158, 162, 184, 193, 210, 216, 280, 287
Beit Haggai 115, 137–38

Beit Hanoun checkpoint 117
Beit Il 75
Beit Jala 115, 119–27, 137, 140–41, 156, 177
Beit Mirsim/Miersam 204–5
Beit Romano (Hebron settlement of) 46, 109, 148, 186–87, 210–11, 214, 217, 231, 244–45
Beit Sahour 115, 119, 121–22, 124–25, 198, 235
Beit Ummar 86, 92, 117, 131–32, 165, 167, 180, 189, 193–98, 231, 239–40, 243–44
Belfast, Ireland 136
Belford, Virginia 231
Belsen 296
Ben Ami, Eliyahu 112
Ben Gurion 67, 190, 233
Ben Israel, Azrael 35–38
Ben Kenaz, Othniel 220
Bender, Nathan 166
Benn/Ben, Aluf 162
Bennett, Ramon 302
Bennet, Zipporah 302
Benvenisti, Meron 16
Benzimann, Uzi 103
Beqa'a/Baqa Valley 66, 80–81, 86, 89–92, 96, 99, 112–14, 117, 131–32, 134, 144, 164–66, 178, 193–94, 203–5, 212–13, 219–20, 231–32, 239, 298
Bereaved Families Network 193
Bergen, Jeremy 58, 98–99
Bergen, Kathy 58
Berlin Wall 296
Berquist, Phyllis 251
Berrigan, Daniel 57
Berruex, Catherine 173
Bethel College 5
Bethlehem 9, 14, 20, 66, 77–78, 104–5, 115, 119, 121–27, 131, 133, 137, 142, 157, 172, 175–80, 188, 190, 196–98
Bethlehem Bible College 121
Bethlehem University 176
Betunya 306
Bias. See "Partisanship"
Bible, role in Palestinian-Israeli conflict 93, 242, 294, 302–6

Biddu 251
Bidya 156
Bir Zeit University 50, 156
Bischoff, Christy 240, 242, 312
Blackhawk helicopters 278
Bnei Avraham 20, 251
Boeing 160–92
Bombings and shellings ix, 47–49, 51, 53–55, 69–73, 115, 118–22, 124–27, 129, 133, 137, 139–42, 150, 154, 160, 166, 171, 176, 180–81, 198, 206, 208–10, 226, 229, 241, 245–46, 277, 282, 293, 315–17,
Bond, Randy 55–57
Bookbinder, Hyman 279
Bosnia 41, 152
Bouwmeester, Jamey 87–89, 93, 127, 213
Boycott 18, 53, 188, 278, 316
Boyer, Grace 97, 135, 147
Brethren in Christ 3–4
Brigith, Ghazi 193
British Mandate of Palestine 17, 76
Britton, Sally 247
Brooklyn, NY 18
Brooks, Gary 219, 223
Brown, Chris 169, 207–8, 215–16, 225–26, 233, 257–58, 261–62
Brown, Michael 236
Brubacher family 78
Brubacher, Gordon 78
Brubacher, Rhonda 78, 179
B'tselem 23–24, 78, 116, 184, 207–8, 213–14, 222, 225, 255, 262, 271
Buchenwald 296
Bulldozer 21, 49–50, 64, 66–68, 71, 79–80, 89, 92–93, 96, 114, 132, 141, 156, 160, 163, 165–66, 172, 179, 181–82, 196, 206–7, 212, 220, 232, 234–36, 278, 280, 313
Bus #18 in Jerusalem (*See also*, "bombings") 47, 52–53, 119, 315
Bush, President George W. 131, 142, 154–55, 205, 227–28, 282
Butt, Phyllis 6
Butterly, Caoimhe 167, 189, 194
Bypass roads 46, 74, 95, 112, 117, 175, 178, 194, 232, 243, 249, 270
Byzantine Empire 16

Cairo 47
Camp David 96–97, 104, 279
Campaign Against the Permanent Occupation 86
Campaign for Secure Dwellings 64–68, 74–82, 86–97, 105, 115, 132, 193, 212, 240, 272, 292, 318
Canada, Canadian government 19, 67–68, 87, 129, 162, 195, 216, 272, 274, 276, 281–83, 298
Canadians 90, 106, 150, 182, 272–73, 281–82; CPTers with citizenship in 106, 150, 182, 216, 281; Foreign policy re: Israel and Palestine 106, 281–82
Canonicus Hebronensis
Carpenter, Cal 262, 265, 269, 274
Carr, Joe 235, 244–45, 247, 264–65
Carse, Henry 176
Caterpillar (*See also* "bulldozers") 160, 182, 278
Catholic theology 320–21
Caton, Christine 173, 176
Cave of Machpelah. *See* "Ibrahimi Mosque"
CCIPPP (*See also* International Civilian Committee for the Protection of the Palestinian People) 207
Center for Economic and Social Rights 26
Chacour, Elias 16
Chafets, Zev 307
Chandler, Matthew 310, 312, 320
Chechnya 39, 316
Chiapas 30, 94, 123, 152, 284, 308
Chicago (*See also* "Christian Peacemaker Teams, Chicago Office") 4–6, 13, 182, 240
Chippewas of the Unceded First Nation 10
Chomsky, Noam 14, 16, 279
Chretien, Canadian Prime Minister Jean 142
Christian Peacemaker Teams (CPT): Chicago office, CPT 14, 19, 56, 70, 72, 74, 123, 140, 153, 160, 164, 179, 241, 283, 292, 295; constituency x, 48, 52, 57, 74, 124, 162, 252, 280, 282, 301, 315; delegations 5–6,

13–14, 18, 30, 67, 81, 89–90, 92, 94, 98, 111, 117, 137, 140, 144, 156, 158, 167–68, 172, 174, 178–79, 182, 187, 190, 210, 231, 233, 240, 242–43, 257, 272, 278, 286, 288–89, 305, 307; history x, 2–8, 258, 261, 271, 322; mandate 4, 15; theological underpinnings 2–5; Toronto Office 191, 276; Training x, 5, 7, 10, 14, 20, 41, 68, 91, 116, 129, 140, 155–56, 164, 187–88, 190, 196, 235, 240, 243, 257, 277, 319
Christian Zionism 47, 104, 300–308
Christians, Christianity (*See also* "Palestinian Christianity"): Anti-semitism in 1–2, 145, 288, 297; Relationships with Muslims 299–300
Christmas Lutheran Church, Bethlehem 126–27
Chupp, Kryss 5
Church of the Brethren 4, 27, 69, 288
Church of the Nativity, Bethlehem 176,
Churches, Peace. *See* "Historic Peace Churches"
Ciaghi, Laura 257
CIPAC (Christians' Israel Public Action Campaign) 302
Civil Administration. *See* "Israeli Civil Administration"
CJPAC (Canadian Jewish Political Affairs Committee) 281
Clark, Jeanne 179
Clausen, Le Anne, 140, 142, 155, 161, 166, 172, 176, 179–80, 185–86, 235
Clinton, Bill U.S. President Bill 96, 104, 125
Closed military zones 27, 33, 91, 93, 113, 157, 247, 248, 262
Closures 95, 105, 125, 128, 132–34, 142, 160, 167, 213, 215, 219, 241, 249, 279, 287, 299
CMS (Council of Moderators and Secretaries) 3–4
CNN 140, 253
Cockburn, David 132, 255
Cohen, Aharon 16
Cohen, Anat 33, 280
Cohen, Ya'alah 170, 289
Collaborators, Palestinian 29, 47, 123

College Mennonite Church, Goshen, IN 92
Colombia x, 30, 252, 177, 277, 283–84, 308, 321
Colonialism 9, 244, 284
Columbus, OH 167
Confiscation of Palestinian land 22, 46, 52, 54, 64, 78, 87–97, 104, 107–8, 111, 113, 121, 129–30, 156, 160, 165–67, 181, 194–96, 203–97, 210–13, 223–24, 226, 236, 238–42, 252, 254, 275, 278, 290–91, 295, 298, 309
Conscientious objectors (C.O.s), Israeli 169–70, 218
Constituency, CPT. *See* "Christian Peacemaker Teams, Constituency"
Consulates, U.S., Canadian etc 22–23, 68, 93, 120, 122, 191, 213, 216, 232, 240, 260–61, 263, 280
Contreras, Joseph 63
Cook, Jonathan 54
Cooperburg, Gary 301–2
Corbyn, Jeremy 282
Cordoba/Cortuba. *See* Qurtuba School
Corrie, Rachel 156, 218, 234–36, 319
CPT. *See* Christian Peacemaker Teams
CPTers: Arrests of 5–6, 21–23, 26–27, 44, 49–50, 53, 56, 66, 79, 84–86, 94, 132, 157, 191, 216–18, 235, 244–46, 254, 293–94, 321; Citizenship issues 277–83; Deportations/denied entry of 45, 51–53, 190–91, 216–18, 245, 290, 294, 319
CPTnet xi, xiii, 28, 47, 68, 73, 99, 117, 191, 261, 323
Crusades, European Christian 2, 16, 300
Curfews, imposed by Israeli military on Palestinians 19, 53–54, 63, 83, 107, 109–11, 115, 126, 128–29, 132, 134–38, 142–45, 150, 158–60, 167–70, 180–81, 186–87, 213–18, 220–21, 224–26, 287–99, 311

Dan, biblical region of 302
Dana families 30, 206, 207, 236
Dana, Abd al-Halim 206–7
Dana, 'Imad 206

Index

Dana, Mazen 41
Dana, Samia 206–7
Dana, Shakir Shukri 30–31, 43, 48, 206–7
Dana, Yazid 'Imad 206
Daoud, Hassan 87
Daour, Naim 272
David, Shmuel, "Shmulik" 23–24
Davis, Bret 169, 182
DCO. *See* Israeli District Coordinating Office
Deheishe Refugee Camp 171
Deir Yassin 172–73
Delegations, CPT. *See* "Christian Peacemaker Teams, Delegations"
Democratic Republic of Congo x, 240
demolitions, Palestinian home 21, 32, 49–54, 64–68, 74–96, 108, 113, 126, 129–32, 141, 156, 160–65, 168, 186, 193–94, 204–9, 211–12, 224, 230, 234, 236, 240, 243, 256, 269, 278, 290, 292, 295, 298, 306, 313, 315, 318
Denmark 155, 187, 189
Deportations. *See* "CPTers, deportations of"
Des Plaines, IL 74
Detainees. *See* "Administrative Detention"
Detention, vs. arrests 26
Deuteronomy, biblical book of 8–9
Dialogue: Christian-Jewish 95, 297, 299; Christian-Muslim 299; With Israeli settlers 55, 288
Didovsky, Rina 112
Diplomatic tours of Hebron 166, 203, 213, 232, 238, 247–48, 315
Drake, Laura 54
Driben/Dribin, Dov 290–92, 295–96
Druse/druze 84, 113, 222
Dubboya Street 17, 32, 34–43, 174, 221, 247, 250
Dura 56, 173–74, 179
Durland, Bill and Genie, 140
Dweiban neighborhood, Hebron 181

EAPPI. *See* Ecumenical Accompaniment Programme in Palestine and Israel
East Timor 145

Eastern Mennonite University 36
Ecumenical Accompaniment Programme in Palestine and Israel (EAPPI) 129, 155, 183, 188–89
Ediger, Duane 5–6, 191
Efrat settlement 156–57
Egypt 8, 20, 232, 303
Eid, Bassam 78
Elections: Israeli 53–54, 89, 130; Palestinian 44, 46, 66, 278, 281
Elon, Amos 16, 103
England 190
Engle, Klaus 217
Epp-Fransen, Diana 181
Escort, military in At-Tuwani 265–67
Europe, Europeans 1–2, 9, 23, 70, 88, 182, 213, 254, 300, 306–7
European Union 92, 208, 279
Evans, Claire 148, 269
Exodus, biblical book of 8, 72, 207
Expulsions 54, 72, 94, 142, 163, 166, 170, 255

F-16s 129
Fares, Qadura 273
Fast, Anita 106–8, 118, 128, 139, 141, 156–58, 158
Fasting, Hebron team 64–67, 94, 99, 107, 177–79, 179, 274
Fatah/Fateh 28, 66, 83, 117, 150, 188, 196, 226, 272
FBI 26, 74
Federman, Noam 25
Fellowship of Reconciliation 188
Filkins, Dexter 222
Finch-Dürichen, Pauline 72, 74
Findley, Paul 279
Finkelstein, Norman 16
Forthofer, Ron 140
Fox, Tom 30, 251, 272–75
France, French 2, 155, 117, 190, 247
Freeman-Maloy, Dan 281
Frey, Mark 57–58, 64–66, 84, 113, 168–73, 175, 178, 295, 298, 308–10
Friedman, Noam 63
Friedman, Robert I. 21
Friesen, Lorne 192, 232–33, 256
Froelich, Aaron 179

Fulk (Fulcher) of Chartres 300
Fundamentalism 300

Gabriel, Angel 103
Galilee 20, 104
Gale, Kathleen 231
Gal'on, Zehava 92
Galt, Johnathan 196–97,
Gandhi 293, 319
Gaza 2, 5–8, 14, 17, 20, 26, 29, 54, 75, 104, 116–17, 120, 124–26, 129, 133, 138, 140, 143, 152, 155–56, 166, 171, 187, 191, 193, 198–99, 234, 239, 242–43, 278, 282, 284, 309, 312, 314, 320, 322
Geneva Conventions 18, 168, 225
Geneva, Switzerland 188
Geniza Documents 16
Genocide 152
Ger, Sojourner, Resident Alien 8–9, 10, 322
Germany, Germans 9, 27, 36–37, 72, 152, 232, 283, 307
Gerner, Deborah, "Misty" 313
Getman, Andrew 111, 116–17, 120
Gibb, Christina 241, 243–45, 249–50
Gilad, Amos 150
Gil, Moshe 16
Gilo, settlement of 121–24
Gingerich, Pierre 74
Gish, Art 45, 64–65, 90, 92, 114, 214, 220–21, 224–25, 230, 232, 239, 241, 246, 252, 269, 288–89, 293, 310–11
Gish, Peggy 176
GITW (intraCPT discussion group) 240, 281–82, 286–87, 298, 310
Givat Ha Harsina, settlement of 49, 89, 91, 97, 148, 157, 165–66, 211–12, 238–39
Givati, Colonel Moshe 183–84
Glass, David 217–18
Golan, Neta 147, 156–57
Gold, Shabtai 169, 219
Goldenberg, Suzanne 172
Goldstein, Baruch Kappel 15, 18–19, 23, 36, 47, 63, 110
Goode, Michael 87, 98–99, 160–61, 182, 191
Goshen, IN 92, 167

Gospel(s) 4, 108, 298; Matthew 29, 265; Mark 51
Graffiti, Israeli settler 32, 71, 183, 233, 279–80
Graziani, Cristina 257
Greece, Greeks 24, 36–37
Grossman, David 95
Gun battles 114–19, 128, 137–41, 148, 160–65, 172–75, 186, 197, 206, 245, 252
Gush Emunim 17
Gush Etzion 194, 211
Gush Shalom 14, 86, 97, 205
Gvirtz, Amos 42, 95

Habiby, Emile 313
Hagel, Senator Chuck 261
Haifa 137, 171–72, 208
Haiti x, 7, 14, 19, 22–23, 30, 44, 54, 152, 284
Halhoul 173, 175, 195–96
Halper, Jeff 50, 75, 77, 87–88, 205, 278
Hamas 22, 28, 47, 50, 52, 54, 69, 71, 73, 90, 150–51, 172, 206, 209, 227, 241, 272, 278, 281, 288
Hanson, Eileen 242–43
Hantash, Abdel Hadi 66, 130, 210, 232, 239, 254, 278
Haram al-Sharif compound 18, 103–4, 244
Harder, Helmut 3
Harel, Amos 97, 184, 195
Hares 190
Haret/Harit/Hart iSheik/iSheikh neighborhood 114–15, 118–22, 180, 211–12, 277
Haret ijaber 164
Ha'aretz 78, 97, 110, 125, 161–63, 186, 204–5
Haroos neighborhood 210
Harper, Prime Minister Stephen 281
Hasbahe wholesale market 46, 98
Hashlomoun, Nayef 221
Hass, Amira 110, 167, 186
Hass, Yoav 169, 218
Hasson, Yossi 76
Hauser, Christine 123
Havat Ma'on/Hill 833 outpost 254–58, 262, 267, 311

HCJ. *See* Israeli High Court of Justice
Hebron Municipal observers 85, 216
Hebron Municipality 19–20, 26, 31, 49, 52, 57, 107, 141, 168, 193–94, 220, 289, 292, 299
Hebron Protocols 58, 111, 215, 279–80
Hebron University 22–23, 26, 30, 32, 45, 55–56, 58–59, 203, 208–9, 226–29, 236, 254, 272
Hebron Rehabilitation Committee (HRC) 20, 208, 213, 247
Hebron Solidarity Committee 15, 22, 26–27, 31–33, 47, 49–50, 54, 318–19
Hegemony, Israeli 104
Heie, Jeff 20–21, 26–27, 29, 65, 288, 313
Hellman, Richard A. 302
Helms, Jesse 43
Hereni, Fatima 256, 275–76
Hereni, Ghanum 256
Hereni, Hafez 256–57, 264, 274–76
Hereni, Saber 256
Herbawi, Afifa 135
Herman, Anne 293
Hezbollah 140, 281
Hicks, Donna 247, 250, 267
Historic Peace Churches 3, 170, 321
Hitchens, Christopher 16
Hitler, Adolf 72, 151, 307
Holland/the Netherlands 72, 155, 188
Holmes, Bob 98–100, 106–7, 111, 116–17, 123, 127, 134, 137, 157–58, 196, 198
Holmes, Keri 89–90
Holocaust, WWII 1, 27, 137, 152, 219, 254, 279, 296
Horowitz, Rabbi Eliahu and Dina 206, 230
Hostage crisis, CPT x, 30, 249, 272–76
Houbrechts, Maartje 262
Hereni, Fatima 256, 275–76
Hereni, Ghanum 256
Hereni, Hafez 256–57, 264, 274–76
Hereni, Saber 256
HRC. *See* Hebron Rehabilitation Committee
HRW. *See* Human Rights Watch
HSC. *See* Hebron Solidarity Committee
Huebner, Harry 5, 316

Hughes, Tracey 140, 221
Hull, Cole 44–47, 49, 54
Human Rights Watch 54, 137–38, 144, 235
Hunsberger, Sally 267
Hurndall, Tom 156, 218, 234–36, 319
Hussein, Saddam 205, 289, 293

il-Ibrahimi Mosque/Cave of Machpelah/Tomb of the Patriarchs 14, 16, 18, 47–48, 73, 83, 110, 135, 146, 161–63, 182, 192, 208, 210–11, 214, 219, 240, 242–43, 285, 309
Ibrahimiyye Boys' School 250
ICAHD. *See* Israeli Committee Against House Demolitions
Iceland 187, 189
Idreis, Ibrahim Khader 24–25
Idreis, Yunis 25
IMRA 290, 294–95
Indigenous communities, North America 10, 152
Indonesia 145
Inquisitions, Christian, imposed on Jews and Muslims, 16, 300
International Civilian Committee for the Protection of the Palestinian People 207
In Harm's Way x, 20, 30, 94, 261–63, 268, 271, 277, 307
International accompaniment organizations 155–57, 160, 176, 187–91; Deportations of volunteers 26, 146, 148, 190–91
International Solidarity movement, ISM 145, 155–56, 167, 178–79, 187, 189–90, 197–98, 218, 234–36, 247, 250–51, 273, 298–99, 319–20
Intifada, First 1987–1993 (*See also* Al-Aqsa Intifada) 18, 21, 66, 116, 184, 316
IRA. *See* Irish Republican Army
Iran/Iranian 227, 293
Iran-Contra Scandal 140
Iraq 20, 30, 41, 189, 193, 204, 218, 252, 257, 272–75, 289, 293, 308, 321
Irish 189, 247
Irish Republican Army 136, 296
Isaac, biblical patriarch 16, 296

Isaiah, biblical prophet 67
Islam 18, 108, 120, 193, 299, 300
Islamic Jihad 73, 209
ISM. *See* International Solidarity Movement
Israeli Civil Administration 23, 27, 48, 75–76, 88, 135, 149–50, 167, 187, 207, 212, 229, 263–65, 270, 316, 318
Israeli District Coordinating Office (DCO) 158, 171, 180, 218, 262, 270
Israeli Committee Against House Demolitions (ICAHD) 50, 64, 67–68, 75–77, 81–82, 86–89, 92, 94–95, 113–14, 131, 205, 278, 292, 298 318
Israeli High Court of Justice 164, 207, 216, 238, 275
Israeli Knesset 42, 134, 263, 266
Israeli Ministry of Foreign Affairs 229–30
Israeli Ministry of the Interior ix–x, 92, 190–91, 216, 218, 239
Israeli Occupation of Palestine 14, 18, 87, 97, 105, 110, 134, 141, 143, 167, 170, 178, 191, 233, 252, 282–83, 310, 313
Israelites 8–9, 207
Italy, Italian 96, 155, 190, 257, 283, 312, 320–21

Jabel Johar 163, 206–7, 230, 236
Jaber/Jabber family 66, 79–80, 89, 99, 112, 129, 156, 162–63, 239, 247
Jaber, Abdel Jawad 79, 89, 93, 112, 149, 164–65, 246
Jaber, Amooni 81
Jaber, Atta 66, 79–82, 87–89, 112–14, 130, 140, 164, 186, 246
Jaber, Ayoub 164
Jaber, Dalia 81
Jaber, Fatmi 144
Jaber, Fayez 80, 86, 130
Jaber, Huda 130
Jaber, Ismael 88, 144
Jaber, Jowdi/Jowedi 149, 164
Jaber, Kaied 88
Jaber, Mansour 112, 116
Jaber, Mahmoud 144, 162–63
Jaber, Rajah 80–81, 87

Jaber, Rodeina 81, 87, 89, 106, 112–13, 130, 247
Jack, Maureen 241, 249, 256, 270, 282–83, 87
Jacob, biblical patriarch 16, 296
Jaffa 22
Jahalin Bedouin 56
Jamjum, Nibin/Nivin 184
Jantz, Harold 3
Janzen, David 165, 248
Janzen, Diane 207, 215, 223, 234, 238, 244–45, 247–48, 257–58, 260–62, 266–67, 269–71, 281, 312,
Jaradat, Ahmad 210
Jaradat, Ghazala 117
Jenin 117, 129, 167, 171–73, 180, 189, 235
Jeremiah, biblical prophet 8
Jericho 7, 32, 115,
Jerusalem ix, 6, 13, 16, 20, 22, 24, 27, 38, 47–50–54, 56, 64, 67, 72, 76–78, 87, 91–92, 94–96, 100, 103–5, 109, 111, 113, 115–16, 119–21, 124, 126, 129, 131, 133, 137–38, 140, 148, 150, 153–54, 156, 169, 172, 175–76, 178, 188–89, 193, 196, 198–99, 208–10, 215, 217, 219, 227, 229, 233–34, 280–82, 289, 300–302, 305, 314, 316–17
Jerusalem Post 40, 92, 99, 121, 196, 262
Jesus of Nazareth 2, 4–5, 10, 70, 93, 108, 111, 126–27, 176, 208, 252, 265, 300, 302–4
Jinba 256–57, 275
Johnson, Rebecca 129, 137, 155, 188
Jordan, Jordanian 5, 17, 24, 36, 38, 54, 81, 227, 302
Judaism 22, 71, 297, 300, 304
Junity 187

Kahane, Meir 72
Kach 18, 33, 40, 68, 72, 74
Kamphoefner, Kathy 20, 22, 29, 31, 135, 169, 181, 186, 196, 210–11, 219, 225, 233–34
Kapenga, Kathy 91, 221, 223
Karmei/Carmei Tzur, settlement of 194–97, 239
Karmiel, settlement of 254

Karmil 256, 264,
Kashmir 272
Kaufman, Gerald 282
Kaufman, Joanne, "Jake" 83–85, 90
Kaufman-Lacusta, Maxine 22
Keeshig-Tobias, Lenore 10
Keller, Adam 114
Kember, Norman 30, 272–74, 276
Kenagy, Ben 90
Kenagy, Lois 3
Kennedy, Bourke 88, 118, 160, 182
Kenney, Jim 167
Kern, Marilyn Rayle 8–9
Keshet, Yehudit 298
Khadijaa Girls' School 192
Khalidi, Rashid 16
Khallet Athba 255
Khan Younis 7, 198
Khoruba Valley 254, 270, 312
Khoury, Sami 216
Kidnapping. *See* CPT Hostage Crisis
Kidron, OH 29
Kifner, John 41
Kincaid, Brett 240–41
Kindy, Cliff 6–7, 20–22, 26–29, 45, 64, 66–69, 167, 182, 191, 288, 313
King David Hotel 281
Kiryat Arba, settlement of 17–18, 30–32, 47–49, 51, 89–91, 97, 144, 157, 160–65, 205–8, 210–12, 238–40, 268, 286, 288–89, 301
Kiryat Shmona 171
Kitchener-Waterloo Record 72
Klassen, Nicholas 245
de Klerk, F. W. 322
Kober, Reinhold 90
Kortenoevan, Irene and Wim 72
Krahn, Natasha 90, 94, 98, 105–7, 118
Kunkar, Umm Elias 122
Kuttab, Jonathan 85–86, 216, 272
Kysia, Ramzi 189

Lamberty, Kim 238, 242, 257–58, 261–63, 265, 268–70, 320
Lancaster, John 27–28
Landau, Uzi 183–84
Lawrence, Mary 148, 158, 168, 173, 180, 186, 192, 194, 215

LDC. *See* Palestine Land Defence Committee
Leah, biblical matriarch 16, 296
Lebanon 5, 38, 54, 172, 253,
Lehman, Ella Mae 63
Lehman, Wendy 13–15, 17, 19–23, 25, 27, 29–31, 34, 37, 39–41, 55–59, 63, 65, 191, 288, 299, 313, 318, 321
Leibovitz/Leibowitz, Elazar 183
Lenchner, Charles 71
Leningrad 296
Lerner, Aaron 290, 294–98
Lerner, Peter 88
Levin, Jerry 140–41, 182, 185–86, 212, 218–20, 239, 241, 246, 250, 252, 254, 265
Levin, Sis 140–41
Levine, Mark 70–71
Levinger, Miriam 17–18, 34
Levinger, Moshe 17–18
Levy, Dina and Gadi 215, 230
Levy, Gideon 78
Levy, Natan 40
Lewis, C.S. 313
Lewis, Harriet 65, 74, 78, 93
Liberation Theology 67
Lieberman, Senator Joseph 292
Likud party, 53–54
Lingle, JoAnne 73, 147, 158, 165, 180, 194, 219, 221
Lis, Jonathan 184
Livni, Linda 177–78
London, England 282, 287
Loney, James, "Jim" 30, 272–74, 276
Lorwin, Yochanan 22
Lucas, Caroline 282
Lugar, Senator Richard 162, 205
Luther, Martin 307
Lutheran Church of the Redeemer, Jerusalem 47, 91, 104–5, 111, 126, 176
Lynes, John 164, 186, 189, 238, 246, 249–50, 281, 296, 298
Lynfield, Ben 116

Maale/Ma'ale Adumim 56
Ma'aref Boys' School 192
Macdonald, Sarah 246

Machpelah, Cave of. *See* Ibrahimi Mosque
Machsom Watch 264, 266, 271
Maghayir al-Abeed 258, 266–67
Mahanea Yehuda market 72
Mahnaimi, Uzi 16
Makhamra, Umm Hani 255
Malachi, biblical prophet 8
Malthaner, Tom 55–57
Manchester College 20
Mandela, Nelson 322
Manley, Canadian Foreign Minister John 142
Manning, David 75
Ma'on/ Maon, settlement of 113, 233, 254–68, 270, 290–91, 295, 312
Market, Hebron casba/casbah
Maroun, Father 177
Martens, Barbara 267, 269
Marzel, Baruch 24–25, 40, 146
Mashka 156
Massacres: of 1929 Jewish community in Hebron 16–17, 104; Baruch Goldstein 15–19; Deir Yassin 172–73; Jenin Refugee camp 172, 189; Netanya Passover massacre 172; Sabra and Shatila Refugee camps, Lebanon 172–73; Tiananmen Square Massacre 54; of Hebron Yeshiva Students in 1980 17
MCC. *See* Mennonite Central Committee
McClanen, Elayne 94, 140, 311
McIntyre, Donald 251
McKinney, Cynthia 279
MCUSA. *See* Mennonite Church USA
Mead, Don 174, 179
Mecca 103
Medina 103
Mediterranean Sea 302
Mennonite Board of Missions 20
Mennonite Brethren Church 3–5
Mennonite Central Committee 3, 20, 78
Mennonite World Conference 2
Mennonites 2–5, 69, 73, 288–89, 310
Meretz Party 49, 52, 54, 64, 92
Methodist 173
Mexico 152, 242–44

Meyer, Rich xiii, 65, 77–78, 81, 89, 91–92, 107, 120–21, 164–65, 190, 196–98, 212, 218, 239–41, 246, 249, 252, 266, 274, 276, 285, 289
Milgrom, Jeremy 9, 42
Miller, Rafi 143
Mitchell Report 142, 279
Mohammad/Mohamed/Mohamed/ Muhammad, Prophet (PBUH) xi, 103, 105, 108, 183, 303, 314
Montgomery, Anne 5, 49–50, 53, 63, 65–66, 122–23, 127, 140, 147, 151, 156–57, 176, 179–80, 189, 199, 309
Moore, Donald 176, 78
Morey, Melyssa 138
Morris, Benny 16
Mortellito, Nicole 137, 140
Mufakara/Mufakra 256, 264, 268
Muhtasib, Ahlam 19–20, 299
Muhtasib, Zleekha 66, 106, 114, 147, 223
Muirhead, David 11, 279–80
Muqata (headquarters): In Hebron 181–82; In Ramallah 110, 171–72, 189, 299
Musgrave, Clarence 176
Muslim Scholars Association 272
Musselman, Nathan 178
Mustapha, Abu Ali 142
Myths, Israeli historical 308–9

Nablus 24, 38, 117, 129, 139, 156, 179–80, 190, 198–99
Nahal Brigade 110, 133, 148, 170, 251, 285
Naiman, Bob 49–50, 52, 55–57, 65, 191
Nasser Hospital 198
Natsche/Natshe. *See* al/an-Natshe
Nawash First Nation in Ontario 10
Nawi, Ezra 257, 268
Nazareth 297
NBC 265
Near, Ken 286
Nephesh (soul) 8
Netanya 139m 172
Netanyahu, Prime Minister Benjamin/ Binyamin, "Bibi" 53–54, 58–59, 64, 67, 86, 89

Netivot Shalom 86
New York Times 41, 123, 138, 149
New Zealand 241, 272, 283
Nijim, Germana 215, 27–18
Nir, Ori 54
Nonviolence x, 3–5, 8, 15, 18, 28–29, 51, 55, 59, 65, 80, 83–86, 107, 152, 155–57, 178, 188, 190–91, 193, 196–97, 215, 221, 228, 235, 251, 253, 257, 267, 27071, 274, 284, 287, 293–94, 314, 316, 319–21
North Manchester, IN 33
Nouwen, Henri 86
Nova Scotia 298
Novick, Peter 279

OCHA 234, 241, 249, 258, 266–68, 271
OD. *See* Operation Dove
Olive Tree summer 155
Olympia, WA 234
Ontario 10, 72
Operation Baby Jesus 176–78
Operation Dove 257–58, 262–63, 266–68, 270–71, 283, 312, 320–21
Orlando, FL 304, 307
Orme, William J. 124
Osama Bin Munqeth School 109
Oslo Declaration of Principles 7
Oslo Peace Process 13–15, 21, 24, 42, 45–47, 51, 53, 64, 75, 90, 104–8, 211, 214, 236, 279, 301
Otniel, settlement of 230
Ottoman Empire 37, 75, 90
Outposts. *See* settlement
Ozeri, Netanel 203–4, 206, 230

PA. *See* Palestinian Authority
Pacheco, Allegra 50, 56–57
Pacifism 2, 3, 74, 119, 144, 288, 294, 316
Palestinian Land Defence Committee (LDC) 20, 92, 292, 318
Palestine Liberation Organization 7, 18, 45, 66
Palestine Polytechnic University in Hebron 209, 226–30
Palestinian Authority 7, 32, 47, 58, 63, 97, 107, 139, 158, 172, 180–81, 189, 217, 258, 273, 316

Palestinian Centre for Rapprochement 156, 235
Palestinian Christians 5, 13, 20, 57, 67, 123–26, 172, 178, 216, 281, 297
Palestinian Ministry of Education 32, 158
Palestinian Ministry of Health 258
Palestinian police 63, 107, 124, 176
Palestinian economy 7, 108, 124, 132, 167, 214, 236, 241, 322
Partisanship, balance, sides, bias 1,9, 18, 23, 68, 74, 113, 123, 196, 278–79, 281–84, 304, 307
Pass, Shalhevet 138
Pass, Yitzhak 138
Passover/Pesach 56, 169, 172, 207, 289, 306
Pauls, Carmen 20, 37, 39, 45
Payne, William 206
Peace Now 86, 160, 169, 262, 271, 318
Pennsylvania 154
Pentagon 153–54
Peoria, IL 160, 182
Peres, Shimon 21, 37, 42, 47, 49, 52–53, 64, 151
Peters, Lorin 248
PFLP. *See* Popular Front for the Liberation of Palestine
Philippines 3
PHRMG. *See* Palestinian Human Rights Monitoring Group
Pierce, Paul 209, 219, 229, 233–34
Pilgrimage of Faith 167
Pledge by Christians to our Jewish Neighbors 297–98
Pleiman, Grace 246–47
PLO. *See* Palestine Liberation Organization
Ploughshares movement 148
Polhamus, Rick 131, 136, 139, 147, 151, 153, 169–70, 176–77, 179–80, 188–89
Pontifical Biblical Institute 176
Popular Front for the Liberation of Palestine 69, 73, 142, 272
Powell, Colin 142, 165, 205, 228
Pritchard, Doug 68, 72, 263
Propaganda 68, 255, 304, 312
Prophets, biblical 8, 71, 167, 297

Protocols of the Elders of Zion 152, 298
Purim 18

Qalqilya 210
Qana 54
Qawasma/Qawasme/Qawasmeh/
  Qawasmi family 118, 120, 317
Qawasme, Hamed 272–73, 316
Qawasmi, Khaled 213–14
Qilqis xi, 92, 95–96, 115, 132, 160, 193
Quakers (Friends) Friends/Quakers 36–
  37, 69–70, 140, 186–89, 234, 298
Quandt, William B. 279
Quartet on the Middle East 279
Quran 105, 314
Qurtuba/Qordoba/Cordoba/Cortuba/
  School 16, 32–33, 35, 41, 43, 55,
  105, 158, 192–93, 214, 231, 247,
  249–50, 272, 287

RAB. *See* Rebuilders Against Bulldozers
Rabai, Juma 255
Rabbis for Human Rights 42, 66, 86, 94,
  132, 187, 199, 262, 270, 298
Rabin, Leah/Lea 42
Rabin, Yitzhak 20–21, 30, 37–43, 46, 58,
  149, 151
Racism 54, 71, 183, 215, 233, 277, 308
Rafah 234
Raheb, Mitri 177
Rajabi, Ramadan 88
Ramadan 124, 136, 214, 252, 281
Ramallah 110, 116–17, 129, 139, 143,
  156, 167, 171–72, 175, 179, 189–90,
  273, 281, 299, 310
Ramle 178, 216
Ramon, Ilan 205–6
Rantis 156
Rashid/Rasheed, Osaid 59, 107, 220,
Raviv, Avishai 38, 40
Rebecca, biblical matriarch 16, 296
Rebuilders Against Bulldozers 67, 89, 92
Reeves, Christopher 232
Refugees, Palestinian 5–7, 16, 54, 63,
  104, 116, 123, 154, 167, 171–72,
  189, 194. 308
Rehovot 318
Reilly, Kathy 280

Rempel, Terry 63–64
Reschly, Sara 57–58, 65, 68–69, 82–85,
  87, 97–98, 131, 213, 241, 286, 306
Reservoir Raiders 88
Reuters 40–41, 123, 221
Ruether, Rosemary Radford
Rhineland 300
Rhodes, Sue 163, 190, 198–209, 221, 237
Rhubarb 310
Riah Abu al-Assal, Bishop
Richmond, VA 152
Rishmawi, George 156
Rishon Letzion 181
Roadblocks, checkpoints 104, 117,
  132–34, 167, 178, 211, 219, 241,
  258, 263, 317
Roadmap to Peace, 205, 227–28, 279
Robbins, Sonia 246
Rochlin, Yona 17
Roe, Dianne 5, 41, 49–53, 64, 73, 88–89,
  94, 111, 115–17, 119–20, 136,
  138, 146, 151, 166, 171, 173, 182,
  192–94, 197–98, 219, 244, 246–48,
  277, 280
Rokach, Livia 16
Rollins, Greg 31, 131, 136, 140, 163,
  170–71, 173–76, 180, 185–87,
  197–99, 207, 213, 215–20, 229, 231,
  233, 235–36, 238–39, 272, 311
Romania 37
Rose, Bill 134,
Roses not Rubble campaign 68, 79
Rosetti, Piergiorgio 257, 260, 267
Rosser, Sister Ellen 55–56
Rossi, Adriano 262–63
Rovera, Donatella 262
Royer, Kathy 3
Roynon, Jim 274
Rubenberg, Cheryl A. 279
Rubinstein, Danny 103
Russia, Russian 39
Russian Compound, Jerusalem 22,
  50–51, 245, 279

Sabarneh, Edna 193
Sabarneh, Leyla 86
Sabbath/Shabbat, Jewish 17, 114, 38, 67,
  100, 113, 161, 164, 240, 296–97

Sabeel Liberation Theology Center 13, 20, 67, 172, 178, 216, 281
Sabra and Shatila Refugee Camps 172–73
Said, Edward 14, 16
Salam, Kawther 49, 135, 137, 143–44, 147
Salameh, Abir 138
Saleh, Imm 172
Samoh, Adel 184–86
Santiago, Chile 126
Sarah, biblical matriarch 16, 296
Sarura 254
Satterwhite, Jim 79, 181, 185–86, 188
Saudi Arabia 115, 302
Savir, Uri 14
Sawadsky, Hedy 5, 37, 39
Sbarro Pizzaria 150
Schiller, Eric 218
Schmidt, Russell 251
Schneider, Frank 167
School Accompaniment: At-Tuwani 257–67, 287; Hebron 32–33, 157–59, 192–93, 248–50
Schramm, Heidi 266
Scott, Diego. *See* Rollins, Greg
Seattle 25
Sefer Hevron 17
Segev, Tom 16–17, 104
Service Civile International 188
Settlements, Israeli: Creation of 14; Expansion 13, 20, 29, 54, 65, 89, 96, 104, 162, 165–66, 196–97, 212, 239–40, 259, 278; Outposts 160, 164, 203, 230, 233, 254, 258–59, 262, 265–67
Settlers, Israeli: Propaganda 289–96; Falsehoods 27–28, 150–51, 197, 288, 293–94; CPT positive encounters with 288–89
Shafer, Don 3
Shaheen, Faris 180
Shaheen, Ibrahim 180
Shaheen, Nader 180
Shahin, Fahmi 44–45
Shalala Street 213, 241
Shantz, Pierre 68–69, 72, 74, 83–85, 122–23, 131, 134, 137
Shapiro, Adam 156, 299
Sharabati family 144, 184–85

Sharabati, Hisham v, 14–15, 17, 34, 38–39, 44–45, 90, 116, 175–76, 179, 181, 185, 252, 257, 272, 313, 316
Sharabati, Yakoutib 181
Sharansky, Natan 92
Sharif, Shehab 115
Sharif, Tarek 115
Sharm el-Sheikh Memorandum 89, 93–94, 98, 104, 279
Sharon, Ariel 18, 100, 103–4, 130–31, 142, 154–55, 161–62, 166, 172–73, 204–5, 210, 212, 236, 279
Shaul, Yehuda/Yehudah 133, 169, 251,
Shawamreh, Salim 131
Shawer, Imad Mohammad 66
Shekhtman, Al 68–74
Shelly, Patty 78
Shepherds, Accompaniment of 267–68
Shin Bet 26, 38–39
Shlaim, Avi 16
Shoemaker, Janet 169, 182, 185
Shreateh, Musallem 55–56, 254
Shuhada/Shohada Street 111, 147–48, 166, 210, 215, 219, 238, 242, 277, 279–80
Shukary, Ahmed 307
Shusaf, Eldad 222
Shuyoukh 180, 194
Sidar, Mohammed 209
Sider, Ron 2–3
Slater, Allan 308
Smith, Char 140
SOA (School of the Americas) 293
Sojourner. *See* Ger
Sooden, Harmeet Singh 30, 272–74, 276
Soroka Hospital 261
Spelling variations, transliterated Arabic and Hebrew x–xi, 137, 343
St. Andrew's Church of Scotland 176
St. Georges' Cathedral, School 67, 104, 176
St. Yves, Society of 27
Stanley, Chelli 247
Star Hotel, Bethlehem 176
Statement of Conviction 30, 288
Stein, Janice Gross 103
Stein, Jerry 182
Steiner, Mary Pannabecker 80
Stigge-Kaufman, Sydney 84

Stoltzfus, Gene 5–6, 13, 44, 69–70, 74, 134, 153, 158, 321
Strasbourg, France 2
Stratford, ON 68
Styrbjörn, Inger 249
Sudan 116
Sultan Family 90–92, 165, 230
Sultan, Fahed 91
Sultan, Lamia 90
Sultan, Omar 90, 94
Surif 194
Surrey, BC 216
Susia (Israeli settlement) 56, 94, 113, 130, 132, 211, 254, 294
Susia/Susiya (Palestinian village) 254, 257
Susskind, Yiphat 49
Switzerland, Swiss 247
Sydney Morning Herald 227
Syria 38

Ta'ayush/Taayush 20, 232, 233, 256–57, 266–68, 270–71, 298, 320
Taba 279
Tahboub, Karim 227
Takrouri Mountain 141
Tantur Ecumenical Institute 78, 178
Tanzim 150
Tarqumia 239
Taylor, Harriet 133, 215, 217, 246
Techny, IL 4–5
Tel Aviv 6, 41, 53, 87, 133, 150, 160, 169, 171–73, 226, 251, 285
Tel Rumeida 21–27, 43, 128, 144, 162, 209–10, 218, 247
Texas 244
Thomas, Michael 176, 178
Thomas, Susan 178
Tibon, Noam 119
Tikkun 71, 74, 152, 154
Tivnan, Edward 279
Tolan, Sandy 26
Tomato actions in Hebron Market 46–47, 79, 90, 98, 236
Tomb of the Patriarchs. *See* Ibrahimi Mosque
Torah 8, 294
Toronto 129
Torture 67, 69, 85, 293

Toytunç, Turtug Cengiz 173
Transliteration. *See* "Spelling Variations"
Tuba 199, 255–56, 258–59, 261–62, 264–67
Tulkarm 129, 167
Turki, Fawaz 16
Tzedekah/Tzadekah, Dov 135, 150
Tzvika, Captain 75

Uhler, Kathie 232, 24648
UK. *See* United Kingdom
Umm Jabriil 255
UN. *See* United Nations
UNESCO 164, 209
Unger, Kurtis 191
United Kingdom (U.K.) 136, 188–89, 247, 272, 281–83, 287, 298; Foreign policy re: Israel and Palestine 281–83
United Nations (U.N.) 18, 40, 54, 65, 97, 104, 125, 131, 140, 144, 172, 234, 241, 258, 267–68, 278–79, 302
United States of America (U.S.) 29; Congress 65, 73, 132, 239, 278–79; CPTers with citizenship in 106; Foreign policy 65, 87, 154, 307, 252, 282; Relationship with Israel 131, 140, 150, 278–83; State Department, September 11, 2001 Al-Qaeda attacks on 152–54; State Department 65, 67, 81, 191, 278, 282
U.S.–Mexico border 242–44
USAID 111, 142, 279

Villota, Luna 247
Voth, Ervin and Susan 19

Wadi al-Ghroos 211–12, 224, 239
Wadi Nasara 164, 240
Wagner, Don 13
Waqf 135
Wall, the/Separation Barrier/Security Fence/Annexation Wall/Apartheid Wall 210, 212, 239, 242–43, 251, 271, 273–75, 282
Washington, DC ix, 14, 29, 45, 152, 154, 278, 284, 297
Washington Post 27, 138
Wasta 317–18

Water issues 21–22, 25–30, 79–80, 88–89, 263–64, 276
WCC. *See* World Council of Churches
We Are the Pharisees 288
Weaver, David 6–8
Weaver, Dorothy Jean 140
Weinberg, Colonel Dror 135, 161,
de Wetter-Smith, Brooks 236
Wilder, David 289, 292, 294,
Wilkinson, Greg 171
Willey-al'Sana, Rosemary 258
Williams Carpenter, Mai'a 210, 240, 257–58, 262–63, 316
Wink, Walter 55
Winslow, Philip 18
World Council of Churches 129, 155, 179, 183, 188–89
World Vision 116
Worshiper's Way/Lane 164, 219, 230
Wye River Memorandum 87, 89, 93–94, 104, 204, 279

Yatta 94, 113, 116, 130, 132, 166, 219, 254, 255, 258, 264, 266, 270, 275, 290
Yeats, William Butler 101, 103, 201
Yehudai Rimmer, Moshe 123
Yesh Gvul 86
Yoder, Bruce 57
Yoder, Mary 164, 170–71, 232, 315
Yusef, Umm 118

Zaatari, Mamdoh Abd al Asem 66
Zaki, Abbas 66, 315
Zalloum family 49, 52, 66, 224,
Zalloum, Wahed 224
Zambia 272
Zeahda, Tayseer 128, 247–48
Zechariah, biblical prophet 8
Zeevi, Rehavam 142
Zelter, Angie 146, 145–46
Zen, Fatimah 255
Zilverschmidt, Beate 95
Zimmerman, Diana 262, 267, 270, 310–12
Zionism, Zionists 9, 104, 143, 172, 254, 281–82
Ziv, Captain Eyal 22–23, 31, 45, 52

Zoughbi, Elaine 14, 20
Zoughbi, Zoughbi 5, 13–14, 66, 121, 123, 322
Zuercher, Melanie 5

www.ingramcontent.com/pod-product-compliance
Lightning Source LLC
Chambersburg PA
CBHW021339300426
44114CB00012B/1003